POLITICS OF LAW AND THE COURTS IN NINETEENTH-CENTURY EGYPT

Politics of Law and the Courts in Nineteenth-Century Egypt

BYRON CANNON

University of Utah Press
Salt Lake City
1988

The illustration on the cover of this book is a full color reproduction of an original political poster dating from about 1919–20. The original is part of a unique collection of early twentieth-century Egyptian posters and leaflets held by the Aziz S. Atiya Middle East Library of the University of Utah. The poster reproduced here represents the figure of Sa^cad Zaghlul, who served as a lawyer and judge in the *ahliyya* courts of Egypt in the 1890s, and as minister of justice in the period before World War I. Founder of the *Wafd* (Delegation) party in 1919, Zaghlul earned an international reputation as an Egyptian nationalist leader until his death in 1927. The Arabic caption on the poster reads: "Have patience, Egypt, for patience is the key to final release from suffering."

Library of Congress Cataloging-in-Publication Data

Cannon, Byron, 1940–
Politics of law and the courts in nineteenth-century Egypt.

Bibliography: p.
Includes index.
1. Courts of special jurisdiction—Egypt—History.
2. Aliens—Egypt—History. 3. Exterritoriality—History.
I. Title.
LAW 347.62'04 88–14315
ISBN 0–87480–279–2 346.2074

TO OUR MEMORY OF THE ALEXANDRIAN KITE FLYER

Contents

Preface

Possibly no single institution in modern Middle Eastern history has received more attention in print than the Mixed Courts of Egypt. The period during which this multinational body presided over legal disputes involving foreigners in Egypt spanned seven decades, 1876–1949. Throughout more than seventy years of mixed court activities, writers of many nationalities surveyed and resurveyed their operations as unique extensions of the legal principle of extraterritoriality that began much earlier, and under very different circumstances, as part of the Ottoman Turkish imperial capitulatory regime. Little was done, however, to explain practical political relationships between the internationally staffed courts and purely Egyptian local civil and penal jurisdictions. We know even less about the social and economic effects of other Egyptian legal reform efforts that the existence of the mixed courts prompted, especially in the early years of their operations. Where links between the major branches of Egypt's secular court system and local social or political questions have been noted, one finds many oversimplifications of the impact of the original 1875 Mixed Court Reform.

For some it contributed immediately to the process of legal modernization and "instructed Egyptians in the constitutional foundations of Western law . . . and civil liberties which became the basis of the nationalist movement" (Nadav Safran, *Egypt in Search of Political Community* [Cambridge, Mass., 1961], p. 36). For others, the effects of the same process of reform were much less clear. When Jacques Berque viewed what he called "the battle over the instruments and symbols of civil law" in Egypt in the 1890s, for example, he found that "native courts" consciously modeled on the 1875 Mixed

Court Reform were "quite out of touch with what was going on in the country" and an example of "contradictions between an imported western type of law and the reality in whose service it ought to be used" (Jacques Berque, *L'Egypte: Impérialisme et révolution* [Paris, 1967], p. 160). It is to offset, or at least to clarify, such apparent contradictions in existing literature that this political and social history of legal reform in nineteenth-century Egypt was undertaken.

The dates opening and closing the main body of this book (parts II through IV) are well known to historians of the Middle East and Europe. The year 1875 corresponds to the initial crisis that would engage fourteen foreign capitulatory powers, first in cooperation, then in jealous rivalry, in dealing with the fading myth of Egypt's political and economic autonomy over three decades. It was precisely at this time that the newly constituted mixed courts began to clash with traditional methods of administration and conceptions of justice under Khedive Isma^cil (r. 1863–79). The courts would continue to play a key role as Egypt's political and financial crisis moved through the experience of the Dual Control, the protonationalist ^cUrabi revolt, and the onset of the British occupation in 1882. The symbolic terminal date of 1904 marks the Anglo-French Entente Cordiale, closing over twenty years of "great power" rivalry between London and Paris over their conflicting self-assigned roles as protectors of Egypt from "irresponsible" opportunists. The latter might be identified variously as the British occupiers themselves, capitulatory powers, like France, seeking special privileges in Egypt, or local political or social elites using the banner of "justice" to camouflage benefits they hoped to monopolize for themselves.

Even before the symbolic dividing line of 1904, however, the reform-weary Anglo-Egyptian administration had more or less relegated legal reform issues—many of which had definitely been at the very center of local and international political maneuvering in Egypt a decade or so earlier—to somewhat secondary status. After 1904, and at least until the rise of formal local nationalist opposition to the famous Four Reserved Points of the period from 1922 to 1936, historians have recorded very little to remind us of the previous centrality of Egyptian legal reform issues before 1900. This is unfortunate since such issues were used by various parties to articulate their particular perception of the nature of justice and its relationship to prevailing social and political interests in each generation, at least from 1850 on.

The first section of this book goes back a full half-century before the founding of the mixed courts to explore precedents that contributed not only to the decision to undertake the famous Judicial Reform of 1875, but also to local perceptions of justice that, once the new system was in place, would seek to justify formal reformism either as a promise to guarantee sociopolitical progress or, conversely, as a device to hamper it. This initial theme, itself quite general, is pursued in successive chapters that cover the history of legal reform in Egypt to the end of the nineteenth century. The picture revealed is one of gradual but clearly frustrating adjustment to the quasi-permanent influence of internationally controlled courts and codes on Egypt's key administrative and private civil litigation by the first decades of the twentieth century. This main framework allows us to discuss justice as a problem of political identity in late nineteenth-century Egypt.

What may be said about the way in which differing perceptions of justice in Egypt contributed to processes of social identity in the same period? Subthemes in this book explore a variety of historical records that should cast new light on the experience of "modernization" as a subjective phenomenon. Each chapter from part II forward contains examples of real people trying to respond to problems created by impersonal "forces of change" represented by formal reform schemes. Such responses, when they can be documented, try to assign sense to processes of change, either as reflections of justice or, to the contrary, as warning signs of injustice. In both cases, differing subjective impressions of the need to defend the cause of justice in nineteenth-century Egypt yield valuable information, if not about social "class," certainly about sources and levels of social identity. Such information can be used to clarify our understanding of changing processes of political identity in any number of developing countries. It also should be used to help us escape outmoded conceptions of the impact of modernization—in this case, legal modernization—on identifiable local social interest groups.

Within its narrowest limits as history, therefore, our subject is the origins and early development of what became Egypt's two major secular judicial systems in the first half of the twentieth century: the mixed and *ahliyya* (local or "native") courts. It examines many peculiar conditions that governed (or obstructed) practical material relationships between these two secular judicial agencies themselves. At the same time, however, it raises questions of subjective conflict between both of these "modernized" administrative bodies and lingering justifications for the maintenance of traditional approaches to justice in Egypt, be they in sectarian (Islamic, Christian, or Judaic) or some other form. Ultimately, it is this dimension of the book's content, which evolves with problems posed in each stage of standard history of legal reform projects, that will fill out the subthemes of justice and sociopolitical identity. Each chapter tests, therefore, the possible motivation of individuals and groups who viewed various legal reform schemes as panaceas to ease Egypt's most evident problems in the last quarter of the nineteenth century. Some of these, as we shall see, had their origins in a general movement from basically agrarian precapitalist economic and social conditions to a situation commonly associated with the forces of integration into a much wider system of economic, social, and political relations. It is equally important (if more difficult, within such a sweeping framework for macroanalysis) to explore the possible motivation of those who branded reformism as a factor contributing to these same problems.

To make a rather specialized Egyptian historical topic relevant for students of other regions or disciplines is not an easy task. Insofar as all court systems potentially involve interests at several levels of any society, however, the study of legal reform questions in nineteenth-century Egypt can add to our knowledge of vital problems of social and economic development well beyond the framework of administrative history per se. In the wider Middle Eastern, Asian, or African context, Egypt's experience provides examples of reactions that the illusive process of modernization—be it in the court system, property tenure and capital investment, or increased professionalism—may have caused in a number of tradition-oriented societies on the eve of the twentieth century. To understand this, one must explore opinions well beyond those expressed by Western providers (and, often, direct beneficiaries) of adopted models for modernization. Certainly, within its own prescribed geographical and historical limits, for example, this book compares the implications of combined judicial and legislative changes in Egypt between ca. 1860 and 1900 for at least three identifiable local groups: political and rural landholding elites; an emerging body of educated Egyptians divided in their dedication to traditional but obsolete local forms of legal interaction and administration; and the mass of anonymous litigants who were the object of many legal and judicial reform schemes during the entire nineteenth century. Because the provisions of mixed and "native" (*ahliyya*) court law affected each of these categories differently, each responded to the supposed challenge or advantages of legal reform in a distinct manner.

It is important to note here that it was not the first but the second group that was most likely to find new ways of contributing—as court advocates, editorialists, or future legislators—to the debate over secular legal questions in the last quarter of the nineteenth century. Given a very long series of disappointments in Egyptian court reforms between 1860 and 1900, it seemed inevitable that many individuals, especially those increasingly involved as professionals in the established Egyptian bench and bar, would lose faith in previously acceptable but naive notions of the inherent value of legal modernization. Indeed, a number of "second-generation" Egyptian lawyers who were exposed to the daily reality of operations in the mixed or *ahliyya* courts consciously refocused their professional career objectives by the turn of the century. Many became much more politically involved in the affairs of their country as it moved into the third decade of the British occupation period. Among these one could list Butrus Ghali, Mustafa Kamil, Saᶜad Zaghlul, and Mustafa Nahhas, all lawyers who became high-level ministers or Watanist (nationalist) opposition leaders in the last decade before World War I. Other professional legalists, including Shaykh Muhammad ᶜAbduh, Qasim Amin, or Ahmad Lutfi as Sayyid, would leave well-known marks on the sociointellectual development of twentieth-century Egypt.

All of these, plus many less prominent figures, had in one way or another concerned themselves at an earlier date with frustrating problems and prospects connected with reforms in Egypt's legal system. After 1900, all had somehow to find politically and intellectually satisfying (or at least promising) alternatives to the way in which the generation before them had seen the complicated international and local politics of legal reform in the second half of the nineteenth century. In some cases, such alternatives simply involved depoliticizing an essentially outmoded administrative reform cause and making the best of what the prevailing system offered. In others, symbolized most prominently by nationalist activists Mustafa Kamil and Saʿad Zaghlul, there was an evident process of repoliticizing the role and relative weight of certain legal institutions in Egyptian society. Whatever circumstances prevailed later, however, knowledge of experiences undergone by a transitional generation of Egyptian lawyers before 1900 definitely helps in understanding how the politics of legal reform contributed to the dual phenomena of social mobilization and national political activism in early twentieth-century Egypt.

It is difficult to offer acknowledgment of, and appreciation for, assistance I have received as this project passed through several stages of transformation. Certainly, a first note of appreciation is owed to the professors who originally inspired me, many years ago, to adopt this subject as the focus of my doctoral dissertation research. The encouragement of Drs. J.C. Hurewitz, John Badeau, and Charles Issawi, then responsible for an excellent graduate program at Columbia University, was an invaluable stimulus, as was the advice of other members of my dissertation committee. Since that time, I have received constructive criticism from too many scholars to be able to mention each name here. Two individuals in particular, however, Dr. Robert Tignor of Princeton University and Dr. Bernard Weiss of the University of Utah Middle East Center, took the time to read the entire work and give opinions concerning its strengths and its weaknesses.

Material assistance for research, writing, and revision has come from several sources. The original project, including drafting of the dissertation, was completed under the auspices of the Foreign Area Fellowship Program of the Social Science Research Council. A return visit to Egypt to work in the University of Cairo Law School Library was sponsored by the Wisconsin Alumni Research Foundation of the University of Wisconsin, Madison. I am also indebted to the Career Development Committee of the College of Humanities, University of Utah, for granting the sabbatical leave that allowed me to make extensive revisions in the much expanded final manuscript.

Finally, my appreciation is extended to people whose contribution to my persistence in reworking this study has much less to do with formal scholarly pursuits than with simple and valuable human qualities. Among these individuals I count scores of Egyptians whose names I never knew or have subsequently forgotten; their help often turned fatigue and despair into renewed enthusiasm for this specific subject and the history of their country in general.

And then there is the person who collected *galets* at Dieppe, blue thistles in Andalusia, and accounts of court politics in the *Phare d'Alexandrie*. Thank you, Dominique.

Note on Transliteration

Transliteration of Arabic and Turkish consonants in this book follows the main lines of the system used in the *International Journal of Middle East Studies*, except for omission of the diacritical mark below the line (on h, s, d, t, z). Initial (but not medial and final) hamzas have been omitted, as have all diacritical marks to indicate long vowels.

Part I

Perspectives on Justice in the Tanzimat Period (1839–75)

1

Historical Introduction

The recent history of Asian and African countries suggests that if terms like "imperialism," "nationalism," and "modernization" do apply to almost all regions, different local conditions should govern the way we use such convenient descriptive categories. Countries in the central Islamic world from Afghanistan to Morocco did, of course, share common features as they moved in stages toward independent nationhood. All became fields for political influence and rivalry among several European powers during the nineteenth century. Such influence was wielded differently according to local circumstances. Both the British and Russian empires, for example, extended military assistance to local tribes to secure political leverage with strategic but unpredictable Afghani or Qajar Iranian "client" states. Within the polygot Ottoman Turkish Empire, quite varied patterns of indirect political imperialism existed throughout the nineteenth century. Historians can easily show how Britain's assumption of control over Cyprus in 1878 involved different motivating forces than France's patronage of the Maronites in Lebanon. In the former case, the Foreign Office aimed mainly at thwarting further Russian moves against the strategically vital "Sick Man of Europe" after the 1877–78 Russo-Turkish War. In Lebanon, on the other hand, emphasis on cultural and religious ties not only increased French influence, but also promised a variety of local administrative and material advantages for Maronite Christians. The latter phenomenon would play a key role in the social and economic destiny of several Levant countries into the twentieth century.

Such forms of Western interaction with traditional Middle Eastern polities did not necessarily convince local populations that they had either to modernize (i.e., adopt European models) or to submit increasingly to indirect foreign control. It is true, however, that European military and educational missions or ventures had attractive effects. Some groups were able to obtain social or political advantages from new circumstances that often bore little relation to local conditions prior to the first signs of Western interest in their regions. Whether such responses led most often to benefits for only a limited minority within the local population or to more general stimuli for long-term change remains moot.

Whatever general scheme is adopted to study the impact of European penetration in eventual colonial or semicolonial zones, one must consider economic dimensions of the same process. A vast literature exists, particularly in dependency theory studies, on the effects of extension—into traditional economies of Asia, Latin America, and Africa—of the material advantages and disadvantages of integration into the commercial capital–based European or world economy. From a solely economic point of view, the replacement of preexisting relationships of production by models associated with commercial capitalism had attractions for certain elements in each "peripheral" zone. In order to realize such economic attractions (or to avoid disadvantages of not responding to Western-inspired factors of change), however, not only changing material relations but social and political relations came into play.

The degree to which "receiver" countries experienced some consciousness of such changes is an internal reflection of the process so inadequately described as modernization.[1] Conscious reaction obviously did not come to all zones subject to European political and economic penetration. In the case of the Ottoman Turkish core of the Middle East, however, enough consciousness did occur to justify historians' assignment of dates and even names to eras of attempted modernization and/or reform. Examples include the Tulip period or Lale Devri (ca. 1702–20); New Order or Nizam-i Cedid reforms (1780s to 1808); and the Tanzimat Reform period (1839–76).

Ultimately, one must question any general theory of modernization experiments that, although perhaps all Middle Eastern, took place in so many distinct geographical and historical settings. Local provinces of the Ottoman Empire, despite many superficial similarities, were challenged by and reacted to the West in different ways. Some authors who concentrated on the "formal" Tanzimat period, for example, skipped over a plethora of different and sometimes opposing central and local institutions in their eagerness to portray a coherent era. Many studies lack a necessary focus on one or two essential indicators of change or resistance to change. It is a major assumption of this book, however, that—once they are separated and studied systematically—such indicators help tie internal topics of administrative reformism to wider analytical problems. These in turn should aim at redefining the interlocking dynamics of historical phenomena previously written off under the general rubrics of "reform" or "modernization."

There may be ground for solving this quandary, not by abandoning traditional conceptions of the Ottoman Tanzimat altogether, but by broadening our understanding of its international and internal political, social, and economic implications. This book suggests, for example, that we should pursue more detailed study of an Ottoman reform dilemma that, in many ways, represented the nineteenth century equivalent of twentieth century governments' well-known emphasis on education as the key to social progress and modernization. In fact, the more closely one looks at nineteenth century Ottoman history, the more apparent it is that a single issue—clarification and redefinition of the role of government authority in various local legal and judicial processes—is a factor common to all regions of the Empire. It is therefore one that should play a central role in any attempt to clarify our understanding of diverse theories of modernization as they may apply in many different regions. The history of Britain's extensive impact on India's judicial organization and traditions could help make this point a comparative one.[2]

The best Middle Eastern model of state institutions clashing with local perceptions of necessary legal procedures in an Islamic environment, however, is still that of the Ottoman Empire. This is true both during and after the Tanzimat era. Within the Ottoman framework, Egypt's experience demands the most attention, mainly because of the wide repercussions it caused, in both political and economic realms for European and Ottoman imperial concerns alike, into the twentieth century. In order to understand how so much attention came to focus on Egyptian legal reform priorities, however, one should first review several peculiar circumstances of the traditional Eastern Question, including the Ottoman capitulatory system, as it existed at the end of the eighteenth century.[3]

THE EASTERN QUESTION AND THE OTTOMAN CAPITULATIONS

The series of bilateral treaties that constituted the Ottoman capitulatory system probably reached their highest degree of efficiency in the seventeenth century. This was before military defeats made the Ottoman Empire vulnerable to a variety of forms of external coercion by both friends and enemies. Initially modeled after much earlier "chapters" (It., *capitula*) of commercial and judicial privileges granted by Mamluk sultans to Italian traders in medieval Egypt, the first capitulatory treaties with Europeans were signed from a position of strength, not weakness.[4] In fact, until the eighteenth century, whatever benefits derived from such Ottoman-Christian agreements were technically reciprocal. Cessation of assumptions of total war (a *de facto* reality in relations between the Turks and Europe by about 1600) brought a need for assurance that commercial intercourse could take place between former enemies without undue risk for individuals or the commercial houses they represented.

Such considerations were particularly important for Europeans in the Levant since, in theory, all local judicial authority was reserved not for a discrete legal branch of the sultan's administration, but for various sectarian bodies. These ranged from minority *millet* courts to the majority Islamic *shari*ᶜ*a* courts (Ar., *mahkamas*) under local *qadis*. It was not only Europeans who claimed that the law of such courts was unsuited for settling their disputes in Ottoman territory: the Ottomans themselves assumed that the jurisdiction of all sectarian bodies was restricted to members of each respective community of believers. There was never any attempt, at least until the Tanzimat era, to devise a "mixed" law from religious or secular sources to meet the needs of "mixed" litigants. Different courts handled cases applying to subjects belonging to sectarian subcommunities. Foreign consulates, meanwhile, handled disputes in Ottoman territory between subjects of the same nationality. Problems arose when disputants were of two different sectarian subcommunities or foreign nationalities, and, of course, when the dispute involved foreign versus Ottoman subjects. In the latter case, the only specific capitulatory privilege allowed was that of a judicial audience chaired by the local Ottoman governor in the presence of a foreign interpreter and consular representative, often the same person.[5]

These and other defects in the early capitulatory regime led to pressures for practical reforms, some of which were eventually incorporated into Tanzimat decrees in the mid-nineteenth century. For hundreds of years, for example, the Ottomans possessed only a very rudimentary body of imperial *qanun* or secular administrative law to supplement the sectarian rulings applicable to Ottoman subjects in their own private affairs. From the sixteenth century onward, only certain privileged provinces enjoyed the possibility of systematic reference to special codes of imperial decrees, or *qanunnahme*s, pertaining to administrative or land tenure questions in their zones.[6] These were supposed to give guidelines for a separate jurisdiction free from sectarian interference in areas of recognized governmental concern, especially in fiscal matters. They embodied neither uniform rules applying throughout the Empire nor provisions for commercial transactions or private contract and property relations that European law would eventually group under the civil umbrella of the Napoleonic Code.

Although technical inconsistencies caused many disagreements over decisions under the Ottoman capitulations, no serious alterations in the system occurred until the middle of the eighteenth century. Even then, when certain European governments began exerting pressure on war-weakened sultans to sharpen definitions of their capitulatory privileges, they were moved primarily by strategic, not yet legal or even commercial, jealousies. The best example of this occurred at midpoint in the eighteenth century, when France and Britain were locked in military confrontations in many areas around the globe. Changing strategic circumstances gave rise to new perceptions of advantages to be gained by manipulating traditional capitulatory privileges. This was particularly true in regions of the Ottoman Empire where potential commercial markets encouraged local definitions of political autonomy from sultanic control.

EGYPT'S STRATEGIC AND CAPITULATORY ROLE BEFORE 1800

In a book published in 1922, François Charles-Roux studied the gradual evolution of French and British interests in the Red Sea and Nile Valley throughout the eighteenth century.[7] His findings suggest several links between long-term European involvement in the Black Sea basin and rising eastern Mediterranean repercussions of France's imperial setbacks east of Suez after the Seven Years' War. Certainly, to the degree that Istanbul had become absorbed in fortifying its European frontiers against Hapsburg and Russian advances since the 1690s, it had to loosen control over key Mediterranean provinces. Both Louis XV and Louis XVI paid close attention to changes in local provincial rule that occurred, particularly in Egypt and North Africa, as a result of Ottoman military preoccupations in Europe.

It was Napoleon Bonaparte, of course, who ultimately converted this aspect of France's Ottoman policy into concrete military terms in 1798. The period beginning around 1760, however, reveals many incipient factors that carried forward to Napoleon's time. Following France's 1763 defeat in the Seven Years' War, the East India Company became the British Crown's direct political and commercial agent in India and east of Suez generally. This forced not only the French but also disgruntled British parties who did not fall under the East India Company monopoly to seek special means to gain, wherever possible, political and commercial concessions along the tightly controlled Ottoman Red Sea trade route to the Mediterranean. The best-known examples of burgeoning interest in Red Sea routes to the Mediterranean were the exploratory voyages of James Bruce between 1768 and 1773.[8] A former British consul in Algiers, Bruce challenged both the East India Company's trade monopoly and British agreements with the Ottomans that prevented competing English (and other European) traders from reaching the Mediterranean via any Red Sea ports above Jiddah. Bruce penetrated the unexplored Abyssinian highlands in an effort to find an approach to the Nile and its Mediterranean ports that would be beyond the control of both Istanbul and East India Company agents.

Even while Bruce was exploring Upper Nile regions, other "renegades" tried to convince the sultan to open Red Sea trade over East India Company objections. They also tried to find local authorities willing to evade the letter of standing Ottoman capitulatory treaties. Such efforts definitely encouraged the emergence of *shaykh al-balad* ᶜAli Bey al-Kabir, who dominated the local Mamluk governmental apparatus in Egypt between 1760 and 1773. ᶜAli Bey's ambitious military intervention to help the sultan "resolve" a local Sharifian dynastic feud in Mecca in 1769 and his own selection of an Ottoman customs collector in Jiddah tend to bear out this suggestion. Within a few years, escalation of the 1768–74 Russo-Turkish

War gave the *de facto* local ruler of Cairo a perfect opportunity to renege on Egypt's annual provincial tribute to Istanbul. Once this was done, ᶜAli Bey went on to conclude his own extracapitulatory agreements with several foreign parties who wished to carry on trade through the Red Sea without suffering inconveniences imposed by the sultan's control.[9]

Although ᶜAli Bey's ascendancy over the Cairo beylicate proved to be short-lived, he created a pattern that affected Egypt's role in Ottoman-European capitulatory relations until well into the nineteenth century. Whether initiative came from British Indian administrators like Warren Hastings, who tried from 1773 to 1775 to set up another chartered company to ply Red Sea trade as far as Suez, or later French missions under Saint-Priest or Choiseul-Gouffier, all parties realized that the continued weakening of Ottoman military strength in Europe had increased Egypt's special importance as a meeting place for European political and commercial interests alike.[10]

OTTOMAN REFORMISM AND THE RISE OF MUHAMMAD ᶜALI IN EGYPT

Few periods of Ottoman history have intrigued scholars as much as the 1805–48 governorate of Muhammad ᶜAli, founder of the dynasty that ruled Egypt until the mid-twentieth century. Muhammad ᶜAli's draconian methods of reconsolidating political control in Cairo following withdrawal of Napoleon's expeditionary force in 1802 became a special focus for historians. Many looked at his forty-year rule in retrospect and concluded that Sultan Selim III's appointee to the Cairo governorate intended from the very outset to carve out a separate Egyptian fiefdom free from serious interference by the Ottoman suzerain.[11] The eventual and well-known Egyptian Crisis from 1831 to 1841 tends to bear out such suggestions. Others underscored Muhammad ᶜAli's success in transforming the productive bases of the Nile Valley's traditional agricultural economy. Indeed, his economic reform efforts, especially the forced reorientation of Egyptian agriculture toward production of cash crops sought by European importers, had the effect of making Egypt once again the most important source for increasing state revenues among all the provinces of the Empire.[12] Since this increased productive potential ultimately served the particular military expansionist aims of Cairo's governor himself, however, there is a general consensus that most local reforms aimed at independent Egyptian state building. Few have tried to interpret the circumstances of Muhammad ᶜAli's methods of rule as an integral subchapter within wider problems associated with the Ottoman Eastern Question. One such problem was the sultan's concern over rising abuse and exploitation of capitulatory privileges by foreign nationals residing throughout the Ottoman Empire.

Brief consideration of international politics by the time of ᶜAli Bey in the mid-1760s already suggested that many interest groups were anxious to redefine the political and economic position of several Ottoman Arab provinces. Istanbul's reaction to this phenomenon by the 1780s included attempts to impose an imperial "New Order." The Nizam-i Cedid aimed at reinforcing central control over military, political, and economic functions deemed necessary to defend the future of the sultanate. In the economic sphere, the Empire had increasingly to concern itself with European attempts to encourage local agreements to contract for exportation of agricultural products that could be integrated into an international cash crop market. In some cases, particularly in Egypt, there was already a sufficient level of reorientation in eighteenth-century trading patterns (hitherto dominated by shipment of the bulk of marketable agricultural commodities to imperial storehouses, combined with east-of-Suez transit trade transactions in spices and coffee) to cause notable slumps in traditional sources of revenue, either for the imperial treasury or for local tax farm (*iltizam*) intermediaries.[13] In Egypt's case, this meant a continuing integration of cash crop commodities (mainly rice, flax, and some cotton at this date) into an international European market as an alternative to previous patterns of internal imperial trade. New Order priorities demanded, therefore, that government participation in, and benefit from, this process be increased. Such priorities could only be realized by rewriting Egypt's administrative law book, or *qanunnahme*, to guarantee that state interests in changing trade conditions would prevail over "slippage" of new sources of profit. Slippage could be either into local intermediaries' hands (the crux of the eternal debate over a multiplicity of decentralized tax farm prerogatives) or into the purses of foreign commercial beneficiaries capable of exploiting various loopholes in the Ottoman capitulatory regime.

The situation described above suggests that the reform of *qanun* law involved traditional administrative interests interacting with traditional individual subjects' interests. It would be premature here to raise questions of a modernizing administrative apparatus defining, through legal structures, the interests of private individuals in an emerging modern sector of the Ottoman polity. At this historical stage in the process, which some describe as the integration of premodern economies into a world market, neither the elements of a modern socioeconomic group nor, certainly, the structural legal bases for a distinct civil law existed. The effects felt once conditions conducive to the emergence of both of these appeared are the subject of each of the succeeding chapters and especially of the conclusion.

It was during the reign of Selim III (1789–1808) that mounting imperial financial paralysis forced reexamination of provincial administrative and economic structures that, like the infamous tax farm system, stemmed from sorely outmoded *qanunnahme*s. The resulting New Order decrees issued by Sultan Selim between ca. 1794 and 1808 were gauged to strengthen central control not only over various military units, but over conditions of internal fiscal and international commercial relations.[14]

If one uses Selim's reform aims as a frame of reference, many of Muhammad ᶜAli's own accomplishments in Egypt after 1805 stand out as local realizations of original Ottoman New Order priorities. In fact, when Selim was himself deposed by conservative forces in Istanbul, the recently installed Egyptian governor was not only confirmed in office by Sultan Mahmud II (r. 1808–39), but possibly encouraged to carry out local versions of centralizing reforms that the sultan himself would have pursued had political conditions at the center of the Empire been more favorable. Evidence supporting this view may be seen in Muhammad ᶜAli's well-known centralization of military and bureaucratic functions in Egypt and, in particular, in his policies toward secular (*qanun*) law and capitulatory treaties after 1805.

APPLICATION OF NEW ORDER PRINCIPLES BY MUHAMMAD ᶜALI, 1805–39

Muhammad ᶜAli's early abolition of outmoded Ottoman Egyptian *qanun* laws clearly followed Istanbul's desire to consolidate as many military and bureaucratic functions as possible in the hands of direct and responsible representatives of the sultan. Ottoman sovereignty had been put to many severe and nearly disastrous tests during Selim III's pioneer New Order reform effort. Now, in the critical period between 1807 and 1815, proponents of strong governmental rule, obviously the model pursued in Egypt by Muhammad ᶜAli, were determined that the essential spirit of the New Order should be kept alive despite Selim's failure at the imperial level. This meant that any bureaucratic structures that failed to shore up the strength of the state would be declared illegal, and a new centralized system would be erected in their place. Ideally, new relationships between governmental and private interests could be calculated to offer tangible benefits for all parties concerned. Replacement of locally autonomous military auxiliaries or revenue-consuming tax farmers by direct agents of the state, for example, could increase both imperial and individual security. What is essential to note here, however, is not specific structural reforms that may have been tried in various provinces of the Empire, including Egypt, but rather several general principles that (ideally at least) permeated the idea of the New Order. These principles, kept alive under Muhammad ᶜAli's strong hand in the eastern Mediterranean until 1840, stand in contrast to the spirit behind reforms in the later Tanzimat period.

As the Ottoman Empire moved into the nineteenth century, it was attempting to reestablish its authority both over imperial subjects' individual secular status and over relations between resident foreigners and individual Ottoman subjects. As a corollary to such alterations in the internal philosophy of government, one would expect a concomitant necessity to reevaluate relations between the Ottoman state and foreign nationals residing or doing business in the Empire. In short, proponents of the New Order were likely to insist that the traditional Ottoman capitulatory regime had become just as inefficient as internal administrative mechanisms regulated by outmoded *qanun* laws. In fact, Selim III's failure to gather adequate support for an Empire-wide reform program before 1808 did not deter the sultan's reconfirmed governor in Egypt from pursuing similar objectives on what was at first a limited provincial scale.

Even a cursory view of events in Egypt between 1811 and 1830 suggests that Mahmud II's governor was dedicated to New Order priorities in his dealings both with local subjects and with foreign capitulatory interests. Initially at least, this dedication coincided with the objectives of sultanic rule. Later, at the end of the 1820s, obviously changing circumstances made Mahmud II regret the wide gap between Muhammad ᶜAli's accomplishments and the reality of his own imperial weaknesses in similar areas. Muhammad ᶜAli began with a concerted drive to regain central control over Egypt's actual revenue-earning potential. To do this, he forcibly revived the Ottoman Islamic theory of state ownership (*miri*) of all agriculturally productive land previously under tax farmer intermediaries.[15] Soon after his first political tasks were accomplished by brutal suppression of local Mamluk interests in Egypt's military and landholding system, Muhammad ᶜAli extended central controls down to the smallest localized units of economic productivity. For town dwellers, this brought a decline in fiscal and administrative autonomy for traditional guilds responsible for the welfare of many artisans and small shopkeepers.[16] For the typical *fallah* cultivator, on the other hand, interventionist policies soon gave the Cairo *diwan*—now the direct agent of state *miri* rights over Egypt's soil—authority to dictate exact terms for planting and marketing agricultural crops. Within a decade after Muhammad ᶜAli's appointment, these controls worked their effect: Lower Egypt became a profitable zone for government-sponsored cultivation and marketing of major cash crops.

From an economic and administrative point of view, it is difficult to overestimate the impact that the introduction of long staple cotton as a cash crop would have on Egypt after 1820.[17] Other innovational aspects of Muhammad ᶜAli's governorate, including cancellation of tax farming and strict methods of military recruitment, were also attempted with limited success by Mahmud II during the three decades of his sultanate. Direct regulation of cash crop agriculture in the Nile Delta, however, allowed Muhammad ᶜAli to use standardized taxes and export monopoly profits to expand controls in directions that were clearly beyond the ken of the unwieldy central imperial administrative apparatus. Although most phases of governmental expansion fell under the aegis of the Cairo War Office, Egypt's governor introduced some new areas of central bureaucratic leverage. Paid officials drawn from military officer ranks undertook responsibilities for public works projects, collection of standard taxes for *miri* land use, and purchase and monopolistic marketing of cotton produced for export.

In short, the ultimate authority of the Cairo governor to regulate nearly every aspect of provincial economic and administrative activity became an accomplished fact. This allowed Muhammad ᶜAli to make many local policy decisions without reference to Istanbul. Eventually the success of aggressive measures tempted Cairo to superimpose its control over neighboring provinces against Mahmud II's apparent desires. Until then, however, use of Muhammad ᶜAli's expanded authority seemed calculated to enhance the governing power of the Ottoman sultanate. The Egyptian Arabian campaign against Wahhabi invaders in the Hijaz (1811–16), expansion southward to establish a new Sudanese province under Cairo's control (in 1822), and intervention to help Mahmud II put down Greek insurrectionists in 1826–27 are all examples that support this suggestion.

Indeed, had it not been for European political determination to defend the "immutable rights" of foreigners to profit from conditions laid down in various capitulations, Mahmud II might eventually have reaped major benefits by adopting Muhammad ᶜAli's methods of regulating provincial economic production and trade. Skillful manipulation of agricultural and industrial production and marketing by 1820 was enabling Cairo to set its own schedule of revenue intake, something that the sultanate had not been able to do since the heyday of imperial power. As a source of taxes that could be turned to military reconsolidation priorities, for example, Muhammad ᶜAli's strict regulation of cotton exports and customs charges was nearly as important as standard schedules for peasant taxes on *miri* cultivation rights.

In the wider service of the Ottoman sovereign, Muhammad ᶜAli himself, along with the New Order governmental philosophy he embodied, might have helped solve the dilemma of the Eastern Question as a whole. Indeed, his successes in military and financial reconsolidation made many parties, including his political rivals in Istanbul, gauge possible consequences if institutions that worked so well in Egypt were taken over and applied throughout the Empire. One example was the sultan's decision to destroy the notoriously inefficient Janissary Corps just prior to his request for the deployment of Egyptian troops against insurrectionary forces in Greece in 1826. This move suggested that Mahmud II felt he had more to gain from recognizing Muhammad ᶜAli as an undisputed and useful master of New Order reformism than from rejecting his meteoric rise to prominence in Egypt.

The Ottoman sultan might also have been tempted, at least until his break with the Cairo governor in the 1830s, to copy Muhammad ᶜAli in reorganizing by fiat capitulatory dealings with foreigners who had helped divert commercial conditions in certain provinces toward economic disequilibrium. It is possible, even, that Mahmud did not look on with total disfavor when Muhammad ᶜAli's disappointment over his thwarted attempts at intervention in Greece led to seizure of the Damascus governorate and its Lebanese and Palestinian dependencies in 1831.[18] Application of firm central fiscal and commercial controls in Syria succeeded in overcoming, during eight years of Egyptian rule, a multiplicity of local political and economic divisions that had sapped the vitality of the Damascus governorate from the mid-eighteenth century forward.[19] That Muhammad ᶜAli exploited gains made in Syria to enhance his own strength at the expense of closer integration into the imperial fiscal and military system obviously soured Mahmud's views by the mid-1830s.

Whatever the sultan's early expectations and eventual disappointments may have been, studies of the Egyptian Crisis between 1831 and 1839 do indicate one thing: commercial adjustments made by Muhammad ᶜAli did correspond to effective application of New Order policies, in both Syria and Egypt. For this very reason, it seems, a second disastrous military encounter between the Ottomans and Muhammad ᶜAli in 1839 provided the crisis scenario needed to create a strong capitulatory front against further Egyptian expansionism. Mahmud's sudden death during the 1839 confrontation with the Syro-Egyptian army, followed by a Concert of Europe decision to impose a return to the *status quo ante* 1831 encouraged Istanbul to abandon commitments to New Order reform priorities and to come into closer coordination with European preferences. In the place of the previous generation's conception of a New Order, assumedly benevolent international intervention led by Britain's Lord Palmerston sponsored a new device to save the Ottoman Empire from its own apparent internal instability. In the same hectic months during which a joint European military plan was devised to confront Muhammad ᶜAli, a second new era, this time of Tanzimat reformism, was tailored to assist Ottoman imperial recovery.

EUROPEAN INTERVENTION AGAINST NIZAM-I CEDID INITIATIVES

Joint European intervention to arrange a new capitulatory *modus vivendi* and to support a new program of Ottoman internal reforms between 1839 and 1841 is a good example of the indirect processes of imperialism introduced in the first section of this chapter. It is impossible here to estimate the full impact of Europe's decision to help rearrange Ottoman-Egyptian relations and to formulate reform programs that would be pursued by several Turkish sultans over the next half-century. It could be argued, for example, that two policy priorities fostered by Britain's Lord Palmerston in particular both aimed at essentially the same objective. Like their predecessors who had dealt with the Eastern Question since 1699, British strategists in 1839 were determined that circumstances behind the Egyptian Crisis should not allow any unilateral gains against the Ottoman Empire at the expense of other post-1815 Concert of Europe powers.

By this date, such potential dangers were obviously not limited to perennially weak links on Istanbul's Balkan flank. French attraction to a North African sphere of influence had grown rapidly since occupation of the Algerian littoral in 1830. In fact, forced detachment of the sultan's westernmost provincial dependency had created numerous misunderstandings over the proper handling of Concert policies toward Mahmud II in his dealings with Muhammad ᶜAli. If anything, Louis Philippe's ministers had tended to encourage acts of autonomy by Egypt's governorate. This could both justify France's own policy of independent dealings with Ahmad Bey in Tunis and raise its chances of becoming a political and economic partner with Muhammad ᶜAli.[20] One of Palmerston's main concerns in dealing with the 1831–39 Syro-Egyptian problem, on the other hand, was to insist on support for the Istanbul regime against menaces of special political or economic status for separate provincial regions. The best means of obtaining this objective, short of serious military intervention, seemed to be to level strong criticism against restrictions on private capitulatory trade imposed by Muhammad ᶜAli since the early 1820s.

All European governments, including France, had experienced frustration dealing with strict controls over import and export markets in Egypt and Syria during the 1830s. Having briefly enjoyed easier conditions of access to exports that reached the Levant via Hijazi caravans, Europeans found Muhammad ᶜAli's system of controls abrasive. When it came to attractive new cash crop commodities, such as Syro-Lebanese silk (exploited under the state sponsorship of the Egyptian governorate in Damascus) or the rising market for Egyptian cotton, many parties complained that Muhammad ᶜAli's interventionism menaced destruction of long-standing Ottoman-European trade cooperation. Since the Egyptian governor paid little attention to sultanic capitulations in his own sphere of Levant trade, European commercial houses gradually abandoned hope of coercive pressure from their diplomatic representatives in the distant Ottoman capital. Indeed, some would have been happier had their governments sought separate agreements directly with Muhammad ᶜAli. In an age of rising pressures for free trade conditions in Britain and elsewhere, Eastern Question political experts in the 1830s faced an apparently insoluble quandary.

A first move to deal with this dilemma was attempted by British policymakers before the Syro-Egyptian crisis of 1839. In August 1838, London's ambassador obtained a bilateral trade agreement between the Ottoman and British governments. British negotiators in 1838 probably felt that, if they gained particularly good terms for the many different firms then jostling to buy goods in East Mediterranean ports, a rise in the volume of British-Ottoman trade would bind the Bosphorus to the Thames politically as well as commercially.[21] If one views these negotiations with the Porte in more general capitulatory terms, however, the 1838 Balta Liman Convention promised to create anything but an aura of free trade and goodwill among third parties. Other governments were bound to come under pressure to update their own capitulatory treaties to prevent the British from reaping advantages from the new scale of lower duties obtained by London's negotiators. On the other hand, the Balta Liman agreement placed Britain in a useful position of leadership in capitulatory matters after 1838. This capitulatory edge was actually used by the Foreign Office to gain allies for a cooperative political front during the 1839–40 Egyptian Crisis.

If a general solution to new Eastern Question political dilemmas could have been reached merely by expelling Muhammad ᶜAli from Syria, then a complete scenario for handling the Egyptian Crisis could have appeared in the political agenda leading to the sultan's September 1840 Convention with the great powers.[22] Lord Palmerston's own conception of the wider causes of instability in the Ottoman Empire, however, definitely went much deeper.

The somewhat contrived circumstances of European reaction against Muhammad ᶜAli in 1839 and 1840 included outbreaks of popular discontent in Christian pockets of the Syro-Lebanese zone.[23] It may have seemed only natural (and convenient) to Lord Palmerston, therefore, that any new Ottoman reform program to replace New Order priorities practiced by Muhammad ᶜAli should emphasize private interests and individual rights, especially where minority subjects were involved. Indeed, this added dimension of "benevolent" sectarian considerations in Eastern Question politics was well timed. It allowed the powers that met in London in 1840 to invite the new sultan, Abdulmecid (1839–61), to absorb lessons supposedly learned by countries that had passed from a situation of arbitrary governmental authority to a commitment to ordered rule by law. By highly idealized liberal standards in post-Napoleonic Europe, the wealth and ultimate security of any state was thought to be measurable in terms of the potential for individual prosperity and security among its subjects. In other words, the most important index of effective Ottoman government, like that of distant regimes in Europe, should be its provision of laws protecting the individual from arbitrary action, whether by the state or by a stronger neighbor.

Whether sponsors of a joint Ottoman-European political front recognized these facts or not, the British evidently insisted that no "mistaken" New Order principles should survive after the powers intervened to save Istanbul from its military debacle against Muhammad ᶜAli in 1839. Thus, as an implicit precondition for convening the special international conference that met in London in 1840, Sultan Abdulmecid was encouraged to issue his famous *Hatt-i Şerif* of Gulhane.[24] In this first major Tanzimat document, the sultan announced that future imperial rule should rest primarily on strengthened judicial protection for the rights of private subjects throughout Ottoman territory. To the premature satisfaction of Foreign Office hosts of the London Conference, this seemed tantamount to guaranteeing that Abdulmecid was ready to modernize the Empire by making individual, not governmental, interests priorities in a new round of imperial reforms.

FINAL TERMS OF THE 1841 EGYPTIAN SETTLEMENT

The following chapter begins to explore the effects Abdulmecid's first Tanzimat decree eventually had on the theory and practice of *qanun* law in the Ottoman Empire, especially in Egypt. For the moment, however, attention should be given to the solution of several other irritating economic problems of New Order practices first established in Egypt and Syria between 1820 and 1841.

The initial convention that European powers presented to both Muhammad ᶜAli and Sultan Abdulmecid in July of 1840 contained political terms and a capitulatory *modus operandi* that were acceptable to all European parties to the London Conference itself. When amended and transformed into an imperial *firman* in 1841, the European Convention for the Pacification of the Levant gave Muhammad ᶜAli the unprecedented right to pass on his responsibilities as Egyptian viceroy to his hereditary descendants.[25] This formal grant of dynastic security assumed, however, certain concessions. Because Muhammad ᶜAli's future governing responsibilities were to be confined to the Nile Valley alone, the powers demanded that Egypt cut back its standing army to eighteen thousand men. Since almost all of Muhammad ᶜAli's important internal reforms had been organized to support a strong military budget, this strict ruling promised to have early repercussions for a number of already implanted New Order institutions in Egypt.

Other conditions imposed by Abdulmecid's 1841 *firman* promised to be less immediate but equally debilitating for administrative and economic structures developed by Cairo since 1820. When it discussed Egypt's controversial status as a subregion within the Ottoman capitulatory system, for example, the London Conference insisted on the suppression of Muhammad ᶜAli's system of government commercial monopolies. To guarantee that foreign material interests would not be adversely affected by awarding *de facto* provincial autonomy to Cairo, the sultan was advised formally to require that "all [capitulatory] treaties concluded . . . between the Porte and the . . . Powers should be completely executed in Egypt. . . ."[26] Next, by urging that reconfirmation of Egypt's obligations within the general capitulatory system should be followed by a new round of most favored nation treaties based on the 1838 Anglo-Ottoman convention, London laid the basis for capitulatory politics that continued to operate for half a century after 1841. Simply stated, Palmerston assumed that disgruntled Concert powers would not dare to upset the new balance of regional political interests he wished to establish, since this would jeopardize mutually attractive advantages in restored capitulatory terms for the Empire as a whole. The first objective was sealed in the London Convention's provision that there would be a joint political and military policy to solve the Egyptian Crisis to the benefit of all, not a minority of interested parties. The second came in a spate of new trade agreements granting each capitulatory power most favored nation status on the basis of the 1838 Balta Liman Convention.[27]

Few parties could have predicted just how long any of these new departures from traditional Eastern Question priorities would endure following the 1840 London Conference. The history of Ottoman relations with Russia over the next three and a half decades eventually proved, of course, that both Lord Palmerston's and Lord Aberdeen's hopes of reviving the "Sick Man of Europe" through Tanzimat reform sponsorship would fail where actual European thrusts for territorial gain were concerned. The playing out of later Ottoman-Russian tensions, as well as British and French diplomatic and military responses (in the crises of the 1853–56 Crimean War and 1876–78 Russo-Turkish War), involved definite reversions to classical eighteenth-century methods of Eastern Question strategy. Events in Egypt during the same thirty-five years after 1841, however, reveal quite different patterns. This applies to the local impact of legal reforms in the Tanzimat era as well as to other forms of penetration of European principles into Egyptian administrative practices. In both of these areas, the ongoing process of integration of the eastern Mediterranean into a wider European economic and political order influenced the effectiveness of many decrees applied in the spirit of the Tanzimat. It also affected the attitudes of various parties, both foreign and local, whose material interests attracted them to definitions of the nature and functions of secular law offered by the first Tanzimat generation.

2

Justice in Egypt from Muhammad ᶜAli to Khedive Ismaᶜil (1820s–60s)

Sultan Abdulmecid's reversal of Muhammad ᶜAli's most ambitious New Order schemes did not automatically end other, less spectacular, aspects of administration he put in place between 1820 and 1841. On the contrary, many well-known principles that became symbols of Ottoman Tanzimat methods were just being tested for practical effect in Egypt at this time. One may even suggest that imperial authorities repeatedly measured their own Tanzimat efforts against the lead the Egyptian province had already taken and would continue, particularly in the area of legal reform.

A good portion of Tanzimat literature describes priorities of Ottoman reform between 1839 and 1875 in terms of purposeful secularization of various branches of internal administration. A general aim of changes, most claim, was to bring wider benefits to the many sectarian subcommunities living under imperial rule. Although such generalizations have merit, it is clear that Istanbul drew several other critical lessons from the experience of Concert of Europe intervention during the 1839–41 Egyptian Crisis.

Almost immediately after Abdulmecid's *Hatt-i Şerif* in 1839, the imperial Tanzimat council tried to respond to the first such lesson by restating the assumed legal bases of Ottoman sovereignty, particularly those associated with the vague provisions of *qanun* law, in formal codified form. Following promulgation of a penal code meant to apply to all subjects of the Empire without reference to sectarian status, work began on the first elements of a Western-inspired commercial code.[1] Such measures were publicized as a first step toward removing local administrative inequities based on outmoded *qanunnahmes*. Informed observers, however, knew well that new imperial legal codes were meant to respond to capitulatory critics of Istanbul's handling of the 1831–39 Egyptian Crisis.

Effective legal protection from penal abuses was an indicator easily understood by European supporters of Abdulmecid's first general Tanzimat decree. The exact scope of the sultan's responsibilities toward individual subjects' material welfare, however, was less easily spelled out in formal edicts. Given the increasingly competitive nature of foreign interests in Mediterranean trade since the 1820s, it was almost certain that an imperial code of commerce was needed to cover much more complicated contracts than either local or foreign merchant communities in the Levant had formerly known. Perhaps the Tanzimat council deliberately set back promulgation of an imperial commercial code year after year in order to size up the actual course of trade following abolition of Muhammad ᶜAli's restrictive trade monopolies. Whatever the actual causes for the ten-year delay, however, it must have been apparent to Ottoman policymakers from the outset that they would soon have to provide wider channels for European forms of credit, bankruptcy, futures contracts, and the like. Without such legislative innovations, bitter disputes were bound to arise between unprepared signers of local agricultural and sales contracts and eager believers in the promise of a new "liberal" economic order under the sponsorship of the Istanbul sultanate. Thus, early promises of personal equality before the law in the *Hatt-i Şerif* of 1839 represented only a partial indication of what would have to be done to avoid repetitions of European diplomatic interventionism in later stages of the Tanzimat.

EXPANSION OF JUDICIAL STRUCTURES IN EGYPT IN THE 1840S AND 1850S

To understand why reforms carried out in Egypt drew early and continued attention from Istanbul, it is important to know how traditional theories of *qanun* law fit in the heyday of Muhammad ᶜAli's governorate. Even though the (pre-1841) Cairo *diwan* was inspired by ironclad New Order precepts, it seems that Muhammad ᶜAli's methods of secular justice in some instances prepared the way for responses to new social and economic and even some political trends that would affect the entire Levant zone by the second half of the nineteenth century.

Owing to a long tradition of overemphasis on Islamic religious factors and their assumed universal influence in Ottoman administration, some writers have claimed that—until special international judicial conventions were introduced in Egypt in the 1870s—court procedures under Muhammad ᶜAli's viceregal dynasty did not extend beyond the limited sphere of the *qadi*'s *mahkama*. Only recently has attention been given to a series of administrative options for different types of litigation introduced by Muhammad ᶜAli and developed throughout the formal Tanzimat period.[2] Studies for Egypt show a pattern that is familiar to students of Ottoman and Islamic history generally: practical administrative requirements always encouraged separation between the (primarily personal status) functions of the *qadi* and secular judicial prerogatives of government. This was especially true where penal or basic fiscal considerations were at stake.[3] Specialists agree that, well before the Tanzimat era, sectarian jurisdiction tended to diminish whenever the power of central political authorities rose enough to offset the traditional influence of the religious classes in many key areas.

The contrary phenomenon is, of course, also visible at specific points in the history of the Islamic Middle East. There are numerous examples of resurgent identification with sectarian legal definitions of state and society, especially when government inefficiency created a high degree of material and social insecurity. In either event, judicial arguments drawn from *shariᶜa* or *qanun* law always depended on the willingness of essentially secular governments to provide supportive administrative structures (fiscal, police, or "moral," as in the case of market supervision, or *hisba*) to give body to any standing or innovative claim of jurisdiction. It is mainly as a result of relatively recent direct associations between Islamic countries and the West that such ebb and flow phenomena have become classified as traditionalist, secularist, or modernizing currents in Middle Eastern history.

Looking specifically at Egypt, we know that Muhammad ᶜAli himself consciously tried to found a system of specialized *majalis* or councils to carry out a variety of secular judicial functions. Although he was only partially successful, Cairo's governor even tried to give to such administratively appointed councils sole authority to hear all judicial disputes involving foreign capitulatory subjects. As we shall see, this was one example of Egyptian administrative reform innovation that Tanzimat leaders in Istanbul attempted to apply more generally throughout the Empire after 1841.

In his own provincial operations in the 1830s and 1840s, Muhammad ᶜAli delegated a portion of his own high executive prerogatives to a single specialized body known as the Council of Egyptian Judicial Rulings (Ar., *majlis al-ahkam al-misriyya*).[4] Whether intentionally or not, the name of this council appeared again in Istanbul's *meclis-i ahkam-i adliye*, which helped administer the first judicial stages of the sultan's famous 1839 *Hatt*.[5] Whereas the Ottoman council was to devise administrative changes and appropriate legal codes for the Empire as a whole, however, the Cairo Council served primarily as a superior court for the Egyptian governorate. It reviewed, for example, petitions against Muhammad ᶜAli's own officials who, in the absence of a distinct judicial branch of government, traditionally settled village-level disputes not clearly reserved for local sectarian jurisdictions. To do this, the Council referred to rudimentary Egyptian *qanun* codes or collections of administrative decrees handed down by Muhammad ᶜAli's *diwan*. The earliest such localized provincial code was the *qanun al-filaha*, promulgated in 1820 to establish peasant rights and obligations as tenants on state-run lands. The major concerns of the *qanun al-filaha* during the 1830s involved penalties for peasant failure to conform to strict government standards of cultivation, taxation, and marketing under Egypt's agricultural monopoly system.[6]

Although individuals who served in the Cairo Council received no special training to qualify as jurists, they could rely on easy access to *qanun* documents stored in the Cairo archives.[7] Most *qanun*s were clear enough to follow, particularly if one had previous experience in dealing with traditional executive agents of the government. Council members assumed that landed property disputes *per se* did not come under their jurisdiction, since the by then predominantly *miri* land tenure regime precluded the possibility of individual ownership claims on cultivated plots. The only freehold ownership (Ar., *mulk*) that was legally recognized in the Ottoman Empire at this time was likely to consist of urban and town properties. The fact that quite specific Islamic legal provisions had always existed to cover such titles, however, made it difficult for the Council to impinge on the traditional jurisdiction of local *qadi* courts over them. Nonetheless, the mere existence of an independent authority to interpret *qanun* decrees and impose decisions on individual subjects and officials alike was a significant *pre*-Tanzimat innovation in Egypt.

Egyptians themselves continued for at least another decade after 1839 to depend on simple provincial officials to settle local nonshariatic disputes summarily. The Cairo Council, meanwhile, technically became the sole competent authority to receive judicial petitions by or against foreigners enjoying capitulatory status in Egypt. The ironhanded rule of the governor's *diwan* especially in the penal domain probably guaranteed respect for this provision as long as Muhammad ᶜAli was alive. In the area of private business dealings, on the other hand, Egypt's governor made at least one early concession to contribute to the spirit of the Tanzimat Council's work toward a general Ottoman commercial code. Anticipating a similar move by the imperial *diwan* five years later, Cairo allowed Egyptians and foreigners to settle their own *commercial disputes only* before two separate merchants' councils (Ar., *majalis at-tujjar*) created in 1845. These first mixed councils were made up of an equal number of Egyptians and foreigners chosen by lot from the merchant communities of Cairo and Alexandria. They could arbitrate disputes between capitulatory and local subjects alike. The specific limits of their competence, however, were carefully spelled out in a rudimentary code of commercial contracts that were by then becoming common between Egyptian and foreign merchants or their agents.[8]

It is difficult to determine whether the commercial council measure was intended to encourage foreign trade or was perhaps a first concession to dissatisfaction with the Cairo Council's technical shortcomings. What it did suggest was that, without yet admitting a need to ask Istanbul for a formal commercial code, the Cairo governorate was prepared to adopt certain European procedures for application to business dealings in Egypt. The fact that only about a dozen special mixed commercial laws were spelled out in 1845, however, indicates a selection that would have excluded any conflicts with either the *shariᶜa* or the Cairo *diwan*'s own growing corpus of *qanun* decrees.

Even before remarkable growth in foreign business activities in Egypt imposed some changes in Muhammad ᶜAli's original judicial system, the Cairo *diwan* had difficulty deciding what types of local conflicts should be handled by the Cairo Council. Muhammad ᶜAli's successor, ᶜAbbas Pasha (r. 1848–54), for example, was the first viceroy to have to find local administrative channels to implement a number of reform directives in different areas passed on by the Tanzimat Council in Istanbul. Perhaps to head off a possibility of conflict between Egypt's grass-roots needs and Ottoman Tanzimat rulings, ᶜAbbas immediately shored up specifically Egyptian methods of administration by publishing a complete set of *qanun* laws which had been compiled earlier by Muhammad ᶜAli. Then, to provide signs of conforming to the Tanzimat's proclaimed aim of expanding judicial options for all Ottoman subjects, five regional councils (Ar., *majalis al-aqalim*) were created in Egypt in 1852 to review and settle petitions presented to district governors (Ar., *mudirs*) according to the prevailing codes.[9]

Like Cairo's High Council, ᶜAbbas's regional councils were comprised of salaried judges named by the *diwan*. These were usually retired army officers or officials who had served in various branches of Muhammad ᶜAli's highly regimented bureaucratic machine. At the same time, some provincial notables, including religious scholars (Ar., *ᶜulama'*) and agriculturists who were beginning to accumulate wealth through a combination of *diwan*-approved rural land grants and ties with the increasingly free cotton export market, were also appointed.[10] Even though such individuals probably lacked the Cairo Council's technical familiarity with *qanun* laws, their knowledge of practical local administrative conditions probably helped speed judicial proceedings. It was only later, when Tanzimat liberalizing trends in property law took root in the 1860s, that Egyptian peasants could complain that Council appointees tended to interpret cases in ways that benefited their own "notable" sector of the rural agricultural community in particular (see discussion on Egypt's First Consultative Assembly and Judicial Procedures in Village-Level Council, below).

Despite apparent technical flaws, then, the theory of a separate secular judicial function existed alongside the *qadi*'s traditional *mahkama* jurisdiction by the time Egypt's governorate passed to Muhammad Saᶜid Pasha (r. 1854–63). One can even suggest that the judicial councils functioning in Egypt by 1854 provided a model for reforms that the Ottoman Tanzimat Council incorporated into its famous "second round" of imperial decrees following Istanbul's involvement in the Crimean War from 1853 to 1856.[11] Formal reaffirmation of Tanzimat aims came in Sultan Abdulmecid's *Hatt-i Humayoun* of 1856. By that date, however, pressures for closer commitments to European forms of administration based on financial and economic development considerations were blurring distinctions between Istanbul's internal legal reform objectives and quite different priorities championed by the sultanate's most important capitulatory allies. Egypt, on the other hand, would still escape the repercussions of increasing European involvement in Ottoman politics and high finances for a few more years into Saʿid Pasha's governorate.

LOCAL SOCIAL AND ECONOMIC FACTORS BEHIND SAʿID'S LEGAL AND JUDICIAL REFORM SCHEMES

Historians can derive two advantages from the fact that many of Egypt's experiences of Tanzimat reformism evolved earlier and along slightly different lines than those of the central sultanate. First, because of the diversity of provinces that were expected to implement sultanic decrees, it is nearly impossible to summarize the impact of imperial edicts in a total Ottoman framework. Several considerations make Egypt an ideal setting for studying Tanzimat legal reform questions from the local rather than the wider imperial level. For one, Egypt definitely experienced several important processes of change that were hardly ever reflected in official Ottoman decrees. Because Egypt was several years in advance of the rest of the Empire in many aspects of both administrative and economic development by mid-century, its population had the mixed blessing of experiencing the potential benefits and disadvantages of such changes before their effects could be gauged either by the Istanbul regime or by interested European parties.

Increasing foreign involvement in the cotton market was bound to give a strong capitulatory and commercial twist to developments up and down the Nile Valley in the 1850s and 1860s. Saʿid's earliest innovations in traditional *qanun* legislation, however, concentrated on questions of tenure and fiscality affecting Egypt's local population. Egypt set the pace, for example, for what became a general mid-nineteenth-century trend toward private ownership of land throughout the Ottoman Empire. As a result, the Cairo governorate was probably the first to experience various conflicts pitting emergent private interests dependent on the still nascent deliberative judicial branch of local administration against the authority of provincial officials who resented sharing key areas of executive privilege. This was especially true when the centralized *miri* land tenure system imposed by Muhammad ʿAli began to cede to new structures fostered by the Tanzimat.

Perhaps it was an uneasy feeling over the possible future consequences of his own decision to extend private land rights that prompted Saᶜid Pasha to suspend ᶜAbbas's local judicial councils, which had been dominated by official assessors. If his aim was to increase individual cultivators' sense of tenure security, however, Saᶜid would only have had to vest responsibility for defining property rights in a judicial body that would be separate from both traditional *shariᶜa* jurisdiction and representatives of formal executive authority. The fact was, however, that no steps had been taken to prepare either new codes or local personnel to assume such responsibilities. Soon after annulling ᶜAbbas's regional boards, therefore, Saᶜid returned full powers of adjudication—now including at least some jurisdiction over *qanun* decrees governing land tenure—to a similarly constituted local council system.[12]

Saᶜid himself never fully faced the inevitable litigious results brought by the changes he made in Egypt's corpus of *qanun* law between 1854 and 1863. In general, additions tended to supplement and support the independent judicial authority of Cairo's *majlis al-ahkam*. Such changes, like those promised but never quite realized at the imperial level, were designed to show both internal and foreign observers that Tanzimat-inspired laws could actually enhance the grass-roots material welfare of the Sultan's private subjects. Viewed from the ideal free market perspective of Europe at mid-century, the long-term welfare of the state was bound to follow automatically.

Naturally, the eventual impact of these reform measures could not have been predicted in the two decades that witnessed the legal recognition of full landownership rights for private subjects and even foreign residents in the Ottoman Empire. From the time this particular concern of the Tanzimat Council took root in Egypt, however, there was some assumption of a concomitant executive responsibility to systematize new legislation in a way that would guarantee that various associated interests, both in land and in commercial prospects connected with it, would not be jeopardized by a reorientation in Tanzimat policy directives. Possibly such rising pressures explain Cairo's decision to convoke its first Consultative Assembly of Representatives only slightly over a decade after Saᶜid's original decrees recognizing private tenure rights in Egypt (see discussion on Egypt's First Consultative Assembly and Judicial Procedures in Village-Level Councils, below).

Saᶜid's own departures from a strict *miri* tenure system indicated an apparent desire to increase security for peasant cultivators who were having difficulties moving from government-controlled to free agricultural marketing in Egypt in the 1840s. Several of his land laws tried to ensure the confidence of peasants who were reticent about continuing cash crop agriculture once market guarantees and necessary maintenance of irrigation facilities, both common features of the 1830s, ceased to be specific responsibilities of the Cairo *diwan*. Rather than grant tax incentives for growers of exportable cash crops, Saᶜid began by offering a greater sense of peasant security on *miri* land—land that was useless to the government without commitments by its occupants to keep it perennially productive. The land law of January 1855, for example, guaranteed that occupants of *miri* lands could, under conditions to be defined by the *shariᶜa* judge, obtain written certifications (*hujjas*) of individually defined usufruct rights. The right to sell or bequeath such titles was thereafter to be formally recognized by either the *qadi*'s *mahkama* or regional council jurisdictions. Thus, without actually granting full ownership rights over the soil, the Egyptian governorate began experimenting in 1855 with ways to use new laws to encourage exploitation of free market agricultural rights by individually motivated local cultivators.[13]

Although Saᶜid's 1855 land law represented an original breakthrough in the overall history of the Tanzimat, it was soon followed by much more comprehensive imperial guidelines. These were then adapted locally to meet Egypt's specific needs. Indeed, once the Treaty of Paris ended the Crimean War, a newly appointed Tanzimat Council took both Abdulmecid's 1856 *Hatt-i Humayoun* and European reform enthusiasts' advice on such matters seriously. A formal law was finally issued in 1858 that ended the traditional concept of *miri* tenure in all agricultural regions of the Ottoman Empire. For Saᶜid, this meant that even more comprehensive legal definitions of conditions for property ownership in Egypt could be undertaken with the assumed sanction of the sultan.

In August 1858, the Cairo *diwan* issued a decree that may initially have been intended as a preemptive response to land legislation priorities set down in Istanbul.[14] In fact, in contrast to the more general imperial decree later in the same year, Egypt's new tenure law expanded a number of already existing landholding rights and obligations that the Cairo governorate obviously wished to keep at the center of its own property regime. Distinctions were made among several categories of tenure. These began with *de facto* freehold granted to a limited number of "dead land" developers or select grantees of converted *miri* land (payers of the ᶜ*ushu*r tax, hence ᶜ*ushuriyya* owners). Next came a less privileged status for hereditary holders of cultivation rights only on former *miri* land who paid a *kharaj* tax (*kharajiyya* lands).[15] The majority of *kharajiyya* tenants had only recently gained the right to pledge officially recognized land use certificates for credit advances and to transfer these same rights and obligations to their heirs.

Saᶜid sought to devise more ways to shore up peasants' attachment to the plots they cultivated. His 1858 law specified, for example, that anyone who maintained a continuous record of cultivation and *kharaj* tax payments for five years running or who undertook to erect useful facilities (storage buildings or waterwheels) could petition to reclassify his land as ᶜ*ushuriyya*. This provision opened the way for more industrious cultivators, particularly those who saw benefit in moving permanently from subsistence farming to full-time production for the cotton export market, to move one step closer to personal independence in the disposition of their labors and land. The main distinction between *kharajiyya* and ᶜ*ushuriyya* tenure, however, was still only a fiscal one. Full title to inalienable ownership awaited fuller clarification of the proper relationship between Egypt's local legislation and registration procedures to be worked out under the 1858 imperial land law.

Many historians consider the 1858 land law an early cause of the steady growth of an Egyptian landholding elite, on the one hand, and an underprivileged class of tenant farmers, on the other.[16] Many later negative effects of Tanzimat-inspired land legislation, however, stemmed mainly from side effects of disastrous central financial policies that began under Saᶜid and extended over the next twenty-five years. Probably only a small minority of astute (not to say guileful) local cultivators managed to turn Egypt's gradually evolving land laws to their distinct private advantage during the coming years of financial chaos in the 1860s and 1870s. Laws on property *per se* were probably a less direct cause of the crisis that was brewing than more subtle features of local *qanun* procedures that accompanied other Tanzimat innovations.

EGYPT'S FIRST CONSULTATIVE ASSEMBLY AND JUDICIAL PROCEDURES IN VILLAGE-LEVEL COUNCILS

Addition of several property decrees to Cairo's growing corpus of administrative laws made it unlikely that either the rudimentary regional councils or traditional *qadi* courts could handle new types of disputes that soon became commonplace. Such gaps may have encouraged Egypt's first attempt, in 1866, to expand the field for auxiliary private participation in the elaboration of new forms of legislation that bordered on what Europeans would call civil law.

We may never know if Saᶜid's successor, Ismaᶜil (r. 1863–79), actually intended to gear his own considerably more famous plans for Egyptian legislative and judicial reform to the expectations of any particular local or foreign interest group in the 1860s and 1870s. Only a few years after Saᶜid's death, the new viceroy's overriding involvement with financial and foreign capitulatory priorities came to overshadow his apparent early concern for the constitutive elements of both central and village-level legal questions. Nonetheless, Ismaᶜil began his governorate with several dramatic gestures that were not reflected generally in the Ottoman Empire until very near the end of the formal Tanzimat period. Whatever other ill-conceived schemes for political and economic reform still tarnish views of the "Maligned Khedive," Ismaᶜil seems to have sensed rising potential sources of social and economic conflict beyond his *diwan* and tried to solve some of them by bending Tanzimat directives to meet local needs. Perhaps the most notable measure along these lines, which was bound to involve local debate over advantages and disadvantages in further innovative use of *qanun* law in Egypt, was his appointment of a small body of provincial notables to form Cairo's first Consultative Assembly of Representatives (Ar., *majlis shura an-nuwwab*) in November 1866.[17]

Although a number of political considerations lay behind creation of the Consultative Assembly, Ismaᶜil seemed most anxious to rally a higher level of rural notable support for new directions in *qanun* legal administration than he could obtain through the local assessors who had served in Saᶜid's regional councils. Such concerns probably stemmed from the growing interconnections among new laws governing private land rights, the supposed limits of council jurisdiction, and Egypt's increasingly obvious central financial problems by 1866.

Between 1863 and 1866, Isma^cil added several new laws to bolster cultivators' sense of the long-term benefit of developing lands that had come available for private ownership by 1858. Better-placed individuals, particularly village headmen or *ᶜumdas*, may already have taken advantage of incentives to accumulate plots under their personal control. Neither they nor representatives of the wealthiest rural families, however, yet formed a substantial political or economic nucleus that could be called a provincial landholding elite. One reason firmer ties to freehold land and commercial investments in its produce were not developing faster was simple: soaring treasury costs for major economic development schemes begun during Egypt's 1860–63 cotton boom had already brought an increase in *ᶜushuriyya* taxes in 1864. At the same time, fears were rising among *kharajiyya* peasants that similar increases might strike them or that other redefinitions of cultivators' obligations to the *diwan* would be imposed in the form of arbitrarily assigned *qanun* decrees.[18]

Ismaᶜil's decision to convoke a Cairo Consultative Assembly, therefore, may have been meant to calm spreading fears in the countryside by involving rural representatives in *diwan* matters of obvious concern to cultivators. Delegates named to Ismaᶜil's first Assembly were probably screened to be certain that they would approve of new directions in administrative decrees. Some, however, may have hoped to reap advantages for themselves by consulting regularly on *qanun* regulations affecting tenure and marketing of agricultural produce. In fact, the original Assembly possessed little real responsibility. It was prohibited, for example, from hearing constituents' petitions for attention to particular judicial grievances or submitting its own new legislative proposals. Both of these functions would have been attractive incentives if Ismaᶜil had been interested only in currying favor with influential representatives of rural agricultural interests. Bringing provincial notables to Cairo to serve largely symbolic consultative functions, however, offered simultaneous counter attractions for the *diwan*: the latter could use interaction with the Assembly to keep check on any tendencies by a privileged few to monopolize advantages offered by new directions in Tanzimat-inspired legislation. This suggestion is borne out by the fact that, until conflicting domestic and foreign pressures for changes in reform priorities drew most of his attention, Ismaᶜil actually widened local bases of support for legal decision making at the village level.

Apparently some individuals who participated in the Cairo Assembly after 1866 were anxious to define and strengthen the grass-roots judicial authority of rural *qanun* jurisdictions. The first sign of this appeared in the session of 1871, when several delegates asked that Ismaᶜil's newly established Ministry of Justice set up a much wider system of small courts. These would hear local cases that could not get a hearing at the limited regional or Cairo Council level and therefore still had to pass before provincial executive officials.[19]

It is not clear what motivations lay behind such requests for more decentralized judicial council operations. The Cairo *diwan* had frequently called on well-placed local individuals to serve as assessor-judges on regional councils since the 1850s. Expanded participation by such men under a wider corpus of *qanun* laws after 1870 not only might have added to the local notables' role as protectors against excessive executive or emergent large landowners' privileges: it also might have contributed to a growing degree of dependency in land-related cases between typical *fallahin* litigants and their more successful peers on the judicial councils. The promise of benefits from such dependence for council appointees could have been camouflaged in different ways. In ideal terms, new Egyptian legal structures appeared to prepare the way for announced Ottoman efforts to establish a standard network of secular (*nizamiyya*) courts throughout the Empire.[20] Service toward this aim, even at a very rudimentary preprofessional level, was a first visible opportunity to prove civic responsibility in the name of the Tanzimat.

At the same time, support for a local version of Tanzimat goals in Egypt's legal system could have been considered a modest buffer against uncontrollable effects if imperial failures brought more direct European involvement in such internal questions. These concerns would naturally have increased as council delegates learned about external pressures on the Cairo *diwan* to adopt courts based entirely on Western codes and procedures (see chapter 3, below). They may even have made maintenance of certain essentials of *qanun* law and procedures at the local level an implicit condition for continued cooperation between the financially troubled *diwan* and the nascent consultative authority of the Assembly after 1870. Without such an explanation, it would be difficult to understand how Ismaᶜil justified appointing a large number of village *shaykh*s and notables to staff an expanded system of village-level *qanun* jurisdictions in 1872. This was only one year before Istanbul approved a Western-inspired plan to become a model for all judicial operations, in civil as well as penal and commercial affairs, in all provinces. Indeed, had it not been for the more famous Mixed Court Reform of 1873–75, the mark left by Isma^cil's response to local *qanun* law reform expectations would probably have been much more obvious during the fiscal and political turmoil Egypt experienced by the mid-1870s.

Several score village courts (Ar., *majalis ad-da ᶜawi al-baladiyya*) were appointed by separate decrees in 1872 and 1873 to hear all minor disputes that could be settled without referring to the distant Cairo Council for reference to the technical provisions of *qanun* law. Such village judicial councils, like their contemporary administrative counterparts (*majalis mashayikh al-baladiyya*), were staffed by village *shaykh*s assisted by locally nominated notables. The latter often served simultaneously as municipal councillors and judicial assessors according to the local administrative or litigious nature of the work before them.[21]

Initially it may have been assumed that principles of *shariᶜa* law would guide village assessors in their attempts to resolve typical local cases that had never been the object of specific *qanun* decrees. Nothing in Ismaᶜil's decrees, however, required the new local councils to refer to the *shariᶜa*, even though villagers had traditionally considered the *qadi* to be the only legitimate judicial authority for solving certain types of disputes. Only those cases of a clearly religious nature, or those raised by litigants who persisted in preferring the *qadi*'s intervention to that of their own village notables, therefore, continued to appear on the local *shariᶜa* registers by the mid-1870s.

Various obstacles prevented an adequate period of testing under normal circumstances to determine the effectiveness of Ismaᶜil's village councils. Almost as soon as the system began to operate, it came under criticism from many different quarters within Egyptian society. Conservative defenders of the inviolability of the *qadi*'s traditional jurisdiction naturally criticized the councils for their apparent disregard of the importance of the *shariᶜa* in the lives of villagers. Less openly, but ultimately very importantly, critics may already have attacked the rising influence of nascent landholding elites, *qua* court assessors, over the grass-roots personal and material affairs of local rural communities. Supporters of a more systematic application of Tanzimat plans for standard *nizamiyya* jurisdictions, for example, would increasingly criticize the use of non-professional appointees in Egypt's evolving judicial system. City-based proponents of such views eventually denounced Ismaᶜil's sidestepping of the obvious need for technical skills to adjudicate complicated property and contract disputes, which were becoming increasingly common in the 1860s. Calls for greater professionalization of the local councils, however, probably had less impact on the rural *fallahin* mentality than criticism of the new jurisdictions on more familiar religious grounds. Even in the latter case, articulate critics of the grass-roots effects of Ismaᶜil's 1872–73 judicial reform decrees took several years to appear. On the whole, therefore, the Cairo *diwan*'s recognition of the councils as binding arbiters of common private and penal disputes was not seriously questioned by *fallahin* litigants during the first years of their operations.

In the still quite simple administrative context of the early 1870s, village judicial councils seemed to conform both to evolving social and economic trends in Egypt since Saᶜid's time and to general philosophical dictates from the Tanzimat Council. First, questions of property tenure and small-scale cash crop investment on credit had taken on a local importance that would have been unimaginable only twenty years earlier. Village judicial councils familiar with the conditions assumed by local contracting parties seemed to be the best way to protect such vulnerable interests from the whims of powerful individuals or officials who traditionally viewed *qanun* laws as an arm of executive administration, not the definition of individual rights and obligations.

Even without being able to foresee the eventual failure of such ideal Tanzimat principles throughout the Ottoman Empire in the 1870s, however, one could have predicted other pitfalls in Ismaᶜil's village council scheme. First, there was an insufficiently defined line of hierarchical authority between the purely local personnel of village councils and provincial-level benches staffed by at least one direct appointee of the Ministry of Justice in Cairo. Such locally nominated councillors not only lacked formal training in the technical provisions of Egypt's *qanun* law: as rural notables they were likely to have indirect personal interests in many cases, particularly those concerning property and marketing of agricultural crops, that came before them. When and if such biases entered council deliberations, the only official nominally authorized to correct possible miscarriages of justice was the local *mudir*—the very agent whose powers of executive intervention had led to pressures for judicial decentralization in the first place!

As we shall see, one solution to this dilemma had been offered as early as 1867 but failed to gain enough support for implementation before the village councils were inaugurated. What ultimately became the famous Mixed Court Reform of 1875, however, did not even originate in the Egyptian Ministry of Justice, but rather in the Ministry of Foreign Affairs. This suggests that a very different legal reform perspective would pull attention away from the grass-roots operations of Isma^cil's local judicial councils just as the impact of evolving free market trends—in land tenure, credit relations, and agricultural commerce—was being felt in Egypt. This different perspective was dominated by concerns for private foreign interests in Egypt's increasing bid to acquire European goods and services, as well as the sale of its exportable commodities. Significantly, such concerns were held not only by Europeans, but also by subsections of Egypt's rural and urban population who were involved in the material consequences of the same trends.

3

European Pressures for Reform

Various factors help explain the unprecedented influx of Europeans to Egypt after 1850 and the rapid transformation of its major towns into beehives of foreign merchants and entrepreneurs. One cause, of course, was the favorable trade regime imposed on Cairo by imperial *firman* in 1841. Following suppression of Egypt's pre-1841 monopoly system, however, foreigners still had to overcome petty administrative obstacles to penetrate Egypt's cotton market. The fact that Muhammad ᶜAli himself persistently refused to brook emergence of independent commercial intermediaries in Egypt's main port cities already made this task quite difficult. By 1845, Cairo had at least seen fit to create simple mixed councils to settle the most common private commercial disputes involving foreigners. Such local measures had already been in operation for five years when Istanbul finally promulgated a European-style commercial code for application throughout the Empire. At about the same date, Sultan Abdulmecid also decided that wider Ottoman interests would be best served by forming similar mixed councils to apply the new commercial code in key provincial ports.[1]

Ottoman refinement of Muhammad ᶜAli's original system of rudimentary commercial justice seemed to have recognizable advantages. Time gained by letting extraordinary jurisdictions deal with capitulatory matters would enable the sultan's Ministry of Justice to concentrate on creating a more comprehensive system of professional Tanzimat courts. Such *nizamiyya* jurisdictions were to receive complete codes of law that would be understandable and useful for all residents of the Empire, local as well as foreign.[2] Although such perceptions seemed realistic even as late as 1853, changed conditions after the

Crimean War definitely dampened chances of success on a comprehensive imperial scale.

Although it is impossible to gauge the full impact of the Crimean War on the Ottoman Empire, certain results of Istanbul's fateful alliance against Russia clearly influenced a second generation of Tanzimat reformers. Initially, the sultan was made to pay the price of Anglo-French military assistance in the war by issuing the famous *Hatt-i Humayoun* of February 1856.[3] Abdulmecid's 1856 rescript reconfirmed his intention to continue the administrative and legal reforms undertaken between 1839 and 1853. Behind public pronouncements, however, new forces were visible that made the second phase of Tanzimat qualitatively different than the first. In almost all cases, new factors that pressed Istanbul to readjust imperial reform aims from 1856 to 1875 had their counterpart in Egypt during the same time period.

By 1857, the Ottoman treasury had already registered a serious deficit following three years of war against Russia. To the surprise of many observers, however, new leadership in the Tanzimat Council did not adopt retrenchment as a priority for the 1860s. Perhaps failing health and declining political prestige had already forced the venerable Mustafa Paşa Reşid, six times grand vizier since 1839, to delegate financial policymaking authority to younger understudies. When Reşid died in 1858, his disciples, led by ᶜAli and Fuad Paşas and Ahmed Cevdet, a highly educated member of the Turkish *ᶜulama'* class, decided to give a revised slant to Ottoman Tanzimat policies in general.[4]

In addition to trying to strengthen Istanbul's diplomatic position in international politics, second-generation Tanzimat leaders favored what came to be rather costly social and economic development schemes they considered vital for the success of all other imperial reform plans. One well-known area of emphasis involved increased expenditures for government-run secular educational institutions, including the Public Education Law of 1869. This act realized Mustafa Reşid's early plans for the Empire's first university (Dar ul Fünün), which had at least partial facilities for modern legal studies.[5] Expansion of educational institutions naturally did not help balance the imperial budget. Since the new Tanzimat cabinet favored simultaneous expenditures for major infrastructural improvements, however, Sultan Abdulaziz (r. 1861–76) had to devise various ways to cover growing deficits. Foreign allies who had saved the Ottomans from Russian aggression in the 1850s again proved quite willing to help.

European governments did not yet involve themselves directly in advising Abdulaziz on the proper management of the imperial budget. Paris and London, however, apparently saw no harm in letting the sultan pay off his most pressing debts by borrowing from both domestic and private foreign financial sources until general financial conditions, especially from increased trade, improved. Even though Tanzimat efforts were becoming costly, budgetary deficits seemed justifiable according to the same political terms that guided the London Convention in 1840: any measures to aid progress in Ottoman social, economic, or military institutions were to be supported for the sake of maintaining the political status quo throughout the Empire. If such progress depended on expanding educational facilities or attracting foreign concessions to mount costly infrastructural improvements, responsible deficit spending, whether by Istanbul or by semiautonomous provinces like Egypt or Tunisia, may have made certain other risks worth taking.

Had Ottoman financial maneuvering between 1861 and 1875 remained a simple question of budgetary excesses, the second stage of the formal Tanzimat might merely have created hard times for taxpayers who had to pay for development schemes that seemed to have no impact on their own lives. In fact, a number of obviously incomplete legal and judicial structures adopted in the Ottoman Empire during this critical period turned financial and fiscal dilemmas into much more complicated problems, especially where capitulatory interests were involved.

Almost all ready capital and skills necessary for Ottoman development schemes from 1861 forward (educational personnel or equipment for rail and telegraphic communications, etc.) had to come from foreign sources. This meant that a new set of potential legal relationships came into being that, because they involved foreign concession and loan contracts, had little to do with earlier patterns of purely commercial relations between Europeans and the Ottoman administration or its subjects. Moreover, the Ottoman state itself and its provincial subsidiaries were usually main parties to contracts involving European creditors or concessionaires. Thus, normal judicial channels for settling disputes (submission of consular petitions to executive agents of the local administration) were not likely to be acceptable to foreign litigants. As the number of foreign plaintiffs against a debt-ridden Ottoman government rose in the 1860s, therefore, a number of capitulatory assumptions needed to be addressed before any other Tanzimat schemes could be carried out effectively. Moreover, once steps were initiated to solve capitulatory dilemmas, it was inevitable that simultaneous demands for similar attention to the legal reform needs of local subjects would mount. This is in part what happened in Egypt, where foreign financial and entrepreneurial penetration advanced at a faster rate than elsewhere in the Empire.

MIXED JUSTICE IN EGYPT UNDER SA^cID PASHA (1854–63)

It was during the nine years of Sa^cid Pasha's governorate that Egypt launched several local economic development projects to match initiatives being planned in Istanbul. The earliest of these involved preliminary acceptance (in November 1854) of a bid by Ferdinand de Lesseps for a private concession to build a Mediterranean-Red Sea canal via the Isthmus of Suez. Britain's concern over the potential political implications of international maritime access to the Indian Ocean from the Mediterranean, however, delayed final Ottoman ratification of his concession for nearly a decade.[6] In the meantime, Sa^cid undertook a number of other projects that brought increasing numbers of Europeans and their capital into Egypt each year. This was especially true after 1860, when the American Civil War closed off Confederate ports to European buyers of American export commodities. Almost overnight, it appeared that expanding Egyptian cotton sales alone might supply enough export tax revenues to finance many desirable agricultural and infrastructural improvements, including the Suez Canal scheme. Under the local boom conditions that prevailed from 1861 to 1864, Sa^cid apparently saw nothing to prevent him from using Egypt's well-filled coffers to demonstrate a friendly economic development rivalry with the Tanzimat cabinet in Istanbul.[7]

As far as relations between Cairo and Istanbul were concerned, Sa^cid's expanding expenses were already being handled along lines that became commonplace under Isma^cil after 1863. In return for approving the Egyptian viceroy's spending beyond realistic budgetary limits for any one year, the sultan accepted optimistic estimates of the future revenue-yielding potential of long-term development projects. Even before collapse of the cotton boom suddenly upset Ottoman-Egyptian budgetary understandings, however, Saᶜid himself discovered that expanded dealings with foreign entrepreneurs carried alarming legal and political, as well as economic, risks. By about 1860, it was clear that a new breed of foreign residents was establishing business ties in Egypt. Alongside the concession market, new types of money-making ventures involving private credit obligations and urban rental contracts were making the simple image of the Levantine trader of Alexandria or Rosetta obsolete. Such trends were already creating a shift in the legal and judicial needs of Egypt's foreign resident community away from purely commercial disputes.

Somewhat awkwardly, Saᶜid tried to reaffirm Egypt's commitment to follow strict Tanzimat procedures to accommodate increasing numbers of both mixed and local grievances recorded by Cairo's Judicial Council. In Shaᶜban 1272 (April 1856), Saᶜid formally recognized the sole validity of the French-inspired 1850 Ottoman Commercial Code for deciding private commercial litigation either between Egyptians or between local and capitulatory subjects in the mixed commercial councils. To retain foreign confidence in the responsibilities of the ten-year-old councils, he instructed the city governor and the foreign consuls of Alexandria to appoint a completely separate (but still unsalaried) appellate council.[8] It was to the presidency of this body, apparently, that the future principal founder of the Mixed Courts of Egypt, Nubar Pasha, was named by viceregal order. Nubar's memoirs, written long after the event, suggest that no serious steps were taken in 1856 to fill the rolls of appellate judges.[9]

Contrary to his expectations, Saᶜid's 1856 decree provided a target for critics of the council system of justice adopted by Muhammad ᶜAli. Foreigners soon complained that, as far as their own changing interests were concerned, there would be little use in reformed mixed councils as long as their decisions were tied to the 1850 Commercial Code. Dissatisfaction with the singling out of commercial affairs as the only area for capitulatory legal renovation was probably the stimulus that led to Crown Prince Ismaᶜil's appointment as Egypt's pro forma judicial adviser in 1858 (not coincidentally, perhaps, the year of Saᶜid's comprehensive land law). When asked how to placate foreign critics of the commercial councils, however, Ismaᶜil had no easy solution. He could only advise sending petitions in totally new areas of entrepreneurial and property contracts to the small body of

European lawyers who were just beginning to be contracted as adjuncts in several central ministries.[10]

In fact, growing interaction with foreigners or their agents residing in Egypt already involved much more than agricultural export contracts. Free market conditions also played a role for concession hunters, since investors obviously tried to find as many devices as possible to maximize returns for contracted services. Even more than bidders for agricultural commodities, concession capitalists needed to evaluate local legal and administrative factors to rate the viability of projects. Once into a contract, neither concessionaires nor Egyptian second parties could make alterations in conditions until a given project was complete. In the case of large governmental contract ventures like rails, bridges, or canals, this could take several years. Under such circumstances, conditions of legal and judicial security in a particular foreign investment area became risk factors to be built into all concession bids.

The lesson Egypt should have learned from these capitalistic facts of life was not difficult to predict. First, it was obviously unwise to undertake, as both Sa^cid and Isma^cil had done, major development expenses that could only have been paid for if the value of cotton exports continued at high early 1860s levels. If prices dropped, as they did in 1864, foreign-earned revenues from the agricultural sector could only have been maintained through cash crop diversification. This represented not only a costly but an unfamiliar practice for Egypt's traditional rural peasantry. Other possibilities would have been tax benefits or relaxed controls over joint investment schemes (to maintain local incentive to produce and foreign investors' enthusiasm to buy in a slump market) or local tax increases. As we shall see, variations of the latter options were eventually tried with uneven success by Isma^cil Pasha.

Mounting capitulatory demands for security make up only part of the financial and legal reform dilemma that gripped Egypt by the mid-1860s. We have already noted that Isma^cil set out with a particular concern for accommodating certain social and economic changes that had begun to occur in Egypt's towns and rural hinterland. Recognition of the Representative Assembly's requests for further decentralization of *qanun* jurisdictions suggests a degree of sensitivity to local expectations of legislative change that matched concern for capitulatory reform pressures. Egypt's growing financial crisis stood to affect all local residents to some degree. It was inevitable, however, that individuals who had actively attached themselves to changing local economic trends over the previous twenty years would feel most vulnerable. They were also likely to try to defend their personal interests in recent land, fiscal, and commercial exchange laws by arguing that certain benefits in Egypt's reform process were somehow irreversible. Study of elements that were beginning to depend on various Tanzimat social and economic trends to improve their material livelihood should, therefore, help clarify the next stages in Egypt's internal political dilemma after 1865. We know that measures were taken to grant increased influence to some groups through the Representative Assembly and local judicial councils between 1866 and 1873. Egypt's nascent landholding elites and several other local groups would have remained sorely disappointed, however, if Isma^cil's revamping of Muhammad ^cAli's provincial legislative and judicial legacy had ended there.

Although no reliable documentation exists to trace specific patterns in private landholdings before the 1870s, high market prices through 1863 probably encouraged a minority of cultivators who had some capital, or who were willing to borrow, to buy more acreage to increase cotton output.[11] Many pledged the assumed value of the product of their labor against commitments to pay for expanded landholdings. Their risk, therefore, resembled that of the central government in its effort to cover development budget deficits through loans. Like foreign entrepreneurs seeking contracts in Egypt, representatives of this nascent landholding elite were bound to try to seek whatever legal protection could be found to protect them against serious losses. Such efforts doubled once price depression hit Egypt's cotton trade in 1864. Examination of the local and capitulatory crises that followed the cotton slump suggests that both the introduction of the Cairo Assembly and attempts to revamp Egypt's system of *qanun* law were reactions to the first signs of such pressures.

JUDICIAL PARALYSIS AND FOREIGN PRIVATE INTERESTS, 1864–66

Soon after Isma^cil became viceroy, it was clear that, far from abandoning Sa^cid's deficit budgeting, he would assume even higher levels of public debt. To some, perhaps, searching for more foreign credit did not seem entirely farfetched. Imperial approval for construction of the Suez Canal (finally obtained in 1863) was bound to be followed by auxiliary contracts to support de Lesseps's main venture. Once the Canal was completed, however, such additional expenses could turn to profit. Revenues gained from transit charges and increased international commercial dealings might even offset the depressed value of cotton exports. To pessimists who couldn't believe in the Canal as a panacea, however, Isma^{c}il's call for additional concessionary schemes was a sign of fiscal irresponsibility.

By 1864 a number of highly vocal foreign residents had begun to worry about internal and international legal complications in Isma^{c}il's public debt policies. Some even called upon their consuls to censure any Cairo Judicial Council decisions in private capitulatory cases that reflected Ministry of Finance priorities, not clear provisions of *qanun* law. Assumption of such jurisdictional prerogatives by diplomatic agents already exceeded literal provisions of the Ottoman capitulations. Things went from bad to worse, however, when consuls who considered the *qanun* law irrelevant to the rising number of mixed breach of contract cases tried to impose decisions based on the laws of their own countries. Such self-assigned capitulatory "judges" then expected execution of their judgment by Egyptian authorities, whether the foreign or local party won its case.[12]

It is difficult to know just when foreign consuls began granting requests to bypass Egyptian courts entirely and to issue their own mixed judgments against local defendants. Such excessive measures probably did not come until it was clear that Isma^{c}il's mounting public debt was undermining the security of both private and governmental contracts in which foreign funds were involved. Similar deterioration in capitulatory procedures had already been noted by the British ambassador in Istanbul in 1858. In the earlier Ottoman case, lack of confidence in Tanzimat reform promises prompted less scrupulous foreign plaintiffs to request ambassadorial intervention to settle private litigation without consulting imperial *nizamiyya* judicial authorities.[13] The desire of most foreign embassies to avoid breaking the assumed consensus of support for the Tanzimat Council, however, ended abuses before the situation became too pronounced. It was probably no coincidence, in fact, that Ahmed Cevdet, the head of Istanbul's *diwan* of judicial ordinances, chose the period between 1858 and 1861 to broadcast his intention to build a more comprehensive system of secular jurisdictions throughout the Empire. Work also proceeded apace in the first years of Abdulaziz's sultanate to complete codification of Islamic civil law (the later famous *mecelle*). This was proposed in order to give Cevdet's *nizamiyya* courts a standard point of reference for disputes that had previously never been handled by secular administrative (*qanun*) authorities.[14]

As long as private interests alone were at stake, success or failure in sidestepping local jurisdiction depended on the personal political influence wielded by either individual plaintiffs or their diplomatic representative. As soon as agents of the Egyptian administration and even Isma^cil himself became the main objects of foreign judicial complaints, however, the situation changed rapidly. Once consuls began to condemn acts that Isma^cil's officials previously carried out without reference to any particular corpus of written law, what had been regrettable distortions of capitulatory propriety in private defendants' cases took on the appearance of violations of Ottoman imperial sovereignty.

The fact that severe signs of capitulatory malaise surfaced in 1866 is historically significant. Capitulatory irregularities may have provided Isma^cil with evidence that Egypt's internal stability could only be guaranteed if bonds linking Cairo to specific imperial Tanzimat guidelines were loosened. This might have been interpreted as a first step toward regaining some of the privileges of provincial autonomy that Muhammad ^cAli had extracted by political and military fiat during the first four decades of the nineteenth century. Post-1863 means of redefining Egypt's relationship to the Ottoman sultanate, however, were bound to be very different indeed. When certain reform guidelines inherited from Sa^cid faltered seriously after 1865, Isma^cil was encouraged to resort to liberalization gestures to respond to as many of his critics as possible.

INTERNATIONAL VIEWS OF EGYPT'S MIXED JUDICIAL REFORM SCHEME, 1866–68

Historians have traditionally attributed the original idea of providing Egypt with fully professional mixed civil, commercial, and penal jurisdictions to Isma^cil's Armenian prime minister, Nubar Pasha. Nubar's own memoirs, although clearly biased and incomplete on many details, convey a similar impression.[15] Contemporary evidence, on the other hand, indicates that the first suggestions for Cairo's famous 1875 Judicial Reform actually came from European sources. As early as 1865, for example, Britain's ambassador in Istanbul sent Isma^cil a scathing résumé of his impressions of consular court practices in Egypt. Sir Henry Bulwer's communication already referred to the possibility of attaching a single province "judicial subchapter," specifically designed for conditions in Egypt, to the general corpus of Ottoman capitulatory practice.[16] In reaction to such warnings, but without an immediate plan of his own, Ismaᶜil invited his first minister to pursue the question further.

Nubar's famous memorandum of August 1867, however, which followed private talks with Ismaᶜil in January, envisaged introduction of a judicial system far beyond what was necessary to sooth European creditors' fears. In an open letter tailored for foreign consumption, Ismaᶜil's first minister called for adoption of the same models that had already been used "so effectively for Egypt's army, railroads, . . . and public services. The competent element, that is to say the foreign element, has been introduced, and this element has served to train the local element. What has been done in the material domain should now be done in the moral domain, namely, in the organization of justice."[17] Nubar's idea of how to achieve such goals involved much more than formation of a special court to handle capitulatory disputes. He originally intended to create a multinational bench at the head of the hierarchy of jurisdictions, including the entire local judicial council system developed from Muhammad ᶜAli's first post-1840 scheme.[18] This sweeping idea may have been intended to allay fears that Egyptian finances would collapse entirely if capitulatory judgments against local defendants were simply added to the mainstream of judicial council property and tax rulings without some common standard to evaluate their total effect.

There may also have been more direct political implications. According to Nubar's memoirs, his original plan sought to alleviate the causes, not merely symptoms, of insecurity among local subjects and foreign residents in Egypt. As broached confidentially at various states of negotiations leading to the Judicial Reform of 1875, Nubar's ideal would have been to establish legal limits on the arbitrary use of executive powers in Egypt.[19] We shall see that this view would eventually be held by proponents of a constitutionalist solution to dilemmas of misrule both by the Ottoman sultan and, in the late 1870s, by Egypt's semiautonomous viceroys. One main point ultimately distinguished Nubar's desire to identify with better government from several of his peers who tried different methods to face Egypt's deteriorating situation. This was his assumption that the most effective check on abusive personal power rested in the administrative apparatus of the courts themselves, not in some form of representative body. Nubar busied himself drawing up plans to give real substance and autonomy to such an apparatus. Meanwhile, a number of developments occurred that, in the eyes of Isma^cil himself, at least, increased his own power to deal with questions of capitulatory and internal administrative importance as an executor enjoying limited sovereignty as defined by several new Ottoman *firmans*.

Such shifts in the definition of sovereignty allowed Isma^cil to carry out mixed court reforms as a semiautonomous international negotiator. At the same time, however, they tended to enhance the perception that authority over all branches of government, including the nascent judicial branch itself, rested with the sovereign authority that created them. Nubar's plan for a major judicial reform was meant to counter this view. Because of political compromises at every stage of capitulatory negotiations between 1867 and 1875, however, the gap between the ideal and reality of judicial authority in Egypt grew wider, not narrower, right up to the last formal year of Tanzimat legislation.

The first redefinition of Egypt's status as a semiautonomous Ottoman province came in the year of Nubar's call to revamp Isma^cil's entire judicial system. A first *firman*, which accompanied bestowal of the unique honorific title of khedive to Cairo's governor in June 1867, altered several terms of capitulatory dependency imposed following Ottoman dismantling of Muhammad ^cAli's powers in 1841. The 1867 *firman* formally authorized Isma^cil to issue separate Egyptian "acts of administration" that he deemed necessary to complement the Empire's corpus of Tanzimat legislation. The sultan included "nonpolitical" foreign conventions, presumably meaning separate judicial accords between Cairo and interested capitulatory governments, under this general rubric.[20] Abdulaziz seemed willing, therefore, to let the new khedive decide whether or not to follow the model of the Ottoman *nizamiyya* court system in his own bid to design judicial institutions to meet Egypt's particular needs. Isma^cil's subsequent actions clearly indicated he wished to pursue a very broad interpretation of the sultan's 1867 *firman*.

Even though the excitement of the 1860–64 cotton boom had clearly subsided in 1867, the Suez Canal project was moving into the final stages of construction. When it became apparent that the Canal

Company was having difficulties filling its original capital subscription lists, the Cairo *diwan* decided to earmark scarce treasury funds to buy up all remaining stock. Apparently, the khedive himself felt that continued commitment of funds for costly infrastructural projects would entice private investors, both Egyptian and foreign, to add their own capital to ancillary development areas. The primary need was for various service enterprises or light industrial production (secondary transport, shipping supplies, etc.). There was an equally strong assumption that expanding foreign real estate purchases, of either commercial buildings or actual crop-producing land, would accompany the prosperity created by full Canal operations.

Both Isma^cil and local landholders in the Cairo Assembly knew, however, that investment would not come from mere goodwill or vague guarantees attached to the Ottoman property laws of 1858 and 1867. Indeed, as long as the Tanzimat Council kept plans to use the *shari^ca*-based *mecelle* as standard Ottoman law on property relationships, even local investors were unlikely to place much stock in Isma^cil's ability to guarantee private deeds on Egypt's real estate market. Chances that foreigners would be attracted to the least liquid sector of Egypt's economy without additional legal security inducements, therefore, were even more remote. Whatever Nubar's higher ideals may have been, therefore, material conditions, especially in areas of mixed economic interest in a free market in land, contracts, and commodities, together with intercapitulatory political rivalries, became the real *raison d'être* of the international court plan ultimately signed in his name.

EGYPTIAN CAPITULATORY BARGAINING AND THE CAIRO CONFERENCE OF 1869–70

Positive international reactions to Egypt's mixed court scheme emerged very slowly between 1867 and 1870. Although the earliest gestures had come from London, it was the French Foreign Ministry that first sought legislative permission to sign a separate capitulatory convention with Cairo. From the very outset, several parties outside the government feared that France might be overly eager to increase its Eastern Question political or financial leverage through some form of capitulatory bargain in Egypt. Paris had gone to great effort over several centuries to build an Ottoman treaty system that guaranteed protection for individual French nationals. A special parliamentary commission found it hard to believe, therefore, that traditionally direct bilateral leverage in Istanbul could effectively be replaced by a new multinational arrangement that would apply to a single Ottoman province only.[21] Such French objections were important enough to spur Nubar himself to travel to Europe to attract support for his plan.

During Nubar's 1867–68 European tour, clarification of the original aims of his mixed court memorandum soon turned to devising compromises to please potential capitulatory signatories. In Paris, Isma^c^il's emissary was forced to abandon a principle of numerical equity that had already functioned for two decades in Egypt's commercial councils: he promised that any future mixed courts would automatically consist of a guaranteed majority of foreign judges. He also pledged that this same foreign-majority bench would have sole jurisdiction over cases between the Egyptian administration and private capitulatory plaintiffs.[22] Such early concessions did tempt less politically dominant European governments. Countries like Holland or Belgium, for example, were quite interested in participating in a single court on which their representatives would have an equal vote alongside the French or British in all cases pitting foreign nationals against the Egyptian government.

Although some technical concessions were granted during Nubar's European tour, the Egyptian still retained his hope of associating a new mixed court system with the local councils that handled "native" justice. Such a combination of capitulatory and internal Tanzimat priorities, however, met objections all over Europe. Thus, when a first joint conference on capitulatory justice was finally held following the Suez Canal inauguration ceremonies in 1869, Nubar had to bend his original plan again to respond to preferences for a hybrid system meeting special, not comprehensive, legal reform needs.

When capitulatory talks began in Cairo, the Egyptians found that European embassies had been busy since 1868 obtaining advance agreement on what portions of Nubar's plan would or would not be acceptable. The French got their way, for example, on the exclusion of local cases from courts that fell under joint capitulatory sponsorship. At the same time, the Paris representative agreed to table the French parliamentary commission's opposition to Nubar's idea that new mixed courts should have penal, as well as civil and commercial, jurisdiction over foreign nationals in Egypt.[23]

One reason Paris yielded temporarily on the politically sensitive question of mixed penal competence became clear in Nubar's revised draft plan based on the Cairo Conference debates. Following French insistence, and apparently against his own will, the Egyptian agreed not only to conform to the Napoleonic organizational model for multiple judge benches, but to provide for a *ministère public*, or *parquet*, in the mixed system. The typically French notion of a *ministère public* had its closest equivalent in the attorney general's office of the Anglo-Saxons, but went much further in drawing overlapping lines between judicial and executive elements of administration. Thus, the task of any future Egyptian mixed *parquet* (containing both foreign and Egyptian *procureurs*) would be not only to take responsibility for preparing prosecution files against foreign accused to be tried by the mixed courts; it would also represent the public interest in any civil litigation involving the government. This means that foreign appointees to a mixed *parquet*, unlike judges on the bench, would have an active hand in observing, and perhaps even influencing, the affairs of any local ministry involved in mixed court litigation. Later events would show that it was this particular repercussion of Nubar's concession, not the future penal tasks of the *parquet*, that attracted French interest in particular.[24]

It must be said to the Egyptian ministry's credit that it did not rely solely on the objective goodwill of capitulatory negotiators to help prepare for the proposed mixed *parquet*. Nubar made it clear that he would expect the prosecutor's office to be equally divided between professional nominees of the several capitulatory powers and Egyptians appointed by Cairo's Ministry of Justice. It seemed perfectly logical, therefore, for the Egyptian government to placate concerns over the scarcity of promising local nominees by promising to revamp the rudimentary legal studies program of Egypt's School of Languages and Administration by adding, for the first time, an adequate curriculum to support a formal program of legal studies.

Overall, the 1870 capitulatory conference achieved most of its objectives. The major remaining responsibility of the Cairo *diwan* was to make certain that all delegates to a full ambassadorial conference, including the Ottoman Porte itself, received a proposal for mixed codes to be applied in Egypt. Indeed, until the attention of all European capitals was suddenly refocused on the catastrophe of the Franco-Prussian War in mid-1870, Nubar divided his efforts between two tasks: collaboration with a French lawyer contracted to draw up the mixed codes and a diplomatic campaign to convince Istanbul to approve Egypt's revised capitulatory regime. It was during his personal meetings with ᶜAli Paşa that Nubar claimed that his plan was an "inevitable and logical consequence of the [Tanzimat] *Hatt-i Şerif*. . . that proclaimed a guarantee of security over the lives, property, and honor of subjects of the sultan." In answer to ᶜAli Paşa's concern that foreign participation on Egyptian courts might make the latter "more a political than a judicial body," the Egyptian tended to believe that *mixité* would act as a neutralizing factor. "The magistrates we will contract," he said, "will carry with them their traditions, which are not political traditions. They will not be of the same nationality, which means they will never be in agreement on any points that go beyond the [strictly professional] sphere of justice itself."[25]

Despite such assurances, second-generation Tanzimat leaders were skeptical of what another Ottoman minister called "Europeanization" of Egypt's legal apparatus. Nubar's memoirs show, for example, that ᶜAli Paşa opposed Cairo's intention to include questions of landed property under the rubric of mixed civil law since, "in the eyes of Muslims, such questions have, if not a religious, at least a sacred character." In this case the Egyptian was finally able to gain Istanbul's agreement in principle only by stressing the material losses (through tax evasion, etc.) that would accrue if the status quo—meaning consular authorities judging arbitrarily without reference to any property codes at all—continued. Nubar failed to specify, however, whether his plans for a mixed civil code would try to integrate European concepts of law with actual practices that had grown out of a half-century of *qanun* law precedents in Egypt.

FORMULATION OF THE MIXED CODES AND THE *MUQABALA* LAW OF 1871

Like organizational stipulations coming from the 1870 Cairo Conference, what became Egypt's mixed civil, commercial, and penal codes were originally designed to please the fourteen foreign ministries needed to approve a separate capitulatory regime in Cairo. Nubar must have felt that rapid reaction, not a complicated process of legislative consultation, would meet this need most effectively. He therefore called on one man, Frenchman Jacques Maunoury (who had served as legal counsel to a French company holding a street lighting concession in Alexandria and then as secretary to the 1869–70 capitulatory conference), to extract a corpus of mixed law directly out of existing French codes.[26]

Even if we assume that Maunoury tried to keep local as well as specific capitulatory legal interests in mind while drafting the original mixed codes, several negative side effects were bound to result from using French law as the basis of Egypt's new court system. First, any European jurist should have been acutely aware that, by 1870, the time-honored *Code Napoléon* itself reflected material and social conditions that prevailed during the first, not the last, quarter of the century.[27] Maunoury, however, may have felt useful political ground could be gained if the codes offered a slightly favorable edge to parties who were attracted to procedures available only under French law. Two examples help illustrate this point.

Even though the Cairo Conference gave no explicit instructions, Nubar probably assumed that whatever mixed codes he proposed should contain specifics covering the most common disputes that had sparked consular judicial intervention in the 1860s. One area involved Egyptian defendants who, after borrowing money from foreigners or their resident agents to expand agricultural landholdings, were unable to earn enough to pay both rising taxes and their creditors. Of all European codes that covered such disputes, the *Code Napoléon*, with its emphasis on lenders' over debtors' rights, promised to be most attractive to foreign creditors in future mixed court litigation.

A second area in which French law seemed appropriate also involved land and credit transactions, but promised potential advantages for both Egyptian and foreign litigants. Napoleonic procedures for property title guarantees had gained wide admiration in Europe since their adoption in the early nineteenth century. Such recognition came from the fact that, since French titles were held in registries of the courts themselves, it was difficult for outside or politically interested parties to use devious counterclaims to influence property litigation. Thus, as an alternative to the notoriously vague *qadi's hujja* (still assumed acceptable as proof of ownership under the Ottoman *mecelle* as well as the council jurisdictions in Egypt), French title law could offer added security for all owners (or buyers and sellers) of property, irrespective of their local or foreign nationality. Neither these laws nor others selected from the *Code Napoléon* were necessarily foreign to circumstances prevailing in Egypt by the 1870s. Their careful application in an experimental mixed code could help prepare the next logical stage of general social and economic development for Ottoman provincial zones that, like Egypt, were outgrowing rudimentary Tanzimat principles launched at mid-century. Because of the crushing condition of Egypt's finances by this date, however, there was little chance that such a revolutionary trend could become established. Instead, emergency local fiscal legislation imposed by the khedive tended to favor limited elements, both foreign and Egyptian, who took quick advantage of legal loopholes even before the mixed codes could be tested.

In reaction to proddings from worried foreign investors in rapidly sinking Egyptian treasury bonds, Sultan Abdulaziz finally issued a special *firman* in 1870 forbidding Egypt to secure further loans merely to service its outstanding debts. With assumed autonomous channels to foreign credit suddenly cut off, Ismaᶜil seemed to have only two internal financial choices by 1871. First, he could raise *all* local taxes despite the probable negative impact this would have on marginal or subsistence agriculturalists. Second, there was the possibility of introducing a special tax affecting only those who might somehow be positively induced to contribute a higher portion of their income toward reduction of the government debt. A third option—a tax levy on foreign businessmen and property owners in Egypt—was conceivable only if the proposed mixed courts successfully proved to foreigners that their material interests would be well protected by a dependable civil code. Out of this quandary, then, came the infamous *muqabala* tax law, drawn up by Nubar's political rival, finance minister Ismaᶜil Sadiq.

Briefly, the *muqabala* law of 30 August 1871 promised a permanent guarantee of full title, plus a perpetual future reduction in yearly assessment levels, to all cultivators who voluntarily paid six years' advanced *kharaj* land tax.[28] For certain peasants, and especially for already well-established landholders, such a promise of tenurial security in the future was attractive enough to justify borrowing funds to pay the still optional *muqabala* tax in 1871. When the only ready lenders to such parties turned out to be *protégés* of foreign-owned credit houses in Cairo or Alexandria, many early *muqabala* payers unknowingly committed themselves to the possibility of future credit litigation under Nubar's still untested mixed courts and codes. For larger local landholding or lending interests, on the other hand, the prospect of securing their own titles or foreclosing on the titles of vulnerable peasant borrowers would be particularly inviting if the *Code Napoléon* could somehow be extended to cover their own property or debt contract dealings. As we shall see, narrow lines of distinction like those created by the *muqabala* law soon became the only guides available to judge if benefits or disadvantages would result from Khedive Isma^cil's sweeping Judicial Reform.

RESULTS OF THE 1873 ISTANBUL CONFERENCE

When the delegates of fourteen capitulatory countries finally met under the symbolic auspices of the Ottoman grand vizier in Istanbul in 1873, the business of reviewing the Mixed Court Charter had become mainly a pro forma affair.[29] The most important compromise yet to come was Egypt's decision to give in to lingering opposition to comprehensive mixed penal powers over foreigners. Rather than try to reverse apprehension over abuses that could not be proved or denied in advance, Nubar agreed to reduce mixed penal competence to a bare minimum. His efforts to omit Napoleonic *hypothèque judiciaire* procedures, which weighted the mixed civil code heavily in favor of creditors and ran counter to Islamic principles of debt collateral, were also rebuffed.[30] Finally, there was one more essential compromise: during a first trial period of five years only, the new system would consist of three tribunals and one appeals court only.[31] Since this made a total of exactly fourteen foreign contractees, contemporaries may have wondered whether it was mere political convenience, not actual judicial need, that sealed the deliberations of the fourteen-member 1873 Istanbul Conference.

INTERNAL AND INTERNATIONAL IMPLICATIONS OF EGYPT'S MIXED COURT CHARTER

Egypt's willingness to compromise so openly with capitulatory negotiators in 1873 is best explained by the sharply declining state of Egyptian finances. Contrary to optimistic predictions, Suez Canal operations had not sparked a new "Klondike on the Nile." Having spent proceeds from previous foreign loans to open the Canal, Isma^cil now had to earmark almost every piaster of internal revenue for servicing debt obligations. In practical terms, therefore, two financial alternatives existed by 1873. Isma^cil had already considered raising funds by making the 1871 *muqabala* law into an obligatory capital levy. A sixfold tax increase in one year, however, would have a devastating effect on Egypt's peasantry. Isma^cil was not yet desperate enough to risk the widespread breakdown in tenurial security that might follow. The only option was to convince Sultan Abdulaziz—as well as existing foreign creditors in Egypt and in Europe—that further recourse to bond sales abroad could be handled responsibly. Successful conclusion of the final round of international mixed court negotiations seems, therefore, to have been a tactic to break Abdulaziz's moratorium on further increases in Egypt's foreign debt. That the Istanbul Conference was followed by reversal of the 1870 *firman* and negotiation of a massive addition to Egypt's European loan balance bears this suggestion out.

Khedive Isma^cil's June 1873 loan was contracted with Oppenheim et Neveu, an Alexandria-based firm that had itself experienced a number of shady dealings in Egyptian finances during the 1860s. The fact that negotiations for a new provincial Egyptian judicial and "single package" legislative regime had been cleared in Istanbul, however, may have helped sell shares in the new loan to investors far from Egypt's shores.[32] In fact, not only Oppenheim but optimists all over Europe began predicting that, once formal mixed courts succeeded in discouraging exaggerated local credit cases against the khedivial treasury, Egypt would be able to meet all of its legitimate public debt commitments.

This observation seems to apply to the early posture of the (1874–80) Conservative government of Benjamin Disraeli. London had gone on record as early as 1866 in support of separate capitulatory arrangements for Egypt. The Foreign Office began to wax impatient, however, when other governments agreed to another increase in Egypt's debt in 1873, but were in no hurry to ratify the new judicial convention that was meant to go with it. Surprisingly, this delay was just as visible in British parliamentary debates as it was in other European capitals during 1874 and even into 1875.[33]

One could assume, of course, that in London's case delays were tied to the unattractive prospect of placing British subjects' interests under an unfamiliar continental system of law. A more substantial cause for the Conservative government's delay, however, probably stemmed from more basic considerations of Eastern Question priorities. First, Disraeli's foreign secretary must have been chary of entering into any conventions that implied a loosening of the bonds of Ottoman sovereignty placed on Egypt by the "Palmerstonian" *firman* of 1841. Although many of the political assumptions of the early Tanzimat period had changed in three decades, Britain remained committed to keeping the Ottoman Empire intact in the mid-1870s. Sponsorship for international capitulatory approaches to a politically separate Egyptian Question, therefore, could have as many disadvantages as possible attractions. The Disraeli cabinet probably would have preferred a solution of Egypt's capitulatory jurisdiction problems within a general imperial Tanzimat framework. Adoption of Nubar's mixed court scheme by the Tanzimat Council itself, for example, might have allowed standard application of whatever codes were adopted not only in Egypt, but in all provinces of the Ottoman Empire. The ultimate source of responsibility over all mixed Ottoman-foreign litigation would be in Istanbul, and Egypt's clear legislative (and therefore political) subordination to the sultanate would remain unaltered.

The precarious state of Ottoman affairs following the death of Grand Vizier ᶜAli Paşa in 1871, however, left little chance of recreating conditions of Lord Palmerston's day. By this date, the sultanate was involved in a financial and political crisis of its own that, if it proceeded to its full and logical consequences, threatened an unpredictable future for foreign interests in all regions of the Empire.[34] Rather than wait to see whether old-line Tanzimat reformers or a newer generation of constitution-oriented critics of the sultan would eventually chart Ottoman capitulatory affairs after 1875, Europeans began reexamining their own Eastern Question policies, including Egyptian subpriorities, in a new light.

What occurred in capitulatory-Egyptian relations in the last half of 1875 appeared at first to be an application of a typical Eastern Question scenario to the particulars of Egypt's provincial financial and legal reform dilemma. While political events in Istanbul early in 1875 focused on the impending collapse of central imperial finances, Germany and Austria-Hungary decided rather suddenly formally to ratify Nubar's draft charter for mixed courts and codes as the basis for capitulatory relations between their governments and Egypt.[35] Although there was no immediate chance that a new judicial system could be launched using judges representing just two foreign powers, separate German and Austrian bilateral initiative sparked widespread fear of capitulatory opportunism.

Without knowledge of the evolution of private European involvement in Ottoman economic affairs since the mid-1850s, it was difficult to foresee how Austria and Germany might gain any serious advantages by rushing Egypt's Judicial Reform along at such a troubled moment in Eastern Question diplomacy. If affairs in Istanbul continued to deteriorate, previous lessons of Eastern Question crises suggested that concerned European capitals would repeat (as Russia ultimately did in 1876–77) long-established modes of direct intervention in Ottoman affairs. The door for such intervention usually opened through the Balkan provinces, which were once again rife in 1875 with the fever of anti-Turkish insurrection. In contrast, Egypt itself held out no particular territorial advantages to powers that might be seeking to bully Istanbul into a more effective arrangement of its imperial financial and political affairs. What Egypt and the mixed court plan in particular offered to countries like Germany and Austria, perhaps, was the possibility of extending to their own nationals a much higher degree of security for their private entrepreneurial ventures abroad than anything conceived in earlier stages of the Tanzimat. Germans and Austrians were not among the most heavily committed foreign entrepreneurs in the Ottoman Empire in the 1850s and 1860s. The growing financial scare in Istanbul, however, combined with the prospects of special capitulatory conditions in Egypt, may have awakened Germanic attention to the possibility of a major shift in investment patterns in the Near East by the second half of the 1870s. In any event, Berlin's and Vienna's watchful capitulatory rivals interpreted their early acceptance of Egypt's Judicial Reform in this light as soon as it occurred.

It was the British in particular who sensed the imbalance that might be created by the signing of Isma^{c}il's first two bilateral capitulatory conventions. Even without formal installation of mixed courts, for example, early application of mixed law in Egypt might create certain legal and economic advantages for German and Austrian residents alone. One of these, the right to form private joint-stock companies according to the provisions of French law, carried an imagined threat that Germans and Austrians could corner major business openings, including property development, that had lain dormant under vague laws covering foreign investments. If a clear but restricted joint-stock regime reduced the legal risks facing Austrian and German companies only, competitive investments by any other foreign nationals in Egypt would probably decline.

Rather than wait to see if such dire predictions would follow partial international acceptance of Egypt's new legislative plan, the British quickly signed the same bilateral conventions that had been offered to Vienna and Berlin in May 1875. Once the Ottoman government announced the first stages of default on its own foreign bond payments in October of the same year, several other European ministries followed suit in staking out firmer ground in Egypt. Neither London nor Cairo, however, could yet be certain that Egypt's capitulatory "revolution" would be realized by the mixed court inauguration target date in December. On the Egyptian side, an untimely falling out between the khedive and his chief minister had caused a cabinet shuffle just as the long campaign for adoption of the Mixed Court Charter neared its end. The man Isma^{c}il chose to assume Nubar's office was Muhammad Pasha Sharif, an Egyptian-born descendant of an Ottoman Turkish *qadi*. Unlike Nubar, Sharif had little practical experience in international politics and was relatively unknown to the consuls who would be charged with the final details of transition to mixed justice. On the other hand, Sharif had contacts in Isma^{c}il's Representative Assembly. This meant he might play a key role in helping Egypt's rural notables adjust to new legislative conditions once the mixed courts and codes on property and contracts were in operation. This characteristic of Sharif's political potential eventually did affect Egyptian attitudes toward carrying Nubar's mixed court scheme to its full logical conclusions. His role in 1875, however, seems to have remained mainly passive.[36]

Although no one knew how legal reform policies might fare under Isma^{c}il's new *diwan*, the last obstacles to acceptance of Egypt's special capitulatory regime had to be overcome in distant European capitals, not in Cairo itself. By November 1875, the British and Russians in particular were wondering why adherence to the mixed courts was still being blocked in Paris. Even though Greece and Italy (the two potential signatories who had the greatest actual number of nationals residing in Egypt) were in a similar position of parliamentary paralysis, French participation seemed politically more vital to the plan's success. One reason for the mixed court scheme, for example, had been to spare Isma^cil the necessity of resorting to even more questionable devices to stave off financial ruin. Since French and British nationals held major shares of Egypt's bonded debt, one might have assumed that, after the bankruptcy scare in Istanbul in 1875, Paris would have turned away from narrow consular protection concerns to recognize "higher" financially and politically stabilizing principles behind Isma^cil's Judicial Reform. As time passed, however, it appeared France was in no hurry to develop an Egyptian Question policy separate from Quai d'Orsay relations with Istanbul. It remained for other supporters of the mixed courts, then, and for the Disraeli government in particular, to convince Paris that France, too, could expect political, and certainly some economic and financial, benefits by adhering to Egypt's special capitulatory reform.

Certainly the most outstanding event in British-Egyptian affairs in 1875 was the British government's purchase of nearly two hundred thousand shares of Suez Canal stock that Isma^cil had originally acquired when de Lesseps's Compagnie Universelle could not fill its capital subscription lists.[37] Disraeli's attempt to justify this unexpected action as an indirect way to relieve strains on Egypt's nearly bankrupt treasury was received with skepticism in the Commons. Aside from questioning the constitutionality of his unannounced act, the opposition objected to committing government funds to an investment project that clearly fell within the domain of private capitalistic initiative. For Conservative regulars, perhaps, British participation in the Canal Company may simply have represented a logical way to safeguard strategic access routes to India. The Liberal opposition, on the other hand, was more likely to argue that the cabinet's venture would pull Britain into the imbroglio of Egyptian internal politics. If nothing else, it seemed unwise to commit treasury funds to Egyptian development schemes when the khedive appeared to be on the brink of financial ruin. The British cabinet clearly sensed its vulnerability on this latter point, and sent Mr. Stephen Cave, MP, on a special mission to investigate the general state of Egypt's finances.

The Quai d'Orsay was clearly piqued by Disraeli's initiative. Foreign minister Decazes resented Britain's acquisition of shares that the French government itself might have purchased had it not been for the possibility of legislative sanctions. The British Government's appearance as a major shareholder in the most important private French company abroad, however, did have one useful side effect: it alerted the Chambre des Députés to the fact that, unless it quickly ratified France's entry into Egypt's Judicial Reform, the job of protecting Suez Canal shareholders' interests in any impending local legal difficulties would lie mainly in British hands. In the face of such an eventual fait accompli, French honor required being able to act at least as effectively as the British, Germans, or Austrians. Even if the London cabinet was temporarily compromised by apparent abandonment of traditional Eastern Question ground rules with respect to Egypt, therefore, Disraeli at least had the satisfaction of learning that Paris would adhere to Egypt's Judicial Reform after 31 December 1875.[38]

Given such new complexities in the traditional Eastern Question, Egypt's Judicial Reform was a unique invitation for European governments to test their leverage with other countries whose trust in Tanzimat reformism had risen during the 1850s and then declined in the 1860s. If one considers the very extensive powers promised to the mixed bench in dealings with the khedive and his administration, questions of leverage were bound to become a matter of serious political concern for both capitulatory and local Egyptian parties. Even if the courts remained aloof from international political intrigue, chances were good that they would become indirectly involved in Egypt's own internal social and economic development dilemma in the mid-1870s. Because the mixed codes were based almost *verbatim* on unfamiliar French law, they were likely to clash with local concepts of private property and contractual relationships that had just begun to take root in Isma^cil's less formal local judicial councils.

To be sure, the Cairo government was ready to argue that Egyptians whose professional or social and economic interests had advanced beyond the rudimentary level of mid-nineteenth-century *qanun* legislation would gain from the Judicial Reform and possibly even enter the new courts as judges and advocates. Those who did would be expected not only to represent Egyptian interests in mixed litigation, but to articulate ways in which modern legal procedures could be used with benefit in the local councils. Ideally, then, the mixed courts would begin to open channels for Egyptians to organize their lives around legal principles that had been unknown to previous generations. In the long run, emphasis on professional judicial organization could mean that changed directions in Egyptian educational training after 1875 might create, if not a separate class of Egyptian secular legalists, at least a new field of social advancement for the sons of families who wished to turn away from standard careers in government bureaucracy.

On a more immediate level, the mixed codes themselves contained attractions for parties who had the perspicacity and means to translate abstract Tanzimat principles into concrete measures. These included European procedures for mortgage transactions, controlled property title registration, and even joint-stock business ventures—all issues that gained controversial prominence in Egypt after inauguration of the mixed courts in 1876. As long as such laws affected only a minority of Egyptians, however, idealists and skeptics alike would question the unfinished aims of Nubar's 1875 Judicial Reform.

Part II

Imposed Innovation and the Formation of Interest Groups (1876–82)

4

The Mixed Courts in the Egyptian Question

When the Mixed Courts of Egypt opened in January 1876, the local Arabic press openly welcomed the "New Justice" that Khedive Isma^cil had provided for Egyptians and foreign residents in the Nile Valley.[1] In fact, despite the last-minute nomination and uneven professional qualifications of some of the Egyptian and foreign judges, initial activities were impressive. The *Phare d'Alexandrie*, a French community newspaper, complimented the courts' quick disposal of disputes created by mere bureaucratic inefficiency. Judgments against the Egyptian government demonstrated independence, while decisions in favor of Egyptian defendants suggested an impartiality unknown under the previous capitulatory regime.[2] The international panic that suddenly reversed this trend, therefore, came from developments that had little to do with proceedings in the courtrooms themselves.

During the first months of 1876, London's Conservative government had been under pressure to publish the findings of MP Stephen Cave's parliamentary mission to Egypt. Partially out of embarrassment over his own controversial purchase of Isma^cil's shares in the Suez Canal, but also to avoid a sudden panic by British investors in Egypt's public debt, Disraeli tried to consider all angles before releasing the parliamentary report for debate. When the findings were published, however, they brought an unexpected turn in Eastern Question policies generally.[3] The ensuing panic also soon affected the status of Egypt's new mixed court system.

Cave was asked to tell Parliament if Cairo could meet essential costs of administration and still service its public and private debts. His findings underlined what many already knew: only stringent management and consolidation of foreign loans at a standard interest rate could avert bankruptcy. The news naturally caused a rapid decline in Egyptian bond values in Europe. Few suspected, however, that such high-level international financial questions would seriously affect the interest of simple creditor-litigants before the mixed courts in Cairo. When similar deficits had brought the imperial treasury to the brink of bankruptcy in 1875, only a short period of panic passed before an international commission was formed to review and schedule funds available for servicing the Ottoman debt.[4] In Istanbul, however, there was no special capitulatory court that could bring additional pressure to bear if diplomatic channels failed. Events in both Cairo and Istanbul during 1876 would show that this difference in capitulatory resilience to financial crisis could be either an advantage or a disadvantage.

Isma^cil's reaction to Cave's report was to delay payment on recent debt coupons, stopping just short of declaring bankruptcy. Then, to shore up foreign confidence, he voluntarily called for an international "public debt commission" in Cairo. As organized in May 1876, Egypt's Caisse de la Dette Publique called for one private nominee each to represent the interests of French, British, Italian, and Austrian bondholders in Cairo. The Caisse's function was to redeem debt coupons on schedule and to transfer payments to bondholders of each nationality in Europe. To assure that enough funds would be available, Isma^cil agreed to earmark tax revenues from several provinces and government administrations for payment to the Caisse.[5] An important contrast with similar solutions already operating in Tunis or adopted later by the sultan was the Caisse's right to sue in the mixed courts if the Egyptian government impinged on the terms of the May 1876 decree in any way. This meant that literally hundreds of European investors, most of whom had never set foot in Egypt, gained quasi-capitulatory protection for their interests overnight under the mixed codes.

Once a formal collection agency had been recognized, Isma^cil tried to consolidate Egypt's total debt at a lower interest rate. The floating and funded debts as of 7 May 1876 (including both the public debt and private loans contracted against the khedivial estates, or *da'iras*) were leveled off at £ 91 million, at a standard interest rate of seven percent.[6] This implied that Egypt could not recognize any claims that were not covered by the decrees of 2 and 7 May without risking financial and administrative collapse. Some bondholders immediately felt uneasy about Isma^cil's consolidation methods, since the 7 May decree favored holders of the floating debt (mainly French) at the expense of previously funded credit issues (mainly British). The most vocal reaction, however, came from locally resident "judgment creditors," who were the first to rally the new mixed courts in support of their private investment interests.

INITIAL MIXED COURT OBJECTIONS TO FINANCIAL REFORMS

The controversy that returned Egypt's Judicial Reform to the forefront of international attention in 1876 involved an Italian resident who had lent money to Isma^cil against a portion of the viceregal estates. Originally Signor Cesar Carpi had merely sued the khedive in the mixed courts for failure to meet back payments.[7] Under pressure from the most aggressive consuls, however, the judges chose his case to test their mandate in light of the 7 May 1876 decree. A first decision in Carpi's favor ruled that Isma^cil's consolidation exceeded proper legislative authority where "individual capitulatory rights" were concerned. Referring to article 11 of the 1875 Charter, the court ruled that placing *da'ira* debts alongside the bondholding debt at a single revised interest rate was an "act of administration . . . infringing on already acquired rights of individual foreigners" residing in Egypt.[8] The judges called for recognition of Carpi's original debt claim (and, by logical extension, those of all other *da'ira* creditors) without reference to Isma^cil's consolidation decree.[9] No one who knew the climate of distrust among foreign creditors was surprised, therefore, when the mixed courts began to receive a flood of minor suits very similar to the Carpi case.

The London government seemed most perplexed by the judges' rapid defense of locally resident foreign financial interests. Disraeli's foreign secretary noted with some bitterness that it was mainly the "lesser powers," whose nationals were only marginally involved in Egypt's bonded public debt, that supported the so-called judgment creditors.[10] Meanwhile, Consul Charles Cookson warned that the mixed courts might actually force Isma^cil's treasury into premature bankruptcy by overzealous defense of individual foreign interests at the expense of Egypt's general solvency. Six months into 1876, the judges had already rendered fifty decisions in favor of *da'ira* creditors. "However," Cookson said, "owing to an understanding promoted by

[European mixed court] advocates to avoid the collapse of the . . . system from which they are [already] reaping a rich harvest," the bench had granted delays of execution.[11]

As one court decision after another was denied execution for fear of causing a general bankruptcy, the foreign judges themselves questioned the point of staying in session. Indignation over apparent capitulatory paralysis coalesced around a Dutch judge, Jacques Haakman, who refused to hear more cases on the grounds that "suspension of execution . . . implied . . . suspension of judicial proceedings entirely."[12] Haakman's boycott caused a number of cases unrelated to the *da'ira* scandal to be tabled long before the first summer adjournment of court hearings in July. Despite Cookson's belief that Egypt could pay its debt coupons *only* if the judgment creditors were constrained, the Haakman incident startled the British just enough to make them stand firmly behind the menaced Mixed Court Charter. At least one stimulus for a show of unity in Cairo occurred in August 1876, when a palace *coup* in Istanbul overthrew the sultan and the last formal Tanzimat Council. Talk of a constitutional regime augured totally different future patterns in relations between Istanbul and the capitulatory powers.[13]

From London's point of view, the possibility of real constitutionalist reforms at the center of the Empire temporarily raised hopes that the financial crisis of Sultan Abdulaziz's reign might be resolved by moderate legislative means. More immediate problems, however, especially Istanbul's awkward attempts to handle charges of violations of personal and property rights of Bosnian and Bulgarian nationalist insurrectionists, actually molded British policy during the first months of Sultan Abdulhamid III's reign. As long as such troubles continued, the most that could be done about pending capitulatory dilemmas was to press for an ambassadorial meeting to confer on the proper relationship between constitutionalist reforms and liquidation of the Ottoman debt. In any event, no foreign parties to a potential new Eastern Question crisis in 1876–77 would have been anxious to raise plans for wider capitulatory adjustments, including the possibility of reimposing Ottoman legislative controls over Egypt, until the political destiny of the new Istanbul regime was clearer. Given the ultimate failure of an all-capitulatory conference in January 1877, the sultan's reversal of the Ottoman constitutionalists, and the outbreak of new Russo-Turkish hostilities in April 1877, such wait-and-see tactics proved to be quite wise.

THE GOSCHEN-JOUBERT MISSION AND DUAL CONTROL

Until resumption of mixed court operations in the last months of 1876, Lord Derby concentrated Eastern Question efforts on central Ottoman political developments. He merely proposed a joint warning to Egypt that the powers expected early execution of all pending mixed court judgments. At this date, Paris was the only European capital to disagree with London's acceptance of the higher necessity of maintaining the Mixed Court Charter intact in Egypt.[14] In October, the French had the satisfaction of seeing their predictions of more serious deterioration in the Judicial Reform materialize. Once the consular holidays passed, the Public Debt Commission filed a mixed court suit against the khedive for failing to pay interest coupons in 1876. The courts handed down a decision authorizing the Caisse to confiscate additional receipts from the Egyptian railways to pay what was due. This was the first move by the mixed courts to protect nonresident bondholders whose interests had never been specifically considered in the 1867–75 capitulatory negotiations.[15]

Rather than try to force execution of the Caisse decision at such a critical juncture in European-Ottoman relations, French and British bondholders soon decided to send two private representatives to devise an alternative to Isma^cil's abortive 7 May debt consolidation decree. This suggests that many bondholders agreed that the only way to return the mixed courts to their original limited judicial role was to eliminate the legislative causes of financial confusion in Egypt. Thus, after reviewing all necessary costs for local administration, bondholder delegates Goschen and Joubert were instructed to establish a new overall debt payment scheme that would be legally safe from attack by the judgment creditors and the mixed courts.

Just as Goschen and Joubert arrived in Cairo, a whole slate of heterogeneous (and some very questionable) legal suits was filed by foreigners who feared that new consolidation maneuvers would harm their rights. This upsurge of claims finally pressed Hussey Vivian, Britain's new consul general, to ask the judges to join "politically disinterested" local diplomats to help break the public debt stalemate as soon as possible. Vivian himself wrote: "There are now 222 private suits . . . against the *Da'ira* . . . I spoke with [British mixed court judge] John Scott . . . to appeal that the judges . . . postpone these cases. . . . All then depends on the success of Mr. Goschen's negotiations and . . . the Khedive showing . . . good will for the settlement of his private affairs."[16]

Soon after this "friendly intervention," Isma^cil accepted new consolidation terms recommended by the representatives of the bondholders. The Goschen-Joubert settlement divided Egypt's debt into four sections, each with a different interest rate and listing of securities. All private debts involving the khedivial *da'ira*s were lumped into a separate category with a payment schedule to be determined later.[17] To help execute this delicate financial process, Goschen and Joubert recommended creation of a more specialized agency to work alongside the Public Debt Commission. Like the Caisse, the so-called Dual Control originally derived its authority from an agreement between the khedive and private representatives of bondholders who resided outside Egypt. Direct foreign governmental responsibility for its operations was ruled out, at least symbolically, by instructions from Lord Derby himself.[18] Since British and French nationals held a majority of the public debt, however, it was naturally assumed that the controllers would come from the London and Paris investors' market.

In fact, appointment of the Dual Control early in 1877 augured a policy shift in London away from post-1841 Eastern Question priorities toward a more specific concern for British political interests in Egypt. There may be some significance, for example, in the fact that the man who was destined to dominate Egypt's internal and international affairs over the next quarter-century, Captain (later Sir) Evelyn Baring, was named at this date to become the first British representative on Egypt's Public Debt Commission. For various reasons, British investors had delayed appointing their representative to the Caisse in 1876. When they invited Captain Baring to leave an important post as viceregal secretary in India, however, the bondholders selected a man who might easily interject indirect British governmental preferences into Caisse deliberations. London's delegate to the Istanbul Conference on the more general Ottoman political and financial crisis in this same period clearly faced unknown quantities in the new sultan and a newly emergent imperial parliament. Lord Derby undoubtedly realized, therefore, that Captain Baring would be well placed and had enough political and financial experience to help formulate a completely separate Egyptian policy if such measures became necessary in 1877.

The Baring family had made its own international fame through the Baring Brothers banking firm in London. Although some influence in government circles could be assumed, the family's political and financial discretion was beyond doubt. Evelyn Baring himself was the only family member to forsake guaranteed standing in London financial circles to embark on a military and administrative career in India.[19] In fact, this unusual mixture in Baring's background may have been a major factor favoring his candidacy for the "unofficial" Caisse job. As the threat of a new round of Russo-Turkish hostilities turned into a reality in the first months of 1877, London bondholders probably felt more secure knowing that the new Egyptian Dual Control structure was supported by a British adviser who had a flair for politics as well as financial matters.

Well before signs of behind-the-scenes political maneuvering actually appeared in Egypt, the Dual Control was asked to test the limits of its authority. Goschen and Joubert had left instructions to avoid future suits involving the Caisse in the mixed courts. In addition, Isma^cil himself wanted to prove his own concern to avert onerous side effects from the terms of the Goschen-Joubert consolidation. He insisted, therefore, that the controllers verify that government tax agents were collecting only authorized revenues and that local cultivators did not suffer in the attempt to pay debt coupons on schedule.[20] This was the first token recognition that Isma^cil's local council jurisdictions could not respond effectively to fiscal and administrative pressures created by the looming financial crisis. Already by this date, peasants who could not pay their debts because of depressed crop prices were being called into village judicial councils by local Egyptian plaintiffs. Technically, British and French Dual Control experts were to look into possible miscarriages of judicial efforts to settle matters equitably. The controllers soon became absorbed in newly resurgent mixed court controversies, however, and had no opportunity (or apparent desire) to become involved in village-level justice.

MANEUVERS AGAINST THE EFFECTS OF MIXED JUSTICE: THE COMMISSION OF INQUIRY OF 1878

Optimists had hoped that the Goschen-Joubert consolidation would return the mixed courts to a purely judicial role and allow more time to tend to administrative side effects of Egypt's financial crisis. New difficulties arose, however, as soon as the Cairo government first tried to follow the vague provisions of Article 12 of the mixed code to make a change in the law governing bankruptcies in Egypt.[21]

Apparently it was the Austrian vice-president of the Alexandria appeals court, Aloyse von Lapenna, who proposed to avoid conflicts between the mixed and remaining consular courts in Egypt by granting unchallenged jurisdiction in all cases of joint-stock bankruptcy to the mixed courts. Lapenna defended his suggestion by arguing that, since investment in joint-stock companies was limited almost entirely to the capitulatory sector, bankruptcies invariably involved diverse foreign litigants. Liquidation procedures therefore rarely came under the jurisdiction of a single consular court or foreign national law. Isma^cil's close advisers welcomed Lapenna's plan as a first move toward "adoption of a system . . . unifying Egypt's judicial authority, which is today too divided."[22]

Whether or not guaranteed extension of mixed bankruptcy law to local subjects might have encouraged more Egyptian joint-stock ventures, these pronouncements alarmed foreign residents. Many saw a danger in letting the mixed courts modify their own codes without prior assurance of full capitulatory consensus.[23] Especially in the wake of Abdulhamid's suspension of the new imperial constitution at the outbreak of the 1877 Russo-Turkish conflict, some feared that any locally initiated changes in the mixed codes would stir up provincial autonomy pretensions in Cairo's ten-year-old Representative Assembly. Tensions slackened, therefore, when Lapenna's colleagues rejected his scheme to apply mixed law to all bankruptcy cases in Egypt. The appeals court's opinion was that, although it would continue to "fulfill a purely judicial . . . mission without concerning itself with the views of other authorities," and despite the wording of Article 12, *consular* authorization was required for any legislative modifications in the mixed codes.[24] Rather than admit that fourteen foreign consuls should have a veto over Egyptian mixed law, Sharif closed the debate without further comment.

The effect of delaying reforms in bankruptcy proceedings was not likely to appear immediately in 1877. When this fiasco was followed by similar opposition to changes in agricultural credit laws, however, the judges' message became clear: the court was quite willing to transfer completely unprecedented quasi-legislative prerogatives to the consular community. If such powers were misused, the results could seriously hamper the efforts of the Dual Control and the Egyptian Ministry of Finance. When it came to mixed laws that touched in any way on economically productive property relationships, like the soon-to-be-notorious "judicial mortgage," concerned observers could already sense future difficulties.[25]

Procrastination forced victims of mixed court paralysis to search for a spokesman who not only opposed the indirect influence of the Dual Control but had enough local political importance to impress worried Egyptian authorities. The judgment creditors' choice of French consul Baron des Michels to champion their cause was not random. Indeed, when it appeared that the French consul would champion all judgment creditors without distinguishing between legitimate and exaggerated claims, his Dual Control colleagues began to suspect personal political motives.[26]

By December 1877, des Michels's criticism had become so bothersome that both the French and British members of the Caisse decided to comment on the legitimacy of claims being made in the mixed courts. De Blignières and Baring opposed, for example, consideration of salary arrears claims from foreign functionaries hired by the khedive as long as no Egyptian official had comparable rights under the local judicial councils. Until the Dual Control actually produced evidence of serious side effects of the financial crisis for the local population, however, the mixed courts seemed bound to go on claiming that strict defense of individual capitulatory rights was a legitimate legal priority.

Since the mixed courts lacked the power to execute their own judgments, of course, the controllers could follow the bondholders' tacit preferences: they could merely stand by while Isma^cil placed judicial condemnations into a future action file. In fact, de Blignières was even prepared to "throw the bailiffs out the window" and pressure the khedive to grant combined financial and judicial powers to a new body that could see further than specific cases involving foreign plaintiffs. Baring, however, felt proof of damages caused by mixed court bias had to be formally produced before asking for what amounted to annulling the Judicial Reform. "It will never do," he told Goschen, "for us to set an example of disregarding the decisions of the law courts. . . . We are pledged to hold a [full financial inquiry including considerations of dependent Egyptian governmental and private interests] or to tell the public that it is not to be. . . . Then creditors may go to the tribunals, consuls may worry the Khedive, and everyone may take his own course."[27]

Similar pressures from the Dual Control soon led Isma^c^il to accept still another private international commission in Egypt. As it was originally conceived, the 1878 International Commission of Inquiry was to employ *both* local and foreign specialists to review the multiple sources and uses of the khedive's revenues. Its report would go not only to the Dual Control, but to responsible ministries in the Egyptian government. The Inquiry was also to examine Egypt's corpus of nonsectarian or *qanun* legislation. This meant that it would be able to review local private property relationships among Egyptian subjects, fiscal laws and collection procedures, and the impact of the mixed codes on both private or local administrative interests. Given the potpourri of *qanun* and mixed law that had been introduced in stages after 1850, the Commission's job promised to be more complex than that of any capitulatory mission before it, either in Egypt or in the Ottoman Empire as a whole.

Apparently to avoid suspicion of any intention to favor public debt priorities, Isma^c^il was encouraged to appoint Ferdinand de Lesseps as chairman of the 1878 Commission. The Canal Company director was a respected symbol of international investment in Egypt. He was therefore unlikely to brook maneuvers that might prejudice resident entrepreneurs or those who had contributed to their risk capital. Moreover, since his company obviously depended on the 1875 Judicial Reform, de Lesseps could be counted upon to shield the mixed courts from unreasonable attack.

It was at the level of daily inquiry tasks, however, that possibilities for give-and-take arrangements with the Egyptian cabinet were visible. Unlike de Lesseps, whose eventual contribution remained nominal, the Commission's British and Egyptian vice-chairmen were both destined to play influential roles in Cairo's growing financial and legal reform dilemma. The choice of Sir Charles Rivers-Wilson, for example, promised not only financial expertise within the Commission, but also practical knowledge of local developments since 1875. The British vice-president's personal association with Egypt was certainly more direct than that of any previous intermediary among the courts, the khedive, and his creditors.[28] Like Baring, Wilson came from a family with long experience in private banking. His own initial career had been with the Exchequer in London. By the early 1870s, he was comptroller general of the national debt. During a temporary leave from this office, Wilson first visited Egypt as an assistant to the Cave mission. After 1875, his career had a number of links with Egyptian financial questions and British political interests in the Nile governorate. In addition to sharing business interests with George Goschen (both were directors of Alliance Life and Fire Insurance, Ltd.), Wilson became the first British member of the Suez Canal Board after Disraeli purchased Isma^cil's shares in 1875. Association with the co-drafter of the 1876 Egyptian Debt Law and responsibility for the British government's interests in the Canal, therefore, were certain to influence his attitude toward Egypt's need for administrative and financial stability. Whether Wilson would recommend more serious Dual Control authority over internal administration, however, was not yet clear when he returned to Cairo in 1878.

The Egyptian vice-president of the 1878 Commission was Mustafa Pasha Riadh. Riadh, like many other officials who had served in Sa^cid's central administration, had acquired wealth and importance by investing in agricultural land.[29] Unlike Nubar or Sharif, Riadh's very limited exposure to foreign commercial and diplomatic circles made him less likely to try to solve problems merely by proclaiming adherence to European-inspired reform schemes. Such common-sense qualities made him an ideal candidate for the 1878 Commission.

By the time support personnel joined the de Lesseps Commission, however, the Ottoman military debacle at San Stefano (March 1878) returned the main focus of east Mediterranean politics to Istanbul. Concern over Russia's victory against Abdulhamid led to the European Congress of Berlin (June and July 1878) and a complete rethinking of the political costs of maintaining stable Ottoman-Balkan borders. Britain's involvement in such priority matters was given a potential new turn after March, when control of the Foreign Office came under Lord Salisbury. The rumored cause for the change was Lord Derby's opposition to pressures to acquire a permanent naval base in Cyprus—an expanded imperial commitment that his successor accepted as part of the Berlin settlement. It was too early, however, to know if Lord Salisbury would risk upsetting other aspects of capitulatory equilibrium east of the Bosphorus to guard against threats to imperial passageways to India. When the Congress of Berlin was over and the Commission of Inquiry began calling for stronger political commitments in Egypt, however, the new foreign secretary definitely began to consider options far beyond traditional Eastern Question parameters.

High-level political priorities in Istanbul throughout 1878 did not mean that Egypt's Commission of Inquiry had been forgotten. They did, however, make it initially difficult for certain consulates to convince their superiors that a British-supported plan to disarm the mixed courts seemed imminent. In fact, it soon became apparent that the Commission had no intention of limiting work to balancing Egypt's budget. Observers like French consul des Michels, who demanded immediate execution of mixed court debt judgments, were alarmed by the amount of time spent on "simple questions of peasant justice." It was surprising, des Michels wrote later, to see "Wilson . . . attempting to give the inquiry a much wider scope than his fellow [Austrian and Italian] commissioners. Always absorbed in social and humanitarian considerations, [he] seemed more concerned with building a legal case against Isma^cil than obtaining information about the resources of the country."[30]

Indeed, when the Commission submitted its preliminary report in May 1878, it already hinted at innovations to help individual debtors protect themselves against administratively imposed hardship. The Commission had probably witnessed some of the paralyzing effects of the earlier emergency tax reforms on the assumed jurisdiction of Egypt's local councils. Both peasants and large landowners had contracted loans steadily since 1871 to pay taxes under the notorious (and now obligatory) *muqabala* law. Their hopes of repaying debts through promised reductions in their tax assessment often ended in judicial council grievances. This occurred either because taxes continued to be levied at pre-1871 levels or because lenders used traditional provisions of the *shari^ca* to seize the produce of private land when debts fell in arrears.

The negative effects of peasant borrowing had begun well before the introduction of mixed law in 1876. Once formal European mortgage arrangements became possible under the mixed codes, however, options existed for moneylenders to obtain more than liens on produce from debtors' property. If some form of foreign association could be worked into the capital sources for loans, local creditors found they could exercise the right of full property dispossession under the notorious judicial mortgage. As applied by the mixed courts, this Napoleonic procedure imposed court auction of any mortgaged property to pay insistent creditors. This held true even if the majority of such creditors (and the likely bidders at auction time) were Egyptians. All that was required was a single foreigner among the list of plaintiffs. Often, however, peasants who had overextended their credit saw the menace of mixed court seizure of their land looming. Such individuals could choose to sell their land immediately to pay their debts. A modest guarantee of sharecropping arrangements with the new owner then completed the vicious circle of contractual and jurisdictional confusion in the Egyptian countryside by 1878.

Given the rising incidence of such inequities, Wilson's Commission naturally wanted to look at mechanisms that permitted privileged groups to exploit legal devices in Egypt's fragmented judiciary. The growing trend toward land title concentration was not caused solely by anomalies in Egypt's legal system. It seemed obvious, however, that interconnections between the imported capitulatory codes and the financial crisis were allowing certain parties to turn special knowledge of the former into a source for personal gain.

All but extreme supporters of the mixed courts recognized that peasants caught up in side effects of Cairo's financial crisis needed an emergency alternative to local council or *mahkama* justice. Who, however, would be ultimately responsible for making changes in *qanun* laws that had no direct bearing on private foreign interests in Egypt? Extremists feared that the British wanted Wilson's Commission to handle such tasks.[31] Given the peculiar combination of traditional executive prerogatives, partial Tanzimat liberalization measures, and capitulatory controls operating since 1876, however, there was no clear channel for making new laws in Egypt. There was some assumption that suspension of the Ottoman Parliament in 1877 left the khedive technically free to promulgate any changes the Commission might recommend. He could also submit proposed laws to Cairo's Representative Assembly for ratification. In either case, any attempted local legislation could be a target for the mixed courts, which tended to see a plot against their charter behind Isma^cil's every move.

THE COMMISSION OF INQUIRY AND LOCAL EGYPTIAN VIEWS OF LEGAL REFORM

Despite glimmerings of controversy over Egyptian legislative questions, the Commission of Inquiry at first concentrated on fiscal inequities in Egyptian agriculture and foreign commerce. Through Wilson, Hussey Vivian learned that the Commission would also bring local and mixed judicial questions to the forefront as rapidly as possible. In his first major dispatch to Lord Salisbury, the consul outlined the changing intricacies of Isma^cil's judicial and legislative options. Surprisingly, he—like the Frenchman des Michels—suggested a simple one-step resolution of the overall dilemma based on the Mixed Court Charter.

According to Vivian, the khedive wanted to preempt the likely thrust of Wilson's final report by providing Egypt with a comprehensive court system to serve the greatest possible number of outstanding needs. The consul did not seem to realize that he was serving potentially contradictory interests when he predicted that the Commission "will propose that the jurisdiction of the mixed courts . . . be extended to natives, so as to give them a . . . means of redress for illegal exactions. . . . The Khedive told me he saw no objection to this, provided that [the originally excluded] criminal jurisdiction over Europeans is . . . given to the courts. But [I don't think he is] in a position to make an act of obvious justice dependent upon any such condition."[32] As soon as the Commission tried to examine the local court system at the level of the village councils, however, it encountered opposition. Whether through naivete or deliberate obstructionism, Sharif Pasha (then minister of justice as well as prime minister) claimed to see no connection between everyday disputes among rural agriculturalists and sources of revenue to service the debt.[33] To support his objections, he claimed that nuances governing simple *qanun*-related disputes and the prerogatives of the *qadi*'s *mahkama* would make it impossible for outsiders to understand local judicial procedures. Wilson reacted strongly to this attempt to shield Egypt's judicial councils. The Commission simply could not leave any area connected with basic property relations unexamined if it aimed at equity for both Egyptian and foreign capitulatory parties. Without even trying to argue, therefore, Wilson pressured Isma^cil to make the Commission's Egyptian vice-president, Mustafa Riadh, justice minister in Sharif's stead.

Suspicion that Sharif had tried to hamper closer examination of the local judiciary makes it more difficult to explain the khedive's next move, which claimed to support judicial fusion. On one hand, it is possible that Isma^{c}il's sudden bid to use the mixed courts as a key to further reform was simply a delaying action. Sparking controversy over even more capitulatory interference in Egypt's internal affairs might have sidetracked inquiries into local council activities. Resulting delays could conceivably have gained favor for the khedive's politics from rural landholders and notables who wanted to maintain the confused system of *qanun* jurisdictions that they themselves dominated. Such an interpretation fits a later "conspiracy theory" that blames Isma^{c}il for the chaos building throughout the country. One should not forget, however, possible altruistic motivation behind khedivial interest in adopting European laws to cover both foreign and local property interests in Egypt. One intent of Nubar's abortive comprehensive scheme ten years earlier had also been to encourage Egypt's emerging propertied elite. There is no definite evidence supporting either one of these two possible explanations for Isma^{c}il's renewed emphasis on the mixed courts as a panacea for Egypt's troubles in 1878. An important added perspective can be gained, however, by examining attitudes in Cairo's first privately sponsored Arabic press, which emerged along with these events.

ISMA^{C}IL'S MIXED COURT REFORM PLAN: LOCAL JOURNALISTIC AND CAPITULATORY CRITICS

As soon as it was clear that Wilson would investigate all phases of Ministry of Justice activities, the khedive publicly reiterated his desire to create a single secular court system for all of Egypt's foreign and local residents. In the absence of a sufficient corps of professional Egyptian legalists, Isma^{c}il felt the judges of the mixed courts themselves were "the body most qualified . . . to propose an arrangement that would agree with the legal and material needs of the local population."[34]

At first sight, this overture to the same bench that had repeatedly condemned the Egyptian administration seemed to run against the basic aims the Commission hoped to accomplish. In fact, by mid-1878, even supporters of the mixed courts could not easily justify expanding their mandate any further as long as so many existing decisions against the government were stalemated. The main object of Alexandria appeals judge Lapenna's response to Isma^{c}il, therefore, was to assure mixed jurisdiction in cases "between *any willing residents* of Egypt," indigenous or foreign.[35] But how could this be done without altering the letter of the capitulatory reform compromise negotiated between 1867 and 1876? Lapenna felt that if a few additional European judges came to Egypt on an individual contract basis, the courts could hold extra sessions to hear any purely Egyptian cases that came to them rather than to the *qanun*-based provincial councils.

Despite the political naivete of this nascent dialogue between Isma^{c}il and Lapenna, a number of presumably impartial observers did indeed support wider reliance on the mixed codes to reduce chaos in local administration. In fact, for the first time since *Rawdat al-Akhbar* welcomed the Judicial Reform in 1876, Cairo's Arabic press integrated legal reform commentary into its columns. Although half a dozen new newspapers had appeared over the previous three years, two trends clearly dominated the politics of Egyptian journalism before 1878. One whole category of subsidized newssheets (*Rawdat al-Akhbar*, *Wadi an-Nil*, and the forty-year-old "official gazette," *Al Waqa'i^{c} al-Misriyya*) combined announcements of government ceremonies or arrivals of prominent Ottoman or European personalities with simple accounts of ministerial activity. More independent journals, on the other hand, often depended on financing and editorial skills from the immigrant Syrian commercial and intellectual communities of Cairo and Alexandria.

Especially since the onset of political disturbances in Istanbul in 1876, stringent Ottoman press laws and restrictions on individual liberties forced a number of already active Syrian and Lebanese journalists to seek more receptive ground in Egypt. Representatives of the Syrian press in Egypt after 1876 included the brothers Salim and Bishara Taqla, who had moved from Beirut to found *Al-Ahram*, and Ya^{c}cub Sarruf, founder (with Faris Nimr) of the pioneer scientific journal *Al-Muqtataf*.[36] The conditions that brought Syrian publicists to Egypt, however, also influenced their journalism. Primary emphasis in *Al-Ahram* at this date, for example, was on the Ottoman Empire, including the Russo-Turkish War and developments in the troubled Balkan and Syrian zones themselves. In order not to incur Isma^cil's displeasure, very little attention was given to Egypt's political and financial crisis until 1878.

Several factors help explain changing views in Arab press coverage of the Egyptian Commission of Inquiry findings. First, political activism within the Syrian Christian community in exile had begun to spark frank discussions of foreign interventionism in Ottoman affairs generally. By the end of 1878, the disaster at San Stefano and prorogation of the 1877 Ottoman Parliament incited political writers (either recent immigrants to Egypt like Adib Ishaq or the famous itinerant activist Jamal ad-Din al-Afghani himself) to focus on controversial issues in the Egyptian environment around them. At about the time Syrian-edited sheets like Ishaq's *Misr* were founded, a first group of Egyptian-capitalized papers also made the same shift. Egyptian journals launched moderate campaigns by comparison to their Syrian counterparts. Some, however, soon became supporters of local administrative and economic autonomy, and even regional constitutionalism, as solutions to the growing Egyptian Question.

The first journal to discuss the legal and judicial dimensions of Isma^cil's dilemma was *Al-Watan*, founded in 1877 by the Coptic journalist Mikhail ^cAbdul Sayyid. Although *Al-Watan* could not have known the details of reform recommendations coming to the khedive from diverse sources, its first editorials were an uncanny prediction of things to come. When rumors of Lapenna's general mixed jurisdiction scheme reached ^cAbdul Sayyid, his reaction was immediately positive. *Al-Watan*'s receptivity, however, contrasted with what might naturally have been expected from frustrated rural or urban property owners, whose primary concern for legal reform was to protect their own material interests. ^cAbdul Sayyid's views were socially and politically oriented. They focused on court reform as the best way to stem further penetration of Egypt by foreign "protectors" in any form. Given the game of influence between the mixed courts and the Commission of Inquiry, codified law, whether mixed or purely Egyptian in origin, represented a guarantee of protection from each. Unlike the Commission, which might expand its foothold by pressuring for *ad hoc* decrees, mixed law had at least the merit of impartiality, whether administered by foreign or Egyptian judges.[37] Without proclaiming full support for the still imperfect mixed courts, therefore, ^cAbdul Sayyid was the first local journalist to favor the broad legislative principles behind their codes over patchwork reforms.

If Isma^cil was pleased to see press support for expanding the 1875 Judicial Reform, his illusions were short-lived. By the time the Lapenna plan reached the Ministry of Justice, various British sources were warning against any dramatic moves that might sidetrack grass-roots Commission reform recommendations. Consul Vivian, for example, quickly dropped his prediction of an easy judicial reform understanding based on the mixed courts. Vivian's revised view stemmed from conversations with Commission head Charles Wilson and a memorandum from Justice (later Sir) John Scott, of the mixed court of appeals. Like Wilson, Scott had previous experience in Egypt before receiving his judicial appointment. Two years before the Mixed Court Charter was ratified, he came to Alexandria to practice law in the consular court system. Unlike most private European lawyers who went on to enter the mixed bar in 1876, he had mastered French and Italian, as well as the basic elements of French law, even before coming to Egypt.[38] Indeed, by the time of his mixed bench nomination, Scott was well known in the local foreign community and even to Europeans who followed Egyptian developments from abroad. In addition to providing *The Times* with a number of dispatches on the plight of the tax-burdened *fallahin*, he had once been nominated by Goschen himself to serve as the British bondholders' representative on the Caisse. His opinion of necessary reforms in Egypt's legal system, therefore, was not likely to be taken lightly by the British-led Commission of Inquiry.

By the middle of 1878, Scott convinced Consul Vivian to "avoid the error of a larger measure of change than is . . . immediately necessary" to assure stability in Egyptian noncapitulatory litigation.[39] The judge believed that the mixed courts should serve only as a model, not an agent, for judicial operations beyond urban centers like Cairo and Alexandria. He was especially wary of situations in which foreign judges with no knowledge of Arabic found themselves applying foreign codes to cases involving bewildered *fallahin* defendants. His preference, therefore, was to organize a training program under which Egyptians with mixed court experience could operate judicial circuits within the decentralized council system. Ideally, the thirty-year-old Cairo Council, or "supreme court," could then gradually evolve codes based on genuine mixed jurisprudence for application throughout the countryside.

Neither Judge Scott nor Wilson made reference to a possible role for the mixed courts in reorganizing local justice. The fact that Nubar Pasha had become Egyptian vice-president of the Commission following Riadh's appointment as justice minister, however, encouraged others to take such prospects for granted.

JUDICIAL CONCERNS IN NUBAR'S 1878–79 MIXED MINISTRY

Contrary to what many had anticipated, the Commission's August 1878 report included quite moderate local administrative reform recommendations. Its openly political attack on the mixed courts, on the other hand, went far beyond expected humanitarian considerations.

In the matter of taxation, Wilson confirmed that the absence of administrative codes enabled officials and moneylenders to exploit rural *fallahin*, despite objections from concerned judicial council judges. Even when laws like the *muqabala* existed, the Commission found that no one outside Cairo knew their specific content. The report was even more vehement, however, in blaming the mixed codes themselves for upsetting Egypt's only recently established private bases for agricultural tenure. The Commission reopened the issue of mixed laws on agricultural credit and decried Egypt's inability to modify even a single article of the mixed code in 1877. Soaring debts stemming from tax or rental increases had steadily increased dependence on moneylenders, many of whom were foreigners or their *protégés* in the provinces. When peasants defaulted, association with a single capitulatory creditor took such cases out of the more flexible (combined *qanun-shari^{c}a*) jurisdiction of the local councils and landed them in the mixed courts. There the notorious judicial mortgage expedited disposal of debtors' possessions by judicial auction. In such cases:

> It is not only . . . livestock and crops which they are obliged to sell . . . it is their land itself. The usurers, to whom the tribunals cannot refuse the execution of contracts which are outwardly regular, are thus becoming owners of large amounts of land . . . while the small property owner . . . is tending to disappear. . . . Nothing shall have been accomplished until a system of judicial guarantees analogous to those in Europe has been instituted. . . . Without examining . . . the means which will permit the functioning of such jurisdictions . . . it will be necessary to take into account the local circumstances . . . and mores of the population as well as . . . guarantees of . . . [judicial] independence.[40]

To reduce such strains, the Commission urged immediate creation of a special administrative and fiscal jurisdiction, to be followed by "common law [penal and civil] tribunals . . . to guarantee respect for individual subjects and their property." Without elaborating, the report indicated that Isma^cil recognized the problem and had instructed the mixed judiciary to "study the means of assuring the benefits of a regular system of justice for the indigenous population."

The Commission's remarks suggested that it was less a report to foreign bondholders than a direct recommendation for action by the khedive. Isma^cil may even have been encouraged to believe that, irrespective of the "unofficial" nature of the Commission's mandate, its British vice-president spoke for Foreign Office desires to speed local financial stabilization. In any event, the khedive would probably never have dismissed Sharif's cabinet overnight and replaced it with the subsequently famous mixed ministry unless he had a clear sense that international political stakes in Egypt had changed considerably by mid-1878.

In fact, Wilson's apparent domination of Commission discussions of Egyptian legal questions did correspond, perhaps fortuitously, to Lord Salisbury's first major revisions in general Eastern Question policies laid down by his predecessors. What was beginning to happen in Egypt, as in Bulgaria and Cyprus that same year, reflected London's increasing commitment to the security of Britain's strategic interests in the east Mediterranean. Of course, when Bismarck called the Congress of Berlin after San Stefano, the major issues at hand had no direct bearing on nominally autonomous governorates in Egypt or North Africa. After Berlin, however, the Ottoman Empire conceded that its continued existence depended on the benevolent intervention of Russia's European rivals. As a result, several parties began to view their own interests in the internal affairs of certain southern Mediterranean provinces in a new light. One can include Lord Salisbury's decision to link the Foreign Office much more openly to Charles Wilson's Egyptian Commission's reform recommendations among the adjustments that followed.

As we know, post–Berlin Congress Bulgaria received a wide international guarantee of local administrative autonomy and Cyprus became a British naval staging base to guard against future Russo-Ottoman hostilities. Other secret understandings soon opened both

Tunisia and Egypt to indirect European penetration that had not been deemed politically acceptable during the first two years of Abdulhamid's reign.[41]

The situation that Britain and France faced in Egypt after 1878, however, was different than anything either had known in earlier phases of the Eastern Question. In the Dual Control and Commission of Inquiry, both powers had agreed to sponsor *ad hoc* private substitutes for direct international political solutions to Isma^cil's internal reform problems. Although Anglo-French interests enjoyed *de facto* controlling influence in both agencies, neither power (and still less Rome or Vienna) could be certain that its preferences would be followed by capitulatory surrogates. In fact, given intensified international rivalries during and after the 1877–78 Russo-Turkish hostilities, miscalculations in pressing for Egyptian reforms might carry more benefit for rivals than for assumed friends. Probably for this reason, French foreign minister Waddington finally lost patience with consul des Michels's blind devotion to Egypt's Mixed Court Charter. Specifically, he rejected the consul's suggestion (at the time of the Berlin Congress) that a formal capitulatory conference should serve as a sort of "international legislative committee" to review any recommendations submitted by Charles Wilson's Commission.[42] Instead, Paris decided to join London to devise an alternative to unwieldy private agencies altogether. The unprecedented mixed ministry solution that emerged was thus one stepping-stone closer to official Anglo-French political responsibility for solving Egypt's capitulatory and financial dilemma.

The Foreign Office had already prepared some ground for responding to the Commission's August 1878 report. As early as May, Vivian learned that London planned to urge appointment of Wilson himself as Sharif's finance minister. The Foreign Office also wanted to impose a unilateral British "Inspectorate General" with wide powers over taxation and judicial administration. If this was impossible, Salisbury expected an effective alternative to simple submission of Wilson's recommendations and a return to the mere power of suggestion that the Dual Control had wielded unsuccessfully for two years. He warned that whatever solution was attempted, it should not be subject to rejection by other capitulatory powers who feared covert intervention on behalf of the British bondholders.[43] When Vivian conveyed London's views to the khedive, therefore, he urged immediate recall of Nubar, vice-president of the Commission, to head a "responsible ministry" to study the Commission's recommendations. He also added that the bondholders would probably agree to suspension of previous Dual Control arrangements if two *European* ministers were invited to join a new cabinet. When Nubar returned to the key prime minister's and justice minister's posts, therefore, Wilson and Ernest de Blignières were immediately appointed to head his Ministry of Finance and Ministry of Public Works.

Such efforts to strengthen the impact of the Commission's recommendations were bound to mark a turning point in Isma^{c}il's troubled khedivate. Even the staunchest critics of the so-called mixed ministry, however, have overlooked the specific role it played in Egypt's decade-old legislative and judicial reform dilemma. This role began almost immediately when the privately contracted British finance minister reexamined the Goschen-Joubert liquidation law.

Although there was little he could do about the main provisions of the 1876 debt law, Wilson tried to convince mixed court judgment creditors to accept Goschen's original recommendation of a gradual *pro rata* liquidation of debts due to them. When Isma^{c}il carried out his part of an earlier bargain and transferred rights over certain viceregal estates to the treasury, however, several judgment creditors protested. Their fear was that the government would use the ceded estates to secure an additional loan instead of indemnifying foreigners who had sued the khedive in court. Nubar hurriedly announced that if Wilson actually secured a special loan with the Rothschild House in Europe, all creditors, not just the bondholders, would receive proportionate compensation.[44] Nonetheless, it appeared that a delicate balance was again forming in which the new ministry's options could easily depend on the unpredictable "legislative" whims of the international bench.

This new focus of attention on the mixed courts offered Nubar an opportunity to argue for what he called "Egyptianization" of the 1875 Judicial Reform. Since Justice Lapenna's earlier suggestions had become a dead letter by this date, the Egyptian decided independently to recall Jacques Maunoury, the drafter of the original mixed codes, to devise a better plan to integrate the foreign judiciary into the Ministry of Justice.[45] The one factor that checked Nubar's enthusiasm for early changes in the Mixed Court Charter was Charles Wilson's arrival in Cairo in December 1878. Within a month, the two European members of the cabinet proposed and obtained a series of priority decrees to reduce administrative abuse through very basic noncapitulatory legislative and judicial reforms.

As far as immediate judicial reforms were concerned, the first round of mixed ministry proposals seemed moderate enough to please everyone. Rumors had it that Wilson would only insist on a special "administrative jurisdiction" attached to the Ministry of Finance. A new *ad hoc* tribunal to handle taxpayers' plaints, he thought, could be made up of Egyptian judges and a single European.[46] The cabinet also discussed the need for government lawyers to represent indigent peasants in the mixed courts. Since 1876, legal services for litigants had remained entirely private and were monopolized by the European mixed bar. The latter body had grown yearly as foreign advocates— some of whom lacked clear professional status as lawyers—streamed to Egypt to cater to European and Egyptian clients. The government and even European journals admitted that Egyptian defendants often paid high fees for completely superfluous services.[47]

Protection of individuals already in court, however, was considered less urgent than preventing desperate actions by uninformed peasants that ended in costly litigation. Wilson himself felt the shortest path was to set up closer controls over fiscal administration. He urged the Commission to use its already accumulated findings to draft a specific fiscal and administrative code to be used by an *ad hoc* Ministry of Finance jurisdiction. Nubar himself yielded to this first suggestion that Europeans, not Egyptians, should formulate any legal reform schemes that might have to pass under the watchful capitulatory eye of the mixed bench.

Even before joining Nubar's cabinet, of course, Wilson had felt that Egypt's recovery from the effects of economic crisis depended on improvement in local, not only mixed, justice. Unlike Consul Vivian and more impatient Egyptian politicians or journalists, however, he resisted suggestions of a simple "one-step" change in traditional modes of settling disputes over agricultural contracts, water rights, or even land exchanges. By recommending new fiscal and administrative jurisdictions as a priority, Wilson and de Blignières limited themselves to alterations in "public" *qanun* law. The original intent of their suggestion was probably to avoid interference in local penal and civil justice. Many Egyptians themselves insisted that guidelines between judicial council and sectarian *mahkama* responsibilities over such matters were not yet clear.[48] There was, however, a problem in depending on Nubar to handle the Ministry of Justice's share of such responsibilities. The architect of the 1875 Judicial Reform was clearly not willing to separate the half-finished product of his earlier labors from the administrative priorities laid down by Wilson. In fact, despite Wilson's recent memo, he risked his political career by reopening the same issues of "extended mixed court jurisdiction" and Egyptianization of the Judicial Reform that Justice Lapenna had raised under different conditions the previous year.[49]

Nubar seemed quite surprised to discover that many parties who might have favored such a plan a year before rejected it in 1879. On one side, Vivian, who had been anxious to see a comprehensive decree affecting Isma^cil's local councils "for Egypt's sake" in 1877, had revised his opinion totally. Now that it appeared that the Commission of Inquiry's known biases against the mixed courts would be carried into the Cairo cabinet by Wilson and de Blignières, the British consul adopted a much less optimistic view of their future. Others felt that serious revisions in the Mixed Court Charter would come in 1880, when formal terms for renewal (or possible abandonment) of the 1875 Judicial Reform would be discussed. Indeed, if the powers behind the Wilson–de Blignières mixed ministry had their way at the end of the 1876–80 trial period, it was possible that the single most important ingredient in Egypt's intensified legal dilemma might be removed by political fiat. Without knowing the actual degree of London or Paris support for Wilson and de Blignières, therefore, few parties were willing to try to reform any phase of Egyptian justice only a year before the 1875 Charter was due to expire.

Meanwhile, Nubar's ideas for court reform struck another unexpected local obstacle. As more time passed and the inefficiency of Commission support for "responsible cabinet government" became more and more obvious, Egypt's first apparent constitutional opposition began to challenge externally imposed legal solutions in any form. The result brought not only Nubar's fall and resignation of the mixed ministry, but more direct foreign intervention against Isma^cil and the reconstituted Legislative Assembly that supported him.

5

The 1879 Representative Assembly

Khedive Isma^c^il's decision in January 1879 to widen the membership and functions of his *majlis an-nuwwab* was probably meant to respond to local sources of discontent with mixed ministry government. Developments since 1876 certainly would have made the twelve-year-old Assembly object that "responsible cabinet government" had rendered its assumed role in the *qanun* lawmaking process superfluous. Local reactions to Egypt's reform dilemma, however, extended far beyond the khedive's symbolic consultative council. Already there were signs of alienation among Cairo bureaucrats and provincial officials whose salaries had been cut to help service the public debt. Some victims of retrenchment could at least hope for assistance from various patronizing sources. Provincial employees of the government might, for example, expect some support from local notables with whom they had enjoyed good relations. Less well-placed individuals or groups that depended directly on the government for salaries, however, were panic-stricken by proposed budget cuts and emergency administrative legislation in 1879. Frustration became open in February 1879 when a group of middle-ranking army officers jostled Nubar and his British finance minister and demanded restored salary levels and normal opportunities for promotion.[1]

If one looks for more widely based interest groups, three identifiable elements seemed ready to support Isma^c^il's projected revamping of Representative Assembly functions. Most obviously, landowners were certain to expect Assembly protection from extraordinary administrative measures that might jeopardize their interests. Such parties would naturally favor clearer definitions of civil law and immunity from government encroachments on legal rights based on private contracts. A second potential group was comprised of self-made or Western-educated intellectuals who had begun to coalesce around Christian and Muslim publicists or *salon* figures in both Alexandria and Cairo. Unlike landowners, such intellectuals approached Egypt's legislative dilemma in terms of larger political issues that had gripped the Ottoman sultanate during the closing years of the Tanzimat.[2] Their attraction to potential constitutional reformist themes in Isma^cil's Assembly, therefore, was predictable. Finally, because of growing signs of influence exercised by a new propertied elite and nascent Western-educated intellectual class, Egyptian *ᶜulama'* were obviously pressed to defend the traditional consultative functions of the Islamic hierarchy as a whole. Ismaᶜil's revamped Assembly was ostensibly designed to provide a public forum for all these disparate elements. Each had its own reasons for calling for an increase in representative government in 1879. Superficially, however, they all agreed that an elected Assembly, not Nubar's handpicked mixed cabinet, should debate any recommended changes in Egypt's *qanun* law.

Obvious political circumstances surrounding Egypt's Representative Assembly prevented it from combining emergency lawmaking with principles of provincial constitutionalism on the Ottoman model. First, unlike abortive constitutionalist reforms in Istanbul, Egypt's 1879 Assembly was the product of sudden khedivial fiat. For nearly a generation, idealist imperial reformers had staked their futures on harnessing executive power by codifying Tanzimat assumptions of civil and penal rights and imposing general constitutional checks on the sultan. By contrast, most members of Egypt's Assembly probably identified with the khedive's methods of rule, in both socioeconomic and political terms. What the abortive Ottoman Parliament and Ismaᶜil's Assembly had in common, perhaps, was a desire to protect both traditional and newly emergent local interests from the dislocating effects of free market trends characteristic of Western finances, property holding, and commerce. In Egypt's case, apprehensions focused on pending Commission of Inquiry legal and fiscal reform recommendations to be submitted to Nubar's cabinet in the spring of 1879. For many Assembly members, these two questions seemed largely inseparable.

Ismaᶜil's decision to sidestep the mixed ministry and to invite his Assembly to draft a full corpus of necessary Egyptian codes gained early support from a wide range of Muslim and even Coptic or Syrian newspaper editors. Some considered the unification of all exceptional jurisdictions under an autonomous Egyptian legislative authority to be a local equivalent of what Tanzimat constitutionalists had hoped to obtain for the Empire as a whole.

As late as 1878, for example, *Al-Watan*'s editors had approved Nubar Pasha's desire to extend the supposed benefits of the mixed codes to Egyptians and foreigners alike. The Coptic-owned daily now argued, however, that only the Assembly should decide whether fully developed foreign legislative models actually fit the needs of a country just beginning to free itself from traditional "oriental" conceptions of state and society.[3] Egyptian landowners and local commercial interests alike would certainly have echoed ᶜAbdul Sayyid's assumption that legislative unification would bring a more realistic fiscal regime. If equity was to be the basis of Egypt's legal system, *Al-Watan* urged the Assembly to do away with foreign exemption from all taxation not specifically provided for in Ottoman capitulatory treaties.[4] Such mention of capitulatory business and property tax immunities certainly appealed to land tax–oriented Assembly members who felt that the countryside's share of Ismaᶜil's debt burden was already heavy enough. At the same time, *Al-Watan*'s frankness probably attracted Egyptians who were not landowners, but supported the logic of sweeping capitulatory reforms over the piecemeal schemes being discussed in the mixed cabinet. Such, at least, was the effect the khedive sought to create.

In February, Ismaᶜil took a first move to frustrate cooperation between Egyptian and European members of the mixed ministry. Claiming that the prime minister had mishandled recent clashes with disgruntled army officers, the khedive called for Nubar's resignation. Contemporary documents surrounding the appointment of Prince Tawfiq in Nubar's place, however, suggest that it came from other sources. Well before this date, both Ismaᶜil and Nubar had publicly sponsored separate schemes to adjust the 1875 Mixed Court Charter so that certain European laws could be extended to the local population. In each case, a storm of controversy had been raised by jealous capitulatory purists. In contrast to Nubar, the khedive was no longer willing to risk another humiliating rejection of judicial reform schemes that depended on capitulatory approval. Instead of seeking a compromise, he apparently broke with his prime minister and aligned with local and European parties who wished to see the mixed courts suppressed altogether. In any event, critical legislative and judicial reform matters such as these, not rising discontent in the Egyptian officer corps, soon captured the full attention of the foundering mixed cabinet until June 1879.

THE TAWFIQ PASHA MINISTRY

By the time Nubar was dismissed, Wilson and de Blignières clearly doubted their cabinet colleagues' commitment to discuss alternatives to conflicting sectarian, local council, and mixed court jurisdictions. Six months' delay had already encouraged Isma^{c}il to play down cabinet initiatives in favor of wider consultation with the Assembly. Two assumptions, however, made this political compromise acceptable to the mixed ministers. First, Prince Tawfiq agreed to encourage consideration of Wilson's earlier recommendation for a revised liquidation law and a judicial plan for fiscal and administrative codes only. There was also a promise to appoint Wilson's original Egyptian assistant, Mustafa Riadh, to both the justice and interior portfolios in Tawfiq's ministry.

Such vagaries continued to sidetrack many of the reform questions raised by Nubar's cabinet at the turn of the year. As soon as Tawfiq's ministry met, for example, Wilson was asked to suspend his draft of fiscal and administrative codes. All efforts were to be concentrated on a final financial report and recommendations for realistic revisions in the 1876 Goschen-Joubert debt consolidation. Apparently London and Paris were anxious to get a reconsolidation law through the mixed ministry before either the mixed courts or the Assembly could raise objections (albeit for quite different reasons).

Several reasons explain why the mixed courts chose this moment to try to influence Egyptian legislative moves that were essentially administrative or financial in nature. First, the judges were experiencing growing paranoia over local journalistic and Assembly attacks on Egypt's fragmented legislative and judicial apparatus.[5] Second, they probably mistrusted the European mixed ministers themselves. Wilson had already condemned past judicial awards to capitulatory plaintiffs as reflecting more pent-up vindictiveness than legal equity. If the mixed ministry had its way, they feared, British or French preferences could prejudice less politically prominent capitulatory interests as much as similar pressures from the khedive himself. In fact, the mixed court stand came just as Vivian's consulate received revealing private requests for "due recognition of *British interests in Egypt's judicial system* . . . before any permanent establishment of the mixed courts in 1881."[6]

From almost all parties' point of view in 1879, the major issue was once again the content of recommended revisions in the Goschen-Joubert liquidation law. If, as many by then predicted, the Commission of Inquiry favored reconsolidation only after a declaration of bankruptcy, many judgment creditors could lose everything.

Two sources of opposition existed, however, that could thwart Anglo-French bids for influence over Egypt's financial imbroglio. First, the mixed courts could again denounce any new liquidation draft as "an act of administration" violating the individual rights of capitulatory residents as defined by article 11 of the Mixed Court Charter (see chapter 3, Formulation of the Mixed Codes and the *Muqabala* Law of 1871). If enough foreign governments were convinced that their own political interests by 1879 lay as much in Cairo as in Istanbul, not only Rome and Berlin but even St. Petersburg might support a defiant legalistic position against the mixed ministry as part of their own Eastern Question strategy.

On the other hand, the Egyptian press itself had become very concerned about the question of legislative autonomy since expansion of the Representative Assembly in January. Supporters of the Assembly shared one thing in common with jealous capitulatory governments: everyone wished to resist any assumption of wider legislative responsibilities by the Anglo-French mixed ministry.[7] On their side, Egyptian supporters of the Assembly felt that Istanbul had severed the last strands of its own legislative sovereignty over Egypt. Abdulhamid had accepted humiliating terms imposed by the European powers without even thinking of resuscitating the short-lived imperial parliament of 1877. From here it was an easy step to assume that future responsibility for realizing aborted Tanzimat reform objectives, including revisions in Egypt's capitulatory regime, properly lay with Isma^{c}il's autonomous provincial assembly. Thus, when Wilson's Commission finally did announce that only bankruptcy, tax reforms, and lower interest reconsolidation could keep the Cairo treasury afloat, normally opposing forces in the mixed courts and the Assembly actually combined temporarily to help Isma^{c}il challenge the mixed ministry's judgment one last time.

Foreign observers were definitely surprised by the khedive's April 1879 announcement that, after stalling three years, Egypt would simultaneously pay its bondholders and local judgment creditors alike. His claim was accompanied by denial of any need to resort to bankruptcy or extraordinary fiscal measures. Isma^cil knew full well that such a status quo position would appeal to Assembly members as well as capitulatory critics of Wilson's "humanitarian" solution to Egypt's debt crisis. His inclination, therefore, was to let these two unexpected allies either share or fight over spoils the khedivate appeared to be offering.

Judging from editorials in *Al-Watan*, nationalist Egyptians already supported the idea that the Assembly should accept responsibility for a variety of legislative schemes that had been promised for a year by the mixed ministry. The most fervent *majlisiyyin* insisted that the Assembly could handle high-level financial reconsolidation laws as well. The Cairo daily denounced any international sanctions, by either the Commission or the mixed courts, against laws adopted to offset the paralysis of Tanzimat reforms in Egypt since 1876. ᶜAbdul Sayyid waxed particularly irate when he compared Egypt's plight with arrangements in Ottoman Bulgaria since the Congress of Berlin. There, the capitulatory powers and the sultan had agreed that recognition of a semiautonomous Bulgarian chamber would speed necessary adjustments left unfinished by Tanzimat legislators. "Why," he asked, "can't they recognize similar autonomy for Egypt's civil [legislative] and administrative apparatus? Egypt is wealthier than Bulgaria . . . has a better system of administration and . . . local courts. . . . If it is argued that treaties still exist between the Porte and Europe [preventing this], we say that it is time to revise these, because of obviously changing conditions. . . . "[8]

Mounting journalistic ferment and prodding from the Assembly gave Ismaᶜil the chance he was looking for to strike at Wilson's tax and reconsolidation schemes. On 7 April, he invited Muhammad Sharif to head a new cabinet. Sharif's now apparent constitutionalist leanings led to an expected reference to executive "responsibility before a chamber whose rights . . . [will henceforth] correspond to the requirements of [Egypt's] internal situation and . . . national aspirations."[9] Ismaᶜil's added request that the Assembly devise its own liquidation law and draft codes "respecting the needs and mores of all different residents in Egypt" led to Charles Wilson's immediate resignation.

Both mixed ministers seemed surprised that the khedive did not recognize that their recommendations actually aimed at reducing obstructions from the mixed courts. Without objecting openly to Isma^cil's Legislative Assembly plans, for example, Wilson's report implied that, once a new reconsolidation was achieved, the Commission itself would handle embarrassing capitulatory aspects of Egypt's legislative and judicial reform dilemma. Ideas for benevolent interventionism included letting the Commission confer with the Assembly on desirable legislative modifications that had failed to pass normal capitulatory channels since 1875. Wilson apparently even thought that the Commission might replace the mixed courts as a "supreme court" over all cases involving the Egyptian government. Many factors, he thought, called for new provisions to "decide without appeal the case of each [judgment] creditor of the government. . . . Such a body may be considered to exist already in the . . . Enquiry . . . who appear . . . as competent as any tribunal. . . . [It enjoys] prestige and the confidence of the creditors. . . . [A separate tribunal] might . . . prolong the present crisis owing to the [complicated] judicial process."[10]

From the resigning mixed ministry's point of view, therefore, resolution of Egypt's unsolved judicial problems still had to be a part of planned liquidation procedures. By calling for an extension of the Commission's mandate to solve such questions, Wilson clearly questioned the continued value of keeping the mixed courts.

The most striking bombshell in the Commission's report was its emphasis on defects and even apparent incompetence in the mixed court regime. Lingering capitulatory anomalies required new arrangements, especially "if the Judicial Reform was allowed to lapse" at the end of its first troublesome trial period.[11] Whatever financial settlement followed a declaration of bankruptcy, for example, Egypt definitely needed to defend itself against blanket acceptance of all pending judicial charges. The Commission proposed that it should itself review mixed court deliberations since 1876 and offer realistic settlements only to deserving private parties. Unscrupulous plaintiffs had learned to use judgment by default to win trumped-up claims at the expense of legitimate government creditors. At first, perhaps, "the tribunals could only suppose that the government was solvent and was merely refusing to fulfill its obligations [by failing to appear]. [But now it is clear that] . . . both the creditors and the tribunals were in error. It is legally indefensible and contrary to equity to administer judgments . . . when the debtor is already bankrupt. . . . The commission opines that all those judgments are null and void. . . . "[12]

Even such explicit condemnation of methods in mixed justice, however, failed to attract Egyptian cooperation with the Commission's liquidation reform scheme. The most obvious reasons for discord stemmed from Assembly opposition to financial and fiscal repercussions that might logically follow. Bankruptcy meant that further loans from the European money market would be, if not impossible, certainly constrained by political concessions, including perhaps a semi-permanent mixed ministry arrangement. At the same time, it was obvious that Egyptian landholding interests were not anxious to abolish inequitable aspects of the land tax regime, including the *muqabala* law, to help reconsolidate government debts. In its own rebuttal of the Commission's report, therefore, the Assembly denied the need for bankruptcy and tax reforms and favored a simple reduction in public debt interest rates.

The Assembly's rejection of Commission denunciations of the mixed courts and its promise of full payment for judgment creditors (both calculated to please capitulatory rivals of Wilson's strategy) were unexpected. The Commission had made specific reform recommendations that it apparently hoped to sponsor jointly with the Assembly. In the end, such conditions were unattractive to the 1879 Majlis. This was not because its members preferred mixed court mentors over mixed ministry guidance. What mattered most was avoiding any confrontations that might upset either the status quo of Egypt's property regime or the (ironically useful) pattern of capitulatory checks that made it impossible for any one country (here Britain or France) to dictate policy through the Egyptian cabinet. Maintenance of laws and procedures guaranteed by the mixed codes seemed to meet at least some of the Assembly's objectives. Indeed, the only local alternative would have involved long and controversial review of possible overlapping and contradictions among shariatic, *qanun*, and imported European laws functioning simultaneously in Egypt. Such a prospect was so unattractive to Assembly members that they avoided the Commission's tempting invitation to censure, and perhaps even abolish, the mixed courts at the end of their first trial mandate.

BRITISH AND FRENCH INTERVENTION TO "SAVE THE REFORM"

Charles Wilson's estimates of changing political interests in the Egyptian Question in 1879 do not appear in his official or published correspondence. A number of new controversial issues existed, however, to raise the hope of firmer Anglo-French support for the Commission's recommendations even after the mixed ministers left Sharif's cabinet. In fact, the general international situation by this date suggested that the spirit of disinterested political *détente* following the Congress of Berlin had already dimmed considerably.

One example of the impossibility of counting on outmoded Tanzimat Eastern Question formulas was a move to renew Chancellor von Bismarck's Three Emperors' League, originally set up by Germany, Austria, and Russia in the early 1870s. Bismarck had justified this military defense arrangement as a necessary evil: bringing the two inveterate rivals for territory in the Danubian Basin into a mutual pact with Germany was meant to reduce the threat of renewed imperial advances against the Ottomans.[13] The Russo-Turkish War of 1877–78 had of course proved the ineffectiveness of the League in tempering St. Petersburg's military policies toward Istanbul. When it was revived after the Congress of Berlin, however, it was hoped that Bismarck's added "Honest Broker" responsibilities would give Germany an important edge in dealing with rival embassies in the Ottoman capital. Rumors also circulated (and were eventually substantiated in an 1885 Colonial Conference in Berlin) that Germany also wanted a role in settling European tensions over exploration and territorial claims in sub-Saharan Africa. For Britain itself, the most immediate cause for alarm in Bismarck's post-1878 policy was the "unholy alliance" between Berlin and the sultan's perennial Russian and Austrian enemies. Lord Salisbury opposed any redefinition of Eastern Question strategies that might eventually invite Bismarck to extend Germany's influence over either land or sea routes leading to India. While the former stretched from Upper Mesopotamia through Iran and Afghanistan, the latter obviously focused on Egypt.

Even without the troublesome existence of Isma^{c}il's Assembly, then, the presumably neutral character of European representation on each of Egypt's ad hoc capitulatory bodies was crumbling rapidly. Indeed, if Egyptian intransigence had not speeded Wilson's resignation, an open contest between Anglo-French policy priorities and supporters of the mixed courts probably would already have occurred in mid-1879 and not, as we shall see, more than a year later. Before European clashes surfaced, however, events in Cairo forced all capitulatory parties, including the perplexed representatives of Britain and France, to rally behind the inviolability of the Mixed Court Charter.

Passage of the Legislative Assembly's alternative consolidation law of 22 April 1879 brought British and French threats of "extraordinary measures" unless other recommended fiscal and legislative reforms were adopted immediately.[14] Rather than wait to see what Britain and France would do, however, the Austrian and Italian (minority bondholders') representatives on the Caisse went directly to the mixed courts for a restraining judgment. This menacing move was enough to elicit Egypt's announcement that, if London and Paris would hold back from intervention, the Egyptians would consider Wilson's and de Blignière's legislative and judicial reforms as necessary adjuncts to their own financial liquidation package. Reconsideration came in the Assembly's last-minute attempt to supplement its own wisdom by creating a professionally staffed legal "council of state."

Since British *chargé* Frank Lascelles was not yet certain of London's preferences in any of these matters, he reported the council of state scheme cautiously. In outward appearance, the Assembly's new draft decree looked like something Charles Wilson might have supported before the liquidation question had blurred all other issues. Although it made no mention of future connections with the Commission, the Assembly was prepared to appoint a *conseil contentieux d'état* divided equally between four European and four Egyptian members. Besides "consulting on all projects of law . . . submitted [by the Assembly]," it would also "judge the acts of public functionaries and sit as an administrative tribunal."[15] The Lascelles dispatches gave no suggestion that the *conseil* plan had many Egyptian supporters. He seemed unaware, for example, that Egypt's more sophisticated constitutional-reformist press agreed that such a body would be a necessary legal and judicial complement to the eager but inexperienced Assembly. For Lascelles, the only immediate advantage seemed to be its promise of increased British and French influence over Egypt's legislative, as well as judicial, priorities!

Gaps between European and Egyptian estimates of the Assembly's intentions would only have been apparent to someone who kept tabs on the contemporary Arabic press. In fact, demands for a more sophisticated apparatus for autonomous legislative action were already coming from several different newspapers. Besides Mikhail ᶜAbdul Sayyid's *Al-Watan*, both the Syrian Christian-edited *Masr* and the Islamic reformist sheet *Mir'at ash-Sharq* had quickly noted the council of state idea and greeted it enthusiastically. For *Masr*, any chance to save the Assembly intact definitely offset the temporary need for European participation in a formal advisory body. After all, Adib Ishaq wrote, a professional council would not be a separate judicial authority mainly concerned with the defense of foreign interests alone. Most important, the professional expertise of a council of state would make it possible to take original Assembly legislative drafts and reformulate them in legal language readily assimilable to the existing mixed codes. Such new laws could be applied throughout Egypt in either the mixed or local council courts.[16] Assembly members seemed ready enough for rationalization of Egypt's legislative apparatus at the top level of interaction with European professional consultants. Many could not forget, however, that elements within their constituencies in the provinces had built up vested social and economic interests through reference to largely nonprofessional judicial proceedings at the village level. This last vestige of immunity from indirect European tutelage should, they insisted, only be altered after Egypt's newfound legislative autonomy had passed a first round of testing.

Such issues, however, were not among the immediate political factors that interrupted Assembly debates and created an open crisis in May 1879. Indeed, wide-ranging discussion in newspaper editorials was just becoming visible when, in the second week of May, the three-year-old legal and political stalemate came to an abrupt end.

On 11 May, Chancellor Bismarck made a move that was predictable, not necessarily in terms of protecting limited German bondholders' interests in Egypt, but because of the shifting balance of political rivalries throughout the Ottoman Empire after 1878. Bismarck announced that Berlin would lead any forthcoming struggle to reverse the Cairo Assembly's financial consolidation law.[17] In so doing he challenged London and Paris either to take threatened "extraordinary measures" or to cede Dual Control responsibilities (and authority to back or oppose mixed court decisions) to the

Wilhelmstrasse. Up to this point, the French and British had waited to see if further legislative actions in Egypt might create better conditions for settling the newest round in the judicial dilemma. The political vulnerability of the original supporters of the Dual Control, however, was now clearly revealed. Bismarck's warning came after England and France had ceded the assumed influence of both the mixed ministry and the Commission of Inquiry to the still undefined authority of Isma^cil's Legislative Assembly. Now their most influential Eastern Question rival threatened to denounce the Assembly's only completed act of autonomous legislation and to intervene unilaterally to shore up the declining prestige of the Judicial Reform. When British and French diplomats in Istanbul intervened at the highest level to obtain Isma^cil's immediate deposition and the closing of the Legislative Assembly, therefore, they moved less to back up their own specific Egyptian policy objectives than to preempt the rising pretensions of others.[18]

The scenario of events reviewed here and in the preceding chapter suggests that Egypt's financial crisis between 1876 and 1879 increasingly affected not only the mixed courts, but European general attitudes toward latter-day Tanzimat reforms in general. Some foreign ministries had originally supported Isma^cil's Judicial Reform primarily to limit abuses against individual capitulatory rights. They soon discovered, however, that as the financial situation deteriorated, the Mixed Court Charter provided convenient channels for exercising political checks on the Egyptian government itself. Such leverage would have been useful to foreign governments generally only if they all agreed on goals to be pursued in Egypt through judicial coercion.

Divided commitments among capitulatory rivals, however, weakened the mixed courts enough to encourage those who feared their potential powers to suggest important changes in their charter. Even if the Control powers might have gone along with measures to lessen the influence of the mixed courts in Egypt's internal affairs, they lost patience when Isma^cil's apparent duplicity thwarted each solution offered, either locally or by "benevolent" foreign experts. By using their influence to put an end to vagaries in Egypt's legislative and judicial reform efforts in 1879, therefore, Britain and France began shouldering responsibilities neither had envisaged during the formal Tanzimat era.

THE LEGAL TERMS OF TAWFIQ'S INVESTITURE

Following the deposition of his father in the spring of 1879, Tawfiq began what was to be an eventful thirteen-year reign. From the outset, the new khedive seemed willing to recognize both Ottoman and European desires to blunt reactions to suspension of the 1879 Legislative Assembly. To shore up their own special position, Paris and London quickly obtained the new viceroy's agreement to restore the 1876–78 Dual Control apparatus. Tawfiq also promised that newly appointed French and British financial controllers could not be dismissed without the consent of their home governments. The controllers' advisory functions were strengthened politically by giving them consultative seats in the Egyptian cabinet.[19] Significantly, the first nominees to gain official backing for the job were Major Evelyn Baring from the Public Debt Commission and Ernest de Blignières, Charles Wilson's French colleague in the ill-fated mixed ministry.

While the Control started redefining its responsibilities, Sultan Abdulhamid was asked to avert any possible confusion over Egypt's need to pursue legislative reforms to deal with its own problems. The *firman* investing Tawfiq made it clear that the sultan respected the khedive's right to promulgate, "in a manner conforming to the general standards of justice, all . . . laws necessary to rule Egypt."[20] Seen from the viewpoint of Abdulhamid's own top councillors, some of whom were veterans of the preconstitutionalist Tanzimat reform generation, such concessions to Egyptian autonomy were badly timed.

Mehmet Paşa Saᶜid was not actually appointed Ottoman grand vizier until October 1879, two months after the terms of Tawfiq's succession had been settled. Abdulhamid's new minister had built his own political career, however, around the same type of legislative and judicial questions that plagued Egypt. Because of this he was bound to have mixed feelings toward the undermining influence of capitulatory privileges and abortive local efforts to offset imbalances that such privileges had caused in such a short time in Egypt and other provinces.

It was under Mehmet Paşa's post-Tanzimat influence, for example, that the imperial *diwan* expanded government schools to train Ottoman (including Egyptian) aspirants in fields that were largely monopolized throughout the Empire by Europeans or European-trained elites.[21] Following establishment of a school of financial administration in 1878, programs based on the European model for legal and commercial careers were founded over the next three years. In addition to reviving emphasis on educational preparation for such newly emergent professions, the new vizier showed signs of resuscitating legal and judicial reform projects suspended since 1876. Thus, the Ottoman Ministry of Justice, itself originally founded to oversee the Empire's earliest European-based legal codes, welcomed Mehmet Paşa's promise of a much wider reorganization. The grand vizier specifically proposed to extend its responsibilities over all provincial *nizamiyya* jurisdictions that were not specifically under the *Şeyhulislam* or separate *millets*.[22] To strengthen this impression, Mehmet Paşa tried to hasten publication of a code of civil procedure for all nonsectarian jurisdictions and reactivated the drafting committee that had given preliminary form to the Ottoman *mecelle* in 1869.

Seen in this light, Tawfiq's investiture *firman* did not necessarily encourage provincial drift away from imperial guidelines for *nizamiyya* legislation. Its terms suggested that Egypt's system of part-*qanun*, part-mixed law had to be altered, and that the khedive should impose necessary local changes as an agent of his imperial sovereign. Indeed, if Mehmet Saᶜid's *diwan* had succeeded with its own proposed *nizamiyya* schemes, Tawfiq would have had many reasons to want to abandon *both* the 1875 Judicial Reform and the tenuously rooted local council system. Any cancellation of original Egyptian contributions to the Tanzimat, however, still depended on realization of what the abortive Ottoman constitutionalist legislature itself had failed to accomplish. In fact, by 1879, Egypt's internal legislative needs had become too pressing to wait for revived imperial Tanzimat aspirations to yield results. Demands for a final financial consolidation had only been delayed, not resolved, by Ismaᶜil's forced removal. Indeed, Khedive Tawfiq could not escape reminders that both disgruntled former Representative Assembly members and important foreign political interests expected major provincial-level legislative reforms at the earliest possible date.

RIADH PASHA'S CABINET AND CHANGING REFORM PRIORITIES

The new thrust of Anglo-French policy in 1879 opened the way for the appointment of Mustafa Riadh to head Tawfiq's first cabinet. Riadh's political name had been made under the protective shadow of Wilson's Commission of Inquiry. No one in the foreign community was surprised, therefore, to hear him declare his intention to reorganize Egypt's local council system and to renew the mixed courts "only after necessary modifications" in their original charter.[23] When Riadh selected a new justice minister, however, such *pro forma* gestures became more substantial.

In contrast to political favorites who had headed the Ministry of Justice under Isma^cil, Husayn Bey Fakhri was the first professionally trained lawyer to serve in Egypt's cabinet. A product of the last generation of local students to profit from Isma^cil's program of foreign educational missions, Fakhri had earned a French *licence* in law.[24] His return from Europe just as Nubar completed negotiations for the mixed courts placed him among the few Egyptian candidates for immediate professional judicial service. Although mixed court judgeships went to older men or those with previous experience in government service, Fakhri was appointed in 1876 as an assistant in the mixed prosecutor's office. What he lacked in actual years of service, therefore, was offset by European training and direct experience of shortcomings of the 1875 Judicial Reform. The new minister also contrasted with Nubar or Sharif, both of whom operated at a high political level and tended to identify mainly with the judicial politics of public debt liquidation. Fakhri himself went directly to an assembly of European lawyers to discuss grass-roots issues that would have to be solved if the mixed courts expected to survive their first "trial" period in Egypt.[25]

The initial reformist concerns of Riadh's ministry brought surprisingly little reaction from Egypt's Arabic or foreign press. On the European side, this may have been because capitulatory interests feared the restored Dual Control more than declarations from the new cabinet. All parties knew, for example, that no local ministry could take more than token measures before Evelyn Baring or his French colleague would weigh everything for possible effects on public debt liquidation, a problem left unsolved after failure of the mixed ministry.

In the fall of 1879, the Controllers called a bondholders' conference in Vienna to plan a revised liquidation law in cooperation with the Egyptian government. If an agreement was reached, the foreign ministries of each nationality involved were to sign the settlement. This would give any new debt law formal status as a capitulatory convention subject to international not Egyptian (or mixed) law. Once in Vienna, however, Baring learned that German and Austrian representatives of the bondholders hoped to use *ad hoc* Egyptian public debt arrangements to gain a wider say in Egyptian political and legislative matters. The Austrian delegate had even suggested recognizing the Vienna conference as a sort of supreme court to sanction any vital Egyptian legislative matter that might be held up by local capitulatory intransigence. Baring's opposition to the Austrian proposal clearly revealed that he had abandoned Charles Wilson's previous optimism concerning internationally staffed "legislative auxiliaries" in any form. He told Lord Salisbury that a permanent capitulatory commission would probably try to take over for itself the internal legislative role the mixed courts had falsely assumed since 1876. Baring warned that, if the British and French wanted to abandon the Mixed Court Charter in 1881, they should not encourage alternative channels for capitulatory attacks on the Dual Control.[26] His private letter to Lord Salisbury was an indirect hint of possible advantages for Egypt and the Dual Control alike if the Judicial Reform merely expired after its five-year test period.

Rumor of another impending clash over Egypt's capitulatory and public debt priorities reached the European press quickly. The Viennese *Messager d'Orient*, for example, clearly suspected Dual Control motivations in raising liquidation law negotiations to the level of a formal international settlement. Not only had Baring and de Blignières removed the liquidation law from the purview of local Egyptian and capitulatory control agencies: they were participating in the Vienna discussions directly alongside two regular British and French bondholder representatives. The Austrian press feared that the same *ad hoc* arrangements (with voting heavily weighted toward British and French preferences) could be applied any time mixed court legislative review ran against Dual Control policy objectives. If the Vienna precedent were extended to take in questions of Egyptian capitulatory guarantees generally, the *Messager* imagined that Anglo-French interests could "assume the responsibility . . . of making laws which would be most advantageous for them. This law would bind the mixed tribunals . . . which will have no choice but to apply, in the name of independent justice . . . legislation . . . imposed by those who stand most to benefit from it."[27]

From the standpoint of the politics of Egyptian legal reform, therefore, the first fear of colonial domination by Britain and France was raised *not* by disgruntled Egyptian parties, but by European rivals who feared political isolation in the labyrinth of the Ottoman capitulatory regime.

DEBATE OVER MIXED COURT REFORMS BEFORE AND AFTER THE BRITISH ELECTIONS OF 1880

The bondholders' representatives in Vienna spent the first months of 1880 discussing liquidation details proposed by the Dual Controllers. The dominant influence of Paris and London and the bondholders' own desire for a lasting settlement practically assured acceptance. When Wilson himself was elected chairman, the liquidation commission quickly produced a settlement reflecting most of the recommendations of the 1878–79 Egyptian Commission. Since the Vienna Conference had a strictly financial mandate, however, there was no attempt to extend discussions to Wilson's earlier controversial denunciations of Egypt's mixed court regime. Once the 1880 liquidation law gained acceptance as a separate international convention, the major justification for four years of mixed court pressure on Egypt's local administration seemed to have been eliminated. For Mustafa Riadh, therefore, the time seemed right to confront the court reform issues that had eluded every Cairo cabinet since the mid-1870s.

The first move to set preliminary terms for renewing the Mixed Court Charter in 1881 came after meetings between justice minister Fakhri and the British and French consuls. Consul de Ring was openly pleased that the Egyptians had not contacted the other powers concerning court reforms until they were "assured of the favorable disposition . . . of France and England."[28] On the British side, Sir Edward Malet assumed the control powers should support Egyptian reform priorities openly once the moment for review of the 1875 Charter arrived. Until then, however, he mainly urged Fakhri to reorganize Egypt's local council jurisdictions. This first step was important, he felt, because "if all efforts at conciliation among the powers fail, and some . . . withdraw from the International Tribunals . . . native tribunals [should] be in existence before which foreigners could bring their suits. . . ."[29] The consul's suggestion that Fakhri appoint "a few . . . mussalman [sic] judges from India to encourage the independence of the local judiciary" indicated that British support for such contingencies should be indirect.

As far as the other capitulatory powers were concerned, most felt that they had little reason to worry about attacks on the Judicial Reform. Failure of the Representative Assembly in 1879 had reduced fears that local Egyptian opinion alone could impose integration between capitulatory and local legal institutions. On the contrary, there was now evidence that the idea of unifying foreign and traditional Egyptian methods of justice alarmed not only extreme defenders of the inviolability of Islamic *shari^c a*, but even liberally oriented *^c ulama'* who had witnessed the chaotic legislative debates of the 1879 Assembly firsthand.[30]

In London, Lord Salisbury depended to a large extent on private letters from Major Baring and Consul Malet to follow Egyptian developments. It is possible, therefore, that the Foreign Office staff itself never formally discussed changing policies affecting the Dual Control. This helps explain why the Liberal party's victory in the spring elections of 1880 brought considerable confusion in London concerning Cairo Agency policies since 1876.

As soon as Lord Granville became Gladstone's foreign secretary, he ordered the first formal Foreign Office review of Egypt's judicial regime since 1876. The law officers were expected to leave political strategy questions to the cabinet itself. In fact, however, the report that came to the Liberal cabinet reflected characteristic political biases among the legalists who drafted it. The same key document also fostered what proved to be shortsighted estimates of changed Egyptian attitudes toward such questions since 1879.

In a section dealing with the effects of the Judicial Reform on the Egyptian populace as a whole, F. S. Reilly's memorandum concentrated on questions of rural litigation. Drawing inspiration from Britain's earlier experiences in India, the law officers felt that cumbersome procedures and overcentralization had harmed peasant interests. The inability of many rural litigants even to respond to court summonses was reflected in an excessive number of judgments by default. The law officers thought that Egyptian confusion over the complexities of French law might be solved by bringing the mixed codes more into "harmony with the laws of England, Germany, and other states whose legislation was not tied to the *Code Napoléon*."[31] Meanwhile, simple logic demanded that the number of judges on the existing benches should be reduced. Personnel released from service in five- or seven-member international benches could then staff much needed itinerant provincial jurisdictions.

Although he stopped short of suggesting open exploitation, Reilly criticized the mixed bench for obstructing efforts to modify the 1875 codes. The courts, of course, defended the status quo out of fear of laws that might discriminate against foreign interests. They should be made to see, however, that a contrary effect could occur. Eventually Egyptians might develop their own property and contract laws with advantages unknown under practically immutable mixed codes. They would then no longer be willing to enter into relations with private foreign interests that would tie them to capitulatory jurisdictions and unfavorable mixed legislation. Foreigners might then be the first to regret the mixed bench's conservative bias and to call for "Egyptianization" of the codes. The only solution, Reilly felt, was to cancel article ll of the Mixed Court Charter completely. Instead of allowing judicial review of any Egyptian laws that might (or might not) affect the "acquired rights of any [specific] foreigner," general principles only should govern acceptance or rejection of future legislation.

Shortly after the Liberal government heard these recommendations, the Egyptian cabinet called for a formal capitulatory assembly to plan modification and renewal of the 1875 Judicial Reform. Whether or not Consul Malet already sensed new directions in London's political approach to Egyptian reform, he was bothered by the way the Dual Control and the French in particular greeted Riadh's announcement. Baron de Ring, for example, suggested that the recent liquidation commission, in which Control views had easily guided nonresident bondholders' representatives, should supervise renewal of the mixed courts. According to the Anglo-French controllers, such an ad hoc body would be qualified to review changes worked out by Riadh's legal advisers. The latter, tentatively including Husayn Fakhri, Octave Borelli and Mr. Mallard (French and English lawyers in Egyptian government service), and several Egyptian officials, were expected to be "entirely devoted" to the presumed goals of the Dual Control.[32]

SOURCES OF EGYPTIAN OPINION IN 1880

The contemporary Egyptian press clearly misunderstood the impact political rivalries had made by this date on the original objectives of the Judicial Reform. Salim Taqla's *Al-Waqt*, for example, simply expected changes that five years' experience had proved necessary. Its editorials referred optimistically to "diverse problems that . . . must be resolved. . . . The powers recognize these . . . and will amend defects."[33] In fact, it was not until Husayn Fakhri named a committee to study defects in both the mixed and local council jurisdictions that contradictions between local public opinion and political reality began to appear. A hint of future tensions should have been visible, for example, in Fakhri's decision to name two French supporters of Dual Control policy (but no British lawyer at all) to his Egyptian-majority advisory committee.[34] According to *Al-Waqt*, however, the members' technical expertise, not a certain proportion of input from different nationalities, would ultimately allow them to "bring the mixed and council systems closer together . . . without resorting to mere imitations of foreign models."[35] Not all Fakhri's appointees, however, agreed. Alfred de Vacher, the French lawyer who had been called to the committee from his post as chief mixed prosecutor, was bent on including "ideas . . . most useful to our own [French] influence" in any Egyptian reform.[36] In fact, such preoccupations would leave complementary alterations in the local council system completely unattended until the French finally felt assured that the future of mixed justice in Egypt would respond to their own political needs.

Until international jealousies nearly paralyzed Cairo's second major capitulatory conference in ten years, the Arabic press tried to remain optimistic about Riadh's approach to Egypt's legal reform needs. In contrast to the political orientation of foreign newspapers, Egyptian editorialists clung to hopes that legal and social reform goals could advance hand in hand. The Arabic press recognized that a strong political effort still had to be made against mixed court encroachments on Egypt's legislative autonomy. Most journalists warned, however, that too much concentration on capitulatory problems could obstruct the need for immediate village-level economic stabilization. Articles from the contemporary press show that personal accounts of rural conditions had become an important channel of recognition for a number of individuals among Egypt's educated elite and even some rural notables. Many Cairo press articles in 1880 and 1881 contained anonymous (and some well-known) individuals' impressions of the meaning of terms that, like "justice" (Ar., *ᶜadl*) or "civil rights" (Ar., *haqq madani*), became main slogans in the broader social and political history of Egypt during coming generations.

Until recently, this phenomenon and the still incomplete story of what one may call early "liberal nationalist" currents of opinion in Egypt have been interpreted almost solely in light of higher-level points of articulation. In fact (in the khedive's cabinet, the army, or the Legislative Assembly), pronouncements were often gauged for direct political impact, usually on foreign observers. Various unofficial impressions of the local problem of Egyptian justice in 1880 and 1881 can offer new perspectives on local forces behind the troubled political events of the same period. In a wider historical context, many of the opinions expressed in the Arabic press at this time would return as reminders of both motivations and contradictions in Egypt's task of social and political modernization for years to come.

It was the Lebanese editor Bishara Taqla who inaugurated what soon became a major theme in Egyptian political journalism by inviting discussion of judicial questions in *Al-Waqt*. Taqla and other Egyptian publicists correctly assumed that readers would have little understanding of the technical legal reform imbroglio. On the other hand, the problems of litigants who experienced the rigors of traditional justice during the most critical stages of the government's financial crisis offered a more newsworthy subject. In simplified form, therefore, the Arabic newspaper served as an unofficial forum for local public debate. Its columns for provincial correspondence provided an ideal invitation for politically aspiring local personalities to air their views and to challenge inequities around them. The content of such articles was uneven in 1879. Developing quality and sophistication in the local press, however, gave birth to ideals that were espoused by the first organized nationalist opposition of the Watan (Fatherland) party in 1881–82 and, as we shall see, by the first professional lawyers' press in Egypt in the decade that followed.

When the question of rural justice first entered the press, Egypt was in the grips of its most serious financial and administrative crisis of the century. Debilitating effects of oppressive fiscal and police pressures on the peasantry were obvious. Material deprivation was one major cause of increasing lawlessness and attacks by peasants against rural private and government property. Under such conditions, a first subject for controversy was bound to be the inability of the Ministry of Justice councils to avert further decline in village security. In fact, the greatest number of complaints registered by 1880 concentrated on arbitrary removal of penal and civil jurisdiction from the councils altogether. Gradually it became common for provincial *mudir*s to reclaim the full (pre-1873) prerogatives of their office and to arrest, judge, and execute penal cases summarily, without even consulting local councils.[37] Many contributors to *Al-Waqt* noted that judicial councils' civil jurisdiction was also disintegrating very rapidly. This created a serious invitation for the *mudir*s to intervene in a wide range of private disputes. Since council bench service involved rural notables and village *shaykh*s whose own interests were often at stake in peasant litigation, encroachment by the *mudir*s in civil affairs was becoming just as controversial as executive prosecution of penal cases.[38]

Certain *mudir*s were even lauded for taking over the jurisdiction of the councils. Although this sometimes protected petitioners from the arbitrariness of the members of the local councils, it had the effect of removing peasant litigation (and the availability of sworn witnesses) from the actual site and conditions of the original dispute. In sum, the desirability of letting the *mudir* assume extraordinary magisterial powers depended on unpredictable factors. It was necessary to know, for example, if council jurors in any particular case were willing to confront the *ᶜumda* or wealthy local landlord with the specific provision of a *qanun* decree. If they were, and if their decisions were accepted by a majority of their peers, there was no advantage (and possibly even more danger of injustice) in having a direct executive agent carry out essentially the same judicial function.

Such controversies became all the more difficult to untangle as incidents of administrative chaos and rural violence continued to rise in number and intensity in 1880.[39] Since the Cairo government was working on schemes to improve conditions of mixed justice but seemed to have forgotten local justice as a priority, discontent was bound to grow. Indeed, judging from the words of an unnamed *Al-Waqt* subscriber in Buhayra, many provincials were beginning to view the political success or failure of the Riadh cabinet in terms of judicial reforms promised, but not yet seriously pursued:

> It is not enough to assume that we have reformed a given *mudiriyya* simply because an upright *mudir* has been appointed. There must be a concern for the organization of the smallest unit of administration. . . . Those in authority should not forget that public opinion is the most righteous judge. . . . Each *mudiriyya* should have a general court and a justice of the peace [*qadi al-sulh*] in each district. He should have a salary that is adequate compensation for work performed, to avoid the temptation of corruption. . . . The residents of the country are patiently awaiting . . . the local council reform law that . . . His Excellence Fakhri is preparing.[40]

Once *Al-Waqt* began identifying the weaknesses and needs of the local judicial councils, other Cairo newssheets also tried to impress the Riadh cabinet with the popular view that "proper administration of justice . . . [represents] the key to all material progress and . . . freedom in the Egyptian countryside."[41] Probably the most respected contributor to the press campaign was the future rector of Al-Azhar, Shaykh Muhammad ^{c}Abduh. Although himself a product of a traditional *shari^{c}a*-based Islamic education, ^{c}Abduh was already noted in Cairo intellectual circles for his social and political reform tendencies. Although the exact degree of his early association with nascent constitutional and Islamic reformist currents in Egypt is still unclear, ^{c}Abduh had definitely followed the course of Isma^{c}il's abortive Legislative Assembly with interest. Whatever his political sympathies before or after this date, Khedive Tawfiq had appointed him to the prestigious post of editor of the Cairo government's official organ, *Al-Waqa'i^{c} al-Misriyya*. Under ^{c}Abduh's influence, a number of articles appeared in *Al-Waqa'i^{c}* that clearly reflected currents of discontent over judicial inequities at a local level.

Only a few weeks before Fakhri convened the long-awaited international commission to discuss the future of Egypt's capitulatory court system, ^{c}Abduh himself published an essay entitled "Respect for the Government's Laws." *Al-Waqa'i^{c}*'s editor did not even hint at the possibility of closing the mixed courts in favor of a unified "national" judiciary. He shared *Al-Waqt*'s concern, however, that foreign advice should be taken only to the extent necessary to integrate capitulatory expectations into plans to guarantee justice for all residents of Egypt.

No discussion of law, ᶜAbduh warned, could be relevant to Egypt's real needs if it was constrained by external political priorities or vested interest groups. If such a situation occurs, he wrote,

> . . . it makes no difference whether the laws are written out or not. . . . Even a country in which legislative options have been highly perfected may thus exist at the same practical level as a country that is barbarous, for the end result in both cases is internal contradiction [*ikhtilal*] and disorder. . . . The Egyptian government has so often prided itself in laying down *qanun* laws and multiple organizations for administering them that one would think that in this country law and practice were in harmony. But it lost the people's confidence when it became apparent that its actual works were not up to the level suggested in the law. The present government is striving to carry out the letter of the law and to direct matters of disagreement to the courts. . . . There can be no advantage whatsoever in laying down new laws that are not in harmony with social practice and the execution of which is not understood by those who are to be protected by them.[42]

Many such views expressed in the Egyptian press seemed based on the assumption that, once the 1880 liquidation law became rooted and the financial crisis eased, the political dilemma of local legal reform would diminish accordingly. The attitudes displayed by representatives to the mixed court renewal talks, however, soon proved the futility of such predictions.

COLLAPSE OF DUAL CONTROL AND EGYPTIAN REFORM PROPOSALS: THE CAIRO CAPITULATORY COMMISSION OF 1880–81

When Fakhri finally released a few mixed court renewal recommendations (including preference for the typically French cassation system of final appeal), a number of parties were disappointed in the apparently piecemeal nature of his special ministerial committee's work. Even the Dual Controllers seemed surprised to discover that handpicked professional legal advisers adhered so closely not only to the mixed courts, but to specific French legal structures.[43] Because they had miscalculated Alfred de Vacher's personal dedication to French interests in Egyptian judicial reform, Fakhri and Riadh had to move quickly to reassure Egyptian observers of their continued sensitivity to both capitulatory and local court grievances. Their alternative options reflected not only the more balanced political goals of the Control powers, but also realistic ways to realize Egyptian goals without depending entirely on foreign models. These ultimately failed, not because of a lack of receptivity among responsible Egyptian parties, but because of intransigence on the part of Britain's and France's political rivals in the mixed courts.

At Egypt's invitation, representatives of fourteen governments met in Cairo in December 1880 to discuss renewal of the 1875 Mixed Court Charter. Riadh himself was conference chairman, assisted by his justice minister and Octave Borelli, the French lawyer who handled Ministry of Finance legal affairs. As in the Cairo Conference of 1869, most powers delegated their consuls.

Even before the commission met, rumors circulated that the "representatives of the [Dual Control] Powers" had pressured Riadh to reconsider the reform strategy recommended to the cabinet by Fakhri's advisory committee a few months before. Indeed, in its first meeting the commission took rumors of Dual Control tampering seriously. Over the combined opposition of Riadh and Charles Cookson, the consuls immediately voted an unconditional one-year renewal of the mixed courts while a subcommittee of their "legal assistants" took up the merits of any reform demands.[44] By transferring their responsibility to the very judges who stood to be affected by revisions in the original charter, the consuls made existing political tensions in effect personal.

The minutes of the 1880–81 subcommittee reveal a pattern of capitulatory jealousies that would plague Egypt for generations to come. To Fakhri's disappointment, even the most logical proposals to decentralize or to increase Egyptian participation in the work of the mixed courts were opposed. For example, the subcommittee rejected a request to reduce the number of judges on the three first-instance courts to free personnel to staff provincial circuit courts. To justify the status quo, the judges insisted that, given diverse levels of technical competence among the powers' nominees for mixed court service, a full five-member bench was the only way to guarantee proper interpretation of the law.[45]

Suspicion of Control "guidance" behind Egyptian recommendations also blocked a request for a superior review court to decide conflicts of jurisdiction between the mixed and the local council courts. Since members of the subcommittee knew that Fakhri's committee had originally recommended two separate lines of cassation to complete the appeal process, they were immediately alarmed. The foreign judges clearly opposed development of a common jurisprudence that might eventually guide both mixed and council court first-instance judgments. When they tried to extract a guarantee that Egyptian litigants could opt for either mixed or local law at the final level of appeals, therefore, Fakhri suspended discussion of the supreme court issue altogether.

Once ruptures occurred over issues that bore the mark of Dual Control sponsorship, all other Egyptian schemes fell on deaf ears. In one case, Fakhri offered to drop the purely honorific appointment of an Egyptian president over each mixed bench in favor of an election opening a position of real responsibility to judges of any nationality. Fear that rivalry might divide the European vote and permit election of an Egyptian judge, however, prompted rejection. The Egyptian minister's resentment of subcommittee prejudice appeared in his reaction to this issue. The government's desire to "raise the level of the Egyptian nation," he stated, made open election of court presidents a basic priority. "But," he went on, " . . . if the commission thinks it can establish two classes of justiciables, those who have the right and those who do not have the right to guarantees, and two classes of judges . . . they should so state. But it should not think that the government will abandon . . . defense of the national dignity."

By the time news of Fakhri's difficulties became public, the foreign community at large had fallen in behind the subcommittee's (i.e., the mixed court judges') staunch defense of the status quo.[46] Thus, in its second series of meetings the subcommittee felt free to table several legislative reforms requested by the Egyptian cabinet. Two areas that stood to be affected—bankruptcy proceedings and real estate credit—had been identified as nascent points of conflict as early as 1876.

The Egyptians noted that a growing number of such cases involved all Egyptian litigants. The unwritten principle of "mixed interest," however, was being applied indiscriminately to take them out of local council hands, even if only a single foreign name appeared in the legal dossier. Fakhri requested a clearer definition of legitimate mixed interest in bankruptcies, joint-stock arrangements, and mortgages. This mirrored his previous contention that qualified local personnel and more effective jurisprudential guidelines could only emerge if Egyptians had a serious chance to share responsibility for such relatively new legal concepts with the mixed courts. The subcommittee's response turned out to be much more than a simple defense of mixed interest: the judges felt that interjurisdictional tensions would never subside until *all* litigation involving joint capital ventures or property title claims came under their aegis.[47] Mixed court domination of the first category of litigation may have seemed logically justifiable in 1880–81. If future investment trends ever yielded more joint-stock initiatives by local Egyptian entrepreneurs, such local interests would be harmed if resident capitulatory subjects refused to buy their shares simply because so-called native companies did not enjoy certain legal advantages guaranteed by mixed law. When it came to suggestions for a single (mixed) jurisdiction over property disputes, the mixed judges were also quick to point out attractive advantages for noncapitulatory interests. A universal title registration procedure (already operating in the mixed courts) would increase security for property owners. Indeed, without identical legal procedures for title clearance, local Egyptians would never be able to compete with foreigners in future sellers' markets.

Confronted with such attempts to impose totally new interpretations on the 1875 Charter, Riadh suspended the conference and accused the mixed judges of wanting to "annihilate the indigenous tribunals just when the government was aiming at efficient justice for local subjects." Ironically, even Octave Borelli, who later followed his government's decision to abandon Dual Control patronage for Egyptian legal reform, denounced attempts to "make Egypt abdicate its sovereign [*sic*] power [by adding] to the special cases in which the original principles of the Judicial Reform were to be set aside."[48]

CLOSING OPTIONS FOR THE RIADH CABINET

If one considers implications of these abortive capitulatory negotiations, broader problems facing Riadh Pasha's ill-fated 1880–81 cabinet become clearer. In many ways, the legal reform question by this date cannot be separated from much-better-known political events in the same period. Undoubtedly what became the historically famous first clash between Riadh and dissident military officers under Colonel Ahmad ʿUrabi occurred only by coincidence very near the date of the breakdown in the international commission's talks.[49] Collapse of Husayn Fakhri's originally very rational judicial schemes, however, probably helped spread a growing feeling of insecurity to different segments of Egyptian society, both urban and rural. It was this general feeling of insecurity that the ᶜUrabists eventually chose as a main theme in their opposition to the Cairo government.

By 1881, the question of local judicial and legislative reform had begun to involve a number of Egyptian parties whose interests had not been seriously considered when Ismaᶜil initiated the era of "New Justice." Indeed, almost every issue raised in the abortive capitulatory negotiations underlined side effects of the mixed courts not only on administrative but also on private social and economic interests. Many of the latter seemed torn between traditionally structured *qanun* law and the attractive but unfamiliar mixed codes. Most frustrating for Egyptian interests were the legal barriers that the mixed judiciary wanted to erect between capitulatory justice and spheres of traditional local litigation. The mixed judges' eagerness to extend select European notions of civil law and property relations (but only under mixed court aegis) camouflaged a serious dilemma: if all property and capital liability disputes eventually came under a foreign majority jurisdiction, what future remained for local modes of social and economic intercourse that did *not* lend themselves to interpretation under the mixed codes?

In short, some form of modification in the existing legal status of Egyptian commercial and real property interests was clearly expected from Riadh Pasha's government. Whether such alterations involved a strengthening of local council jurisdictions or wholesale adoption of the European mixed codes may not have been considered that important by a minority of successful Egyptian landholders in 1881. For them, the most vital concern was protection from executive mismanagement of provincial finances and administration. On the other hand, many local contributors to the Arabic press recognized that the government needed to be concerned not only with the needs of Egyptians who had already come in contact with the civil and commercial codes of the mixed courts, but also with obsolete methods of justice in traditional rural areas. Many parties, including *Al-Waqa'i*ᶜ's editor Muhammad ᶜAbduh, agreed that neither the foreign personnel nor procedures of the mixed courts would necessarily be involved in seeking the best response to Egypt's many-sided legal dilemma. No article appearing in 1880 suggested that such commentators had lost confidence in the government's promise to correct imbalances between the exclusive Judicial Reform and less sophisticated methods of justice in the Egyptian village. Optimists may even have accepted the high-level maneuvers of the Riadh cabinet as necessary to put the mixed courts in their place before turning to the plight of the average *fallah* in court.

When Riadh and his British and French supporters failed to make any headway against capitulatory intransigence, however, many local parties began to resent the effects of the Ministry of Justice's abortive policy. A small but vocal section of the Arabic press had become intellectually and politically compromised in its reactions to Egypt's poorly prepared experimentation with Tanzimat legal reforms. At a more general level, thousands of local agriculturalists found themselves facing even worse conditions of physical and legal insecurity as the fiscal crisis and legal paralysis of Tawfiq's khedivate continued unabated. As a result, the initial consensus on Husayn Fakhri's methods of legal reform began to disintegrate. This occurred just as new and much more openly contradictory political priorities gripped Egypt in 1881.

6

The Egyptian Nationalist Constitution: Law before a Popular Tribune (1881–82)

By the spring of 1881, Mustafa Riadh could turn in few directions without encountering some form of dissatisfaction with his ministry. Although the effects of a more balanced public debt schedule were visible, *fallahin* who had insufficient land to participate in cash crop agriculture still found tax burdens extremely oppressive. Simple peasant grievances, however, were probably not major concerns for Riadh's cabinet. Tensions in the air by mid-1881 reflected discontent at a significantly higher level. Although the problems of governing Egypt caused discontent among the humble and privileged alike, delayed solutions often hurt discrete special interest groups more perceptibly than the rural masses. Dissatisfaction existed not only among influential landholders and political elites who were Riadh's personal rivals, but also in the bureaucracy, the professional military, and the local intelligentsia. Among the latter were representatives of both traditional Islamic and secularly oriented "liberal reformist" tendencies. In their separate ways, each of these would contribute to the instability that dominated Egypt's affairs until the open crisis that came in the spring of 1882.

It is essential to remember that, between May 1879 and September 1881, the Cairo cabinet tried to solve a number of problems, from debt consolidation through reform of mixed and village-level justice, without relying even on a symbolic "council of notables" to share responsibility for success or failure. After failure of the 1879 Assembly, Riadh governed without communicating with representatives of urban or provincial notables who, in normal times, had been accustomed to pledging loyalty to some political leader in the khedive's entourage. Each failure thus encouraged demands from traditional *majlisiyyin* for a return to council consultation in all reform matters.

Dissatisfaction with mismanagement of Egypt's affairs was also spreading to other sources by the second half of 1881. The frustrations of higher-ranking bureaucrats and representatives of Egypt's nascent urban intelligentsia (teachers in government schools, journalists, etc.) were bound to enter any debate over reformism. Positions taken by such middle elites differed considerably from those of more-established traditional notables, even though both tended to fuse eventually as *majlisiyyin* critics of the 1879–81 cabinet. A study of Egypt's internal politics in this period indicates that the origins of support for formal constitutional government lay mainly among newly articulate bearers of influence in Egyptian society. Fortunately, various representatives of less-established professional and bureaucratic callings began to use the Arabic press to express their views of such issues at this time. We are able, therefore, to document a number of points of disagreement, especially on the subject of legal reformism, between this nascent group and more traditional bearers of political influence. Among the latter were rural landholding and religious notables who also flocked, albeit for different reasons, into the ranks of opposition to Riadh's three-year-old cabinet.

A summary review of groups who played key roles in Egypt's renewed political crisis between 1881 and 1882 must, of course, include one more disgruntled party: the Anglo-French agents of the Dual Control. We have seen that Riadh had been willing to tolerate some Control rearrangement of local reform priorities before renewal of the Mixed Court Charter in 1881. The collapse of joint plans in the 1880–81 capitulatory commission meant that the Control would probably insist on revisions in Riadh's strategy. Dominant French and British interests, however, assumed that any revisions would be evaluated primarily for usefulness in mixed court renewal negotiations, not for their relevance to the local reform debate that was taking form in the local Arabic press.

Meanwhile, even if the Cairo ministry had looked to Istanbul in 1881 for guidance, it would have found a very changed scene. Less than two years after the burst of enthusiasm caused by Mehmet Saᶜid's revival of Tanzimat reformism, Abdulhamid's sultanate seemed much more intent on launching high-level military and economic renewal plans. By this date, issues of legislative consultation and justice were already being handed back to civil servants and political officials, most of whom sought promotion for loyal service, not innovation.[1]

POLITICAL ORIGINS OF THE FIRST "NATIVE" COURT SCHEME

Despite signs of both internal and international political isolation, Riadh still enjoyed some support for his legal reform efforts from British and French agents in Cairo. One reason Anglo-French diplomats continued to sponsor the increasingly unpopular Cairo cabinet may have been because they blamed themselves, as much as Riadh, for the fiasco of the 1880–81 capitulatory reform negotiations. In fact, Paris was embarrassed by Consul de Ring's apparent collaboration with supporters of mixed court aggressiveness. Soon he was replaced by someone who would respect Anglo-French Dual Control policy priorities.[2] Riadh asked de Ring's successor for a guarantee that the French would oppose passage of any of the 1881 commission's drastic reform suggestions during the temporary twelve-month extension of the Mixed Court Charter. Both London and Paris were willing to comply if only to stifle the arrogance other powers had shown during the capitulatory commission sessions. Agreement to freeze the 1875 Charter without changes for another year, however, carried conditions.

Lord Granville's ambassador in Paris had already begun to weigh the cost of complicating Dual Control responsibilities by raising Egypt's judicial question to the same political level as financial priorities. By June, Anglo-French diplomats in Cairo were echoing the same condemnations of mixed justice that Charles Rivers-Wilson had unsuccessfully written into his reports two years earlier. According to the vocal British ambassador in Paris, revived and revised Dual Control interests made it "essential that [Britain and France] should come to an understanding . . . on the direction to be given to the [suspended] International Judicial Commission. . . . It is quite impossible to leave questions of so much social, economic, and political importance to be dealt with indiscriminately by a commission in which all powers . . . are represented without regard to the importance of their interests in Egypt. . . . "[3] Lord Lyons concluded that London's own consul general should suggest the best way to obtain Egypt's basic legislative and judicial goals before the one-year renewal of the Mixed Court Charter expired.

The choice of Edward Malet as an intermediary interpreter of British reform priorities in Egypt between 1881 and 1883 eventually caused considerable problems for Foreign Office strategists. Malet began by claiming a wide sphere of technical expertise in both mixed and local council court affairs. He had no hesitation about warning Lord Granville against listening to jealous "Egyptian hands," even British civil servants in Cairo, on such matters.[4] As he began to propose bases for what actually became semiofficial British Egyptian policy on legal reform for the next decade and a half, however, Malet himself depended on Granville's new appointee to the controller general's post in Cairo, as well as on Riadh's own preferred French legal adviser, Octave Borelli.

Appointment of Sir Auckland Colvin as controller general in Egypt seemed to fit a logical political plan.[5] Colvin's arrival not only corresponded to new directions in British capitulatory policy; it occurred just as two Cairo "old hands" since the mid-1870s—Justice Scott and Major Evelyn Baring—left for colonial service in India. Both men would return to Egypt to play key roles under the later British occupation regime. Between 1881 and the demise of the Control in 1883, however, it was Auckland Colvin, in collaboration with Edward Malet, who had the task of making post-Tanzimat policy in Egypt more effective and acceptable to the Gladstone government in London.

The new controller's responsibilities were still mainly financial in nature. It goes without saying, however, that a man with extensive Anglo-Indian experience was likely to tie local finances, public works, and stabilization of judicial administration together. This would have been considered a bare minimum of interdepartmental bureaucratic rationalization on the subcontinent. In Colvin's case, the apparent success of British methods of legal reform in India had made a strong mark. In fact, his enthusiastic impressions of India's judicial progress since 1860 caused him to overlook obvious differences between the Raj's unhampered political prerogatives and Britain's jealously monitored role in the affairs of the Ottoman Empire. Some of Egypt's local economic and administrative problems did, of course, resemble those that had gripped the subcontinent prior to the Great Mutiny of 1857. For an "India hand," it was easy to conclude that the material welfare, and therefore the overall political stability, of Egypt's population would be enhanced by Indianization measures, not only in public works and finances, but in justice as well.[6]

When Colvin first contacted Foreign Office policymakers, however, he was probably told that Indian tactics did not fit either the Egyptian or the general Eastern Question formula. Instead of simplification and sponsorship for time-tested "native" procedures of law, the residual legacy of Tanzimat demanded continued attempts to shore up standards of justice following familiar European models. Unlike the foundering Tunisian beylicate that had just succumbed to the pressures of a foreign protectorate, Egypt and most other Ottoman provinces still seemed unlikely ground for direct colonial competition. Thus, continued legal reform efforts along original Tanzimat lines could have clear benefits for British policy. By helping to reaffirm the 1856 Treaty of Paris (and simultaneous *Hatt-i Humayoun*), British dedication to Tanzimat legislative and judicial models in Egypt could shame others who might be tempted (as Jules Ferry had been in Tunisia) by overtly expansionist ambitions.

Auckland Colvin was not the last British official to hear Foreign Office career men recall the international political logic of supporting 1839–76 principles of Ottoman reformism. One finds recurrent references to the ideal goal of autonomous legislative and judicial structures in Egypt years after the collapse of the Tanzimat government in Istanbul. A primary aim of London's patronage at the time of the 1839–40 Egyptian Crisis had been to prove the Empire's ability to raise its administrative standards and avoid politically volatile capitulatory intervention.

Indeed, Egypt's own nearly disastrous experience in the spring of 1879 very nearly confirmed Lord Palmerston's earlier predictions: in the absence of a standard body of Ottoman civil and administrative law, tensions within the Concert of Europe system could foster dangerous small-scale interventions in the Near East. Similar crises or near crises during the Tanzimat (Crimea, 1853–56; Mount Lebanon, 1858–64; Tunisia, 1864–69; and Bosnia and Bulgaria, 1876) all had their origins in a breakdown of confidence in local administration and threats of foreign intervention to defend the capitulatory status quo. During these major crises and again during the crisis in Egypt in the spring of 1879, Britain had been forced to sanction exceptional and costly joint international actions to avoid collapse of local order. Lord Granville now made it clear that, in order to avert any further drift toward "Tunisification" of any other Ottoman regions, Istanbul should encourage important provinces to return to local Tanzimat legislative and judicial reform models. It was on this general basis that London collaborated with the ill-fated ministries that succeeded one another in Egypt from summer to summer in 1881–82.

On the higher diplomatic level, Sir Edward Malet assumed that London favored eliminating the suspended international capitulatory commission entirely and defining more direct Egyptian legislative and judicial responsibilities for the Dual Control itself.[7] The new British controller general himself, after conferring with Malet, agreed to discourage any confusion between Egypt's realistic internal needs and experimental foreign legal structures adopted in 1875. Auckland Colvin was particularly wary of visibly strong sentiments in Egypt favoring one-step adoption of the mixed codes for application in a single countrywide jurisdiction. He warned against the chaos that would result from introducing complicated codes that were "too far in advance of the existing local administration and separate from it." He seemed convinced that Riadh realized the futility of such approaches to legal reform and was prepared to establish a totally autonomous system of "indigenous tribunals administering laws in harmony with the degree of development which . . . is within practical reach."[8] Such views underscored experience with post-1857 India Office policies and contrasted with the high-level political risk taking (at least in capitulatory matters) practiced by his predecessor, Evelyn Baring.

Although Colvin attempted an original assessment of Egypt's legal problems, his dependence on Edward Malet for detailed information irritated a number of parties. In contrast to the high-level clique beginning to form around Malet, Colvin, and Riadh, a number of self-appointed advisers began to besiege Lord Granville with arguments *against* separating capitulatory and local judicial affairs. Many critics gathered under the banner of a British auxiliary commission, founded at the time of the Mixed Court Charter renewal negotiations. Several reports submitted to Lord Granville in 1881, however, suggest that this auxiliary commission's membership had shifted from the British community in Egypt to individuals with direct political influence in London. Its views seemed to be in clear sympathy with the one-step comprehensive legal modernization scheme originally expounded by Riadh's fallen political rival, Nubar Pasha.[9]

In fact, as early as mid-1881, there were signs that Nubar was regaining some of the high-level political influence he had lost at Khedive Isma^cil's hand two years before. The former minister's British sympathizers and his main Egyptian rivals were aware that Nubar's chances of making a political comeback would increase as long as Egypt's legal reform dilemma remained unresolved. No one should have been surprised, therefore, when participants in Lord Salisbury's earlier Egyptian policy (including Charles Rivers-Wilson himself) began communicating Nubar's criticism of Riadh's "misguided" judicial methods directly to Lord Granville. On the contrary, it would have been surprising if, when tensions finally led to Riadh's ouster in September 1881 by a "constitutionalist" cabinet under Sharif, the new government did *not* immediately sponsor major plans for legal reformism. Such a move was inevitable, if only to head off a new leadership challenge by a politically ambitious Nubar Pasha.

Wilson's private correspondence with Lord Salisbury provides evidence that Nubar tried to convince London to abandon local court reform in Egypt to stimulate return to gradualist objectives of the Tanzimat era.[10] He preferred a commitment to make the mixed courts the sole basis for legal reform policy under the Dual Control. With Wilson's tacit approval, Nubar outlined the disadvantages of makeshift methods to separate the European-dominated mixed codes from the mainstream of Egyptian social and economic developments in the 1880s. To make his argument stronger, he planted the (not unfounded) idea that Britain's Dual Control partner was already making plans to profit politically from the quandary Riadh faced.

Nubar felt that both controllers, but especially de Blignières, had deliberately exaggerated the menace of extending the mixed codes to areas of purely Egyptian litigation insufficiently covered by *qanun* law. With an uncanny power of prediction, he urged Lord Granville to make the future of the mixed courts the keystone of British Egyptian policy before the French did the same for their own special political advantage. To make his point seem urgent, he concluded that

> the principal thing is for you [the British] to know what you want. The French know what they want, and that is to destroy the independence of the courts, and to render them dependent on the administration, since the administration is largely in their hands. . . . Do you wish . . . to have justice organized according to the principles which I estab-

> lished, namely, under independent tribunals deciding the rights of each individual according to laws made and to be made? In that case, keep the existing regime and make it better. For that, . . . tell Riaz [*sic*] to revise the plan he has already presented and he will do it. It is because of you that he is where he is, and he will gladly do what you ask.[11]

EGYPTIAN PRESS VIEWS OF JUSTICE IN 1881

When Sharif Pasha was appointed Tawfiq's second prime minister in September 1881, it was already clear that court reform would be near the center of any new political crisis that might occur. It is necessary to belabor this point, if only for the sake of historical accuracy. First, Egypt obviously did suffer a major political breakdown once Sharif's cabinet gave way (in January 1882) to openly antiforeign elements supporting Colonel Ahmad ᶜUrabi. A great deal of effort has been expended by historians to understand how and why Khedive Tawfiq's regime was irreversibly shaken from the top down to the lowest level of *markaz* administration until foreign troops intervened in Egypt in June 1882. Overconcern with cabinet-level politics in this period tends to separate the rapid ascendance of ᶜUrabi's Hizb al-Watan and the restored Legislative Assembly from many grass-roots issues. Because local and capitulatory legal reform was definitely one of these issues, its inclusion in the still fragmentary political record of 1881–82 is not only useful, but necessary.

Nationalist and xenophobic pressures affected each of the cabinets that succeeded one another in Cairo in the last months of 1881 and the first half of 1882. One cannot fully understand how Egypt's national court decree of November 1881 fit into this larger political picture, however, without asking how it tried to respond to the disillusionment of three groups: Husayn Fakhri's Ministry of Justice, the ᶜUrabi-led Hizb al-Watan, and behind-the-scenes supporters of Nubar's approach to capitulatory reform. Indeed, the way in which Sharif's new cabinet actively pushed this particular issue suggests that it was as important as more highly publicized causes for the return of extreme constitutionalist demands and the final collapse, in 1882, of political and administrative order in Egypt.

Egyptian press accounts in 1881–82 do not establish a direct connection between internal political malaise and the threat of foreign exploitation by means of the still unreformed capitulatory regime.

The Cairo cabinet naturally faced many pressures to avoid repetition of the foreign interference that had reversed Egypt's chances of legislative autonomy at the time of the 1879 Assembly. The climate of opinion concerning Ministry of Justice responsibilities, however, had changed perceptibly in two years. The main thrust of discontent appearing in the local press from mid-1881 on substantiates this suggestion. Disgruntled individuals at various levels of Egyptian society were beginning seriously to question the costs of leaving local legal relations under *qanun* law and the limited interest groups that benefited from it. Indeed, even if a much larger confrontation had not occurred between ʿUrabi's Hizb al-Watan and defenders of the capitulatory status quo after 1881, any Egyptian regime would have had to confront this problem.

Although there was widespread criticism of Egypt's traditional legal apparatus at this time, there was no clear consensus on what should be done to ease frustrations, particularly at the rural village level. Like the inchoate entity of the Hizb al-Watan itself, early participants in the polemics of legal reformism and constitutionalism in Egypt wore coats of many colors. Opinions took on diverse shades according to local interest groups that stood to gain or lose from adoption of different proposed reforms. Rural peasants themselves, of course, had no direct channels to make their views on such issues heard. Other potentially articulate spokesmen, however, for Azhar-trained *ʿulama'*, rural landholding or administrative elites, or the rebellious *fallahin* officer corps itself, gained frequent access to the Egyptian press. Because of this, and because of their recognizable (if unequal) social and political status in more popular circles, their views provided useful grist for both supporters of the Hizb al-Watan and their more conservative rivals.

The typical contributor of newspaper reports on Egypt's legal system in 1881 seems to have been a regular reader or subscriber living near a provincial administrative center. Relative isolation and a paucity of official information meant that he would have known very little about earlier hopes to increase interaction between rural judicial councils and the foreign-sponsored Judicial Reform. In fact, many provincial commentators favored options that had little or nothing to do with the possibility of a sweeping legal reform plan originating in Cairo. If one considers what Foreign Office and Dual Control advisers were pressing for at this date, however, this was precisely the indicated direction for any political clique that had pretensions of succeeding Riadh Pasha.

In most cases, parties alarmed by declining conditions of village justice expressed concern for the least-advantaged rural litigants. This was the case in several articles written by anonymous *wakil*s, or advocates who spoke in behalf of litigants in local council sessions. Paid proxies had existed in both *mahkama* and *qanun* jurisdictions long before professionalism became an issue in the Egyptian court system. In fact, the functions of a typical *wakil* probably involved less formal educational training in the actual practice of the *shari*ᶜ*a* or *qanun* law than those of the better-known Islamic notary, or *shahid*.[12] It would be wrong, therefore, to speak of such individuals as representing particular types of client interests, or as bearers of a professional bias. Nevertheless, proxy exposure to the actual grass-roots effects of confusion in rural and urban litigation probably gave them, more than any other identifiable group, a real cause to criticize popular Tanzimat-inspired slogans like "justice" and "civil rights."

A case in point shows how this particular group's disillusionment with hollow Tanzimat rhetoric could be turned to political advantage by Egypt's nascent constitutionalist opposition party. "No one with any degree of insight," wrote an anonymous *wakil* in the delta town of Tanta,

> will deny that the aim of the civil laws [*qawanin nizamiyya*] is to protect the rights of the individual subject. To the extent this is accomplished, there is no need to intervene in [separate cases of litigation]. But I have before me a case that reminds us of the lack of respect for law by minor functionaries. The dispute involves lands belonging to several peasant cultivators. The case had to be transferred to the [provincial-level] council at Tanta, but when I requested the current land titles from its president, he declared they were being held in suspension. . . . Each time we call his attention to the laws, he refuses to cooperate even in the simplest matters. Recently I directed a complaint to the Ministry of Justice, who in turn sent an order to the president of the council to carry out the government's circulars dealing with these matters. Despite this [the negligence continues]. . . . The pressures on individual litigants go on mounting. . . . I don't understand how it is possible for one man to refuse to carry out the orders of a just government.[13]

There was no suggestion here that basic justice required total replacement of rural judicial councils or even the *qanun* laws they were meant to apply. This was in apparent contrast to cabinet-level officials who were willing to adjust their own conceptions of necessary legal reform to fit externally induced political considerations. Most editorialists felt justice could be improved merely by replacing incompetent or venal magistrates with more qualified and disinterested individuals from among the provincial notability.[14] *Al-Watan* minced no words when editor ᶜAbdul Sayyid wrote:

> Looking at the letter of *qanun* laws we find them based on truth and integrity . . . resembling in this respect the laws of the more advanced countries. . . . The difference [between the Egyptian judicial and legal apparatus and that of Europe] is that their minor functionaries are dedicated to the carrying out of their responsibilities. . . . [True reform involves] better appointments to administrative posts. If there are transgressions, let the courts try the administrative officials themselves to provide an example to others. . . . [Why change the laws?] How many police agents flaunt the law, and how many secretaries do not even consider it? We feel that laws based on supposed inequity . . . but in force are better than laws based on justice that are cast off and forgotten.[15]

Small wonder, then, that the political factions that finally unseated Riadh's two-year-old cabinet took immediate steps to create a new and popular image of justice ministry priorities.

SHARIF PASHA'S ABORTIVE 1881 NATIONAL COURT DECREE

By the end of the summer of 1881, it was clear that the Cairo cabinet had failed to satisfy local and international expectations that had developed since Khedive Ismaᶜil's deposition in 1879. Some of these expectations came from veteran Egyptian elites who, like Riadh himself, had been close to gaining positions of major influence in khedivial politics when the 1879 Assembly collapsed. Although no one in this select coterie of potential ministers or cabinet heads held anything approaching systematic nationalist or constitutional views, it may have been useful for some to rebuild their political image (for foreign as well as local observers) by lamenting the demise of the first Majlis. Each cabinet failure, whether in providing better standards of justice for local peasants or in answering the grievances of ill-paid bureaucrats and army personnel, brought opposition pledges of dedication to issues the Assembly had supposedly attempted to raise. Any number of Riadh's elite political rivals, therefore, could have been willing converts in 1881 to the popular call to change Ministry of Justice priorities.

Riadh's dismissal in September 1881 came as a by-product of what several parties, including the Dual Control, considered to be unreasonable delays on a number of issues affecting different political interest groups. The most general of these was a local expectation that a restored Assembly, rather than the Dual Control, should guide essential financial and legislative affairs. Further down the list, and probably even below controversy over judicial injustices at the village level, was the issue of canceled promotions and back pay for pensioned-off middle-ranking army officers. Even if the officers' complaints were joined to those of disgruntled civil employees, the likely base for recruitment to their specific political cause remained limited in both number and potential influence. When Tawfiq had to replace Riadh with someone who could respond to the major problems of 1881, therefore, he was bound to seek a person qualified to deal with grievances expressed by both the 1879 Assembly and the Dual Control itself. Thus, the khedive called upon Muhammad Sharif, prominent member of the *diwan*'s entourage since the 1850s and critic of both Riadh and Nubar Pasha, to form a cabinet. The appointment carried a clear injunction to make civil justice for local subjects a priority in all executive offices under his control.[16]

One need not look far to find the source of Foreign Office confidence in Sharif Pasha. Sir Edward Malet must have spent a good portion of his summer leave building a case for solutions to Egypt's legislative and judicial dilemmas that would involve little political cost to London or the Dual Control. By the time he returned in September, Malet carried authorization to invite Sharif to decree an end to traditional local council jurisdictions in Egypt. In their place, the fully professional civil courts planned but never realized during the Tanzimat era would finally have a chance to be tested in Egypt. That Sharif soon accepted the main lines of Malet's invitation is a matter of documented fact. When his cabinet submitted its recommendations for review by a restored and presumably sympathetic consultative legislative authority, however, it soon became apparent that constitutionalist support for Sharif's ideas was only partly articulated.

London received its first impressions of the changed political situation in Egypt after Consul Malet met Muhammad Bey Qadri, the sixty-year-old man who now filled Husayn Fakhri's justice portfolio. The new minister's private and public life prior to 1881 revealed parallels and some important contrasts with that of his predecessor. Although both Fakhri and Qadri were fluent in French, the latter had obtained his skills as a student in the Khedivial School of Languages and Administration. There he pursued what his biographer called "purely secular studies," including some notions of European law.[17] His first employment and the first published examples of his scholarly work (under Sa^{c}id Pasha and Isma^{c}il Pasha) were connected with the language school, where he served as a translator. Throughout his student years and after, however, Qadri's preferred field was Islamic law. Indeed, although never a formal student, he associated personally with Azhar *shaykhs*, even though he worked in an entirely separate field. In contrast to the French-trained Fakhri, therefore, Qadri was well known among traditionally educated circles before he became minister in 1881. Possibly because he had pioneered translation of European legal texts for the Egyptian school system, he was named, like Fakhri, to fill a judicial post in the mixed courts after 1876. Despite this, Qadri never abandoned his orientation toward *shari^{c}a* studies and the possibility of shoring up Egypt's legal system by systematic codification of Islamic law. These views were to stand him in good stead later, when the time came to convince the 1882 *Majlis al Nuwwab* that some cabinet members had minds of their own and were not too narrowly tied to Dual Control sponsorship.

In the first month of Sharif's new government, however, the British consul used various routes to find similarities between Qadri and his predecessor. Dual Control priorities depended on Sharif's commitment to legislative and judicial reform continuity after Riadh's downfall. Qadri himself did nothing at first to disappoint this expectation. He reminded Malet, for example, that he had been a member of Fakhri's abortive 1880 committee on capitulatory and local council reforms. Whatever Qadri's political motives may have been at this point, he argued that one of Fakhri's mistakes at that time had been to ignore reform options offered by experienced Egyptian colleagues. He gained Malet's sympathy by claiming that he himself would have avoided the fiasco of the 1880–81 capitulatory reform commission by putting local justice in order first. Once this was done, the goal of depoliticizing the mixed court system would come more easily. Step one (which sounded like a combined cue from Sharif and Malet himself) would be to "assimilate the charter of new Native Courts [the councils] . . . to that of the Mixed Courts. . . . " Necessary "modifications in the mixed codes" adopted for such courts would be added as passed, depending on their usefulness in purely Egyptian litigation.[18]

From Malet's point of view, this approach offered the best chance of bringing reforms to the mixed courts themselves. He urged the cabinet to limit its initial policy, however, to requesting a second temporary one-year extension of the Mixed Court Charter, still without revision, at the end of 1881. His supposition was that the Dual Control would need another year to prepare the political ground before submitting a new reform plan to the representatives of the fourteen capitulatory powers. At this stage, therefore, the British consul chose to stress humanitarian aspects of Qadri's proposals. This may have been to avoid arousing capitulatory suspicion of British bargains with the new cabinet. He told Lord Granville, for example: "If the [formal capitulatory] commission is reassembled, I fear the native scheme will again have to make way. . . . The establishment of justice for natives appears to be more pressing than the reform of the mixed courts. . . . [The latter are] working satisfactorily, and it will not prevent the regular administration of justice if [their reform is] held up."[19]

As far as dealings with Sharif were concerned, this optimism, if somewhat hypocritical, was apparently not far off the mark. When it came to measuring Qadri's willingness to cooperate, however, the British consul should have considered the broader local political environment within which Cairo's key ministers had to work. If Qadri was at all sympathetic to the constitutionalist promises Sharif had made when Riadh resigned, he would have been busy (as external evidence suggests he was) building confidence that he would stay within legitimate boundaries of legislative authority as defined by a new Assembly. Malet's mistake was to underestimate serious local differences of opinion over the importance of such consultative legislative processes for the success of any legal reform scheme. Thus, a full month before any alternative suggestions could have been made by an elected Assembly, he assumed Qadri would stand aside while Sharif instituted a comprehensive system of local courts based point for point on the model of the 1875 Judicial Reform.

EGYPTIAN POLITICAL REACTIONS TO SHARIF'S *AHLIYYA* COURT DECREE

As promulgated on 17 November 1881, Egypt's *ahliyya* court decree had all the superficial trappings of a European judiciary.[20] The new local (literally, people's) system included a four-level hierarchy of courts throughout Upper and Lower Egypt. Jurisdictions ranged from single-judge tribunals at the district level to a supreme court in Cairo. There was also to be an attorney general's staff to prosecute penal cases and to represent the government in civil cases. This conscious copying from the mixed courts made it clear that Ministry of Interior officials (*mudirs* and *ma'murs*) would no longer have quasi-judicial responsibilities preparing penal and civil litigation. The entire scheme, including sixteen provincial tribunals and two appeals jurisdictions in Upper and Lower Egypt, called for more than one hundred new professional judicial posts. An equivalent number of less formal judges' functions under the abandoned council system would automatically end.

Curiously enough, the man who had most actively encouraged changes in Ministry of Justice policy expressed the first misgivings when the *ahliyya* decree appeared. Somewhat naively, Consul Malet informed London that "the scheme [was] evidently the work of a French draftsman, and seems . . . unnecessarily cumbersome, intricate and vague. Some organization of a simpler kind would have been more desirable."[21] Malet saw a number of difficulties unless Sharif agreed to consider two essential supplements. First, Egypt needed formal procedures for appointing professional judges or an announcement that it would temporarily depend on foreign jurists in key spots. Second, one could expect confusion until a standardized code of *ahliyya* law was devised and promulgated. Unless a new code specifically superseded all residual bits and pieces of *qanun* legislation, Sharif's courts might have to "recognize all laws . . . that do not contradict their own codes and [possibly even] the old laws of Mehmet Ali, or . . . Turkish laws which are supposed by some to be in force in Egypt."[22]

The only (surviving) Arabic newssheet to lend unequivocal support to the *ahliyya* court decree was *Al-Watan*. Editor ᶜAbdul Sayyid countered *The Times*' disparaging view that "Egypt should first guarantee the practical application of the laws . . . before worrying about political rights under a constitution" by insisting that the courts would protect private rights that were inseparable from the political principles of constitutionalism.[23] Although *Al-Watan* claimed that "laws appropriate to the . . . present state of Egyptian society" were ready, it overlooked the obvious fact that Sharif had merely decreed an organizational restructuring of the courts. No guidelines for revised codes had yet been discussed. This single contradiction opened the breach that led to Sharif's failure and helped bring the final political crisis of pre-occupation Egypt a few months later.

The brewing controversy was epitomized in a series of articles in *Al-ᶜAsr al-Jadid*, an Alexandrian daily published by Salim Bey an-Naqqash. Author of a later major testament in support of Egypt's abortive 1882 Legislative Assembly, Salim Bey was already known as a member of the local literary and social reformist coterie that had hosted Jamal ad-Din al-Afghani during the latter's 1871–78 sojourn in Egypt.[24] *Al-ᶜAsr al-Jadid* naturally welcomed editorials from very much the same politically concerned Syrian and Egyptian literary circles. Most contributions involved liberal political themes, with stress on constitutionalism as a panacea for the Ottoman Empire as a whole. Some tried to tie basic judicial questions to the same idealized matrix. One such article bore the name of the Syrian expatriate Adib Ishaq, mentioned in chapter 5. On the eve of Sharif's *ahliyya* court decree, Ishaq propounded an abstract reform philosophy that saw in effective legal institutions the source of social and political as well as administrative progress. "It is impossible to secure a full system of rights," he wrote,

> without a concomitant sense of duty [*wajibat*]. The contrary is equally true. . . . In all cases, the relative degree of [individual and political] duties varies in direct proportion to the degree of rights enjoyed. . . . The right of freedom assumes the responsibility of guaranteeing justice. The right of free choice assumes honesty. . . . This suggests that both civil rights [*huquq madaniyya*] and political rights proceed from sacrificing some part of the interests of the individual. . . . [Each individual] must respect the integrity of the collective law . . . and stay within its limits. We are now at the stage where we can set down laws and procure the benefits that accrue from them, such as the defense of civil rights. This will help the government carry out a program of public welfare.[25]

Despite variations in philosophical orientation, Ishaq's peers agreed that as many social groups as possible should be involved in formulating any changes in Egypt's legal and judicial institutions.[26] Some contributors to the Arabic press in the last month of 1881, including Shaykh Muhammad ᶜAbduh, actually urged maintenance of Egypt's existing traditions of *qanun* law, subject to responsible revision by the new Legislative Assembly. His "Legislative Authority and the Law" appeared to be an attempt to close the growing breach between Sharif's Dual Control–conscious cabinet and devoted supporters of the Majlis. ᶜAbduh accepted Ishaq's contention that secular legislation reflected a social contract between a governing authority and individuals who depend on government to oblige society to conform to rules of law and order. *Al-Waqa'iᶜ*'s editor added that "good" *qanun* law should be based on the sum total of individual needs and responsibilities of the members of the society to be governed. The usefulness of any legal system, he concluded,

> depends on agreement as to what is essential to the general welfare and . . . the enlistment of individual concern [literally, *ijtihad*] by means of consecrated guidelines that are . . . never neglected. . . . It is in this fashion that the soundness of the laws is established, and it is impossible to carry them out in practice if this goal is obstructed in any way. To accomplish the ideal, all classes of society should select representatives [*nuwwab*] to carry out this responsibility for them. [Once promulgated by their representatives] . . . the law becomes familiar, both intellectually and in practice. . . . Thus, if only a few members of society are ignorant of the law that governs them, it will do no harm, since it emanates from them as a whole, and therefore will be easily understood. . . . As representatives serve as the tongue of those they represent . . . how could they leave the law as mere ink on paper, without concern for the vital intellectual and practical value that is its essence?[27]

Thus, there is ample evidence that press editorials in 1881 opposed any attempts by Sharif to alter Egypt's basic legal system before obtaining a broad consensus. In practical terms, this meant Assembly review of any modifications needed to rationalize and complete Egypt's uncodified *qanun* law. When warnings to this effect were clear at the end of 1881, Qadri tried to respond in part to the cabinet's critics by emphasizing the necessary relevance of Islamic law to the codification process.[28] Obvious discontent over stop-and-start handling of vital issues like the *ahliyya* reform, however, probably helped push many otherwise moderate critics into the wider nationalist opposition that confronted the prime minister and his Dual Control sympathizers head-on at the turn of the year.

Only weeks before a newly elected Assembly reconvened (in January 1882), Sharif's government announced a compromise. According to the *Phare*, the "wise delay involved in selecting judicial functionaries" prompted Qadri temporarily to staff four new courts only, in Cairo, Alexandria, Tanta, and Mansurah. To deal with the problem of transitional justice in the provinces, the legal department of the Ministry of Finance (Borelli's office) had been advised to send delegates to advise the *mudirs* on judicial procedures. Before compromises ended, the cabinet and "several members of the chamber of delegates" reputedly indicated a willingness to accept a few foreign judges to fill critical *ahliyya* bench positions.[29] Although each of these measures would be denounced once the Assembly convened, Sharif felt he was prepared to court Dual Control and local critics' approval simultaneously: on 1 January 1882, he announced indefinite suspension of the troublesome international capitulatory commission of 1880–81 and renewal of the Mixed Court Charter for *one more year only*.[30]

It seems clear that responsibility for pushing Sharif to rush the *ahliyya* court decree through rested with the Dual Control. Auckland Colvin's and Malet's main goal in calling for native courts had been to discourage further attempts (by supporters of Nubar's views) to tie Egypt's entire secular judicial system to the mixed courts. This goal seemed partly guaranteed by temporary extension of the 1875 Charter while the new court system began operating. What Sharif's cabinet had not counted on was vocal resistance to blanket acceptance of the mixed courts as the model for a new hierarchy of jurisdictions. When the issue of legislative approval for the *ahliyya* courts came before the reinstated Assembly in 1882, this resistance produced heated debate. Defenders of the status quo of less formal judicial councils or stronger emphasis on shariatic models for Egyptian justice openly challenged superficial conformity to Dual Control legal reform preferences. The resulting international political crisis toppled Sharif's government and transferred responsibility for implementing legal reform to the first openly nationalist government in Egypt's pre-occupation history.

THE ANGLO-FRENCH DUAL NOTE AND COLLAPSE OF CONSTITUTIONAL JUDICIAL REFORM EFFORTS

The famous Dual Note of 12 January 1882 tried to shore up political clout behind the Dual Control by specifically warning the Legislative Assembly that its consultative powers did not include the right to tamper with Egypt's annual budget. Anglo-French threats "to guard . . . against all . . . complications, internal or external," that might stem from financial mismanagement under the guise of constitutionalism put Sharif in an even worse position than Riadh Pasha had faced only months before.[31] With the Assembly in session, the cabinet had to answer many critics at once, all clamoring to defend Egypt against more threats of foreign intervention. Rather than meet the challenge head-on, Sharif ceded cabinet leadership to more extremist parties who rejected the 12 January Dual Note as a violation of constitutionalist principles and Egyptian autonomy. When Mahmud Pasha Sami accepted the responsibility of forming a new government, he made the fateful decision of appointing the most outspoken opposition leader, Colonel Ahmad ʿUrabi, as undersecretary for war. This nearly guaranteed that a nationalist-oriented Assembly would demand even fuller autonomy from Ottoman and Anglo-French control alike. While the attention of British and French diplomats was diverted to preparations for a new crisis over finances, however, an equally delicate issue became clear: many parties in the Assembly were prepared to force both the mixed and local legal reform question, not just finances, to the forefront of the impending confrontation between Egyptian nationalists and the Dual Control.

Old hands who had witnessed the vicissitudes of Dual Control politics since 1878 were quick to warn Gladstone that any extension in Cairo's legislative autonomy would create the same capitulatory dilemma faced by the Conservative government three years before.[32] Egypt's 1879 Assembly had seemed set on precipitating a clash between unofficial opponents of the highly politicized mixed courts (mainly British and French) and supporters of the capitulatory status quo. At that time, London had, willy-nilly, backed the 1875 Mixed Court Charter: no adequate local courts existed to counterbalance the mixed judges' steadfast opposition to any changes that might affect the monopolistic scope of their imported codes. In contrast, by 1882, the Dual Control itself had welcomed Sharif's *ahliyya* decree as a harbinger of comprehensive civil and penal legislation that would apply throughout Egypt. Any hope that Gladstone might have had to exploit this essential difference between 1879 and 1882 disappeared, however, when Mahmud Sami's cabinet delegated authority to implement Sharif's judicial plan directly to the Legislative Assembly.

By mid-February 1882, the Assembly passed a draft constitution prepared by the Hizb al-Watan. This document stressed shared authority between the khedive's appointed executive agents and elected representatives in the legislature.[33] The only sections of the constitution that referred specifically to judicial functions were articles 39 and 40, which gave any subject the right to petition the Assembly if he failed to obtain proper justice from "the existing civil courts or administrations." Meanwhile, the representatives suspended further implementation of the *ahliyya* court scheme until they could make certain that its codes and procedures properly fit Egypt's needs.[34] Even though the Assembly restricted its own pronouncements to matters of *ahliyya* justice, the Sami government did nothing to dispel rumors that its nationalist legislation might be extended to foreigners as well, especially if the Mixed Court Charter was not renewed at the end of 1882.[35]

Leaving preparation for the coming struggle over budgetary autonomy to a very worried Dual Control, foreign newspapers tried to convince the Sami government it was moving too fast toward the objective of unified civil legislation for all inhabitants of the Nile Valley. The *Phare d'Alexandrie* delivered the most direct blow by criticizing Egypt's lack of legislative experience and professional jurists to carry out Sharif's plan:

> It is not enough to institute courts, unless there are . . . capable judges, sure of themselves and of the law they are to apply. . . . It would . . . be better at this juncture to leave things as they are, since justice is not an institution with which one can experiment in an offhand manner. . . . Is it in Egypt's interest to have two justices and two races, one of which invokes Islamic law and the other European law that is different [from the former] only because no one has yet tried to conciliate them? . . . Egypt does not yet have a written law . . . and yet it must come to that if it wishes to undertake serious and lasting reforms. [The realistic way of resolving the problem is still to attach Egyptian chambers to the mixed courts and expand the competence of the latter.] Then theory and practice could move ahead simultaneously, and initiation to the

> cases and healthy practices of the European magistracy . . . will come about promptly and effectively.[36]

Although Consul Edward Malet knew that the *Phare* was exaggerating the threat of wholesale application of *shari^ca* law in the courts, he realized the Assembly was robbing the Control of influence over capitulatory and local legal reform. By March, prospects for an early reaction against the Mixed Court Charter were lessened by a decision to relegate all court questions to a judicial subcommittee of the Assembly. The British were very worried, however, that the belligerent attitudes of the Hizb al-Watan would carry over to the judicial sphere in general. If nationalist currents prevailed and the *ahliyya* reform turned into a bid to unseat the mixed magistracy with no transitional regime whatsoever, Malet knew that the Dual Control would once again have to revert to unquestioned support for the multinational Judicial Reform.

Events moved so rapidly into the summer of 1882 that harried foreign consular agents, but fortunately not the local press, lost sight of the fate of the *ahliyya* court plan in the hands of the constitutional nationalists. Since the Assembly intended to review Sharif's November 1881 decree only after debating recommendations for a comprehensive law code, a caretaker ministerial committee was named to apply whatever interim measures were necessary to maintain judicial order in the provinces. This body consisted of Octave Borelli, Husayn Wasif, and Butrus Ghali. The last two were French-trained Copts who had seen previous service in the mixed prosecutor's office. During the two months that remained before complete chaos descended, the ad hoc ministerial advisers vacillated between innovation and protection of local tradition in what was left of Egypt's provincial judiciary.

Until the Assembly made up its mind about Egypt's national codes, Borelli and his Egyptian aides could make no definite plans for appointments to the *ahliyya* courts. Their inclination was to maintain the pre-1882 local council system at least temporarily. Alarmingly sparse appropriations for Ministry of Justice operations in 1882 ruled out more extensive bench appointments. Where pressures for better justice were immediately apparent, there were some attempted innovations based on the November 1881 *ahliyya* decree. To Borelli's surprise, however, cabinet-level suggestions to regularize penal procedures and reduce previously unchecked executive powers of prosecution in the provincial council system were not very popular with the newly convened Assembly.

When it became apparent that political instability was causing a breakdown of order in the Egyptian countryside, Borelli's committee tried to detach a number of police officers serving under the *mudirs* for service as salaried prosecutors under the Ministry of Justice. Recognition of such a specialized function may have been seen as a first step toward setting up a separate prosecutor's office with minimal standards of formal legal training. The Assembly, however, was apparently not prepared to risk untested Ministry of Justice responsibility for penal infractions in villages where many delegates owned extensive croplands. Instead of clearly separated police and judicial prosecution functions, it approved experimental appointments of Ministry of Justice "delegates having sufficient knowledge to oversee criminal prosecution by the *mudirs*." The Assembly's most revealing identification with traditional executive prerogatives was its rejection of the judicial delegates' right to argue for or against the *mudirs*' prosecution dossier once court sessions actually began.[37]

A few reports survive suggesting continued exchanges between the Borelli committee and the Cairo Assembly until the latter recessed indefinitely for the summer. The only concrete actions taken by the Sami ministry before it resigned were high-level appointments to courts that still lacked a clearly defined organization and codes.[38] Further steps were apparently blocked pending Assembly approval of a fifty percent increase in the ministerial budget to pay for a fully professional provincial court system.

Many contradictions in the legal reform strategy of the Mahmud Sami government resemble problems faced by Riadh from 1879 to 1881 and by Sharif's brief 1881 cabinet. All paid some lip service to the need for reorganization of grass-roots provincial justice. Ultimately, each Egyptian government since 1879 (actually, since 1873) had to abandon such pledges when issues involving mixed court judicial or legislative grievances assumed overriding political importance. Representatives of the Dual Control recognized this dilemma after the abortive international capitulatory commission of 1880–81. Once Dual Control support against capitulatory interference seemed guaranteed, each succeeding Egyptian ministry agreed to place local justice first. Finally, and very clearly under pressure from the British and French, Sharif decreed creation of an entirely new system of local courts obviously primed to receive European codes of law. By the end of 1881, however, obstructing factors that paralyzed reform efforts came from local not foreign sources.

Egyptian nationalist and constitutionalist rhetoric in 1882 aimed not only at constructing workable *ahliyya* courts to protect the rights of all Egyptian subjects. At its peak, the pro-Majlis press extolled "civil law" as "the purest expression of individual and social values" and implied that "true justice" would not be done until all barriers to equality before the law were eradicated.[39] Such rhetoric could be leveled against either remaining Egyptian sectarian immunities from standard Ministry of Justice jurisdictions or the separate status of foreign interests under the Judicial Reform of 1875. Thus, one cannot easily conclude that the 1882 Legislative Assembly would have proclaimed support for any particular type of legal code when it returned from its recess. We know from the record of confrontation between the Majlis and foreign protectors of Egypt's fiscal status quo, however, that the major capitulatory powers were not willing to wait to see what "true justice" would finally be done under the guise of Egyptian legislative autonomy. Publicly expressed reasons for foreign intervention against the ʿUrabist-led Assembly reflected a desire to protect financial and budgetary functions covered by the Dual Control arrangement, not alarm over Egyptian rhetoric concerning private litigation in the civil courts.

For Great Britain, in particular, fear of a serious breakdown of order in Egypt had both an international capitulatory and a national strategic dimension. A crisis leading to the sudden collapse of both the Dual Control and the mixed courts could leave London without effective means to assure other capitulatory powers of the security of legitimate foreign interests in Egypt. Loss of the mixed courts would also have had an immediate impact on the legal interests of the Suez Canal, the vital waterway that linked Britain to its imperial possessions east of Suez. Thus, initial Anglo-French threats of force against Majlis extremists were linked to much larger considerations that had little direct connection with local debates over the transitional meaning of justice in Egyptian society and politics.

When the crisis of June and July finally came, foreign observers and Egyptian political leaders alike all but forgot the war of rhetoric that had accompanied presentation of the *ahliyya* court plan a few months before. By the time Assembly extremists demanded that the largely powerless khedive resist further foreign interference in Egypt's affairs, effective civil and penal administration had already come to a standstill in many provincial centers. Early in June, the *Phare d'Alexandrie* reported from Mansurah that administrative and judicial affairs had stopped completely and "everyone, including consular agents, police, doctors, and [both local and mixed] court personnel," was packing, leaving full responsibilities to a very bewildered *mudir*.[40] Isma^cil Pasha Raghib, Mahmud Sami's replacement as cabinet head at the end of May, provided only the shadow of a promise to "prepare new laws and submit them to the vote of the Chamber of Notables [*sic*] . . . to determine the rights and obligations of . . . all classes of the governed . . . and to give to these reforms a national character in conformity with the needs of the country."[41]

As soon as actual violence broke out, attacks against foreign residents in Alexandria forced the Raghib government to abandon all talk of restoring normal civil government and penal jurisdictions. After 11 June, responsibility for order became a military question. Because the Egyptian army was in the hands of Colonel Ahmad ᶜUrabi's extremists, the foreign powers, and Great Britain in particular, saw no solution in sight short of direct military intervention.

Part III

Political Adjustment and Professional Opinion (1882–90)

7

Legal Bases of the New Order: International and Local Perceptions (1882–83)

Unilateral British operations against Ahmad ʿUrabi's insurgent forces were carried out in several military encounters between ll July and 13 September 1882. Once minimum security was restored, General Garnet Wolseley confirmed the khedive's sole authority to rule—an authority backed by occupation troops under British command. He also made it clear that the 1882 Majlis was to be suspended indefinitely. These actions converted the khedivate into a de facto protectorate under a British army of occupation. Under such circumstances, neither the London Foreign Office nor any European ministry in whose name the British had acted demonstrated the slightest interest in the fact that the Egyptian Assembly had tried, however unsuccessfully, to serve as a forum to debate abstract questions of justice, politics, and society.

The sudden transformation of Britain's formal presence in Egypt, however, immediately incited reactions from capitulatory rivals. The most vehement, including France, feared abandonment of Britain's long commitment to "Palmerstonian" principles of equal rights and responsibilities among all parties to Eastern Question political and commercial priorities.[1]

Publicly and in diplomatic circles, Gladstone tried to soothe nerves by stressing the temporary nature of the occupation. At the same time, he reminded critics that not only the British but other governments and trading interests depended on protection of the strategic Suez passage. For some Eastern Question hands, this was either an acceptable rationalization or concealment of aims for imperial aggrandizement, according to one's anglophilia or anglophobia, respectively. Closer observers expected mention of long-pending Dual Control legislative and administrative frustrations, including charges of manipulation of the law in both local and mixed courts, among the problems England would try to resolve before withdrawing. In fact, these considerations would occupy policymakers just as much as stereotypic imperial security issues over the next two decades of Britain's occupation of Egypt.

In the fall of 1882, London began to remold its image of moderation by dispatching its ambassador to the Porte, Lord Dufferin, to Cairo. The ambassador's task was to size up failures in Egyptian reformism and to recommend ways to meet Britain's limited objectives under the revised situation of military occupation. Dufferin sought to convince foreign observers that he would avoid heavy-handed unilateral tactics in trying to obtain what the Dual Control had itself failed to achieve over the previous five years. Unfortunately, one problem in understanding the Dufferin Mission is that such announcements represented only the barest tip of the iceberg. The deeper one delves beneath Lord Dufferin's public recommendations, the clearer it is that a peculiar brand of local and international *Realpolitik*, not rational devotion to either Anglo-Indian experience or Tanzimat symbolism, was at the root of British policy after 1882. This observation applies particularly to the history of capitulatory and local legal reform methods over the next two decades at least.

EMERGENCY JUDICIAL ADMINISTRATION IN 1882

Civilian advisers who followed General Wolseley's forces could easily see that military support for Khedive Tawfiq's restoration was only a first step toward rectifying damages caused by the 1876–82 debacle. In the wake of the ʿUrabist insurrection, basic functions of government, from the taxation and distribution of agricultural commodities to restoration of sequestered private property, lay vulnerable to exploitation by self-appointed agents of a new order. While deployment of British forces to key provincial centers was still under way, the only alternative to chaos was martial law.

Having announced that its forces were acting in the name of the khedive and ultimate Ottoman sovereignty in Egypt, however, London was under pressure to replace military justice with whatever legally constituted local court bodies had been responsible for keeping order before 1882. The situation was especially tense where property contract interests were concerned, since the British depended on Egypt's rural notables to provide informational support and services to their courts-martial. It was not surprising, therefore, that Tawfiq was encouraged to call on Muhammad Sharif, the moving force behind the November 1881 local court decree, to form a cabinet even before ᶜUrabi met final defeat in September 1882. Since Sharif's former minister of justice Muhammad Qadri had lost Dual Control support by refusing to bypass shariatic law in the abortive 1881 reform, his younger French-educated predecessor Husayn Fakhri came back to lead judicial affairs. Following what had become standard protocol since Khedive Ismaᶜil's days, Tawfiq urged Sharif to consider the "progress of . . . justice" as the first step toward developing "liberal institutions . . . compatible with Egypt's present social and political conditions."[2] Immediate surrounding conditions, with wholesale arrests for suspected looting and complicity with the ᶜUrabists still going on, served to render this pronouncement purely symbolic.

Foreigners in Egypt felt at least two extraordinary jurisdictions, one to try Egyptians accused of criminal offenses during the rebellion and another to deal with destruction of foreign property, would have to be approved before returning to the pre-insurrection capitulatory status quo. Controversy over the first demand arose immediately when General Wolseley tried to remove responsibilities in these areas from his courts-martial. Critics balked at his claim that the khedive's administrative agents could handle public security better if they did not have to rely on supervision by British officers without formal police training. Late in September, a compromise was reached by forming special commissions under the presidency of loyal provincial *mudirs*. These bodies were to gather local information vital for prosecution and send dossiers to central courts-martial in Cairo and Alexandria.[3] Although all judgments came from military tribunals, Wolseley's critics thought involvement of Egyptian interior officials in *any* prosecution procedures was unwise.

An equally urgent task was the review of indemnity charges from foreigners who had lost property during the summer's violence. London could be sure of objections from rival consulates if occupation authorities tried to act as intermediaries between foreign plaintiffs (many of whom were themselves British) and the Egyptian government. Miscarriages would be just as great, however, if such politically charged questions were turned back to the mixed courts when and if they reconvened in the fall of 1882. Indeed, by midsummer, both French and British members of the Caisse were busy reminding London of earlier difficulties they had in convincing the mixed courts to separate individual foreign grievances from wider capitulatory interests in Egypt's financial solvency.[4]

Rather than face charges of favoring Dual Control public debt liquidation priorities, the Foreign Office agreed to an ad hoc arrangement for foreign indemnities in September 1882. As originally conceived, a special indemnities commission composed of representatives of the Egyptian government and several mixed judges (representing aggrieved nationalities only) began reviewing indemnity claims.[5] Although the ad hoc body used mixed court property registers and chambers, indemnities cases were not to overlap with regular court proceedings and were to continue independently even if the mixed courts were revised substantially or canceled after January 1883.

POLICY CONSIDERATIONS AT THE TIME OF LORD DUFFERIN'S ARRIVAL

Issues like these may have seemed unimportant beside larger international political questions raised by Britain's unilateral intervention in Egypt. Any mixed court claims recognizing or rejecting essential Egyptian legislation affecting foreign interests, for example, would now have to pass an entirely different sequence of capitulatory review. It was a material fact that Britain could, if it so decided, impose solutions to internal problems that had contributed to the collapse of khedivial government. If Lord Dufferin so advised and the Foreign Office agreed, Britain's backing for Dual Control reform priorities in Egypt could end overnight, leaving only *Realpolitik* to guide relations among the occupant, other capitulatory powers, and the Ottoman sultanate.

The 1882–83 mission of Lord Dufferin proved that such dramatic policy changes were not under serious consideration. It did serve warning, however, that London would not separate internal Egyptian questions, including solutions to the 1876–82 legal reform dilemma, from priorities to be resolved before ending the military occupation. Policymakers who backed Dufferin assumed that, even if temporary extension of the occupation faced opposition at home and abroad, there would be no point in withdrawing without some guarantee that 1882's internal and capitulatory chaos would not recur. It remains something of a mystery, however, why several important issues did not immediately become "trade-off" items with parties who, for various reasons, were anxious to see an early end to the occupation regime. To be sure, certain former Dual Control concerns, including land tax reform and essential public works projects, were quickly transferred to British stewardship until desired objectives could be met. Other vital priorities like legal and judicial reform, however, did not receive equal attention.

One reason for London's reticence to use legal reform openly as a bargaining chip may have been high sensitivity to issues that had held obvious political attraction for both France and Britain before the crisis of 1882. It was not yet known whether the former Dual Control partners could agree on a modus operandi for reaching pre-1882 goals under the unilateral sponsorship of the Foreign Office. Until the situation became clearer, more harm than benefit might have resulted from including sensitive political issues like the mixed courts in the main body of British occupation policy. Moreover, by the time Lord Dufferin arrived in Egypt, some of his closest advisers, including Sir Edward Malet, saw fit to assure him that, as far as legal reform was concerned, a plan already existed to meet minimum needs within a fairly brief period of time. Britain's consul general soon followed up with suggestions on how to reduce the political influence of the mixed bench without openly manipulating the sacrosanct capitulatory charter. London quickly approved these overtures, noting with pleasure Malet's (still unconfirmed) assurance that Cairo would use existing mixed law to resolve future litigation in new *ahliyya* courts.[6]

Although Lord Dufferin was to examine the feasibility of recommendations from various sources, factors like these made his eventual hand in forming Egyptian judicial policy extremely awkward. His later famous report defining Britain's limited responsibilities under the occupation shows that Dufferin mainly followed suggestions from veteran protagonists in the legal reform dilemma. Outside of his scheme for a limited legislative council to replace the defunct Majlis, his main original mark was made in dealing with rising French suspicion of British political goals in Egypt.

Until late fall of 1882, Paris tolerated London's handling of the post-insurrection situation, since mutually accepted Dual Control policy lay behind Gladstone's decision to intervene. By December, however, when London decided unilaterally to take over Dual Control responsibilities for Cairo's finances, the French had to reassess their attitudes overnight. Even before ruptures developed over the Control's future, however, the Quai d'Orsay had already prepared for clashes over capitulatory questions and Egypt's judicial future in particular.[7] It was the British opposition both to the right and left of Gladstone that gave the first warning that previous Anglo-French agreement in these areas would quickly evaporate under the occupation regime.

According to parliamentary critics, Britain's new position in Egypt should allow imposition of Foreign Office conceptions of original Dual Control capitulatory reform priorities. MP George Campbell, for example, argued that the Mixed Court Charter itself should be dissolved as part of an internationally sanctioned bargain ending the temporary occupation. In fact, on questions like this, radicals even joined conservative critics of the Liberal cabinet. Both demanded (for different reasons) more direct British intervention to settle matters the khedive seemed incapable of resolving on his own. As in March 1882, when it had supported the Judicial Reform against the Cairo Assembly, the government faced Campbell's denunciation of mixed courts for "rich Europeans" and the inevitable question whether, "in view of the early expiration of the . . . international tribunals, [London] will . . . refrain from again giving to courts, practically foreign, jurisdiction over the government . . . and power to seize and sell the land of Egyptians, free from the control of any legislature."[8] Despite Charles Dilke's response that England was "only one power out of fourteen" that had signed special capitulatory accords with Egypt, the Foreign Office soon wired to ask whether Cairo had any propositions concerning the future of the mixed courts after February 1883.[9]

Under these circumstances, Lord Granville must have been surprised to learn that Sharif had already proposed a five-year extension of the mixed courts to 1888. Malet, somewhat embarrassed, described the move as an attempt to regain the confidence of foreign residents following the summer's crisis. Tawfiq's prime minister, however, apparently viewed judicial reform questions, like the much more famous

Sudan issue that led to his downfall a year later, as bargaining chips to gain allies in several different camps.

The French were the first to capitalize on Egypt's offer as a means of compromising Dufferin's mission. In fact, a full month before London decided to abandon the Dual Control, they were already prepared to change camps entirely on the major issue of mixed court reform. Their consul himself echoed interpretations of mixed justice that, in the days of Dual Control common objectives, had led to his predecessor's downfall. In Raindre's own words, the mixed courts

> certainly merit more than a renewable lease from year to year . . . . It would be to our advantage to give them . . . permanent status. The day may come when they will be one of the principal obstacles to the establishment in Egypt of one exclusive foreign influence. We should begin to arm such auxiliaries and make certain that when the . . . hour comes for reorganizing the Egyptian judicial system, the mixed tribunals will have the necessary force to absorb rather than be absorbed.[10]

When the French Chambre learned of Anglo-Egyptian cancellation of the Dual Control, it became equally eager to take advantage of Britain's embarrassment over mixed court renewal. London's ambassador in Paris reported a warm welcome for Sharif's five-year extension proposal, especially from *député* Jacques Maunoury, the lawyer who had helped launch the Judicial Reform ten years before. Now *rapporteur* for the mixed court extension bill, he urged strict maintenance of the 1875 Charter since, "by virtue of the . . . convention, France has a foothold in Egypt; she has influence in the most important branch of the administration and the one on which all others depend."[11]

British policymakers were painfully aware of the truth of Maunoury's statement. Until Lord Dufferin somehow devised a comprehensive reorganization scheme that the powers and Istanbul could accept in place of the unwieldy Dual Control, London possessed only military and—even after appointment of a formal financial adviser in February 1883—very shaky budgetary control over Egypt's internal affairs.[12] When the French began rebuilding their own policy based on powers of obstructionism inherent in the Mixed Court Charter, therefore, Sharif had to be warned against giving premature assurances to supporters of the capitulatory status quo. To make his position clear, Lord Granville claimed that London would agree to "consider extension *for more than one year* only when reforms have been carried out."[13]

POLITICAL POSITIONS IN SHARIF'S CABINET AND LORD DUFFERIN'S RESPONSE

Formal Egyptian discussions of local and capitulatory legal reforms began just before Lord Dufferin's arrival in Egypt. Husayn Fakhri's call for a new committee to draft changes in Egypt's traditional council system met with opposition from his former chief Muhammad Riadh, then interior minister in the new cabinet. Although Riadh had previously avoided any association with the abortive constitutional front that replaced his 1879–81 government, he was the first to recall that Sharif's earlier *ahliyya* reform decree could be implemented without delay.[14]

Fakhri's objection that the 1881 decree overlooked essential points, particularly regarding jurisdiction over public officials or the government itself, did not alter Riadh's insistence. Even though waiting might help bring *ahliyya* justice into closer harmony with local needs, he claimed, "it still will not help free us from . . . the foreigners. Perhaps later we shall be forced to carry out a reform . . . that will be attributed to [foreign influence] and everyone will assume that, were it not for the Europeans, our judicial system could not function. . . . " By yielding to London's suggestion that a few foreign judges could help speed the transition along, Riadh warned, "we shall open a door we shall never be able to close. . . . If we compare our people and the level of our civilization with the people of Europe . . . it is obvious that qualified Egyptians will be able to administer justice at a comparable level, but in an Egyptian setting. If we bring in foreign judges we shall have the same problem as in the mixed courts and be unable to change a single . . . law without their consent."[15] Riadh's remarks caused disagreement over the risk of adopting an imported system of law without relying to some degree on European legal professionals. Finally, the justice minister was asked to review changing conditions of justice since 1881 and to submit reasons for either adopting Sharif's original *ahliyya* scheme or starting afresh.

Fakhri's report declared that Khedive Isma^{c}il's locally devised judicial council system had definitely helped clear distinctions between the respective spheres of *shari^{c}a* and *qanun* law during the 1860s and 1870s.[16] Their rudimentary organization, however, prevented the councils from reflecting changing needs, especially where private contract or credit legislation was concerned. Now that the possibility of a one-step change in both law and the courts was again at hand, however, he saw no harm in adopting the mixed court model (Sharif's 1881 plan) or even imported European laws for the projected *ahliyya* system. The only alternative to this approach had been raised by the rebellious 1882 Assembly, which

> thought it advisable to draft a civil law following the principles of the . . . *shari^c^a*. This task was assigned to Muhammad Qadri. . . . It is not yet completed. . . . Would it be possible to apply such a law to people in their dealings with one another nowadays, whether between themselves or with foreigners, or should we try to refer to the [existing] *qanun* law to adjudicate complicated actions like sales, rent, or confiscations? And if some claim that the civil law should follow the *shari^c^a* [because it is closer to the customs of the people], then there is even more reason to judge penal matters according to the holy law. The difficulty . . . of this under present conditions in Egypt is evident.[17]

Fakhri argued that, even if a borrowed legislative model facilitated the first stage of *ahliyya* justice, the experience and intelligence of a local professional judiciary would eventually create jurisprudence that lay halfway between European law and basic Egyptian social and economic needs. In the cabinet as a whole, however, acceptance of this rationalization rested on quite different grounds. Reactions to recommendations to revive the 1881 *ahliyya* decree suggested that promises of British political cooperation had not only been heard, but taken at face value. Sharif welcomed what he took to be an invitation to "form our own courts . . . so that we will be able to do without the mixed courts *after three or four months*. This will be preferable to letting them go on, and continuing the disgrace [the foreign courts] bring to us. . . . The law of the native and mixed courts should be one, and if changes are made, they should be made in both, or not at all."[18] The short-term political success of this particular aspect of post-insurrection policy was registered when Sharif decided to cancel his call for a five-year renewal of the Mixed Court Charter. In its place, the Egyptian cabinet announced a *third* one-year extension until January 1884.

Lord Dufferin himself had no direct hand in Egyptian cabinet plans to form a new *ahliyya* court committee by the turn of the new year. His only recorded intervention ended after an unsuccessful suggestion that Nubar Pasha's experience in such matters warranted naming him head of any legal reform body.[19] In fact, the cabinet's defensive reaction created a countereffect that Lord Dufferin seemed slow to comprehend. Instead of his political rival Nubar, Sharif chose the French lawyer Octave Borelli to direct his special committee. This move gave the Quai d'Orsay a source of leverage to oppose excessive British influence in Fakhri's ministry and, eventually, to bargain over conditions of mixed court renewal.[20]

Partly because the French had already revealed their own political interests in Egypt's legal affairs in *Chambre des Députés* debates, they fully suspected Lord Dufferin's apparent lack of concern for Sharif's manipulations. In fact, any claim of British neutrality in the court question had already been compromised by publication of a note that Dufferin's *chargé* had communicated directly to the sultan in Istanbul. Mr. Wyndham assured Abdulhamid that Britain still supported Tanzimat-inspired reforms in Egypt. As soon as London was satisfied that Tawfiq could realize these on his own, the need for continuing the occupation would cease. His view of recently revived *ahliyya* court plans, however, confirmed French suspicions that the judicial question was as high as military and fiscal control on the list of British priorities in Egypt. Wyndham's memo revealed that Dufferin's real purpose in supporting *ahliyya* courts was to solve the bothersome problem of Egypt's special capitulatory status. The British diplomat told a worried Abdulhamid that, "considering . . . it contrary to proper law and equity to judge several million native subjects according to a jurisprudence that is foreign to them, and only applies to two or three hundred thousand Europeans [*sic*], England tends . . . to separate itself from the principle of mixed tribunals and favors . . . indigenous tribunals. . . . Judicial reform will tend toward an entirely Egyptian organization."[21]

Even though Granville and Dufferin knew that such policies involved high international and local political stakes, they continued to depend on persons whose biases actually increased their risks. This is clear from Dufferin's acceptance of Sharif's obvious rush to implement the 1881 *ahliyya* court decree. The British ambassador pretended not to be worried by the fact that the new courts would receive European codes that were "faulty in many respects."[22]

Such remarks suggest that Dufferin based his opinions on those of Edward Malet and Sharif, both active architects of the abortive 1881 *ahliyya* decree. His idealistic conclusions had to be altered, however, when the ambassador realized that things were being pushed too rapidly without adequate technical supervision. Late in January, for example, the English judges on Fakhri's committee warned that future *ahliyya* courts might adopt existing mixed law without modifications to fit local litigants' needs. Overnight, therefore, Dufferin had to insist on the appointment of London's preferred judicial reform expert, Nubar Pasha, to correct "misconceptions" that might have been aired by Fakhri's French legal aide, Octave Borelli. At the same time, the ambassador suggested that London should nominate "a good Chief Justice to be the directing spirit" behind a plan meeting essentially Egyptian not complicated foreign capitulatory needs.[23]

EGYPTIAN AND BRITISH SKEPTICISM

Nubar's return at this date suggests that Lord Granville assumed that firm support for the founder of the mixed courts would be appreciated by both Egyptian and foreign political interests. Because his return bore the mark of Foreign Office patronage, however, and also because he did not receive an actual cabinet office, Nubar avoided identifying too closely with Dufferin's mission until he had more assurance that cooperation would yield personal political advantages. In fact, Isma^c^il's former minister was willing to seek such advantages from any source, local or foreign.

According to French Consul Raindre, Nubar was alarmed that Borelli had pushed for blanket adoption of French law without concern for its possible effects on Egyptian society. The Armenian minister inaugurated his return to political prominence by declaring opposition to "slavish imitations" of European laws that had definitely proved harmful after six years' application in the mixed courts.[24] In fact, there was nothing new in the list of items he wished to exclude from the draft of procedures Borelli had prepared for cabinet consideration: most came from the report London's law officers had prepared for reform and renewal of the mixed courts in 1880. Nubar argued that the notorious judicial mortgage, for example, was beyond *fallahin* comprehension and should not be included in local contract law. He also questioned awkward provisions in the abortive 1881 *ahliyya* decree that called for special jurisdictions to look into administrative irregularities. On this point, defense of mixed court procedures providing for judgment of officials by regular members of the professional bench promised better protection of the separation of powers principles Lord Dufferin was then building into Egypt's new "Organic Law."

Despite this last-minute Anglo-Egyptian initiative, the French seemed confident their own indirect contribution to judicial sections of Dufferin's main plan would remain intact. Consul Raindre assumed Borelli's original collaborators in the *ahliyya* court plan (Sharif and Riadh) would still carry the day politically. "Nubar may be disillusioned," he wrote,

> when he sees the work of Borelli Bey on the older code. Our compatriot is not one of Nubar's disciples and . . . he will attempt to give to this . . . code certain allures showing the collective paternity that changing circumstances have caused. We should, however, support certain of Nubar's proposals. Anything that establishes close assimilation between the mixed and native courts . . . may lead . . . to a unification . . . and menace the last citadel of Egyptian independence, the mixed courts.[25]

The general public, of course, knew nothing about such intrigues. Without other sources of information, many relied on Lord Dufferin's public reports, which promised that any new laws would be made "as congenial to the habits and prejudices of the people as circumstances permitted."[26] When such simplistic pronouncements reached the Arabic press, however, there was skepticism against rhetoric borrowed from the early 1881–82 constitutionalist movement. Alexandria's *Al-Burhan*, for example, urged sensitivity to local needs and the limited legal understanding of most rural litigants, factors that had been set aside in the confusion following Sharif's first *ahliyya* decree.[27] Such warnings, however, seemed tame once London's first official nominee for Ministry of Justice service arrived in Egypt. Sir Peter Benson Maxwell came to Cairo in April 1883 as *procureur général* (not, as Dufferin had suggested, "Chief Justice") in the planned local courts. Unlike previous unofficial judicial advisers, Maxwell had a law degree and experience as a judge in India.[28] Because of his exposure to methods of "native justice" on the subcontinent, Sir Peter had difficulty from the outset appreciating Egypt's reform dilemma. In fact, he startled London's ambassador by immediately proposing abandonment of a sweeping *ahliyya* plan in favor of practicality and simplicity. Dufferin was particularly perplexed to hear a defense of common law methods instead of trying to match the French-inspired mixed courts at their own game. Maxwell was against codes and preferred letting judges use "their own . . . common sense to evolve a body of law. I soon . . . convinced him [Maxwell] of the absurdity of the plan. The one thing necessary here . . . is a strict, definite code. . . . As I had given instructions to . . . render the procedure as simple as possible . . . I was very disappointed to hear my little truculent judge denounce the whole thing as 'rubbish' and . . . the production of . . . fogies . . . forty years behind other people."[29]

Although the ambassador opposed unnecessary delays before implementation of his Organic Law for local government during the temporary occupation, he did take some of Maxwell's warnings seriously. Just before the Dufferin Plan was formally accepted in May 1883, he realized that, despite promises from Nubar and Sharif, French or "Frenchified" members of Fakhri's committee still favored a Napoleonic model for all Egyptian courts. Instead of using his influence to stop hasty moves, however, the British ambassador delegated this responsibility to Maxwell. Thus, even though the Dufferin Plan contained a neat schema for input to the Cairo executive from a select and presumably manageable local Legislative Council, at least three factions—a clique favoring Sharif's original 1881 decree, supporters of Nubar, and a "little truculent judge" from the Indian Service—all felt that London should depend on their particular interpretation of Egypt's needs for legal reform.

Eventually the impossibility of satisfying such mutually exclusive expectations would undermine confidence in the new Legislative Council and other idealistic aspects of the Dufferin Plan as well. Many European critics felt that the 1883 Organic Law, with its awkward adoption of the earlier constitutionalist slogan "Egypt for the Egyptians," was meant to announce the probable price for reintegrating the Cairo khedivate into a loosely bound Ottoman imperial structure. Consul Raindre in particular suspected that the Legislative Council and *ahliyya* courts were designed to transform the occupation into a *de facto* protectorate. Instead of fearing Gladstone's alternative to "Tunisification," however, the French expected his policies to fail. It was possible, perhaps, that a passive handpicked Legislative Council would merely look on while British advisers imposed new laws to be applied by *ahliyya* judges. Then, once artificially contrived native courts and codes were in place, Raindre said, a "new Egypt" would rush to "stand up in opposition to the mixed and consular courts like an impatient heir. The English will try to . . . help it get its succession. But . . . probably . . . the corruption of the indigenous magistry . . . will lead . . . to a total miscarriage in Dufferin's *ahliyya* plan. . . . This would be to the benefit of the international jurisdictions, and . . . a veritable reverse for English policy."[30]

PRACTICAL VERSUS POLITICAL PERSPECTIVES IN MID-1883

By the time a revised version of Sharif's 1881 court reform was promulgated in June 1883, local administrative affairs in Egypt were suffering under the shock of a spreading cholera epidemic. Growing chaos prompted informed observers to expect changes in the Dufferin Plan, perhaps even renewal of martial law, just to guarantee order and a minimal livelihood for Egypt's rural population.[31] Despite signs of a new nadir in public security in mid-1883, however, local parties were already looking ahead for ways to protect their interests under the proposed *ahliyya* system. One can only speculate about concerns at this early date for future effects of new laws on urban or rural property holdings. Debate over possible professional employment benefits, budgetary fluctuations, and bureaucratic rearrangements, however, surfaced even before the courts became a reality.

Discussion centered on the qualifications of personnel to staff a European-style judiciary. Middle functionaries in several departments naturally expected there would be an opportunity for experienced or loyal officials to transfer into the court system. These same hopefuls were apparently also first to decry Husayn Fakhri's proposal to channel all bench appointments through a central examining board in the Ministry of Justice. Announced plans for professional training (including courses for bailiffs and court recorders at administrative schools in Cairo) aroused rhetorical support in the local press, but few responses from other ministries.[32]

Anyone who questioned the rush to implement the local court scheme as the first phase of the Dufferin Plan became the object of rebuffs from either Sharif or the majority Liberal party in Parliament.[33] The man who felt the effects of the Anglo-Egyptian judicial reform bandwagon most directly was Maxwell, London's unhappy assignee to the Ministry of Justice. When Maxwell gave Husayn Fakhri his glum predictions of confusion under the *ahliyya* plan, he expected the British consul to help orchestrate harmony. Instead, Sir Edward Malet immediately sided with the Egyptians (as Dufferin had done earlier) against the "little truculent judge" who felt "unable to direct a system of which he disapproves and with which he is inadequately acquainted. The Minister, . . . however, thinks it is easier for one legal officer to master a foreign system than for eighty Egyptian judges . . . to . . . administer a justice the rules of which are foreign to their whole legal education [*sic*]."[34]

In fact, Maxwell's criticism went much deeper than Malet was willing to admit. He objected mainly to wholesale borrowings of French law for Egyptian courts. He did recognize that any local system that aimed at replacing the mixed courts would eventually have to master European codes. Common sense, however, suggested that many of Egypt's most pressing judicial needs had never even been a real concern for the lawyers who had worked on the original mixed codes or the new *ahliyya* plan.

Two items of Maxwell's practical advice had apparently been set aside by Malet as "foreign to [the] . . . whole legal education" of prospective *ahliyya* appointees. The British lawyer felt local codes should include extremely simple procedures for typical cases of peasant justice. Without some departures from French models, procedural confusion was bound to multiply minor *fallahin* appeals all the way to Cairo. Maxwell complained that neither London nor the Egyptian cabinet was seriously concerned about professional input to help local judges avoid an eventual appeals imbroglio. When his request for several British nominations to the new bench was turned down, for example, the adviser was told that an Egyptian mixed court judge had already visited several "neutral" European countries to recruit for nearly all senior positions. His disappointment in learning that fourteen Dutch and Belgian judges had already been appointed confirmed suspicion that Lord Dufferin wanted mainly to avoid political recrimination from the French. Since only one of Maxwell's British nominees was accepted for appointment, the "little truculent judge" assumed he had misunderstood the extent of his authority and offered to resign even before the *ahliyya* courts began operations.[35]

EVELYN BARING'S RETURN TO CAIRO

In September 1883, Sir Evelyn Baring was recalled from his secretarial post under the viceroy of India and appointed British agent and consul general in Egypt. Many of Edward Malet's critics felt the appointment reflected Lord Granville's conviction that the head of the Cairo mission should be a trained financial expert. The former

Caisse member's first serious challenge, however, was to resolve disagreements with Maxwell over Egyptian legal reform.

Baring admitted that Maxwell's arguments were "weighty," but felt the Egyptians correctly opposed delaying one of the two major reform components of the Dufferin Plan. He decided to test the influence of his new office by inviting both parties to compromise. "A little pressure" brought the same promises given earlier to Malet: the Egyptian ministry would make several (still unspecified) changes in the "native" codes. Meanwhile, they would send delegations to settle the backlog of minor *fallahin* disputes that had built up since 1881. Once the slate was cleaned, Fakhri predicted that *ahliyya* litigation would give Egyptian judges the higher-level judicial experience needed to stem the tide of cases that had earlier ended up in the mixed courts. Baring was sufficiently impressed to boast, somewhat naively, that he had "concluded [his] original task of supervising the preparation of the new codes."[36]

It is difficult to know whether similar trust or behind-the-scenes politics prompted promulgation of Egypt's new codes during Maxwell's temporary European leave in November 1883. British correspondence indicates that, after "solving" the local court question, Baring himself spent the rest of the year preparing for the coming debate on the Mixed Court Charter, due to expire again in February 1884. As for the Cairo cabinet, it became involved in controversy over increasing losses of Egyptian territory to Mahdi Ibn as-Sayyid ᶜAbdullah's rebel forces in the Sudan and left many internal political issues dangling. In fact, for a full month, no one even tried to answer charges that the Ministry of Justice had tricked the British by enacting laws that were mirror images of the mixed codes.[37]

Among Egyptian journalists, disappointments focused not on technical but on moral contradictions. Cairo's recently founded *Az-Zaman*, published by an Egyptian Armenian, led the way in criticizing Europeanization of Egypt's existing legal traditions. It may have been no accident that Alexandre Seroufian's argument against wholesale borrowing from the mixed courts resembled those of other Christians (principally the editors of *Al-Watan* and *Al-Waqt*) who had sympathized with secular currents during the pre-occupation constitutionalist movement. He wrote, as Adib Ishaq had in 1881, that:

> legislated law [*qanun*] is not a material . . . but rather a subjective thing that defines the way Europeans order their lives. They should not criticize us for our way of ordering our own. We have . . . our own *shariʿa* as well as the Ottoman imperial law for those who have chosen it. . . . We are astounded when we hear foreigners complain about the absence of justice in Egypt. Are the ones who complain . . . judges of the mixed courts, or others who do not understand our holy and our legislated laws?[38]

When the Foreign Office finally asked for details of Baring's supervision of Lord Dufferin's legal reform directives, however, timing, not content, was the first concern. Even after Maxwell had personally visited permanent undersecretary Sir Julian Pauncefote and repeated his lonely objections to Sharif's scheme, Lord Granville urged "pressure, if not a threat to change personnel at the Ministry of Justice," to have a new judicial system functioning in Egypt *before* discussions began over renewal of the mixed courts in 1884.[39] After Malet's successor received this warning, he had another embarrassing surprise: although fourteen Dutch and Belgian judges had been appointed (and paid) since midsummer, no Egyptian nominations had yet cleared Fakhri's ministry! The Cairo Agency used pressure, therefore, to assure that forty-six Egyptian appointments would be processed in the last week of 1883.[40]

Since the original *ahliyya* plan now suddenly appeared to have been overly ambitious, Baring reported that a court of appeals and five tribunals only (in Cairo, Alexandria, Mansurah, Tanta, and Benha) would open in January 1884. No local district tribunals were to be introduced until qualified personnel received adequate training. Technically, this meant that the circumscriptions of some thirty small town courts (originally planned to receive the mass of *fallahin* summary disputes) had to be temporarily covered by five provincial city courts in the Delta zone. One additional fact made it evident the new system would mainly serve the more-developed town and commercial agricultural sectors of the population. Upper Egypt, which had experienced minimal contact with European commercial interests, received no new tribunals at all. As a last-minute gesture to deeply rooted Egyptian traditions (but mainly because of budget and staff shortages), all up-Nile provinces were allowed to remain under the uncodified judicial council system.

Anyone without some knowledge of the politics of Egyptian legal reform might have questioned Baring's assumption that only five tribunals could handle litigation generated by over three-quarters of the country's population. After repeated pledges to save Egyptian civil and commercial litigation from capitulatory encroachments, however, London needed some tangible proof to offer, especially to Ottoman imperial authorities in Istanbul. In fact, Granville's permanent undersecretary hinted that Egyptian judicial policies were tied to much larger international political considerations when he specifically urged the return of Nubar Pasha to serve as prime minister under the occupation. If, as Julian Pauncefote predicted, Sharif resigned over Egypt's loss of Sudan Province, Nubar's characteristic unwillingness to separate "native" from capitulatory reform considerations could help prepare the next logical stage of the Dufferin Plan.[41]

REDEFINITION OF CAPITULATORY STRATEGY BY JANUARY 1884

Public attention had focused mainly on political and financial issues in Egypt since the defeat of the ʿUrabists in mid-1882. Nonetheless, all but the most naive observers knew that many domestic questions, from increased public works projects to protection of individual and government interests against commercial fraud, depended on the cooperation of the foreign resident community. The first item that obviously demanded attention was public security and penal prosecution of Egyptians and foreigners alike. Already in the summer of 1883, Egyptian cabinet members had insisted that any local police reform efforts would fail as long as foreign offenders remained completely immune from prosecution in Egyptian criminal courts.[42] Those who were most disgruntled claimed that many crimes, especially in urban areas, involved capitulatory accomplices. Unlike "strawman" involvement of individual foreigners in Egyptian civil cases, however, penal collusion did *not* lead to judgments by the mixed bench. Instead, individual consular responsibility meant, at best, judgment under one of fourteen different extraterritorial legal systems with no participation by Egyptian police or professional judicial authorities. More often, it meant temporary repatriation followed by a "cooling off" period and reentry into Egypt by troublemakers ready to devise new shady dealings with other foreign or local parties.

There was no question that occupation officials shared the Egyptian government's desire to end the existing imbroglio of conflicting penal jurisdictions. Suggestions made by Britain's veteran consul in Alexandria, however, fell far short of expectations in Sharif's cabinet. Consul Cookson adamantly supported any move that would bring foreign offenders into a court "in which the [Egyptian] government . . . is represented." He admitted frankly that it would be some time before the local system could handle such responsibilities on its own. The prevailing British view, which Sharif reluctantly incorporated into a circular memorandum, was that consular missions should surrender all remaining extraterritorial penal jurisdictions to the mixed courts once they had won general confidence.[43]

Anglo-Egyptian desires to improve standards of penal justice through the mixed courts provided opponents of the occupation an unexpected invitation to strengthen the 1875 Judicial Reform. Consul Raindre, obviously hoping to regain influence that had disappeared with the Anglo-French Dual Control, assumed that Sharif's request would necessitate a full international commission (like that of 1880–81) to review the penal question along with "other necessary mixed charter revisions" occasioned by the events of 1882.[44] Ultimately, however, it was London's new appointee to the Cairo Agency who convinced London that the possible benefits of penal regularization might be worth the risks of reconvening a full capitulatory reform commission.

For a time after his reassignment to Egypt, Evelyn Baring seemed to hope that higher-level political pressure, combined with silence on the future of the Mixed Court Charter after 1883, would bring reform concessions from the key powers.[45] After two months, he changed his estimates. First, the new consul saw that one effect of encouraging immediate promulgation of the "native codes" had been a flood of unexpected mixed mortgage litigation. Lenders who feared imminent abrogation of the mixed courts or suddenly imposed changes in their laws besieged the Cairo mixed bench with foreclosure proceedings against Egyptian borrowers. When he reported the shock of the onslaught, Baring did not consider the possibility that creditors were reacting to the hidden implication of a next stage of legal reform after the Dufferin Plan. Oddly, he as much as apologized for aspects of the 1875 Judicial Reform that earlier British experts had consistently and openly opposed. "Unless I am mistaken," he wrote, " . . . it is only during the last year or two that the full consequences of the establishment of the mixed tribunals and the action of Western law on an ignorant population . . . have begun to be felt. During the first few years large sums of money were lent. Now these debts are coming due, and the European creditors are demanding payment or dispossession."[46]

There was in fact a much more concrete explanation for Baring's apparent change of heart concerning mixed court defects previously considered irremediable. Paris was sending a new consul to replace Raindre and, presumably, would press for immediate transfer of all remaining consular penal jurisdictions to the mixed bench. This single concession was so important for occupation administration that Baring urged "anticipation" of future cooperation by offering something more than a token one-year extension of the Mixed Court Charter. On the basis of the French penal reform feeler, London quickly ordered a five-year renewal "in full reliance that the . . . government will vigorously push on the . . . opening of the Native Tribunals." Simultaneously, the Foreign Office gave in to requests for a new international capitulatory conference in Cairo, provided that penal questions and the controversial judicial mortgage received priority attention.[47] The British thus ended 1883 with an assumption that, at least in capitulatory reform matters, they could revive some of the spirit of Anglo-French cooperation that had prevailed before 1882. Lord Granville hoped that good sense would encourage France and other foreign rivals to see that reasonable concessions on the future of mixed justice would help foster local political and financial stabilization. This in turn would speed Britain's stated goal of leaving Egypt at the earliest feasible date.

The material contained in this chapter provides a useful new perspective on the contemporary and better-known 1883–84 debate over Britain's responsibility to help Egypt retain Sudan Province and Muhammad Sharif's resignation, presumably over the loss of Khartoum. In fact, when Sharif, Husayn Fakhri, and Sir Edward Malet were all ultimately removed by the outset of 1884, three prime actors behind the abortive capitulatory negotiations of 1880–81 were replaced by veterans of legal reform under Khedive Isma^cil. At least two returning veterans, Evelyn Baring and Nubar, found themselves by this date tempted to view the mixed courts in a totally different light than had been possible in earlier Dual Control days. Hope was rising that France's key cooperation in capitulatory reform essentials would ease Britain's tasks without making it necessary drastically to change existing judicial structures. This could save unnecessary additional budgetary allocations to the Cairo Ministry of Justice. Also, unlike the situation that prevailed at the time of the 1880–81 capitulatory fiasco, unwarranted and troublesome pretensions of secondary powers arguing over minor capitulatory concessions would presumably not be tolerated by France: the Quai d'Orsay's primary policy aim in 1884 was to speed Britain's withdrawal from Egypt.

On his part, Nubar was obviously prepared to support a new round of negotiations before renewal of the Mixed Court Charter. If successful, his new ministry could gain the distinction of having rewon Egypt's freedom from indirect foreign legislative and judicial as well as direct military control. His own unique Tanzimat creation would thus be restored and recognized, not as a device of international intervention in Egypt's affairs, but as a guarantor of legitimate foreign and local legislative and judicial needs. One question, then, remained: what responsibility would Nubar hold for the separate "native" court system, devised and only partially implemented by an obviously rival ministry?[48]

8

Nubar Pasha's Campaign for Justice

The most obvious reason favoring Nubar Pasha's return to office in 1884 was that, unlike Muhammad Sharif, he did not hold strong opinions for or against retention of Egypt's rebellious Sudan Province. Rather than risk his political future on issues that had to be decided at higher levels in the Foreign Office, Nubar looked forward to attacking problems he was best qualified to solve. No one was surprised, therefore, when he ended Husayn Fakhri's one and one-half years of service as Sharif's minister of justice. When this change was gazetted, the local foreign press advised recent Ministry of Justice appointees to brace themselves for "a radical change in the [*ahliyya*] courts, which, hardly installed, must already be redone from top to bottom."[1]

The most cynical critic was Octave Borelli, Cairo's de facto legal adviser until Benson Maxwell filled the newly created attorney general's post in 1883. Borelli knew well that Evelyn Baring had collaborated with Dual Control efforts between 1876 and 1882 to disarm, or possibly even cancel, the mixed courts. He also suspected that the new Egyptian ministry did not like Britain's apparently sudden agreement to renew the mixed courts any more than the outgoing cabinet, but for different reasons. Nubar would have preferred to ask for increased Egyptianization of the mixed bench as part of the capitulatory trade-off that was occurring. Instead, his first act as prime minister was to accept a five-year continuation of mixed justice without any a priori conditions. This raised rumors that cooperation assumed recognition of his own long-term plan to make the 1875 Judicial Reform the sole basis for all high-level litigation in Egypt. Borelli's newly founded French newssheet *Le Bosphore Egyptien* as much as invited him to aim at that goal and to leave the artificially created *ahliyya* courts to whatever fate awaited them: "Did Nubar sign this renewal decree, which assures justice for foreigners, without a certain degree of bitterness? . . . The Reform is safe. But the regard of all those who want real justice, common to all inhabitants of the country, turns toward it. Its . . . benefits should extend to all Egyptians. Will we not have the joy of bringing the honor . . . to Nubar, and saying to him, this time, *sic vos et vobit*?"[2]

ANGLO-EGYPTIAN DISAGREEMENT OVER *AHLIYYA* JUDICIAL AND POLICE METHODS

The British were clearly not receptive to French hints of premature moves toward "judicial fusion." The Agency was relieved, therefore, when Nubar announced that, while he himself concentrated on efforts to reform the mixed courts, matters of *ahliyya* justice would be handled by his Coptic undersecretary, Butrus Ghali.[3] Recognition of Ghali's responsibility at this time was important for several reasons. First, criticism from Maxwell promised to be as embarrassing to Nubar as it had been to Sharif. Maxwell simply would not agree that the needs of local Egyptian justice could be served by using superficially camouflaged French law. His repeated attacks on attempts to "bend usages of the people . . . to rules which . . . commend themselves to the legislator as convenient, without being based on any important principle" raised much ire in Cairo. In fact, his jibes made Baring suggest that Lord Granville should consider replacing Maxwell with someone who had Nubar's prior approval.[4]

Meanwhile, the consul tried to lessen tensions by playing up the legal abilities of someone who could afford to be neutral in feuds between Nubar and Maxwell. Of all potentially qualified Egyptians, Ghali seemed to fit such a role. The thirty-seven-year-old son of a former secretary in Isma^cil's administration spoke four languages, including Turkish and English.[5] His first government work had been as chief of the cabinet's translation department. He began specializing in legal affairs after 1876. His good record earned him the job of deputy minister when Husayn Fakhri first headed the Justice Department (1879–81). He managed to hold that post under Muhammad Qadri as well, until radical currents brought down the government in 1882. He returned as soon as Sharif was reinstalled in the fall of the same year. Butrus's experience under all three major ministries since 1876, therefore, potentially armed him to handle a number of key judicial tasks in Nubar's stead.

The undersecretary's new prominence in the daily management of ministry affairs allowed higher-level Anglo-Egyptian concentration on a few priority issues in 1884. First, perhaps, was preparation of mixed court reforms to achieve penal equity and extract a capitulatory price in return for Britain's early withdrawal. Another issue of immediate concern was control over spreading lawlessness in the Egyptian countryside. Unlike matters of civil justice, police organization was early recognized as something that could not be solved by the Cairo ministry without open assistance from various occupation agencies. Contemporaries and historians alike have underlined problems pitting interventionism against "self-help" in Egyptian Ministry of Interior and police operations. Little attention, however, has ever been given to ways in which Anglo-Egyptian compromises in this area inevitably affected other branches of local administration. It is now apparent that the British recognized numerous pitfalls in local penal justice well before professionally trained advisers like Maxwell and Clifford Lloyd were attached to the Ministry of Justice and Ministry of the Interior, respectively. Convenient separation of their actions under two different departments hinders our understanding of how penal policies in the two ministries overlapped each other and higher judicial questions simultaneously.

Although the so-called Lloyd Controversy focused on a different set of disagreements than those within the Justice Department, the interior undersecretary's criticism of police organization caused similar reactions from the head of the Egyptian cabinet.[6] Soon Nubar was arguing that excessive British concern for local police functions, like Maxwell's obsession with the local court system, might distract his ministry and the Agency from their joint commitment to obtain important capitulatory reforms in 1884. He worked very hard to convince Baring that subordinate British advisers—including Maxwell and Lloyd alike—lacked the political insight to adjust their efforts to facilitate such larger Anglo-Egyptian policy priorities. In retrospect, the Agency's decision to support Nubar's demand for compromise from both Maxwell and Lloyd overestimated Egyptian commitments to plan responsibly for the next stage of capitulatory negotiation. Just as importantly, it also allowed local elites to extend, for a number of years, a dual system of justice that served their interests, both in penal repression and in increasingly vital Egyptian property and contract disputes.

Clifford Lloyd left a difficult post in the Irish Constabulary in 1884 to enter a similar situation of civil unrest and lawlessness in rural Egypt. His Irish experiences help explain why Lloyd focused so quickly on Egyptian police methods and relations between police and court authorities. He showed an antilegalist bias characteristic of someone whose professional concerns emphasized direct repression of lawlessness. In contrast to the views of the Egyptian cabinet, and in apparent agreement with Maxwell, Lloyd felt the *ahliyya* court decrees tried to accomplish too much too quickly. Both felt that retaining certain familiar patterns of interaction between private subjects and executive authority (symbolized by the *mudir*) was a necessary compromise that more idealistic reformers needed to recognize. Maxwell preferred to support something modest like justice of the peace jurisdictions staffed by professional judges who could handle both simple civil and penal cases. Clifford Lloyd's training as a law enforcement agent, on the other hand, made him lean toward placing more responsibility with the provincial *mudir*. Those executive agents' police and magisterial powers could, he thought, be supervised by a British-staffed "inspectorate general."[7]

Lloyd seemed convinced that propertyless *fallahin* in rural districts had very little stake in the more complex legal guarantees offered by the new codes. The main problem in the countryside was one of increasing material deprivation that made Egypt's peasants vulnerable to temptations of lawlessness. This was encouraging widespread theft and armed attacks, phenomena which had gone on since the "revolutionary" drama of 1882. The undersecretary's proposal to place more emphasis on magisterial functions for the *mudir*s implied that some of the problems of social dislocation and spontaneous criminality came from hastily applied judicial reforms. Lack of serious attention to obvious incongruities in the new penal codes seemed to substantiate Lloyd's suggestion. He could have argued, for example, that higher-level reformers tended to concern themselves mainly with civil justice, and especially with contract law affecting the interests of propertied groups.

Urban elites or absentee landlords whose material or political interests stood to gain most from the replacement of old *qanun* structures by European law probably considered penal questions to be at best necessary distractions from the main thrust of legal reformers' efforts. In fact, in 1884, local journalists began to show approval for Lloyd's tendency to separate jurisdictional questions into executive penal and judicial civil components.[8] Nubar, on the other hand, tried to remain steadfast in defense of his original idealistic hope that justice in Egypt should be recognized as an indivisible whole. His reasoning was probably not based solely on fears of a return to reactionary vested interests in executive control over Egypt's rural peasantry. Rather, Nubar's definitions of justice almost automatically had their source in the mixed court system he had created. Both he and higher British authorities were sensitive to the fact that some sympathetic tolerance for mixed court reform, especially in the still untested area of penal justice, was just beginning to appear among earlier skeptics who had opposed the 1875 Mixed Court Charter. Nubar also knew well that potential capitulatory negotiators kept their own frames of reference, and therefore willingness to cooperate with next stages of reforms, narrowly adjusted to recognizable Western legal standards, not factors of traditional Egyptian rural administration. By the spring of 1884, therefore, Nubar willingly accepted interior minister Thabit's resignation and assigned to himself simultaneous responsibilities for *both* the justice and interior portfolios.

Egyptian officials clearly hoped Nubar would help resolve the rising feud between the Ministry of Justice and the Ministry of the Interior by removing both Maxwell and Lloyd from their rival undersecretarial positions. His first step was to try to remove any impression that the affair was simply a British personnel problem by interviewing the *mudir*s and then interpreting their views of post-1882 conditions to the Cairo Agency. When a meeting of *mudir*s was held, it appeared that rural governors were totally opposed to foreign-inspired changes in local administration, whether in new judicial or traditional executive spheres.

Most *mudir*s remembered that 1881–82 proponents of constitutional reforms attributed rising administrative irregularities to arbitrary intervention by Interior officials in matters that were inadequately covered by *qanun* laws. Now that new judicial institutions had been created, the governors wanted to avoid suggestions that continued lawlessness stemmed from their own incompetence or abuse. They complained that chances of keeping order had been reduced by the loss of penal responsibility to the attorney general's staff and to Lloyd's British-officered constabulary. Both administrative innovations were unfamiliar to the rural population and poorly coordinated with the traditional offices of the *mudir*s or district *ma'mur*s. Even if Lloyd's inspectorate general plan was accepted and Egyptian police regained some responsibilities of penal judgment lost to the courts, rural disorder would probably not abate. The *mudir*s felt that Lloyd's inspectors, like judicial agents, would follow high ministerial conceptions of proper administration and ignore time-tested methods of preventing, or at least discouraging, disrespect for government authority.[9] Several governors listed minimum traditional powers they needed to help reestablish order. These included the right to jail persons suspected of brigandage or theft and to try "all minor penal offenses" without necessary reference to *parquet* procedures or distant *ahliyya* court benches. The *mudir*s also requested the unappealable right to judge any minor officials found negligent in their duties.[10]

Nubar was not at all displeased to see the *mudir*s add another controversial dimension to the rural brigandage issue that had brought Maxwell and Lloyd to loggerheads. Baring's private letters to London were already conveying an urgent need to respond to Lloyd's (and also other Interior officials') plan to strengthen extrajudicial controls over rural crime. Siding with Lloyd against Maxwell's view of the "inalienability" of *parquet* functions in criminal justice, Baring claimed (somewhat belatedly) that he had predicted rural judicial chaos when Sharif's reform was introduced "in too great a hurry." When he arrived, " . . . everything was so far advanced that I could not interfere, and I was being pressed on all sides not to delay the new codes. . . . But both Lloyd and I hinted that too little power was being left to the mudirs. Cherif, supported by Maxwell, would not believe us. The result is that we must now go back and give powers of summary justice to the executive. . . . "[11]

When London's response came back, Baring discovered that his adversaries had also used the private pouch to warn against abandoning ideas that enjoyed support among London's law officers. Undersecretary Pauncefote personally conveyed to Lord Granville Maxwell's separately written defense of Egypt's first trained body of full-time jurists.[12] At the same time he reminded his superior that the *ahliyya* codes and local legislative council system had been put in place to defend against further capitulatory encroachments on the khedive's provincial autonomy. To admit they were not working and to return to pre-Tanzimat forms of justice in noncapitulatory-related administration would only widen the gap that had led to the establishment of separate mixed courts of law. Pauncefote recommended, therefore, withholding support from *both* Maxwell and Lloyd and letting Nubar "establish his own way" of providing judicial guarantees for all sectors of the local and foreign resident communities.[13] When Clifford Lloyd realized both Baring and the permanent undersecretary were assuming equal expertise in judging his and Maxwell's estimates of grass-roots reform needs, he resigned in protest.

FELONY COMMISSIONS AS AN EXTRAJUDICIAL OPTION

Lack of clear instructions from the British forced Nubar to move independently to stop further deterioration in rural penal justice. His plan of action, which became Egypt's first felony commission decree, helped soothe Baring's ire over London's rebuff of his own support for Clifford Lloyd. Also, by identifying brigandage as a separate problem for special agencies in the Egyptian administration, it held out the promise of letting the *ahliyya* courts prove themselves in other key areas. Ideally, this adjustment would allow them to play a serious role in capitulatory reform discussions in 1884.

On paper the first felony commission decree of April 1884 removed serious penal prosecutions, especially rural brigandage, from the still only partially staffed *ahliyya* courts.[14] This was supposed to free them to attend to less spectacular but essential application of civil, commercial, and misdemeanor law. The same decree called upon the Ministry of the Interior to appoint a high official to preside over felony deliberations and to receive criminal dossiers directly from rural *mudir*s and police who made arrests. Nubar promised, however, to name trained judges from the Cairo court to the commission. He assured early critics that the judges' presence would guarantee that otherwise unappealable decisions would not be handed down by Interior officials without some reference to the penal code.

The only person who reacted negatively to Nubar's redistribution of rural penal responsibilities to "save up" the limited professional judicial capacities of local court personnel was Maxwell. After a year in Cairo, the attorney general had begun to reconsider his original preference for "no codes at all" in Egypt. From Maxwell's altered point of view in 1884, Egypt had a great deal to gain by encouraging the small handful of trainees who had begun professional careers in the new court system. Some of these were willing to run the risk of departing from traditional channels for career advancement according to one's ascribed social status, high administrative or political office, or traditional educational accomplishments. Warning against "once again placing power into the hands of corrupt and ignorant men and taking it away from trained and unprejudiced . . . magistrates," Maxwell felt the opinions of such men concerning the future of their profession and its potential contribution to much wider questions of social and political reformism should no longer pass unnoticed.[15]

Local political maneuvers helped table further discussion of Maxwell's observations before they could reach the level of controversy unleashed earlier by Clifford Lloyd. The occasion came when Nubar announced he was transferring responsibilities for preparing the first annual report on *ahliyya* court operations to a fully Egyptian committee under Ghali. As Nubar obviously expected, the Agency tried to avoid embarrassing political repercussions that would be caused by Maxwell's exclusion: Baring asked London to reassign the only officially contracted British jurist in the new courts while Maxwell was away from Egypt on seasonal leave.[16]

Given certain characteristics of Egypt's internal situation and the international capitulatory climate, it is not difficult to suggest why Baring let Nubar "establish his own way" of handling Ministry of Justice affairs at this stage. First, the British Agency was already hinting that, because of public insecurity outside town centers, chances of implementing planned fiscal and public works reforms were decreasing daily. Although he never stated so openly, Baring must have recognized that such schemes depended on acceptance of British-sponsored programs by rural landowners and provision, by expansion of their agricultural activity and taxes, of sufficient revenues to support them. Nubar was already conveying landowners' concerns—in fact reflections of similar worries in the 1882 Legislative Assembly—for maintaining direct executive means to protect their property and produce. Baring must have felt a grass-roots penal compromise could not be avoided, if only to retain local support for higher-priority issues. Certainly the most important of these in his eyes as well as Nubar's was the job of preparing joint mixed court reform demands to be presented before the end of 1884.

CAPITULATORY BARGAINING AND REPOLITICIZATION OF THE MIXED COURTS UNDER NUBAR

When Nubar returned to the premiership in 1884, several foreign powers had begun to relax their guard against the anti–mixed court biases that had dominated cabinet affairs for nearly five years. Consul Camille Barrère was particularly pleased to see that the French judge on the Alexandria court was discussing the new climate for reform with his foreign colleagues. After reviewing priorities with the Quai d'Orsay, Judge Martin-Sarzeaud actually published, in an international scholarly journal, a set of proposals for consideration by all signatories to the original 1875 Judicial Reform.[17] On one hand, the French no longer denied the very questionable technical qualifications of certain foreign appointees to mixed court judgeships. On the other, they now recognized inequities caused by the extreme centralization of mixed court proceedings in three Delta urban centers only.[18]

The French thus seemed ready to accept reforms in 1884, including decentralization and even Nubar's idea of "native chambers" to help sort out questionable cases of mixed interest. These stood little chance of success, however, until London was convinced that Paris would not use them as opportunities to expand extrajudicial capitulatory interference in Egyptian affairs. Unfortunately for those who had rising hopes, when the mixed courts themselves showed the first evidence of conforming to British expectations, foreign jealousies outside the courtroom repoliticized their position overnight.

For over a year and a half, a main worry of Egypt's Ministry of Finance had been to handle 1882 foreign indemnity claims without jeopardizing budgetary stabilization efforts. Occasionally Anglo-Egyptian financial advisers had stopped payment of indemnities, either because funds were earmarked for priority stabilization plans or because certain awards appeared unreasonable. Finally, after holding back for two years, the mixed courts themselves began reviewing charges that failure to pay indemnities bills so long after the event constituted a separate legal grievance. They agreed that a new round of civil suits against the government should consider substantially higher figures, because of financial losses incurred by delays. In March 1884, the Cairo court's landmark Tedeschi decision granted a new award to an indemnities plaintiff that caused considerable alarm for the British financial adviser.[19]

Although the total sums involved were much less significant, Evelyn Baring easily remembered how the public debt crisis from 1876 to 1880 had turned mixed court defense of private creditors' claims into a diplomatic imbroglio of major proportions. Immediately after the Tedeschi judgment, therefore, he convinced various capitulatory governments to include prorated indemnities in a revised version of the pre-occupation (1880) liquidation law. The Agency then carried the Tedeschi case to the Alexandria court of appeals and won.[20]

Government success in the Tedeschi case was an example of growing technical expertise among Egyptians on the attorney general's staff as well as a sign of professional integrity and political independence on the mixed appeals bench.[21] Capitulatory "hard-liners," however, saw in it a sign of collaboration with Anglo-Egyptian financial preoccupations. Although it was generally smaller powers like Italy and Greece that used court tensions to magnify their own leverage in the Egyptian Question, collapse of Tedeschi's suit sent ripples not only to Rome and Athens, but to Paris as well. Apparently the news caused the Quai d'Orsay to reconsider risking good relations with smaller countries whose support against Britain could prove essential, either in Egypt or in other geographical zones, including sub-Saharan Africa and Tonkin. When other issues arose, French diplomats did not want London to be able to remind France's former capitulatory allies that Paris had not stood by their otherwise marginal interests in the Egyptian Question in 1884. It was not because of Signor Tedeschi or any other indemnities claimant, then, but because its Egyptian policy assumed French leadership of a tacit alliance among Britain's capitulatory rivals that Paris returned to open political defense of its interests in the mixed court regime. Before either the British or Nubar saw this shift coming, the French managed to benefit enormously by playing a dual role in the capitulatory reform process.

Even before the shake-up caused by the Tedeschi case, French Consul Barrère had felt the same type of local pressures that had made Baron de Ring break with Dual Control reform preferences and support openly interventionist powers for the mixed courts in

1880–81.[22] Such roughshod and open political maneuvering seemed inappropriate, however, in 1884. Nonetheless, as soon as Nubar assembled the consuls to discuss capitulatory reform, Barrère suggested that a subcommission of mixed court judges only, not diplomats, should sift out reform recommendations that would benefit the capitulatory community as a whole. Because the British knew that Justice Martin-Sarzeaud had already broached quite moderate French reform priorities, they agreed, hoping that the professional objectivity shown by the mixed bench in the Tedeschi case would carry over into a separate subcommission.[23]

From a strictly technical point of view, the judges' work did meet Anglo-Egyptian expectations. With a few exceptions, Martin-Sarzeaud's revised statement of the Foreign Office's 1880 reform memorandum, including a recommendation to close all remaining consular courts and transfer full penal jurisdiction over foreigners to the mixed courts, was adopted. Another major concession came in the subcommission's insistence that "the Court of Appeal . . . should introduce into the codes . . . by their own initiative or by a demand from the Egyptian government" new laws that responded to changed private or administrative circumstances since 1875.[24] Indeed, had other factors remained equal, the plenary consular meeting's enthusiastic approval of the subcommission's recommendations probably would have led to major changes in Egypt's Mixed Court Charter before the second year of the British occupation ended. As it was, the plan lost British favor and collapsed as soon as it became apparent that certain powers were busy devising ways to turn reform to their own political advantage.

When Camille Barrère predicted success for Martin-Sarzeaud's plan, he already hinted privately that Paris could expect to impose several conditions. Specifically, if the Alexandria court of appeals and the mixed prosecutor's office stood to play a more important role in lawmaking and penal matters after 1884, the French wanted to be sure that their stake in those two key bodies would increase accordingly. Martin-Sarzeaud had already recommended that seven new justices (five Europeans and two Egyptians) should be appointed. The French hoped to gain in these new appointments and also wanted to realize long-standing desires to gallicize Egypt's *ministère public* from the top down, beginning with appointment of a Frenchman to the upgraded prosecutor's slot. Accordingly, Barrère began to wheedle representatives of less important powers politely by promising to help them get more influential appointments if they would accept increased French representation on the high court.[25] Martin-Sarzeaud struck upon a convenient mechanism by noting that two of the seven proposed additions to the appeals bench were already on the Ministry of Justice payroll in the form of auxiliary judges, one French and one Greek. He proposed to make both of these full appeals justices. Although such a move would give France the unique privilege of having two justices on the Alexandria court, the Greek consul gladly concurred.

It was only when special capitulatory commissioner Mr. Egerton submitted his report that Lord Granville and Baring realized that, even though a number of jurisdictional concessions were on the way to resolution in 1884, the other consuls were following French preferences for a stronger Alexandria court of appeals that they themselves hoped to dominate. Surprisingly, Nubar had hastily appointed the French and Greek substitutes to full service on the mixed bench to save these first signs of French willingness to trade compromises.[26] In fact, once Lord Granville learned that no one had tried to check France's double representation by some essential political trade-off, he decided that the price for reform was becoming too high. In the summer of 1884, therefore, word went out to key embassies to suspend the spirit of cooperation that had come with Nubar's government and once again to delay formal adherence to Cairo's mixed court reform plan.

BRITAIN'S SELF-CRITIQUE IN MID-1884

Abandonment of much needed capitulatory reforms, plus several other Egyptian policy problems, caused serious difficulties for Gladstone's government during the remainder of 1884. Certainly the most sharply debated issue, both in Egypt and Westminster, was the problematic fate of Egyptian forces fighting the Mahdist rebellion in the Sudan. Confusion surrounding General Charles Gordon's relief expedition and British military expenditures to secure Egypt's internal and international security led opposition members to question Lord Granville's assurance that the originally stated objectives of the occupation still held.[27] This led to additional queries concerning Egyptian administrative reform efforts under budgetary restrictions imposed by the 1880 liquidation law. Opposition MPs focused on the costly consultative "Egyptian Assembly" in Cairo, continuation of the unreformed mixed capitulatory regime, and apparent chaos in Egypt's system of penal justice to make their points.

MP Sir George Campbell, who had strongly criticized Dual Control policies, asked for information on Cairo's symbolic legislative council and rumors of tacit British sponsorship for brutal penal prosecution methods. Did the British plan to make reasonable adjustments in such untenable "autonomous reform institutions" once pending renegotiation of the 1880 debt law freed their hands? What chance was there to salvage remnants of the Dufferin Plan should new debt law negotiations fail? Lord Fitzmaurice's responses in Westminster indicated that he was not certain just how Anglo-Egyptian authorities planned to proceed. Then *The Times* printed letters by both Lloyd and Maxwell leveling charges of political duplicity and deficiencies in the recently installed Egyptian penal codes. These set off attacks against Sir Evelyn Baring himself. MP Coleridge Kennard asked, for example, why Maxwell had not been officially invited to offer his views of the local political reasons for termination of his contract. He also wondered why the Agency had done nothing to investigate Clifford Lloyd's charges that executive officials were being shielded from prosecution for using torture to extract confessions submitted to Egypt's new "brigandage commission."[28] As controversy mounted, MPs particularly concerned with Egyptian legal reform began repeating Maxwell's public denunciation of Evelyn Baring's "grave dereliction of duty" in handling Egypt's internal affairs.

Baring managed to avert censure for his role in Egypt's aborted legal reforms largely because the London Conference on Egypt's public debt collapsed in August 1884. Despite attempts to convince an international conference to loosen the terms of the 1880 liquidation law, France reacted to rejection of its mixed court reform overtures by vetoing Lord Granville's financial requests outright. For watchdogs over London's already strained Exchequer, this setback spelled more difficulties than any other issue in Gladstone's Egyptian maneuverings. Everyone knew Cairo needed budgetary flexibility and long-term credits to carry on public works development projects until Egypt's tax base rose enough to make the khedivate self-supporting. Without the international cooperation Lord Granville had requested from the London Conference, even less costly but essential administrative budgets would soon have to be cut back. Recently installed *ahliyya* courts, for example, could not hope to expand outside a few Delta towns for years to come.

By mid-1884, many political activists in Britain were ready to raise these aspects of the Egyptian dilemma to supplement attacks on Gladstone's home rule approach to the Irish Question. During the last six months of the 1880–85 Liberal government, therefore, the Foreign Office had either to defend its original occupation policies or to take more drastic measures to achieve financial and administrative goals. Conservatives and liberals alike realized that continued delay merely strengthened radical demands for immediate and unconditional withdrawal, something neither major party was likely to admit.

In fact, informed observers who considered imperial strategy within a wider regional framework must have recognized that Britain's presence in Egypt from this point forward counted for much more than the general public realized. Only two years before, the Foreign Office had looked to Ambassador Dufferin to rationalize the occupation along lines laid down by Lord Palmerston during the heyday of the Ottoman Tanzimat. Events that had taken place in Egypt and east of Suez since Sharif Pasha's replacement by Nubar, however, were becoming important enough to affect traditional British Eastern Question policies. The impending "victory" of Mahdist forces in the Sudan was not in itself likely to cause new directions in occupation tactics during the second half of 1884. At this date, at least, retention of unexplored expanses of the Upper Nile promised to be not only too costly, but without major political advantages, either for Britain or for other foreign interests, including the Ottoman sultanate.

By contrast, experts on either side of parliamentary opposition lines could see that Lord Granville's decision to use British forces to occupy Berbera on the Gulf of Aden during the summer of 1884 was directly in keeping with a long-standing imperial objective of controlling Indian Ocean access to the Suez.[29] Once east of Suez sea-lanes became subject to British surveillance from both sides of the Gulf of Aden, the strategic importance of the Mediterranean access to Suez was bound to increase far beyond anything imagined when Benjamin Disraeli occupied Cyprus in 1878. Especially in view of new signs of colonialist appetite in both France and Italy in the mid-1880s, Britain's presence in Egypt was losing its initially rather vague relevance to traditional Eastern Question policies. Now it was easier to see how France's tightening of its recently installed protectorate in Tunisia or Italy's open designs on Eritrea could easily run counter to Britain's strategic interests in the eastern basin of the Mediterranean.[30]

Thus, there was considerable political incentive for Gladstone's government to use its position in Egypt in ways that would have trade-off value in a much broader international political and high-level financial field. Despite rising public controversy over awkward issues like the Sudan relief expedition, the lord head of the Admiralty came to Cairo in the fall of 1884 to explore possible new terms for British policy in Egypt. Even though circumstances finally appeared right to abandon original and outmoded Tanzimat-era Eastern Question tactics, however, the British failed to obtain their goals. Once again the legal reform imbroglio posed obstacles that neither Gladstone nor his Conservative successor could overcome during the next phase of the occupation regime.

CAPITULATORY IMPLICATIONS OF THE NORTHBROOK MISSION AND EGYPTIAN OPINION

Gladstone's appointment of Thomas Baring, earl of Northbrook, to lead an investigatory mission to Cairo promised to be controversial from the outset. At least one sign of reorientation in cabinet assessment of the Egyptian Question was the fact that Northbrook came to his assignment from the highest position in the Admiralty, where concerns for imperial defense obviously extended far beyond Cyprus and Suez. Gladstone may also have preferred a man who would not depend on coaching from traditional Eastern Question policymakers. As a former viceroy of India under both Gladstone and Disraeli (between 1872 and 1876), Northbrook had firsthand experience of political rivalry between proponents of "native reforms" and more direct means of protecting Britain's strategic interests beyond Istanbul. By the time he became head of the Admiralty in 1880, Northbrook leaned in the direction of the latter. He definitely supported a stronger British military presence in Egypt and was among the four cabinet ministers who originally pressed for General Gordon's emergency expedition to Khartoum.[31]

The Liberal cabinet's search for fresh policy recommendations in the fall of 1884, however, was more immediately financial and legalistic in nature. International rejection of debt law reform in the summer of 1884 had unleashed strong public criticism of the unimpressive record of the Dufferin Plan since 1882. Lord Granville realized, therefore, that the lord of the Admiralty's report on Egyptian finances and legal reform could have much more political weight than any previous Foreign Office recommendations originating at the ambassadorial level.

From the outset of Northbrook's visit, London insisted his only aim was to prove that necessary administrative services could not be provided by any regime that had to conform to Egypt's 1880 liquidation law. After conferring with outgoing financial adviser Colvin, however, Northbrook unexpectedly chose an English-trained Muslim judge from India as his sole official aide in Egypt. Some observers thought that Samiullah Khan was coming not to examine the still uncertain effects of "native justice" under the occupation, but rather to rubber-stamp radical measures in any branch of Egypt's judicial system whose operations could affect the financial solvency of the government.[32] For the *Daily Telegraph*, this meant a single stroke against the mixed courts and assumption by London of unilateral responsibility for foreign capitulatory interests in Egypt. The Telegraph's correspondent wrote:

> As Egypt cannot accept a loan or reduce the interest on her public debt without acting contrary to the law of liquidation or exposing the government to proceedings . . . before the international tribunals . . . people here anticipate that Lord Northbrook will either abolish the latter or obtain the same end by downright annexation. . . . It is notorious that several members of the English Government consider no satisfactory arrangement . . . possible whilst the international tribunals afford a basis of action against the Egyptian Government.[33]

Although the overall impact of Lord Northbrook's mission fell short of such extremist expectations, several of his actions helped ease opposition criticism of Granville's Egypt policy. He began, for example, by advising Nubar to disregard sinking fund provisions in the 1880 liquidation law and to use surplus revenues from assigned government departments for rising costs in other vital areas. This was clearly inviting a new round of confrontation with two ad hoc creations of the pre-1882 era, each of which seemed determined to hamper British reform efforts. Indeed, the immediate reaction of the Public Debt Commission and the mixed courts did just that. Northbrook assured Nubar that any new crisis precipitated by the

Debt Commission could be resolved much like the earlier Tedeschi indemnities case. This time, however, the liquidation law was judged to be clearly separate from the 1875 capitulatory conventions. The Alexandria court rejected government defense of its emergency moves and even threatened to sue individual ministers for earmarked monies they had spent unless repayment came immediately.[34]

Aggressive mixed court involvement in the sinking fund scandal responded in several ways to Nubar's expectation that London should and would adopt a harder-line policy in 1885. The renewed financial crisis dramatically emphasized the fact that, as long as remnants of ad hoc capitulatory arrangements from the Dual Control period stayed in place, any hope of improving local administration would remain a chimera. When it came to immediate policy changes to save local fiscal reform and public works projects, therefore, Northbrook could be expected to press very strongly for British intervention in Egypt's judicial and public debt regime.

The Foreign Office actually used these implications in Northbrook's November 1884 report to menace its critics. Results were more immediate than anything British financial advisers, including Evelyn Baring himself, had been able to accomplish during the entire period of Dual Control–mixed court rivalry between 1876 and 1882. Within two weeks, and before the Gladstone cabinet itself concluded that Northbrook's recommendations were too interventionist to serve the Liberal government's troubled political cause in 1884, France decided to resume debt law negotiations. It also allowed suspension of mixed court sinking fund judgments until budgetary pressures could be resolved by a new liquidation settlement.[35]

The Foreign Office's firm backing for Lord Northbrook in this first stage of confrontation with the Caisse impressed Nubar's cabinet. Even though the source of influence that avoided an open crisis over the sinking fund was on the Rue de Rivoli, Egyptian actors in the near scandal were clearly shaken. The incident had shown once again that the mixed courts would not hesitate to identify with international political and financial concerns that had little or no connection with the limited civil code placed under their aegis. Especially for high officials who faced possible seizure of their property to pay for emergency expenditures of earmarked funds, the importance of having Britain help "tame" the mixed courts was now quite apparent. No one yet understood how this rather sudden recognition of common objectives between the British and the Egyptian cabinet would be integrated into Northbrook's attempts to have his views officially adopted in London. Nubar's immediate call for a new British nominee to fill Maxwell's vacant post, however, suggested that, for the moment, the cabinet's special emissary carried more political weight in Cairo than Evelyn Baring himself.[36]

With each sign of reassessment in British policy during the last months of 1884, newspapers like *Al-Watan* and *Al-Waqt* regained some of their pre-1882 verve and called for local Egyptian adjustments to simple Tanzimat-inspired legal reform models. Just as in the 1880–82 press campaign, it was a Christian-edited newssheet that set the tone for debate. Armenian publisher Alexandre Seroufian insisted on the complete impersonality of the law and called for clearer separation of sectarian and civil interests in the courts. During Northbrook's visit, *Az-Zaman* repeated clichés used by nationalist factions in 1881 and later borrowed by parliamentary critics of continued Dual Control legal reform tactics in Egypt: abolition of the mixed courts would be necessary if Lord Dufferin's Organic Law was to help create "autonomous" Egyptian institutions.[37] Once the sinking fund scandal gave evidence that the Foreign Office shared this conviction, Seroufian redirected *Az-Zaman*'s approach. The new thrust was meant to help Northbrook's assistant, Samiullah Khan, determine why Dufferin's local legal reform plan was not working effectively. In fact, for everyone but Nubar, the time seemed right openly to criticize the *ahliyya* courts as a first step toward preparing them for a more important role.

The Arabic press did not adopt the same simplistic charges of bench-level corruption that foreign critics used to explain Egypt's faltering local court system. Besides mentioning handicaps caused by excessive geographical centralization, newspapers published letters decrying auxiliary services and organizational defects that the judges themselves were powerless to correct. High fees (derived mechanically from schedules set years before for the mixed courts), loss or inaccuracy of legal documents prepared by court agents, and uneven quality among individuals claiming to be court lawyers were all factors discouraging confidence in the post-1882 legal system.[38] When *Az-Zaman*'s correspondents followed Samiullah on his investigation of court operations outside the capital, however, respondents to inquiries often overlooked such practical questions. Instead, most focused on the judge, who was supposed somehow (by such biased spokesmen as the *mudirs* and *qadis* in *shari*ᶜ*a* courts!) to be personally responsible for both the spirit and effects of codes handed down from Cairo.[39]

The Arabic press agreed that the recognized professional status of any new judges should make them the only officials authorized to review courtroom irregularities, including charges against advocates serving court litigants. *Az-Zaman* thought the lack of government training programs, not personal deficiencies, was the main cause for professional failings in the judiciary. "The real problem," it said, "is that the ministry has not established a law school [*sic*]. . . . So far there is no difference between the training of those replaced and the new judges. . . . Wouldn't it be more logical to appoint those who have studied law in Europe as teachers and institute an obligatory course for all appointees? The government should realize that it will not shame judges already appointed by formal efforts to teach them the laws."[40]

Supporters of increased responsibility for professionally trained legalists in the court system were obviously distressed by the only concrete ministerial action taken before Lord Northbrook's departure. When Nubar announced that the 1884 Cairo felony commission would be extended to 1885 and that provincial branch operations would be run entirely by *mudirs*, even the *Egyptian Gazette* echoed *Az-Zaman*'s concerns. Both papers opposed increasing dependence on ad hoc bodies that now judged and even hanged "brigands" without reference to *ahliyya* personnel or codes.[41] For *Az-Zaman* (soon to be taken to court itself for antigovernment slander), what Nubar was doing was an affront, both to the new *ahliyya* courts and to Egypt's ᶜ*ulama'*, whose word on legal issues had always somehow to be kept in mind. Predicting that the government's ad hoc appointments would only lead to more complications, Seroufian wrote:

> We should only appoint individuals who have . . . studied the laws. . . . It has been said that there is a lack of qualified people but . . . some of the Azhar ᶜ*ulama'* are competent for *ahliyya* judicial service. Since the principles of shariatic law are at the basis of secular civil law, they could offer socially familiar ways for solving many problems. . . . If real results are desired, . . . the appointment of such learned men is preferable to the appointment of engineers and officials who have been dismissed from other government offices.[42]

Lord Northbrook was never invited by the London cabinet to unveil more than the main lines of his markedly interventionist scheme for occupation policy for criticism by Gladstone's political rivals. *Az-Zaman* could not have known, therefore, that, even though the already hated brigandage commissions were extended with tacit British approval, the first stage of a trade-off in Anglo-Egyptian responsibility for local justice had been made before the head of the Admiralty left Cairo. In fact, Northbrook offered to increase British political input into all future Egyptian capitulatory questions, ranging from the debt law through reform of the mixed courts.[43] In return, he clearly expected both Nubar and Baring to stop insisting that British advisers "too wedded to English law" were harming plans for improving both mixed and *ahliyya* justice. Lord Granville received hints of this when Baring himself went through a new stage of semantic transformation. By November 1884, when Bombay court judge Raymond West was recommended by Lord Northbrook to become the new *ahliyya* attorney general in Egypt, Baring had rationalized earlier "mishandling" of Maxwell's dismissal only a few months before. He now claimed it was no longer the imagined political dangers of English law but concern for demonstrated flaws in "Roman law" that should determine the man and the methods guiding the Cairo *procureur*'s post.[44]

EGYPTIAN JUDICIAL POLITICS IN THE LAST MONTHS OF THE LIBERAL GOVERNMENT

Had the Liberal cabinet followed policy revisions suggested by Lord Northbrook, Evelyn Baring might have found many points of agreement with Raymond West during the latter's six months of service in Egypt. He would also have shared any credit due for finding a way out of contradictions in the Dufferin Plan and defining new conditions for Britain's occupation regime as early as 1885. As it turned out, however, during the entire first half of 1885, the Gladstone cabinet was absorbed in attempts to reforge party unity and retain a parliamentary majority. The government resigned following the Commons' rejection of its proposed general budget in June 1885. Until then, few political leaders had time to turn from internal issues like Irish home rule or the franchise and redistribution of seats bills to wonder whether Lord Northbrook's report was worth another divisive controversy or not. Even major news from Egypt, including the fall of Khartoum in February and Granville's announcement of preliminary capitulatory agreement on revision of the 1880 debt law, did not receive the attention that would have been automatic two years earlier.[45] Given this short-term turn in parliamentary politics, the Cairo consulate suddenly started to play down its earlier agreements with Northbrook. In fact, when a new British attorney general made recommendations that were very well received locally in Egypt, Baring suddenly found himself trying hard to avoid being identified, with Northbrook, as an interventionist or "Indianizer."

Raymond West's appointment represented only a small part of Lord Northbrook's recommendations for increased intervention in several areas. The Egyptian foreign press had not forgotten, however, that, two years before, the job West now held was deemed vital by the British for strengthening *ahliyya* law and preparing Egyptians to take over the temporary mixed court system.[46] Once West arrived, however, it became clear that the Bombay judge maintained some distance between his work and such higher-level politics of legal reform. His first report to Nubar did register alarm that, after some cautious overtures in 1884, Egyptian litigants with important civil suits were staying away from the *ahliyya* bench. Literally hundreds were presumably waiting for an opportunity to bring property transactions before the mixed courts.[47] West suggested early on that the dilemma was organizational and not necessarily due to double standards between mixed and local Egyptian court personnel. He provided statistics showing that, because no summary jurisdictions had functioned since 1881, a small number of important cases in the four provincial courts were competing with hundreds of minor *fallahin* disputes. Thus, although the higher appeals bench had been quite busy during 1884, its cumulative jurisprudence still reflected the rudimentary legal interests of litigants whose cases were really out of place in Cairo.

Already in his first report, West argued for recognition that there was an almost separate category of "native justice" that did not require the full gamut of *ahliyya* procedural law. He also criticized several hasty decisions Nubar had sponsored, apparently merely to prove that he was busy dealing with dilemmas caused by the Dufferin Plan. Only weeks after West's arrival, and probably as a result of his insistence, the government began reconsidering some early appointments to the new bench and canceling contracts with judges whose technical incompetence clearly hampered court operations.[48] At the same time, West disagreed openly with Nubar over expanding felony commissions to judge serious crimes that the regular courts could not yet handle effectively. His opposition to brigandage commissions was, like his view of civil justice, based on the long-term aim of building up Egyptian skills to deal with more weighty and technical cases that skeptics claimed were beyond local competence. Creating an ad hoc authority over felony violations was likely to have the opposite effect: where application of codified procedures by professional judges could make the difference between equity and major miscarriages of justice, Nubar was expanding exceptional jurisdictions.

West actively sought opinions beyond the Egyptian cabinet and his fellow Anglo-Egyptian officials. His ideas were openly discussed, therefore, by several local interest groups just beginning to express their views on justice. He found unexpected support in the token Cairo Legislative Council, whose members could not officially initiate reform schemes, but who tried to debate cabinet policies on their own. In mid-1884, the Council voiced misgivings over the absence in Egypt's codes of provisions for the most commonplace village-level misdemeanors. Its chairman, Hasan Effendi ᶜAbd al-Raziq, even presaged West's views by recommending adoption of a separate set of laws to handle such cases without having to rely on complicated *ahliyya* penal procedures.[49] When West sidestepped Nubar's Ministry of Justice and asked Council members their opinion on other questions, they responded quite eagerly.[50] A bit more time had to pass before evidence of input from other local parties appeared. The stress that West's final (August 1885) report placed on the Khedivial Law School and conditions of advocacy before the *ahliyya* courts, however, suggested a similar pattern of contacts in the Ministry of Education and even in private law offices in Cairo.

Despite storms of local controversy when Nubar extended commission of brigandage operations in both Lower and Upper Egypt, London never forwarded instructions either to support or to reject West's summary civil and penal proposals.[51] Official silence continued right up to Gladstone's resignation in June. This was particularly discouraging for Evelyn Baring, whose local mandate had become dependent from month to month on higher-level political developments in London. There were also signs of malaise among Egyptian parties who began to imagine diverse implications of West's reform efforts on their own lives. Judging from accounts in the local Arabic press, the British adviser managed to produce a larger number of ministerial decisions affecting local court personnel than at any time over the previous two years. First there were high-level appointments, including the promotion of a Khedivial Law School graduate, Hamdullah Emine, from West's office to the Cairo *ahliyya* bench and a similar appointment for Qasim Bey Amin, who had just earned a *licence en droit* in France.[52] West's hand could also be seen behind the establishment of a Ministry of Justice council to discipline negligent bailiffs and recorders. Another decision allowed advanced law school students to attend court deliberations as assistants to West's own *parquet* staff.[53] In fact, some members of the Egyptian cabinet were so impressed with these changes that they began raising the question of immediate transfer of competence over contraventions (*not* felonies and brigandage) to district *ma'mur*s. Such a step would have been in keeping with West's idea to free professional jurists to accumulate a record of expertise in serious cases comparable to their counterparts in the mixed courts.

BARING'S ROLE IN UNDERMINING THE "WEST PLAN"

By the time Raymond West submitted his final report on mixed and local justice, a new Conservative government had taken over in London. In some ways an assumed apolitical expert like West may have been relieved at the change, since it freed him from any assumed service to either Northbrook's or Granville's Egyptian policy biases. Gladstone's departure, however, did not mean that an interim government under Lord Salisbury would know how or even want to depoliticize ten-year-old Egyptian reform questions. Moreover, even though Salisbury began his first term as prime minister by dispatching privy councillor Sir Henry Drummond-Wolff on a special Egypt-related mission to Istanbul, two national elections over the next twelve months still separated the Conservatives from firm political control in Whitehall. Pending assurance of a parliamentary majority and Drummond-Wolff's elaboration of a comprehensive basis for the Conservatives' own Egyptian policy, therefore, the new cabinet still called for expert opinions on medium-range aims for the Cairo Agency.

Raymond West's August 1885 report fit these objectives well. He argued that Egypt's hope for an eventual single system of justice at the highest level would not be harmed by recognizing a separate "native" tradition free from the complexities of codes adopted between

1875 and 1883.[54] This time West even alluded to wider political considerations he knew were foremost in the minds of those who made Anglo-Egyptian policy. He was direct in attacking the mixed courts' hostility toward the Egyptian government and their "disdain for the people and institutions of the country." The capitulations themselves he called "an encroachment . . . since the original political situation which brought them has now passed away," leaving "insolence . . . of Europeans toward the native official, not the tyranny . . . of the latter" as a chief worry in different ministries. His general call to "assist Turkey in maintaining its sovereignty in Egypt" followed typical Eastern Question phraseology. He apparently thought, however, that Britain could best achieve that goal by encouraging Istanbul to study Egypt's particular experiences with legal reform since 1876 and to turn them into imperial priorities nearly a decade after the closing of the Tanzimat Council. Thus,

> the Empire should adopt its own codes of civil law founded on European models. . . . Nothing makes a man feel . . . outside the circle of sovereignty . . . more than . . . his ignorance of how to proceed when he has suffered some palpable wrong. Similarity of legal consciousness, on the other hand, tends to consolidation by producing a sense of national identity, as was seen in the Roman and new British Empire. . . . Something here might be borrowed by Turkey at large from Egypt and, in the interest of the former, the continued existence of any striking contrast between "standard" Ottoman laws and ad hoc arrangements [like Egypt's brigandage commissions or the mixed courts?] is to be . . . avoided.[55]

It is difficult to gauge the effect of such thinking on the first stages of negotiations between Lord Salisbury's privy councillor and the Ottoman Porte in 1885. Soon after Drummond-Wolff outlined preliminary conditions for British withdrawal, however, and just as West was busy drawing up a codified version of his summary justice scheme, London decided to grant the Cairo Agency totally independent initiative in Egyptian legal reform strategy for the first time since the spring of 1884. On 6 November, Lord Salisbury announced that "circumstances" that had prevented changes in the mixed courts since mid-1882 no longer prevailed. Instructions soon followed to prepare several of the abortive 1884 capitulatory commission's proposals for circulation and ratification by the powers. These pinpointed revisions in mixed law on judicial mortgages, agricultural bills of exchange, and commercial securities. Thus, it appeared that the Conservative Foreign Office aimed at alleviating the largest number of individual private grievances, both Egyptian and capitulatory, before reopening capitulatory debate over the future of the Mixed Court Charter itself.[56]

The fact that two full months passed before Nubar answered Salisbury's note suggests that he resented London's handing down of priorities that were not his own. A more serious indication of trouble to come, however, was Nubar's desire to direct attention away from grass-roots procedural questions back to his own traditional "sweeping" panacea for court reform.

Although the British Consulate neglected to inform London of the fact, Nubar's first move after receiving Salisbury's policy statement was to announce his intention to work once again for early "fusion" of mixed and *ahliyya* justice.[57] As this obviously ran counter to West's report and ignored London's preference for immediate procedural changes in the mixed codes, Nubar needed only to wait for reactions from the British Agency. Although no record of private dealings survives, Baring must have worked very rapidly to garner necessary Egyptian backing for Salisbury's modest three-point mixed court plan. What is certain is that he paid for Nubar's change of heart by helping to bury local reforms already supported by the Egyptian legislative council and a nascent body of Cairo lawyers themselves. This helps explain why, even before Nubar again widened brigandage commission operations against rising public objections, informed local sources ruled out the "prospect of any great change being made in the native courts" with or without the benefit of advice from the attorney general's office.[58]

In fact, West's plan to simplify and decentralize summary justice was quickly nipped in the bud by Nubar with the Cairo Agency's tacit approval. Even the local French press seemed surprised to learn that, when the Egyptian minister denounced plans for single judge summary courts as "too radical and involving more extensive reforms than . . . necessary," the *procureur* received no backing from Evelyn Baring.[59] Instead the consul argued privately in support of Nubar's promise that local court paralysis could be eliminated by "working the present system vigorously," and adhering to the Dufferin Plan.[60] Most revealing was his support of Nubar's renewed drive for "legislative unity." This concern translated into a desire "not to root up"

French laws that, according to the consul's obviously shifting estimates, fit Egypt's patterns of administration. West's intention to "implant an entirely new system" ran counter to Egypt's need for "a procureur . . . not a legislator. . . . Termination of West's contract may give rise to an outcry that. . . . English officials here are not sufficiently supported and that nothing is being done to reform the law courts. . . . Therefore I proposed . . . to institute a commission of Europeans and Egyptians to examine West's very elaborate plan. This would, I think, *pave the way for West's departure*, which . . . is inevitable."[61]

FOREIGN AND EGYPTIAN OPINION FOLLOWING RAYMOND WEST'S RESIGNATION

Raymond West resigned his post in Egypt just as Nubar's cabinet met to consider his draft revisions in local court procedure. Although surprised reactions came from many quarters, the strongest was that of Cairo correspondent Charles Moberley-Bell. In an attack aimed at the Foreign Office, *The Times'* future editor predicted that West's scheme would

> be relegated to the pigeon holes of the. . . Ministry of Justice unless her Majesty's Government insist on [its] serious consideration. . . . The reports . . . assert the existence of a state of things that, in Naples or Bulgaria, would have aroused the . . . indignation of England. . . . They refer, not to abuses which England has failed to redress, but to abuses *created* under the Anglo-Egyptian government. . . . The honor of the English Government demands . . . a strict inquiry into these allegations.[62]

The Arabic press could not afford to be as direct in its criticism, but papers like *Al-ᶜAlam* and *Az-Zaman* were clearly pessimistic. West's failure, they felt, would probably be followed by new guidelines for those sectors of the legal system that benefited mainly foreign interests. Egyptians would be asked to continue to persevere under a combination of outmoded traditions and innovations that had never been clearly understood by the majority of the population.[63] It was perhaps to oppose rising cynicism that several local lawyers chose this date to found *Al-Huquq*, Egypt's first private organ to examine possibilities for social and professional advancement through modern legal reform.

The decision to print a specialized legal journal seems to have been a side effect of Raymond West's brief service in Egypt. In fact,

Al-Huquq's first issue acknowledged local lawyers' debt to West for encouraging them to form a committee to debate "the rights and duties of their profession, as is done in other advanced countries."[64] Although little specific information has survived concerning the individuals who founded *Al-Huquq* in 1886, two personalities, Amin Shumayyil and Saᶜd Zaghlul, may be singled out as revealing prototypes. The first, who remained editor until his death in 1897, was the member of a Syrian Christian family with business interests in Egypt since the 1870s. He migrated to Egypt in the early years of Abdulhamid's reign and soon developed an active interest in the political and social problems of his adopted country. The second personality was, of course, a native Egyptian whose early years as a court lawyer most certainly played a role in preparing him for his more famous political career after 1900.

The case of Amin Shumayyil is an interesting example of the way in which Egyptians of different origins, as well as Syrian immigrants, gradually came to connect abstract Ottoman Tanzimat pronouncements with their own personal stakes in local court operations. Like most individuals who entered the new profession of advocacy in Egypt during the 1880s, Shumayyil possessed extensive experience but no formal legal training. Unlike some of his Egyptian colleagues who enjoyed either high social station or a professional education, however, he had the advantages of a Lebanese Christian who knew something about European society, ideas, and—perhaps most importantly—methods of business. The older brother of the more famous Syrian Arab literary figure Shibli Shumayyil followed up a secondary education in missionary schools by interpreting for a Maronite bishop who visited Rome in 1848 and 1849. This qualified him to serve as the bishop's assistant in Istanbul during the early 1850s. He next traveled to London and Liverpool, where family textile trade connections encouraged him to open an outlet with his brother Bishara.

In 1860, the family established a three-cornered trade in Syria, Alexandria, and Liverpool. Amin himself was responsible for Alexandrian affairs during the American Civil War. These years undoubtedly provided many occasions to witness clashes between European and Tanzimat concepts of law and private commercial enterprise and the reality of Egypt justice under the capitulations. After six more years in England (1869–75), he returned to trading interests in Gharbiyya Province in Egypt. In 1885, only a year after the opening of the *ahliyya* courts, Shumayyil decided to turn his knowledge of European legal practices and government regulations to lucrative use by assisting Egyptian clients as a *muhami*. At this date, he probably met Sa^{c}ad Zaghlul, another "self-made" advocate who opened a law office in Cairo in the same period.

Zaghlul's case was somewhat different than Shumayyil's. Following elementary and secondary studies in the traditional provincial school system, he left Gharbiyya Province, where his father was a village headman, to study at the Azhar in the late 1870s. Association with Shaykh Muhammad ^{c}Abduh, who was then editor of *Al-Waqa'i^{c} al-Misriyya*, led to his first job as a member of the official journal staff around 1880.[65] From this he moved to a position as an aide in Tawfiq's Ministry of the Interior. By 1882, just as the chaos of the constitutional nationalist movement peaked, he was serving as director of the legal department of the same ministry. This experience during the transitional period between the local council and *ahliyya* court systems prompted him, together with Husayn Saqr from the same government department, to launch (in 1884) a private practice representing Egyptian litigants before the new judiciary. Several years later, Zaghlul decided to improve his skills as a lawyer by pursuing formal studies in the Khedivial Law School. This made him one of the technically most qualified contributors to *Al-Huquq*'s columns during the late 1880s. It also made possible eventual appointment (in 1892) to the Cairo court of appeals and a high-level career in government and politics after 1900.

Whatever professional future was held out to *Al-Huquq*'s original collaborators, its initial editorials bore a mark if not of naivete then certainly of idealism. Shumayyil's description of the responsibilities of Egypt's first generation of private advocates, for example, reflected attachment both to Tanzimat rhetoric and to the same ideas that Raymond West had tried to integrate into his 1885 reports:

> Each people and state possesses a characteristic set of laws. Every judge and lawyer must therefore first know the laws of his own country and then study, as far as is possible, the laws of other countries. . . . In the Ottoman Empire there has always been the science of *fiqh*, as well as a number of other laws [*qawanin*] that have been necessary due to the number of different people in it and the different types of legal relationships that inevitably occur. Our Sultan has ordered that the books on *fiqh* be supplemented to bring them up to date, and that important sections of European laws be published throughout the Ottoman

> lands. . . . A thorough study of the basic principles of these laws is necessary, because it is precisely those general principles that tie each individual action to the various and related guidelines from which analogies and comparisons [with Western law] can be made for future government in Egypt and the Empire generally.[66]

The problem idealistic legalists encountered in 1886 was much the same as that of any academic or specialist: their newspaper was read infrequently, if ever, by nonlawyers. What concerned other types of influential people was not how Raymond West had stimulated local lawyers to establish a journal of law and what ideas were expressed in that journal, but how the void created by West's resignation would be filled. Thus, while the Foreign Office tried to placate critics in Parliament and *The Times*, the Cairo Agency tried to restore confidence in its handling of top-level Justice Department priorities, especially where clashes between mixed and *ahliyya* jurisdictions were concerned.

A good opportunity came when the exiled ex-khedive Isma^cil sued the Egyptian government in the *ahliyya* courts for losses incurred when his estates were ceded to guarantee the 1878 Rothschild loan. This alarmed the Agency for two reasons. First, there was always a fear that Isma^cil's obvious personal influence might sway the judges' decision. Second, even if deliberations were objective, a favorable decision might encourage a run on the courts by other Egyptians who had lost fortunes during the period of fiscal chaos between 1878 and 1882. This could spell disaster for the new terms for debt liquidation obtained in 1885. Baring had little trouble, therefore, persuading Nubar to delay the proceedings until the case could be transferred to the mixed courts, which could be counted on to reduce Isma^cil's claims to reasonable proportions. Ironically, this was done by having the (foreign-staffed) Ministry of Finance legal section argue that cases affecting the public debt in any way were ipso facto mixed and fell under the 1875 Charter! Such arguments obviously received support from the foreign community and ultimately caused Isma^cil to abandon the courts and accept arbitration for a much smaller claim. The only local newspaper to resist was *Al-Huquq*, whose editor recalled earlier, less spectacular, cases against the government treasury that had stayed under local jurisdiction. The new lawyers' journal feared that introducing questionable principles of mixed interest in such cases would bring "new defeats for the country" just as the local courts were beginning to gain independent stature.[67]

Other parties, however, had special reasons to encourage Nubar to use mixed interest to sidestep the jurisdiction of the *ahliyya* judges. French Consul d'Aunay, for one, assumed that the West fiasco had seriously disillusioned Egyptians who were tiring of the vagaries of British guidance in legal reform. The fact that the ex-khedive's case had jumped from one to another jurisdiction and then completely out of the courts led him to try to embarrass London once again by pushing for the abolition of "native justice" altogether. Repetition of intervention in similar cases in the future, he reported, "will throw . . . discredit on the native tribunals. Actually it is difficult for the government, who themselves find them corrupt, to persist in imposing the native tribunals on litigants. The . . . consequences of the incident should be, if not the suppression, at least the fusion of the native with the mixed courts. . . . Nubar favors this, and assures me that Pauncefote . . . shares his views."[68] D'Aunay added confidentially that unspecified "functionaries in the Egyptian service" were ready to draw up a "modified fusion" proposal that would consolidate earlier gains the French had made on the mixed court of appeals.

FAILURE OF NUBAR'S 1886 FUSION PLAN

The coincidence of a new court reform plan so soon after West's departure caused Paris to wonder about possible duplicity in British and Egyptian motives. Foreign minister de Freycinet, himself a veteran of earlier Dual Control strategy, suspected any move that, behind a guise of improvement in administrative standards, might increase Egyptian control over the mixed courts. Before he could get more information, however, Nubar had opened the fusion question to public debate. On 5 May 1886, he announced that the "mixed judges were ready to participate in a single superior appeals jurisdiction, provided that the principle and functions [of the Mixed Court Charter] remained intact."[69] When d'Aunay asked Nubar if he actually intended to alter mixed court operations without prior approval from the powers, the Egyptian seemed so sure of himself that the consul finally understood that the plan had indeed been hatched with Agency support.

Nubar's 8 May 1886 private memorandum to Evelyn Baring was ostensibly intended to explain Egyptian reasons for rejecting West's local court scheme. It began by candidly recalling contradictions caused by the Liberal government's partial sponsorship for Dual Control reform options in 1880. Lord Dufferin's task, Nubar claimed, had been to take over the Control's idea that a completely new system of European-style courts would reduce the dominance of the mixed courts in Egypt's internal affairs. For three years the Cairo Ministry went on assuming that, "if the powers refused to free Egypt from all [nagging capitulatory] obligations . . . imposed upon her . . . , England would support the . . . government in denouncing the mixed court convention. The grounds for this would be that an independent judicial system had proved itself capable of functioning according to . . . the principles of the mixed tribunals. . . ."[70] West's proposals had been dropped because they ignored this last objective. In their place, Nubar drew up a partial fusion plan to guarantee immediate equality between Egyptians and foreigners at least in major cases of civil law. To make fusion appear particularly attractive, he offered a superior court reform that would have attracted any policymaker who wanted to be certain that relations between the mixed courts and the Egyptian government would not deteriorate once the occupation ended. Superficially, the Egyptians were admitting that hopes in 1883 for a completely autonomous European-style court system had been premature. Until a more fully competent body of local jurists could be trained (in fact one of the main thrusts of West's grass-roots plan), the cabinet was ready to settle for a new combined superior court that would take all Egyptian appeals immediately.

Here Baring drew conclusions that proved his own support for Nubar's plan. Although original appointments had brought Belgian and Dutch judges into the *ahliyya* courts, no rule technically prohibited adding *British* nominees to a combined appeals bench. If such extracapitulatory appointees could serve simultaneously as full members of a combined appeals court, their influence over other nationalities' mixed court justices would make fusion politically very attractive, with or without a British commitment to withdraw.[71]

Baring became so attracted to the idea of appeals court fusion that he failed to note important disagreement on the subject, especially within local Egyptian circles. Arabic newssheets probably did not realize that the real aim in adding more British judges to an expanded mixed appeals court was to counteract the dominant representation France had won on the same bench two years before.

What they feared most was that politically motivated reform zealots might lose the few advances the *ahliyya* courts had begun to make on their own. The issue even caused *Al-Huquq* to drop its claims of purely objective professionalism to remind Nubar that the mixed courts had failed to change with obviously changing conditions of Egyptian government and society. Partial judicial fusion would help very little unless there were simultaneous changes in capitulatory controls over the Mixed Court Charter itself. Anything short of this, the lawyers' journal claimed, would be

> admitting that we cannot reform our own courts . . . and that we must appoint foreigners to carry out our own affairs. . . . They will gain control of our judicial institutions, which are most basic to the life of a nation, and become our judges. . . . We shall have frustrated the hope . . . of obtaining by ourselves the knowledge . . . necessary to better our courts. This hope will have been born despondent and despairing, and will end in utter submission. Once the hope is dashed, we shall not find among the men of the country the will to learn the requisite legal sciences, and shall . . . therefore lose the means of establishing autonomous local institutions.[72]

Despite such widespread negative reactions, Baring worked into the summer to try to convince London that partial judicial fusion should be actively supported.[73] Finally, when it appeared that nothing else could draw Foreign Office attention away from Gladstone's preparation for a new round of elections, Baring tried alarmist tactics. He told undersecretary Pauncefote that if the mixed courts were not encouraged to adopt Nubar's fusion plan soon, he would have to press for interventionist measures that made Northbrook's leanings toward "Indianization" appear moderate. Given an unfavorable recommendation, he warned, " . . . the best alternative will be to name an English *procureur* [the third!] and several English judges. The number of *ahliyya* judges will have to be reduced . . . to provide funds for this change. Nubar is quite prepared to act on these lines. He . . . talks of going to England to choose his men."[74] If Nubar actually did promise to cooperate with Baring's new threats to intervene in the Egyptian Ministry of Justice, it was only after an increasingly suspicious mixed bench itself refused to consider his fusion scheme without prior capitulatory approval.[75]

Baring's French rivals themselves never learned the full extent of his disenchantment with the Gladstone government's last-minute failure to support the fusion scheme. Consul d'Aunay was clearly pleased, however, to report that the mixed bench had remained loyal to the principle of protecting court autonomy from external pressures. He, like Baring, seemed unaware of rising Egyptian concern for legal reform and related professional and social issues that went far beyond the narrow circle of cabinet politics. Cynically dismissing government efforts to involve more Egyptians in the work of the mixed courts, for example, he wrote: "Nubar claimed that the native judges could aid considerably in a fused system, but those already on the mixed bench are only able to relate *hadith*s, since they don't even know the Muslim legislation [*sic*!]. All one can expect of them is not to become a hindrance in the work of the courts."[76]

GLADSTONE'S COLONIAL AND LEGAL REFORM LEGACY TO LORD SALISBURY

The role that Egyptian legal reform played in Liberal party politics between 1884 and 1886 illustrates both a problem and a useful perspective in understanding British post-Tanzimat policy generally. The period beginning with Lord Northbrook's mission and ending with abandonment of the Anglo-Egyptian judicial fusion scheme revealed a general phenomenon that would continue under the Conservative government elected in 1886. Both the sinking fund scandal and Evelyn Baring's menace to fire Egyptian judges to Anglicize the local courts suggested that threats were justifiable if their ultimate aim was to weaken the influence of the mixed courts. Several such warnings had been launched on this assumption and then withdrawn by the Liberal government between 1882 and 1886. It was quite likely, therefore, that overriding concern for the potentially disruptive role of the mixed courts would exercise the same influence in British Egyptian policy once Lord Salisbury gained the parliamentary majority he held from 1886 to 1892.

In fact, examination of Drummond-Wolff's abortive mission and its aftermath reveals several little-known angles in the cyclical scenario of British anti-capitulatory interventionist threats. These included one that the Liberal government may have prepared, but had never confronted directly in its Egyptian policy. Eventually the Salisbury government would have to abandon serious hope of negotiating withdrawal from Egypt largely in exchange for capitulatory trade-offs affecting the mixed court regime. By that time, however, a new generation in Egypt and elsewhere in the Ottoman Empire had become convinced of the irreversible nature of the legal system that had been implanted since 1876. Such convictions would come not only from self-satisfied political elites and conservative landowners. Increasingly, input also reflected views of individuals who had trained for professional legal careers that, in the 1890s and even after 1900, could be effectively pursued only in the Egyptian province of the Ottoman Empire.

9

British Definitions of Priorities (1888–90)

No history of Britain's occupation of Egypt omits mention of Sir Henry Drummond-Wolff's mission to Cairo and Istanbul in 1887. Most, however, ignore the diverse interests within Egypt itself that were affected by Lord Salisbury's second round of attempts to settle the quandary of the five-year-old occupation regime. Certain aspects of negotiations that led to the abortive 22 May 1887 convention setting Anglo-Ottoman conditions for British withdrawal, especially an article covering the post-occupation status of Egypt's mixed courts, have all but disappeared from the record.[1] In fact, during the phase of his mission that came after Lord Salisbury's return to Downing Street in July 1886, responsibility for steering British capitulatory policy fell almost entirely on Henry Drummond-Wolff's shoulders. Once again, British short-term transfer of responsibility for long-awaited judicial and legislative changes incited reactions from various private and political interests in Egypt.

PREPARATION FOR OTTOMAN NEGOTIATIONS: WOLFF'S UNDERSTANDING WITH NUBAR

While in London in the summer of 1886, Nubar Pasha tried to discover why the Foreign Office had rejected his judicial fusion plan as a prelude to Wolff's negotiations. Soundings yielded results only when Lord Iddesleigh succeeded Rosebery as foreign secretary. Iddesleigh told Baring he would stress continued financial and military security and—behind these often-repeated guidelines—place all branches of administration "on a better footing . . . by modifying those portions of the capitulations which . . . impede the government in its most essential features."[2]

Drummond-Wolff, who was by then in Egypt, felt that the last pronouncement would tempt the powers to break the Egyptian capitulatory deadlock, if only to encourage an Anglo-Ottoman withdrawal convention.[3] Ironically, this same chance of a breakthrough caused Evelyn Baring some consternation. He feared that, if Rosebery was actually planning an early withdrawal, continued reliance on legal reform bargains would never foster a genuinely stable post-occupation capitulatory regime. This fear increased when Baring realized that Nubar had not yet even tried to find a serious alternative to the combined court of appeals scheme. To avoid letting the Cairo cabinet steer Wolff toward another makeshift fusion plan, he privately suggested removing Nubar from office and starting afresh, especially where future legislative modifications were concerned.[4]

If the Egyptian minister knew about Baring's change in attitude, no signs of disappointment were recorded. Once the powers accepted the mixed procedural changes Salisbury had channeled through his cabinet late in 1885, Nubar felt secure that the British would use his services for additional piecemeal reforms as soon as possible.[5] In fact, just before leaving Egypt for Istanbul, Wolff decided on an open trade of concessions to salvage Salisbury's original 1885 reform strategy. Compromise involved Wolff's promise that Egypt's most important capitulatory legal interests would be protected in any final Anglo-Ottoman convention. In return, Nubar agreed to take immediate steps to increase efficiency in Egypt's local court system.[6]

In fact, the Egyptian cabinet gave a draft of simplified *ahliyya* codes, including Raymond West's earlier court decentralization scheme, to the Legislative Council for debate. Nubar stated that his chief aim was to move toward ending all extrajudicial brigandage commissions.[7] Indeed, during the entire period of Wolff's absence, he followed the main lines of Raymond West's earlier recommendations. The Legislative Council quickly ratified a plan for district-level courts under one trained judge assisted by two assessors chosen among the local notables.[8] Just before this scheme passed, the Cairo lawyers' press congratulated Nubar for accepting what West had argued a year earlier: "Lawmakers . . . should be certain that any proposed changes will not harm the . . . people . . . by allowing permanent defects to become established with time. . . . All these complicated legal mechanisms . . . have come to our country too early. . . . The revision of the laws in a single move and the suppression of the former traditions in order to imitate everything European is something that wisdom . . . should not have allowed."[9]

Such signs of support for his *modus operandi* with Nubar encouraged Wolff to include a capitulatory section in his first round of talks at the Porte. His correspondence shows that the Conservative Foreign Office aimed at more drastic changes than had been attempted at any time in the previous decade. When the high commissioner asked London if he should alter or even abolish mixed court jurisdiction over Egyptian governmental administrations before withdrawal, the answer revealed a very aggressive anti–mixed court spirit in London. Salisbury first urged cancellation of mixed jurisdiction over all government cases "if we can get it, [since] . . . it is the only way of breaking the power of the Caisse."[10] Later, realizing this might destroy the spirit of compromise Wolff wished to foster among British, international, and Egyptian interests, he added: "As to the powers of the mixed courts . . . I think . . . we shall not obtain as much as I have asked for. But I wish to raise the question . . . to lay the foundation for refusing to renew the courts if we do not get some satisfaction."[11]

From Cairo, Evelyn Baring reminded Salisbury that, if Britain chose to return internal autonomy to Egypt, mixed courts would still be quite necessary to protect private foreign interests under the local administration. Limiting them too overtly might invite a return to the anarchy of the 1860s. To avoid this, Baring saw no alternative but to use Wolff's mission to facilitate moves to build international control factors into not only the judicial but also the legislative branches of any post-occupation regime. Most parties already expected a demand to end the criminal immunity of foreigners by expanding mixed court penal jurisdiction. It was Baring, however, who drew attention to another reform need that might offset this loss of consular powers and actually increase foreign sponsorship for a carefully drafted Anglo-Ottoman convention ending the occupation. The Agency now felt ready seriously to widen the influence of the mixed courts in Egypt by creating "some machinery [within the Mixed Court Charter] for making laws applicable to Europeans [to] take the place of diplomatic action."[12] Nubar had already asked for some sort of "special body" to oversee application of new laws to foreigners and Egyptians alike. Baring's sudden willingness formally to involve the mixed courts in the legislative process, however, seemed designed to attract support for Wolff's negotiations at any price, no matter what Cairo's

Legislative Council or other sources of articulate Egyptian opinion thought of the idea.

THE FOREIGN COMMUNITY AND DRAFT NEGOTIATIONS IN ISTANBUL

By early 1887, foreigners in Egypt knew that capitulatory priorities definitely formed part of Wolff's mandate from London. French Consul d'Aunay was especially pleased by the rumor that the British were ready to set up a local "multinational council" in Egypt to channel new laws into the mixed and local codes simultaneously.[13] As far as d'Aunay was concerned, Paris should support Wolff's Ottoman negotiations *if* the proposed withdrawal convention contained an attractive capitulatory article. An indication of his newly cooperative attitude came when Alfred de Vacher's resignation from the influential post of mixed attorney general was not followed by an immediate demand for replacement by a Frenchman.[14]

By March, Wolff forwarded draft terms for an Anglo-Ottoman convention on Egypt's status after Britain's withdrawal. The first sections, of course, dealt with obvious military and strategic questions, including conditions for reoccupation should "internal peace or external security" again be threatened. In addition, the high commissioner included a capitulatory article to be cleared with "Egyptian legal authorities." Its main stipulations were that

> the capitulations . . . be at once . . . modified . . . to render foreigners . . . amenable to the criminal jurisdiction of the mixed courts. . . . For changes in the penal code and [all other legislation affecting the reformed mixed and *ahliyya* jurisdictions] . . . a council is to be established consisting of members of the mixed courts, to be chosen by the courts themselves, two Egyptians . . . and [several] members of the *Caisse*. This council shall decide . . . acts of legislation proposed . . . but it should have no right of initiative. . . . During [the remainder of] the occupation, the President should be an Englishman.[15]

Apparently the grand vizier at first opposed the addition of foreign-sponsored legislative innovations that resembled, like the Caisse itself, emergency capitulatory adjustments in the last harried stages of the Tanzimat regime. To obtain cooperation, Wolff had to request permission to "take up technical alterations with some specialist" who could explain the impossibility of simply abolishing judicial and legislative precedents that had built up in Egypt since 1875.[16] Once the Porte accepted his draft article, Wolff's own share in pre-evacuation preparations for mixed court reform was complete. From that point it became the responsibility of the Cairo Agency to provide a method to implement the Anglo-Ottoman plan.

Actual conditions surrounding court operations in Egypt should have indicated that the capitulatory thaw in the spring of 1887 was premature. Ink was scarcely dry on the only modest legislative changes allowed during the entire first decade of the Judicial Reform. Now, just when diplomatic representatives were beginning to feel comfortable at a higher level of bargaining, the local Egyptian end of Wolff's new plan ran into unexpected problems.

An ideal opportunity for skeptics to react came halfway through Wolff's visit to Istanbul. In March 1887, Nubar announced that he had ordered investigation of the financial activities of French mixed appeals judge Martin-Sarzeaud. Consul d'Aunay's own confidence that a public scandal could be avoided waned when the judge resigned rather than face an inquiry. As France alone possessed the privilege of double representation on the high court, the consul expected an inevitable Anglo-Egyptian demand that a judge of another nationality fill the vacancy. He therefore asked Paris to press London to avoid embarrassing French interests in the mixed courts just as negotiations were coming to a head in Istanbul. Before a response came, Martin-Sarzeaud set sail, leaving foreign residents puzzled over the resignation of two of France's most influential representatives in the mixed courts in less than six months.[17]

In Egypt the sudden need to replace de Vacher and Martin-Sarzeaud became a public issue overnight. Even moderate newspapers assailed what had apparently always been a system of political spoils in making mixed court nominations. *Al-Huquq*, for example, shocked both the British and French when it questioned the continuing need to appoint foreigners of any nationality to judicial posts for which qualified Egyptians were available.[18] This set off vigorous defensive editorials in French newspapers. *Bosphore* editor Octave Borelli, who had seen Nubar use political leverage in the courts several times, claimed (erroneously) that

> the government of the khedive has just declared that upon expiration [of the second five-year term of the Mixed Court Charter] in 1889, it does not intend to renew the experience. The Judicial Reform will therefore have lived its full term, unless the powers consent to emasculate it through internal modifications, and to permit it to become an instru-

> ment of underhandedness. . . . Now the [Egyptians] are pursuing a single goal: to be free of the obligation to accept judges chosen by the foreign governments. In the final analysis, isn't he who choses the judge the master of justice?[19]

In fact, no one fully understood the actual degree of connection between the Istanbul negotiations and Nubar's attempts to make gains in the mixed courts before an expected British withdrawal. Lord Salisbury himself apparently first discovered local Anglo-Egyptian departures from Wolff's general capitulatory goals when he received Nubar's proposals for post-convention reforms. The Egyptian plan clearly bore the mark of Baring's concern for practical administration, while Nubar's hand appeared in the more obviously political details of court organization. Even before mentioning Wolff's known priorities, the Egyptian insisted on two ministerial demands: Egypt's right to appoint judges to the mixed bench with no necessary concern for proportional foreign representation and complete immunity of the *parquet* from capitulatory interference.[20]

Although Nubar placed primary emphasis on future court appointments, he also passed on practical legislative and administrative expectations that originated in the British Agency. This was clear when it came to the draft convention's plan for a multinational legislative council to review changes in the existing codes. Cairo asked Wolff to limit very strictly areas in which significant mixed interests made some form of prior foreign approval necessary before new laws could be applied by the mixed or local jurisdictions. Taking his cue from Baring, Nubar argued that certain categories of local administrative bylaws should automatically apply to all residents without passing through capitulatory channels. He failed to mention that several of these, including acts governing port and river navigation, and policing public establishments (hotels, gaming houses, etc.), covered areas in which foreign resident interests were in fact dominant. For more important laws affecting mixed interests, Nubar backed Wolff's plan for a special multinational legislative council "composed in such a manner as to give sufficient guarantees to the powers."[21]

By the time London received Anglo-Egyptian suggestions, Wolff himself already sensed that Baring and Nubar were trying to bargain for increased leverage in the mixed courts after withdrawal. After reading Cairo's dispatches, he objected to any changes in methods of staffing the mixed bench just as he himself was trying to reduce the political role of the courts through broader capitulatory negotiations. At a time when France's cooperation in Istanbul had become a vital concern, the high commissioner recognized that "if we are to ask for the modification of the capitulations and the surrender of privileges . . . it would be difficult to ask the powers at the same time to diminish the powers of the local [word illegible] to whom the consular jurisdictions and the international legislation [*sic*] are to be transferred."[22]

Although Wolff's warning cleared the air in official circles, momentary gains were lost when opponents of any concessions to the French publicly congratulated Baring and Nubar for their influence over the capitulatory reform proceedings. By mid-May, d'Aunay was so discouraged that he withdrew support even from the broad capitulatory reform proposals being considered in Istanbul. When the draft of Nubar's scheme reached him, he branded large sections, including the "simple" bylaws clause, as "totally unacceptable" until Nubar eased pressure on established French interests in the mixed courts.[23]

Seen from London and Istanbul in 1887, it seemed that essential imperial and strategic interests were being sidetracked by renewed politicization of legal reform questions in Egypt. Already Lord Salisbury had authorized a compromise with France by promising withdrawal three, instead of five, years after ratification of the Anglo-Ottoman convention. Now, at the last moment, Wolff signed the 22 May agreement *minus* the intended capitulatory article. In its place, Wolff annexed an ambiguous protocol calling upon both signatories to "address the powers with a view to the establishment in Egypt of a 'local and uniform jurisdiction and legislature' [*sic*] applicable to foreigners."[24] This decision not only reflects Wolff's fear of France's suspicion of the Anglo-Ottoman convention: it proves that Lord Salisbury was prepared to leave Egypt in 1890 without a firm guarantee that future capitulatory crises would not precipitate great power intervention, a phenomenon that had already occurred in 1879 and 1882.

BARING'S FIRST PLAN TO INTERVENE IN PENAL JUSTICE

Nubar clearly felt betrayed by London's rejection of capitulatory suggestions from Egyptian authorities who stood to be responsible for their own internal legal affairs in three years' time. After having finally taken steps to change important sections of the *ahliyya* codes, he hinted that his earlier bargain with Wolff no longer held. Overnight, staffing of new district-level summary jurisdictions was suspended. Just as signatures were being placed on the Istanbul convention, Baring observed that Nubar had ceased cooperating and suggested that London might consider not just another judicial head, but a new man, perhaps Riadh Pasha of the Dual Control days, to fill the prime minister's post itself.[25] Before serious consideration could be given to his bitter request, however, French and Russian diplomats were already busy subverting Ottoman ratification of the Drummond-Wolff Convention. All main lines of the Conservative government's Egyptian policy, therefore, were seriously blocked.[26]

The Egyptian press had little idea why the Anglo-Ottoman convention or the abortive capitulatory article it originally contained had failed. It lost no time, however, condemning suspension of local court measures begun the preceding winter. An example of already rising expectations was the favorable reception of examination procedures to accept individuals claiming status as professional advocates. This precedent, which Nubar had encouraged during Wolff's negotiations, reportedly cut by two-thirds the surplus of unqualified Egyptian lawyers.[27] Baring's *chargé*, Gerald Portal, feared that such partial reforms were beginning to alienate different classes of the local population. Some, seeing marked improvement in certain administrative departments, such as rail transport and irrigation, could not understand why judicial affairs, where both government and private interests were at stake, lagged behind. Portal seemed surprised that in Cairo, where needs were obviously greatest, Nubar maintained only one examining judge to serve the attorney general in preparing criminal prosecutions. He then revived Baring's old cyclical rationalization for the apparent failure of Anglo-Egyptian court reform efforts:

> I know there are many objections to the appointment of an Englishman to watch the native administration of justice, but [circumstances seem to demand] the presence of an European authority who . . . without taking part in the conduct of affairs . . . would prevent . . . waste of time [and corruption]. . . . [Many], seeing this scandal . . . lay the blame on England, without [inquiring] whether this . . . branch is watched by an English inspector, or . . . left in native hands.[28]

In the face of a growing consensus that his usefulness in judicial matters had run its course, Nubar tried new tactics. In October, he appointed Charles Legrelle, one of the original Belgian judges on the local bench, to the second key post under a very vulnerable Egyptian attorney general. Legrelle's move was followed by a rumor that Raymond West's Egyptian associate and interim successor, Shafiq Bey Mansur, would soon resign.[29] This would place control over the entire prosecuting branch of the local courts under a European appointee, who, being Belgian, could not be displaced by mere Foreign Office preferences.

For Baring, the main issue was less how to lend support to qualified Egyptian judicial appointees like Shafiq Bey (who finally did resign) than to show Lord Salisbury how local political obstacles could paralyze Egyptian administration. He told Tawfiq that politically motivated appointments (not only Legrelle's, but also the sudden advancement of undersecretary Butrus Ghali's brother from a beginning post to a top position under the attorney general) had probably prompted Shafiq Mansur's resignation. Baring warned the khedive that, unless cooperation improved soon, he would inform London that questions of security and requests from "almost all classes" of the local population demanded "active English interference in the administration of justice."[30]

In fact, the Agency was already laying groundwork for serious revisions in local penal justice. In the fall of 1887, Baring and General Frederick Stephenson had called for a court crackdown on local offenses against English occupation troops. When he talked with the khedive about Nubar's alleged mishandling of the Legrelle and Ghali appointments, therefore, Baring warned that General Stephenson would soon have to "take the law into his own hands" if nothing was done to impose stricter penal investigations.[31] In another case, the Agency requested permission to act itself on complaints from the (British-controlled) Bank of Egypt and the Anglo-Egyptian Banking Company that "dilatory proceedings" in local investigations of forgery cases were prejudicing private parties' willingness to invest in noncapitulatory business ventures.[32]

By now Baring thought he had enough evidence to test London's willingness to appoint another Englishman to the attorney general's post he himself had helped vacate twice since 1884. To avoid reoccurrence of the misunderstandings that had led to Maxwell's and West's resignations, this time the Agency felt that only someone with prior direct experience of Egyptian affairs should be considered. Baring thought that John Scott, who had left the mixed court bench to enter the Indian judiciary, would be willing to serve and align his own legal reform priorities with those of the Agency.[33] What Baring did not mention was that, without a total change of policy and creation of a formal judicial adviser's post, Scott's job could involve little more than limited input into the work of the *parquet*.

RETURN TO PRE-1887 POLICY AND CAPITULATORY PRIORITIES

At least until the end of 1887, Lord Salisbury tried to keep the door open for eventual acceptance of the Drummond-Wolff Convention. He discouraged any sign of alterations in occupation administrative methods that might prejudice that possibility. Evelyn Baring himself was told that, if there was to be any change of direction in Anglo-Egyptian policy after Wolff's setback, it should stress obvious capitulatory not local legal reform priorities. This meant reviving earlier methods of obtaining capitulatory concessions that might help speed an end to the occupation, under proper conditions, after a few more years.

It was Nubar who first proposed that the best strategy would be to await expiration of the Mixed Court Charter and then make any reinstatement dependent on the powers' acceptance of conditions originally drafted into the Anglo-Ottoman convention. Baring added privately that Nubar's symbolic assistance would no longer be needed after expiration to represent what were actually British expectations of minimum capitulatory reforms before withdrawal.[34] In fact, the winter of 1887 found Baring busy preparing selected sections of Nubar's earlier capitulatory circular for presentation to the powers for "voluntary" ratification in 1888. Several chances arose to attack Nubar's erratic handling of court issues that were by then regularly debated in the Egyptian press. Baring either did not know, however, how critical such questions were becoming for local opinion or purposely passed them over.[35] He was perplexed to learn, for example, that Nubar was apparently ready to drop earlier identification of local bylaws that, in Baring's view, needed to be freed from any form of review by representatives of foreign interests.[36]

Even though Nubar succeeded in winning an extension of Foreign Office confidence in his usefulness as a capitulatory negotiator, he no longer doubted that Baring was set on ending his political career. He tried, therefore, to counteract growing enmities by finding another influential local political ally in the foreign community.

Because the British and the French had been at loggerheads over occupation policy since 1882, it was not surprising that Nubar made overtures to the new French consul, Count d'Aubigny, during his last tenuous months as prime minister. Since Nubar's political style always involved some form of maneuvering around mixed court questions, he immediately tried to bargain with d'Aubigny over terms for Mixed Court Charter renewal in 1889.[37]

By this date, however, both London and Paris had decided to try once again to deal with differences over Egypt at a higher bilateral level. While his ambassador to Paris tried to reinstill the spirit of Anglo-French compromise of early 1887, Lord Salisbury warned Baring not to go beyond the law officers' long-since publicly stated and moderate capitulatory reform priorities. The French foreign minister was equally curt, advising d'Aubigny to avoid any new "combinations or confidences," not only because of embassy-level Anglo-French discussions, but because no real advantages had ever been realized through special mixed court dealings with Nubar in the past.[38]

One is tempted to conclude that by this date many parties who depended on the Mixed Court Charter for political leverage were reconsidering the effectiveness of such tactics for the coming decade. Nubar Pasha's political barometer, traditionally set according to the capitulatory climate, was thus reaching its nadir at this point. Promises of deals over mixed court renewal in 1889 no longer seemed to interest the major signatories to the 1875 Charter. Thus, even though Evelyn Baring may have felt some satisfaction when Khedive Tawfiq had a personal falling out with his Armenian prime minister and dismissed him in June, this key transition probably would have occurred on the Egyptian side in any event. Tawfiq's choice of Nubar's successor, however, had the ironic effect of finally giving the freedom to choose capitulatory reform priorities he had sought since the outset of the occupation.

EGYPTIAN PUBLIC OPINION AND JUDICIAL MOVES BY THE RIADH CABINET

A cloak of secrecy seems to have surrounded both internal and international politics during the last months of Nubar's cabinet. This bothered parties who wondered whether London would stand by the aborted Drummond-Wolff Convention or impose new local priorities under an extended occupation. Even before Nubar's dismissal, *Al-*

Qahira printed letters from subscribers worried that suspended Anglo-Ottoman negotiations meant that initiatives taken since 1884, including establishment of a legislative council, new courts, and the beginnings of a local lawyers' profession, had served no purpose. One writer argued that the mixed court system in particular was meant

> to settle disputes involving foreigners in areas where, formerly, no suitable laws existed for such specialized cases as patents and the like. . . . It was not intended that the arrangement would become permanent and that the local population would passively accept them until they became immutable to the point of being religious obligations. . . . Here . . . the people are deprived of the right to enjoy their own public and private laws because the foreign national comes first. If a local subject raises a complaint against one of them . . . or if a local national is killed [by a foreigner] he merely says: "I am protected." . . . How can the government prevent corruption as long as these conditions continue? It is like a sore in the body of the community and the necessary way to cure it is by abolishing the capitulations. No doubt the integrity of the [capitulatory] countries will force them to agree to that need.[39]

Al-Qahira itself felt Britain would win support by following the example of the French in Tunisia and declaring formal abolition of Egypt's capitulatory regime with or without Ottoman imperial agreement.[40]

While the Arabic daily press called for increased British intervention against the status quo of the mixed courts, *Al-Huquq* tried to represent the assumed professional, not political, concerns of its readers. The lawyers' press was well aware of one main obstacle in convincing foreigners of the future of legal reform commitments in Islamic countries: there was continuing insistence by sectarian authorities (Islamic and Christian alike) that *no* civil proceedings should be carried out without reference to personal status jurisdictions. The latter, without formal codes, still remained separate from the secular governmental system that had evolved over the previous fifty years. By admitting that difficulties in the local courts stemmed as much from clashes with sectarian jurisdictions as from capitulatory encroachments, *Al-Huquq* apparently wanted to convince foreigners that they could expect new efforts to achieve processes begun, but never completed, by original Tanzimat reformers. In the spring of 1888, just before Nubar's dismissal, Amin Shumayyil wrote:

> We know that [provisions for separate communal status and jurisdictions] hamper the ability of the civil courts to carry out justice. We

> hope that responsible religious authorities will not look with disapproval upon our attempts to do away with any of these procedures that may harm the rights of individual litigants. It will be in the interests of the country to do so before the harm becomes too firmly entrenched. . . .
>
> This situation exists only in the Ottoman states. In European states all subjects have equal rights and under a single legislation, whatever their [religious or ethnic] origins. . . . Without such a system, no justice is possible, because each party views its interests in a different way. With time, all the religious communities . . . become absorbed in pursuing their separate goals, and they regard as political tyranny any attempt to remove the distinctions between them. This runs counter to natural law, which ultimately governs over all.
>
> There are, then, a *number* of "special regimes" standing in the way of national independence. Let our effort be toward unification of our own laws and our methods of carrying them out the same way under all conditions.[41]

By midsummer 1888, Shumayyil's specialized newssheet was joined by a second specialized journal edited by and for Egyptian lawyers. Nicula Tuma, editor of *Al-Ahkam*, was also a Lebanese Christian *immigré*. His previous experience as a minor public functionary in Egypt enabled him to offer services as a "self-made" advocate in 1884.[42] Also like Shumayyil, Tuma had had no formal legal education from the time of his secondary schooling under the Jesuits. His early vocation had been as a teacher and assistant editor of Butrus al-Bustani's well-known Beirut journal *At-Taqaddum*. This exposure, plus ties with the Islamic reformist journal *Mir'at ash-Sharq* shortly after leaving Lebanon, convinced Tuma that he could combine skills to help analyze many Egyptian legal reform questions. In reality *Al-Ahkam* entered the growing debate very hesitantly in 1888. It aired mainly opinions about common practical difficulties of judicial procedure and left statements of wider political or social reform significance to *Al-Huquq*. Despite such differences, however, the existence of two specialized papers by mid-1888 guaranteed that Ministry of Justice activities after Nubar's dismissal would be scrutinized more closely than at any time since 1882.

When Tawfiq named Mustafa Riadh to fill Nubar's post as prime minister, no signs of surprise or opposition appeared in the British correspondence. Riadh had served as cabinet head following the ouster of Khedive Isma^c^il in 1879, at that time answering a need for a conservatively oriented and cooperative prime minister. Returning justice minister Husayn Pasha Fakhri was another supportive symbol of this same "new image" in the new Egyptian cabinet. In fact, from the very outset Riadh promised to restore public confidence in Cairo's ability to establish order in the provinces. As premier and interior minister, he took charge of redefining the responsibilities of the *mudirs* and rural police. Fakhri, meanwhile, was to review local civil and penal jurisdictions. A first attempt to answer disappointments over court paralysis came in a meeting with both *shari^ca* and *ahliyya* court judges in Cairo.[43]

These deliberately public remarks helped the local Arabic press forget that, as far as mixed court policy was concerned, Riadh was getting off to a bad start. In fact, neither the cabinet nor the British were at all prepared to handle a controversy mounted by the Caisse that showed how vulnerable Egypt still was to capitulatory interference. The most important conflict of jurisdiction question since 1884 broke as soon as Nubar fell in June 1888. The object of debate was a mixed court ruling that future litigation between Egyptians and *any* administrative section of the government that had part of its budget assigned to public debt amortization should fall under mixed jurisdiction.[44] The test case involved the customs bureau, one of the most critical local administrations not only for occupation finances but also for Egyptian commercial houses in Cairo and the provinces. Both *Al-Qahira* and *Al-Huquq* predicted that the judgment would "lead to entanglements." Only the lawyers' press, however, deliberately threw the issue down as a challenge to Riadh's new cabinet. Comparing the rift over customs to an earlier failure to block mixed court competence over all litigation involving the khedivial estates, *Al-Huquq* concluded that

> what was meant to be a benefit for foreigners and Egyptians alike [the installation of "parallel" civil and commercial jurisdictions] is rapidly becoming a burden . . . because [if customs matters even involving Egyptians only are linked to the mixed courts automatically] one after another of the government's activities will be construed as mixed. The *ahliyya* courts will become a place for the poor people alone. . . . Basic justice requires that only when it is impossible for one body to reach a proper decision should a case be transferred to another jurisdiction. The system of justice since 1876 . . . removed [any normal system of appeals with the superior *tamyiz* jurisdiction enjoyed in other Ottoman zones], which was a mistake. It would be better to return to the old system. . . . If we must keep two separate jurisdictions, we should at least set up a high court based on a foreign or Egyptian majority according to the

> nature of the original litigations, so there will be no further doubt as to the justness of final decisions.[45]

Despite these signs of difficulty, Riadh's government made progress in other areas to offset the loss of more ground to the mixed courts. Improving conditions of local justice both soothed the ire of the Cairo lawyers' press and widened the circle of supporters of cabinet policies among different interest groups in Egyptian society. Before naming new personnel to staff rural jurisdictions abandoned since 1881, for example, Fakhri promised to make existing local courts more effective. The government's intent, he stated, was to reduce strains between traditional administrators and the professional judiciary. His only specific target at this date was elimination of the unwieldy post of examining judge, an idea first broached by Raymond West himself. A second plan went ahead when the Cairo appeals court began administering a standard qualifying examination and eliminating unqualified advocates from the *ahliyya* chambers.[46]

As soon as Fakhri turned his attention to standards in advocacy and legal training, interesting reactions appeared in the local press. First, unlike the more technical questions of jurisdictional and procedural reforms, anyone could see how lawyers affected interests at every stage of the judicial process. Defending the fading interests of many self-made Egyptian lawyers, *Al-Ahkam* argued that a good general education, plus practical experience, should enable serious applicants to meet the standards the new government proposed. Tuma regretted that Nubar's previous emphasis on social rank had made practical experience a secondary qualification for bench appointments. He claimed that most high posts were filled by the sons of the wealthy or those who had been fortunate enough to study law abroad. When such students returned, they, "like the foreign judges on the mixed bench," either ignored or showed open disdain for local customs that colored the content of Egyptian litigation. Yet, because of their supposed technical competence, judgeships were offered to these candidates first.[47] Tuma's bitterness against the standards of professionalism Fakhri was trying to introduce naturally increased when, shortly after this date, he failed the Cairo court's exam. *Al-Ahkam*'s editor was obliged to move his practice to a new district court in Asyut, where requirements were less demanding.

ANGLO-FRENCH MIXED COURT BARGAINS

British correspondence on legal reform issues was very active during the first few months of Riadh's new ministry. It was June's capitulatory scare, however, not apparent reversal of Nubar's "do-nothing" attitude toward local justice, that dominated Agency concerns. Baring's first meeting with Husayn Fakhri dealt solely with mixed court matters and produced an agreement to retain Nubar's year-old draft, "with some unimportant alterations," as the basis for renewing the Mixed Court Charter in 1889. A ritual return to hard-line tactics appeared in talk of a "temporary" extension of the mixed courts for two years only.[48]

When Baring delivered a copy of updated capitulatory reform priorities to Lord Salisbury, however, two items that Nubar had sponsored in 1887 were clearly altered. An earlier proposal to transfer all remaining consular penal jurisdiction to the mixed courts was trimmed to include only seven minor offenses.[49] What Baring probably intended was to offer a penal compromise in return for a break in the legislative reform deadlock. During the summer diplomatic recess, therefore, he obtained authorization from London for a definition of specific mixed court responsibilities to review and accept new Egyptian laws to be applied by both mixed and local jurisdictions. Apparently Lord Salisbury realized that the occupation was going to drag on and that there was a serious need to escape foreign capitulatory controls over every piece of legislation the Agency wished to introduce via the local cabinet. He agreed, therefore, that if future laws, gauged "to improve the administration of justice in the mixed courts, [were] not inconsistent with the fundamental principles of the system, and [did not] contravene any treaty obligations," Egypt should not need to depend on any additional capitulatory agency to amend local legislation.[50]

Reception of the first restatement of Anglo-Egyptian capitulatory reform priorities since Nubar's dismissal was uneven. French *chargé* Denant was particularly pleased that the new ministry had dropped Nubar's attempt to gain the right to appoint mixed judges without prior capitulatory agreement. On the other hand, he felt that efforts to alter the original wording of article 12 of the civil code were a poor substitute for suggestions of an "international legislative body" that had surfaced, then disappeared, during Drummond-Wolff's 1887 negotiations.[51]

Such unexpectedly strong local opposition caused the British Agency to worry that a charter renewal fiasco like that of 1884, when the new occupation regime won no changes, would be doubly embarrassing if repeated in 1889. The quickness of Baring's defensive reaction, however, surprised Foreign Office advisers who had helped him draft what seemed to be a quite moderate renewal scheme during the summer recess. One month after the plan's publication, Baring had Riadh withdraw *both* the penal competence and general legislative compromises. Rather than face another hostile renewal campaign "without anything definite having been settled," the new maker of Anglo-Egyptian capitulatory policy offered a five-year extension in return for simple acceptance of the bylaws clause he had carried over from the abortive Drummond-Wolff Convention. In a show of bravado that did nothing to conceal a new willingness to compromise, Baring talked about a mere six-month renewal unless his conditions were met.

Foreign Office consternation at Baring's stop-and-start methods was compounded by hard-line critics in Parliament who opposed any Egyptian capitulatory concessions. When Sir Charles Dilke tried to defend London's bargaining position in last-minute renewal negotiations, however, he was reduced to reporting that, although changes were at hand, they would be limited to practical and minor administrative matters.[52]

It was in Cairo that the political impact of Baring's handling of the mixed court issue was most direct. The French now recognized important differences between Baring's revised request to implement simple bylaws and necessary capitulatory protection for foreign capital and property interests established under the original 1875 mixed codes. All consulates, including the French, were aware of a growing need for closer regulation of private trade in pharmaceutics and spirits, both areas dominated by small-scale foreign shopkeepers. D'Aubigny conceded that capitulatory "immunities" often harmed both Egyptians and foreigners by obstructing uniform standards that protected the public under normal conditions of administrative law. He therefore recommended acceptance of the bylaws proposal not as a condition but as a useful supplement for mixed court operationsduring the next five years.[53]

Other powers, however, had reasons for wanting to keep capitulatory bargaining from becoming a series of mere bilateral agreements between the French and British. Because new bylaws would mainly affect hundreds of shopkeepers and tavern and hotel proprietors who were subjects or *protégés* of politically less dominant powers, the reaction of their consuls was particularly important. In fact, to save the day, the Foreign Office had to answer Belgian, Spanish, and Portuguese demands for a new "collective" court of appeals slot to look after the interests of their nationals. Salisbury did this by promising to raise the issue in a "technical commission" *after* renewal of the 1875 Charter in 1889.[54] A much more serious compromise followed Greek and French bids for recognition of their own special privileges beyond the letter of the Mixed Court Charter. This time, Baring himself responded without any prior consultation with the Egyptian cabinet.

Greek reactions came very quickly when, as part of plans to increase public respect for the local courts, Riadh declared that "all assumed foreign subjects . . . especially Greeks" who failed to produce locally registered evidence of capitulatory status would henceforth be treated as Egyptians and fall under the *ahliyya* law.[55] The Greek consul immediately protested attempts to intimidate legitimate Greek subjects and *protégés* and to bring them under purely Egyptian jurisdictions. Baring consented to forward the charge to London, but felt it was difficult to back either side in the dispute. The Agency had no doubt that the size of the Greek community merited special consideration and possibly even a recognized post on the mixed court of appeals. Too many local subjects escaped the legitimate jurisdiction of the local courts through favors delivered by the Greek Consulate.[56]

Hesitance to restrain Riadh in his reform zeal nearly jeopardized Baring's attempt to make mixed court renewal conditional upon acceptance of very simple changes in the 1875 Charter. By mid-January 1889, Athens threatened not only to reject the bylaws annex, but to abandon the courts entirely if Riadh tightened conditions of capitulatory status for Greeks. Last-minute pressures on Greece to moderate its demands presented serious but not insurmountable problems for London's ambassador in Athens.[57] The Greek question, however, was only the first sign of split priorities between the Agency's now totally ad hoc capitulatory policy and the altered judicial reform posture of Riadh and Husayn Fakhri.

Early in January 1889, Comte d'Aubigny himself decided to raise "technical points" to help assure French ratification of terms for mixed court operations between 1889 and 1894. Although the French had denounced Nubar's earlier attempts to influence bench appointments, d'Aubigny now adopted the same tactics: he asked Riadh both to grant permanent status to the "temporary" French mixed attorney general and to guarantee that a retiring judge (France's unique second seat on the mixed court of appeals) would be replaced by a nominee of his choice.[58]

Baring's reaction to these last-minute developments was open indignation. Having already suspended most of his own additions to Egypt's official reform circular, he was inclined to reject any promise of ratification that involved further favors.[59] On the French side, d'Aubigny felt the British were boxed in, since they had already promised special consideration for the secondary powers' "technical requests" in return for adherence to 1889–94 terms of renewal. It was only when he learned that Fakhri planned to name a Belgian to the mixed attorney general's post, however, that the French consul decided to go directly to the British Agency.

In several private talks with Baring, d'Aubigny this time offered a financial trade-off in return for continued French predominance on the Alexandria appeals bench. Specifically, he agreed to the appointment of a Belgian attorney general provided that France retained two justices on the high court. If Baring accepted this, The French public debt commissioner would "close his eyes" if the Anglo-Egyptians wished to raise the salaries of certain high British officials above the stipulated ceiling of £E 2,000.[60] The British consul apparently lost little time adopting Nubar's former habit of confusing judicial and extrajudicial matters. Even before he received instructions from Lord Salisbury, he reported that Riadh agreed to the French bargain on judicial appointments, but did not comment on the salary increase option. The new *de facto* adviser to the Ministry of Justice, however, made it clear that he would insist on d'Aubigny's offer "for our own reasons."[61]

These outward signs of a quickly adaptable capitulatory *modus operandi* certainly did not guarantee that the Egyptian cabinet would be satisfied with the new division of labor between mixed and "native" reform responsibilities. London may have been encouraged to think that, having found a way to reach bilateral understandings with the

French, similar methods could solve other defects in the 1875 Mixed Court Charter and actually improve foreign community relations with the Egyptian ministry. The fact remains, however, that, after having criticized Nubar for the same or similar tendencies, Baring had opened the door to parties who would now feel free to seek British sponsorship for other special court adjustments. If such bargaining spread, as it did, Riadh and Fakhri had one possible consolation: Baring would soon be too busy with capitulatory infighting to be able to impose British controls over local reform initiatives that were now clearly under way.

Part IV

Rising Expectations and Social Deceptions

10

Local Initiative by the Riadh Ministry (1889–91)

Communication gaps between the British Agency and several Egyptian special interest groups became increasingly noticeable halfway through Mustafa Riadh's 1888 to 1891 ministry. Many serious difficulties of the later 1890s originated in 1889, largely because of British failure to recognize widening Egyptian support for successful reform strategies adopted by Nubar Pasha's successors. As this process continued, legal reform issues that appeared narrow or bureaucratically compartmentalized in the 1880s took on different and politically quite significant form in the second decade of the occupation.

The British Agency did not mention activities in Riadh's Justice Department until after serious concessions had been granted to obtain a third five-year renewal of the Mixed Court Charter. In a summary of reforms under way in 1889, Baring reported that the government, having largely recovered from financial limitations of the 1880s, would finally open courts in Upper Egypt. He conceded that the local judiciary, "although still defective," had improved and was ready to serve new rural areas. Extra costs, he added without hesitation, would "be met by an increase in . . . court fees."[1] Baring was apparently unaware that the Egyptian Legislative Council had reviewed court fees in 1889 and registered opposition to the already high costs of justice. The Council felt that pegging *ahliyya* fees to high mixed court schedules had kept, and would continue to keep, many litigants out of the courts. Justice minister Fakhri was obviously favorably disposed to such soundings, since he himself was proposing to pool mixed and local court receipts, "borrowing" from the former to help pay new personnel needed to expand the latter.[2]

While this debate continued in the Legislative Council, the Cairo press announced the first application of a "lawyers' statute" to cull out unqualified advocates. *Al-Huquq*, whose editor had been asked with nine other Egyptian lawyers to help implement the regulation, called for tighter standards to protect Cairo's most rapidly expanding "modern" profession. Shumayyil argued for a reduction in the number of lawyers to a maximum of two hundred individuals, out of seven hundred then claiming status as advocates. Even a preliminary announcement recognizing sixty openings before the Cairo appeals court alone seemed inflated. *Al-Huquq* warned that "this [high] number in a country that has only had established secular courts for about four years, and a modern law school even more recently . . . would indicate one of two things. Either Egypt is a land in which qualified men . . . can come forth in a very short time . . . without schooling, or the examination is not strict enough, and therefore follows the lax practices of the past."[3] In fact, Fakhri soon admitted he had overestimated the number of applicants able to pass formal examinations. This tightening of standards, plus the announcement that examinations would also be used to select judges for new courts in Upper Egypt, strengthened *Al-Huquq*'s confidence in the new ministry's professional intentions.[4]

The best summary of Egyptian efforts to improve local justice appeared in Charles Legrelle's comparison of recent court activities with the record for 1884–87. The Belgian attorney general's report indicated that more peasants and town dwellers had brought disputes to the courts in 1888 than in any previous year. One reason was that delays had been reduced by speeding up procedures for minor suits. Legrelle also felt that qualitative developments in local litigation had begun to affect mixed court operations. He reported, for example, that fewer Egyptians with complex civil suits were arranging *ad hoc* association with foreign "strawmen" merely to avoid the local courts. While the trend had not hampered legitimately mixed cases, it was increasing the practical experience of the local judiciary and bringing more substantial Egyptian civil litigation under *ahliyya* law. Legrelle noted that even some foreigners had submitted claims to local Egyptian benches rather than carry minor litigation at higher costs to mixed courts in Cairo or Alexandria. The second generation of local magistrates, he said, had already made:

> improvements . . . in the preparation of judgments. The cases are better studied and . . . logically deduced. . . . The "new justice," remembering the abuses of the past, wanted to be independent. [Thus, between 1883 and 1888] . . . sentences were based on what appeared to be equitable, rather than on the law, and an excessive number of [faulty] judgments were subject to appeal and further delay. Now the transition period has passed; more than forty magistrates are graduates of European law faculties, while eleven others, all members of the *parquet*, are graduates of the Khedivial Law School. . . . [5]

Legrelle's optimism was buttressed by findings on *fallahin* disputes, which usually fell somewhere between summary justice and more complex cases provided for in the 1883 codes. The most obvious improvement to serve this need was establishment (in Shibin al-Qum and Damanhur) of the first summary courts in Egypt since suppression of the local judicial councils in 1881. By setting lower fees for the summary courts, Fakhri was trying to attract village litigants whose interest in European-based law was taking form, but who shied away from the expenses of more formal jurisdictions. On the other hand, he had already helped reduce the number of truly inconsequential disputes by introducing a minimum fee for cases formerly settled without charge. Although Legrelle himself did not make this point, the implication was that rural village cases that did not fit *ahliyya* procedure and had clogged the courts since 1883 were being diverted to much simpler methods of settlement.

HUSAYN FAKHRI'S NEW POLITICAL PROMINENCE

By the middle months of 1889, Husayn Fakhri was clearly becoming the most publicly acclaimed minister in Riadh's cabinet. In addition to making many effective administrative changes, he, above all people, seemed most interested in ways in which court reforms could affect existing and future local interest groups. Fakhri made repeated visits to the Khedivial Law School and suggested broadening the curriculum to allow students to move into various levels of Ministry of Justice employment, not just the magistracy proper. Such developments attracted support from Cairo journalists who felt that reduction in bureaucratic elitism and favoritism would build the morale of Egyptian students who were hoping to enter new areas of professional and government service in the 1890s.[6]

The justice minister's activities, however, revealed only one aspect of Riadh's approach to legal reform problems inherited from Nubar's time. On some questions, the prime minister seemed to be in more of a hurry than Fakhri to prove progress toward priorities laid down at the outset of the occupation. On others, his approach was more traditionalist, if not actually reactionary. One indicator of differing views showed that Riadh still hoped that rapid gains at the highest levels in the local courts would tempt the British to help whittle away mixed court dominance in the most important areas of civil justice. When he announced intentions to keep to original (1883) provisions for a second *ahliyya* appeals court in Upper Egypt and a "supreme cassation court" before setting up more summary jurisdictions, for example, the justice minister was clearly displeased.[7]

Egyptian Arabic press accounts also indicate that Riadh delayed several of Fakhri's nominations to new bench posts in Upper Egypt. He preferred to give assurance that nonprofessional officials would eventually handle the bulk of minor cases and leave only important issues to trained judges. As long as there was no Anglo-Egyptian position on such questions, the local press tended to condemn these and any other signs of concessions to pre-1881 traditions of Egyptian justice.[8] Soon, however, it became apparent that occupation authorities were indeed sympathetic to compromises with the letter of the 1883–84 codes when it came to rural summary jurisdictions. Just prior to the target date for closing the notorious brigandage commissions, British police inspectors Johnson and Coles insisted that separating out "*fallahin* justice" was the only way to avoid overloads that had necessitated transfer of emergency penal powers to the *mudirs* in 1884. Instead of encouraging Fakhri and others who hoped to expand the staff of the attorney general as a means to train future summary judges, the inspectors urged use of Egyptian police officers to compile summary prosecution dossiers. Both Fakhri and judges on several Egyptian courts criticized Riadh's apparent willingness to consider what was essentially Clifford Lloyd's (1884) scheme for Ministry of the Interior participation in lower-level judicial affairs.[9]

Even though the hated brigandage commissions were formally abolished and three new first-instance courts opened in Asyut, Bani Suwayf, and Qena in June 1890, the events incited surprisingly little notice in the press. Despite the lukewarm response, the ministry did fulfill its promise to appoint bench personnel following a ranked list of finalists in standard qualifying examinations. Several jurists named to these first new courts in Upper Egypt, including Qasim Amin, Husayn Thabit, and Sa^cad Zaghlul's brother Ahmad Fathi, were destined to pursue quite famous careers. More important than the future fame of a few, most of Fakhri's other appointees had studied law in the Khedivial Law School on encouragement from Raymond West. Their entry into the judiciary just as a later version of West's summary justice scheme was about to be tested seemed to be an auspicious beginning.

Not long after opening courts in Upper Egypt, the minister of justice tried to enhance recognition of professional accomplishment at higher levels in the Egyptian judiciary. When it came to placing persons with more advanced training in appeals posts, however, Fakhri ran into political complications. His own idea was to appoint seven more substitute Egyptian judges to the Cairo appeals bench immediately, so that they could gain experience that would be needed when a second appeals court opened in Asyut.[10] When Lord Salisbury learned of the proposal, however, he took it upon himself to strike a bargain that might meet two separate but presumably reciprocally attractive objectives simultaneously. In return for granting Fakhri a free hand to expand the senior ranks of the local judiciary, the Foreign Office asked to place at least two of its own nominees in prominent positions on the Cairo appeals bench. Salisbury was convinced that the presence of two more English judges at the highest level of local justice for a "temporary period of about five years" would bolster foreign confidence in an obviously improved system.[11]

Neither nominee put forward by the Foreign Office had any training in the French law applied in Egypt's courts. Cameron and Willmore, however, were both consular officials and well known in the capitulatory community. London thought this might help communication between Fakhri's higher courts and the mixed judiciary. Impelled by this logic, Riadh ended by inviting the two British consular agents to fill posts Fakhri had tried to reserve for promotions from intermediate levels of the local judiciary.[12]

FAILURE OF THE 1890 TECHNICAL COMMISSION AND DEADLOCK OVER PROPERTY JURISDICTION

Over a year passed between renewal of the Mixed Court Charter in January 1889 and the meetings of the technical commission Baring had promised after concluding bargains with several powers in the last weeks of 1888. Until the technical commission met, the only openly optimistic views came from the Egyptian Arabic press, which was clearly impressed by changes in the local courts since 1888. Especially *Al-Huquq* and *Al-Mu'ayyad*, the unofficial organ of Riadh Pasha and his party, expected recognition of advances made after five years' delay, as well as specific adjustments during a "final" five-year period of mixed court operations.[13]

Since it was seen in this light, former mixed court judge John Scott's return to Cairo following Evelyn Baring's renewed request for a new "formal but temporary" judicial adviser was not initially resisted by Riadh's cabinet. Scott's arrival just as the technical capitulatory commission convened added to the impression that the British and Egyptians had finally agreed on different types of equally important reform, each demanding quite firm political commitments.[14] As we shall see, if Scott's revision of views he had formed in the late 1870s had been left to operate by themselves, this impression might have carried forward into the 1890s. As it was, a complete fiasco of "technical reform" in the mixed courts in 1890 repoliticized the entire *ahliyya* court system and, with it, Scott's contribution to ministerial policy.

Once the technical mixed court commission convened in March 1890, agreement was quickly reached on at least one issue that had lost much of the political sensitivity attached to it ten years before. With British support, the Egyptians called for a new "court of conflicts." This superior court was to settle disputes of jurisdiction between the mixed and local courts solely on the basis of actual litigants' nationality. Most capitulatory representatives by now accepted the need to stem obvious abuse of strawman tactics to bring so many otherwise purely Egyptian cases into the mixed courts.[15]

Capitulatory sensitivity to proper maintenance of the principle of mixed interest was clearest when it came to real estate law. This was an area in which foreign investments in Egypt, through land development and mortgage finance firms, were expanding most rapidly after 1890. Development ventures, like the British-registered Aboukir Company founded in 1888, were involved mainly in land recovery through drainage projects or subdivisions in new urban suburbs. Mortgage companies, especially the French-controlled Crédit Foncier Egyptien, found themselves taking over large amounts of agricultural land from Egyptian borrowers who could not meet payments. Most mortgage firms usually held foreclosed land just long enough for some appreciation and then sold it to reap a modicum of profit.[16] Naturally, such companies came under mixed law whenever they dealt with Egyptians who either contracted to buy land they offered or took out mortgages to purchase land on the general market. Because they felt they had a vested interest in any and all issues affecting Egyptian property values, however, big companies like the Crédit Foncier stretched the matter of mixed interest, even in private land litigation between Egyptians, to the extreme. Thus, they created an uproar when Riadh, hoping to remove the same type of abuses that had been recognized in strawman cases, asked the technical commission to rewrite Article 9 of the original Mixed Court Charter.

Article 9 allowed for mixed court competence over "real estate actions between all persons, *even those of the same nationality*."[17] Without such specific wording, consuls might have kept to the pre-1876 tradition of claiming the right to hear property disputes between their own nationals in Egypt. This practice, based on the literal provisions of earlier capitulatory treaties, was still recognized and acceptable after 1876 when two foreigners of the same nationality were involved in their own civil disputes in Egypt. In many such cases, application of the disputants' own national law was not likely to impinge on basic Egyptian interests. Litigation over real estate, on the other hand, involved disposition of units of revenue-producing wealth that were physically inseparable from Egypt. It was unthinkable that any foreign consulate should apply one set of laws (for example, Greek) to Egyptian property when members of their community owned it, only to shift jurisdiction to a second consulate and another set of national laws if other foreigners (Italians, for example), "even of the same nationality," purchased the same property a year later! From 1876 through the 1880s, therefore, capitulatory residents had accepted a single mixed law to govern *all* their property relationships. The Egyptian government followed the same logic in 1883 and adopted local codes incorporating mixed court property laws.

Despite near equality in the two codes governing property disputes, however, neither Egyptian nor foreign owners willingly accepted maintenance of separate mixed and *ahliyya* jurisdictions. Foreigners who counted on predictable levels of security (and therefore value) for property titles of land they bought from Egyptians felt the only way they could rest assured was to have mixed judges handle all "real estate actions between all persons, even those of the same nationality," *including Egyptians*. Their pressures were certainly not resisted by Egyptians equally concerned about legal technicalities that might affect the value of their property in a changing and speculative market. This had led to an ever rising number of "native" title and mortgage registrations with mixed court recorders. Once such Egyptian titles were recorded, judicial review of any litigation over them, even between parties of the same Egyptian nationality, was automatically assumed by the mixed courts.

Egyptians might have had several reasons for wanting their property under mixed court jurisdiction. Some may simply have been unwilling to risk confusion in the *ahliyya* courts over the legitimacy of their own title deeds vis-à-vis *hujja*s, or statements of ownership that were traditionally (and still could be) obtained in the Islamic *mahkama*. The *hujja* had never been recognized by the mixed judges, who adhered rigorously to the letter of their own codes. In local deliberations, on the other hand, judges often took claims based on *qadis*' previous acts into consideration and granted judgments that drew inspiration from both the written code and Islamic practice. The Egyptian lawyers' organ *Al-Huquq* frequently complained that cases bogged down when it became necessary to refer to the *mahkama* for essential documents for which no systematic registration procedure existed. Although only a few articles stated it openly, problems like these increased pressures to spell out rules to guide judges' decisions when shariatic principles or documents had some overlapping role to play.

Foreigners, of course, could rest assured that no new legislation along these lines would enter the mixed codes. Egyptian property owners, on the other hand, could never be certain that changing perceptions of local social and economic reform needs might not bring changes in *ahliyya* law that would place their holdings on quite a different legal basis than that applied through the mixed courts.[18] Any local titleholders who feared that such local legislative adjustments could someday exclude their property from a wider market would have been doubly anxious to opt, along with foreign owners, for the apparently immutable Napoleonic provisions of mixed law.

Such rationalizations might have helped extend the jurisprudential principle of mixed interest to guarantee both foreign and Egyptian access to a single legal environment for property exchanges. It was much easier, however, for mixed benches simply to exploit the peculiar original wording of Article 9 of the Mixed Court Charter. The 1890 technical commission did just this. It openly told Riadh that the mixed courts had a specific textual mandate to hear purely Egyptian as well as mixed property disputes. In response, Consul Charles Cookson accused the commission of wanting to strip the *ahliyya* courts of their most important legal functions. The British did not confront their traditional French rivals openly on this issue. Cookson's alarm, however, was amply justified by Consul d'Aubigny's private estimate that literal application of Article 9 "in a country whose entire wealth rests in its soil would give . . . the Reform enormous authority" and influence over Egyptian economic development far beyond the confines of the courtroom.[19]

Once Husayn Fakhri realized that the technical commission would oppose or distort Egyptian aims on all real estate questions, he withdrew discussion of Article 9 from the agenda. In reprisal, the foreign delegates dropped earlier support for a high court to review all other types of jurisdictional conflicts. Rather than waste time trying to get the commission's cooperation on remaining Egyptian proposals, Cookson called for adjournment and submission of the "few modest improvements" left intact directly to foreign governments for approval.

Baring's summary of the commission's collapse resembled his anti–mixed court bias at the height of the financial crisis in the days of the Dual Control. Unlike the situation between 1879 and 1883, however, there was now practically no chance Britain would react to its newest capitulatory disappointment by abolishing the Mixed Court Charter outright. Some foreign parties may have feared another threat not to renew the Judicial Reform when its 1889–94 term expired. Between 1890 and that date, however, a great deal could and would occur. What is most important in distinguishing earlier disappointments from this one, however, was the fact that Egyptians definitely knew that real changes in local justice had been carried out since 1888 without increasing dependence on foreign assistance. The British could not be held individually responsible for failing to harness aggressive tendencies that obviously still dominated capitulatory questions. It seemed reasonable in 1890, therefore, to expect them to wait four more years for a simple "expiration" of the Mixed Court Charter. Riadh's earlier willingness to allow two new British judges in Cairo appeals posts sought by qualified Egyptians and acceptance of John Scott's "temporary" appointment as judicial adviser were still linked to such an understanding.

POLITICAL SHIFTS BEHIND JOHN SCOTT'S ADVISORY MISSION

Once Anglo-Egyptian strategy in the 1890 technical commission failed, any presumed need for a British judicial adviser to prepare closer relations between the mixed and *ahliyya* courts waned overnight. Quite aside from obvious Egyptian disappointment, Evelyn Baring was dismayed to find that John Scott had been busy during the commission's abortive sessions and had drawn his own conclusions concerning the needs of Egypt's courts. According to the Arabic press, these generally fit in with opinions held by the local ministry.[20] What disturbed the British Agency most was that neither the cabinet nor Scott seemed prepared to make adjustments to fit new conditions imposed by the commission's adjournment.

After reading Scott's report, Baring had to admit that a number of useful reforms had already been undertaken without the need for intervention. Two recent changes—establishment of a disciplinary council to hear charges of negligence in prosecuting functions and extension of single-judge summary jurisdictions—were identified as priorities before Scott arrived.[21] The adviser's suggestion that the judges on the Cairo court of appeals should supervise the lower judiciary also carried forward an idea discussed many times in the Egyptian lawyers' press. Overall, then, nothing suggested serious opposition, either from local Egyptian lawyers or from Husayn Fakhri himself, to cooperating with Scott. Disagreement had to come, then, from someone with particular reasons to oppose, or at least alter, local reform methods that were becoming an accepted part of government operations by 1890.

On the day he sent John Scott's mainly complimentary report to London, Baring wrote a separate private letter requesting permission to give the judicial adviser authority to participate directly in cabinet discussions.[22] Signs that Riadh would resist any increase in British responsibility for Egypt's internal governance, however, made it necessary to clear the matter with Lord Salisbury first. When he returned from his London leave in the summer of 1890, Baring had in effect created in the *ahliyya* courts a new scapegoat whose apparent weakness could justify several forms of "benevolent" intervention. Not surprisingly, Scott proved to be an early convert to a new policy that, although it ran counter to his own earlier estimates of the local courts, promised to double the importance of his position overnight.

Husayn Fakhri was obviously still moving ahead with reforms the British had backed publicly only a few months before. John Scott's reorientation of his originally positive views of local court affairs, therefore, probably should have been announced in stages. Instead, whoever helped write Scott's new memorandum in November had no qualms about scuttling several gentlemen's agreements concluded with Riadh between 1888 and 1890. Somehow, "reflection" over the summer now led the judicial adviser to conclude that "no reform [would] come . . . on the country's own efforts [owing to] . . . the arbitrary interference . . . of those who rule and the senility . . . of those who are ruled."[23] With this rather surprising shift to open denunciation came Scott's revised plan for formal and direct advisory functions.

On the surface, the only new feature in Scott's plan was the introduction of supervision of local justice by special extrajudicial agencies. First among these was to be a Committee of Judicial Surveillance headed by an English inspector general with a small staff of Egyptians, to help the Cairo appeals court supervise the lower courts. This was a function most professional jurists and the Cairo lawyers' press deemed essential. Another committee was to screen and nominate all candidates for judgeships. Scott topped off his proposals by suggesting that the *ahliyya* court of appeals could only measure up to its full responsibilities if two or three more English judges were added to its ranks.

Apparently, London's only serious worry during the mini-crisis that followed was that any local criticism of British pressures on the Ministry of Justice might unleash more unwanted capitulatory surprises, especially from the French. Soundings at the Quai d'Orsay, however, yielded about the same attitude Baring hoped for and received from the Foreign Office itself. As long as appointment of a permanent judicial adviser did not imply full ministerial powers, Ribot saw no reason to determine whether Scott was continuing or breaking with reform efforts that had surfaced since 1888.[24] Neither the French nor the British correspondence contained the slightest hint that any sector of the Egyptian population, beyond the central ministry, might object to such maneuvering.

When the Egyptian cabinet received Scott's new proposals, local parties that were growing impatient with such frequent shifts in legal reform policies reacted in various ways. The daily press argued more or less as it had in 1883. *Al-Watan* repeated that Lord Dufferin's original reform scheme had been implemented with the aim of "abolishing the mixed courts and creating [one system of] courts . . . like those found in other countries . . . some of which are below Egypt in the quality of their justice."[25] If Scott did not depart from that objective, temporary expedients, even foreign judges in certain higher posts, might be necessary for a policy that was in both British and Egyptian long-term interests. By contrast, the Cairo lawyers' press saw little connection between the new surveillance scheme and assumptions implanted earlier, and growing, within professional judicial circles. "Certainly the existing system is incomplete and defective," *Al-Huquq*'s editor wrote,

> . . . but we should not deceive ourselves by thinking that foreign advisers, with their ignorance of Arabic, will be able to straighten the tortuous path. We must have our own judges. . . . When Egypt will be truly governed by Egyptians and prepared morally and intellectually to run a complete judicial system, [the proposed single-judge circuit plan without an external surveillance committee] will provide direct benefits. In the meantime, none of these goals, especially full independence of the local judiciary, will be attainable until the mixed courts are annexed to the local system.[26]

Husayn Fakhri was clearly impressed by opinions expressed in the Cairo press. He asked several Egyptian and European private advocates for advice on how to respond to the judicial adviser's proposals. This sense of unity may have pushed Scott into offering a compromise denial that he wished to control appointments to both the proposed surveillance committee and the Cairo appeals bench.[27] Baring, by contrast, refused to bargain. Rather than face the embarrassment of a cabinet pronouncement against Scott, Baring went directly to the khedive. He persuaded Tawfiq to use his own higher offices, plus one final compromise, to convince Riadh of the desirability of new directions in court reform. The predictably docile khedive bargained only briefly before participating in what became a very controversial precedent. On 11 February, Baring reported that Tawfiq felt that the cabinet would be favorably impressed if, instead of adding two new British judges to the Cairo appeals bench, Scott agreed to the return of Belgian attorney general Legrelle to his earlier Cairo court duties. This would reduce the need for British assistance to one judge and make it possible to appoint "a very competent Egyptian" to the top prosecutor's post. The khedive talked to Riadh about this prospect, stressing the possibility of appointing another prominent Egyptian jurist to the directorship of the Khedivial Law School. The cabinet finally conceded and approved Scott's permanent appointment along with his basic reform plan.[28]

FRENCH BARGAINING BETWEEN MINISTRIES

The first serious objection to Anglo-Egyptian methods of compromise came not from Egyptian but from external sources. From Paris, foreign minister Ribot warned about underestimating the political implications of Baring's interference in cabinet decisions via Abdin Palace. Ribot's main concern was not the effect of Scott's appointment on the Egyptian courts *per se*. He worried more about future British manipulation, through Tawfiq, of other administrative matters that might impinge on the rights of French residents, mixed court vigilance notwithstanding. When Consul d'Aubigny carried this protest to the khedive, however, he found Tawfiq more anxious to offer the French conciliatory arrangements than to risk "reprisals from the occupying power" if Scott did not have his way. He promised, for example, to recommend that one member of the new judicial surveillance committee be a Frenchman.[29]

Baring soon learned that the French were looking for piecemeal concessions to help soothe their nerves over use of khedivial influence to steer cabinet decisions. The Agency therefore speeded appointment of a senior Egyptian judge to complete the surveillance committee and suggested another way to assuage French political sensitivities.[30] This move to name an *ahliyya* judge to surveillance work earned some appreciation. Egyptian pride, however, this time in the Ministry of Public Education, paid a price for British efforts to restore their image of measured benevolence in judicial affairs.

Baring knew that financial adviser Elwin Palmer had been under pressure to free funds to replace Victor Vidal, director of the Khedivial Law School between 1873 and his death in 1888, with a new French nominee.[31] One prospective candidate (former government lawyer and outspoken defender of the capitulatory status quo Octave Borelli) would have been equally unpopular with Egyptians and the British. When the name of Paris law professor Edouard Testoud was broached, however, Baring quickly advised London that *two* prestigious appointments (Testoud's plus a new French director of the Egyptian Museum) might attract Paris much more than another round of backbiting over Scott's appointment. Since Palmer was the only person who could allocate salaries for such posts, Baring was confident the French would also drop threats to use the Caisse to block increased funds to pay for surveillance committee operations. While this possible combination was discussed, the names of two well-known Egyptian judges submitted to education minister ᶜAli Pasha Mubarak as candidates for the law school directorship were held in limbo.[32]

By mid-March 1891, it was clear to Riadh that the British were actively easing tensions with the French over a number of ten-year-old disagreements concerning legal administration. D'Aubigny's *chargé* tried to lessen disappointment by promising the Egyptian that Paris would protest vehemently if Scott tried to assume the same level of quasi-executive authority enjoyed by the financial adviser. Riadh cut him short, however, by concluding that French policy was guided by "personal interests," not by any serious concern for Egypt's internal autonomy.[33] Such implicit charges against the khedive in his dealings with both the British and the French were strengthened by even more obvious signs of bargaining. Within a short time, Tawfiq resumed the pre-occupation khedivial practice of presiding over cabinet meetings. In the first such "higher executive" session, Scott's proposals, including promotion of a second Belgian judge to the Cairo appeals bench and appointment of a third British judge to the same court, passed with only minor discussion.[34] As of this date, the appeals bench, like the mixed courts, had a majority of foreign judges: three British and two Belgian, with another Belgian (Legrelle) as attorney general.

Foreign resident reactions to these developments reached a higher level of anglophobia than at any point since 1882–83. Main foreign concerns were not what increased British influence in court affairs would do to Egyptian interests, but whether the changing situation would affect the capitulatory status quo.[35] To some extent the Agency's next move, which shifted attention from the higher-level court system to conditions of grass-roots native justice, helped reduce fears of a British-sponsored challenge to the mixed courts. The confusion that this juggling act caused, however, ultimately created more problems in the second round of Egyptian reactions to the "Scott plan."

Colonel Herbert Kitchener, aide to the British military commander, was called upon to reorganize Egypt's rural police force just as the Marquis de Reverseaux became France's new consul in Cairo. De Reverseaux was surprised that Egyptians did not protest Kitchener's new supervisory role over the *mudirs*. If one needed to attach a label to Kitchener's activities and their relations to Scott's efforts in the courts, however, the term "Egyptianization" probably applied best. In fact, Kitchener indicated he was favorably impressed with Riadh's sense of division, especially between summary penal procedures and more important penal and civil concerns in the courts, well before Scott's arrival.[36] Despite rising objections to involvement by the Ministry of the Interior in judicial matters from several local judges and lawyers, Riadh could see attractions in what would soon be called the Kitchener plan. Ultimately, it was not schemes being put forward simultaneously by Scott and Kitchener but the methods London's agents used to get their views accepted that alienated the entire Egyptian cabinet.

This became clear when the French consul warned that the British were again counting on the khedive's cooperation to encourage adoption of a new round of reforms despite cabinet opposition. This time, however, Paris had advance assurance that silence on issues apparently unrelated to identifiable capitulatory concerns was worth risking: within a week after Riadh's resignation for reasons of health (but actually to avoid the embarrassment of more imposed solutions from Scott and Kitchener), the French learned of the nomination of Paris law professor Edouard Testoud to head the Khedivial Law School. De Reverseaux called this a sign of British "moderation" and political objectivity in "purely administrative" matters.[37]

By resigning at this time, Riadh could be fairly certain that supporters of increased police and judicial authority for local executive agents would soon gain satisfaction and remember his ministry for it. Opponents of this trend, on the other hand, might overlook the fact that Riadh himself had originally sponsored similar elements in the so-called Kitchener plan. They would applaud his resistance to the obvious political bargaining process that accompanied its introduction. Parties who might back the outgoing minister on these grounds included Egyptian professional judges, the now much better organized *ahliyya* lawyers' "bar," and several outspoken individuals in Cairo's Legislative Council. Meanwhile, Tawfiq's selection of the pliant and reputedly anglophile Mustafa Fahmi to replace Riadh guaranteed that if there was to be any further controversy over the Scott-Kitchener plan, it would come from parties with direct stakes in the outcome of reforms, *not* from the cabinet itself.

"NATIVE JUSTICE" AND HUSAYN FAKHRI'S MOVEMENT TO THE OPPOSITION

A number of people wondered how John Scott himself managed to rationalize disruption of what had finally begun to look like an Anglo-Egyptian consensus over legal reform priorities. After talking with foreign minister Tigrane Pasha, who had chosen (along with Fakhri) to stay on in Mustafa Fahmi's cabinet, the French consul concluded cynically that the man Baring had nominated to be judicial adviser

> has a very fickle mind . . . and agrees with the last person who offers a suggestion. He has changed his . . . reform plan several times. . . . If Scott thinks that the best justice can only come through fusion [of the mixed and native courts] he has given up the idea. . . . In any event, these preoccupations are irrelevant today, as the judicial adviser is completely devoted to questions of police, village watchmen, and the like. He and Kitchener have proposed a plan . . . that is a pell-mell of administrative and judicial questions . . . with no political interest because they do not concern the mixed courts.[38]

De Reverseaux's last point in particular explains why a broad front, including Egyptian Legislative Council politicians, private lawyers, and journalists, tried to resist the Scott-Kitchener plan. Malaise was spreading over what appeared to be cosmetic measures to make up for Anglo-Egyptian inability to adapt legal conditions to fit changing needs in the 1890s.

It is quite probable that, had the British Agency contented itself with simple cabinet approval for an alternative "native justice" plan, this latent controversy might have climaxed with Riadh's resignation. Instead, Baring tried, unsuccessfully, to obtain Legislative Council approval for the Scott-Kitchener plan. Although the Council itself had already called for continued extension of summary jurisdiction involving division of responsibilities between formal courts and executive officials, it refused to disagree openly with Riadh's "party of opposition." Lack of cooperation obliged the British to turn again to

Khedive Tawfiq to exert pressure for immediate implementation of the Scott-Kitchener plan.[39]

From the Legislative Council, criticism of Baring's handling of the summary justice question spread to Shaykh ᶜAli-Yusuf's daily *Al-Mu'ayyad* and the Cairo lawyers' press. One might have expected *Al-Mu'ayyad*, which had already expressed a general bias in favor of traditional executive authority, to welcome a British-sponsored version of Riadh's own earlier summary justice scheme. In the end, however, both papers implied that covert political pressure on the Legislative Council had weakened many parties' already lukewarm acceptance of British advisers in three key Egyptian ministries.[40]

John Scott was aware enough of resentment against Kitchener's emphasis on rural penal justice to try to point to other advantages under the revised summary court system. By midsummer 1891, for example, a decree finally made a special chamber of the Cairo court of appeals into a superior cassation court.[41] For anyone who had watched Baring's recent success in adding several foreign judges to the appeals bench, however, the move looked doubly suspect: *de facto* control over its decisions might easily fall to a simple majority of British judges selected to sit in the separate cassation chamber. Fakhri must have concluded, therefore, that expectations of full integration of local professional competence and jurisdictions in the *ahliyya* system, just like hopes for similar gains against separate capitulatory justice, had been abandoned by the judicial adviser. By the time Scott returned to Cairo from leave in January 1892, he found that Fakhri had not only resigned, but made hostile public remarks opposing interventionist trends in occupation policy in general.[42] Coming as it did in the same month as Khedive Tawfiq's death, this latest upset encouraged even moderates to call for firmer resistance, if not from the docile Fahmi ministry, perhaps from the new khedive, ᶜAbbas II.

CHANGING GOVERNMENTS AND POLICIES IN EGYPT AND EUROPE

It would have been difficult to predict local reactions to Husayn Fakhri's resignation on the basis of Mustafa Fahmi's selection of his ministerial replacement. Nomination of Judge Ibrahim Pasha Fuad seemed to continue the precedent set by Riadh in 1879 when he selected Fakhri himself out of a then limited number of Egyptian legalists trained in France. Indeed, Ibrahim Pasha's length of experience in the Egyptian courts, where he had been appointed first-instance judge in 1884, was only rivaled by Butrus Ghali, who (although without formal legal training) had been justice undersecretary in every ministry since 1884. In contrast to both Fakhri and Ghali, however, Judge Fuad was accepting for the first time a post in which political *savoir faire* obviously could affect the carrying out of his responsibilities. This fact may even have been considered a positive reason for the British to support his nomination: Fuad's professional aloofness would mean he had never built up a network of understandings with (and therefore potential support from) other high-level political leaders in or out of office.

One other consideration, however, raised suspicions that this latest cabinet appointment was not based on strictly professional qualifications. Ibrahim Fuad had only recently advanced to the presidency of the Cairo court of appeals, as part of the decision to name three new British judges and elevate a chamber of the court to cassation status. His "promotion out" of the court, therefore, could have been seen not only as reward for a loyal judge: it vacated a leadership post that figured prominently in Husayn Fakhri's bid to make the court the keystone of an integrated national professional system. This led skeptics to assume that Ibrahim Pasha's place would soon be taken by a British judge.[43]

If one combines all these developments by the end of 1892—use of khedivial pressure to impose reforms, growing involvement of Interior officials in local judicial administration, and reductions in the responsibility of professionally trained Egyptians at both the lower and upper levels of the *ahliyya* judiciary—it seems obvious that the ground was ripe for a wide range of negative Egyptian reactions. In contrast to the situation during the first decade of the occupation, however, reactions to changes in legal administration after 1892 were bound to be more socially penetrating and more seriously political in nature. In the first place, by this date it was clear that certain issues that had seemed very vital when the local court system was set up were no longer as relevant for debate. This change had both international and internal Egyptian dimensions.

Internationally, Egyptian issues that heads of state had earlier considered for their potential impact on the delicate Eastern Question had taken on very different form by the 1890s. Most European interests in the Ottoman Empire were increasingly guided by considerations that, although they did not exclude concern for the role of law in Ottoman politics, contained a new combination of economic and political emphases. One of these, involving changing modes of economic and financial involvement in the Ottoman Empire, is discussed in the next and concluding chapters. One could see at the same time, however, a major shift in European political maneuverings that presaged new dimensions in the Egyptian Question for the remainder of the century.

Several changes affecting the interests of European powers in both Africa and Asia occurred soon after the fall from power of Chancellor Bismarck in 1890. Kaiser Wilhelm's assumption of more direct responsibility for Berlin's foreign policy created at least two watershed conditions between landmarks of German history at the outset and after the end of Abdulhamid's sultanate (in 1878 and 1914, respectively). One of these would lead to closer involvement in the military affairs of the Ottoman Empire by the turn of the century. The other increased European attention to potential German colonial expansion in Africa. Both processes would strain great power rivalries until, by 1904, a readjustment of relations occurred between France and Britain: the Entente Cordiale. The Entente allowed the future allies of World War I to bury their differences and to prepare to meet the kaiser's growing imperial challenge in Africa, the Near and Far East, and, of course, Europe. Britain's movement first toward, then away from, a direct colonial clash with France in the 1890s had definite consequences for the Egyptian occupation. Beyond Egypt, this movement also affected methods traditionally used by both powers to balance their respective interests throughout the Ottoman Empire.

Almost all historians agree that one major source for instability in great power relations during the 1890s was a reawakening of competition for influence over southeastern Europe. Tensions naturally involved Austria and Russia, the two traditional Eastern Question protagonists whose clashing interests in the Balkans eventually ignited World War I. Germany's decision in 1890 not to renew Bismarck's Reinsurance Treaty with Russia, originally designed to prevent the possibility of a two-front war against Germany, appears to have encouraged what the Iron Chancellor had feared most: closer relations, including west-to-east economic and financial transfers and, eventually, closer political and military ties between France and Russia.[44]

Although Wilhelm's reactions were numerous and complex, a growing Ottoman emphasis in Germany's *Ostpolitik*, including military missions to Istanbul, was one result. As far as London's interests were concerned, changing German foreign policy left no real doubt that the British presence in Egypt and Cyprus had a heightened strategic importance. Thus, British policy toward the Egyptian occupation would have entered a new stage in the 1890s in any event: increased German naval capacities (and therefore the strategic significance of Istanbul and Suez) had started to become an overriding joint concern for all future allies and enemies in World War I.

The rearrangement of priorities that gradually led Britain to enter the spirit of Entente Cordiale should, however, also be traced on the African continent itself. Here again, politics of imperial rivalry had no specific direct bearing on the problems of Egypt's internal governance. Because inter-European relations since the mid-1870s always had effects on high-level politics in Egypt, however, tense conditions elsewhere in Africa could easily be reflected in operations of the Public Debt Commission and the mixed courts. Britain had often faced these bodies as catalysts behind internal Egyptian economic and political crises of both minor and major proportions. Now London was particularly unwilling, because of Egypt's increasing strategic importance, to let tensions elsewhere in Africa serve as an invitation to other nationalities to use similar tactics in the 1890s.

It is not necessary to outline here the full process of colonial expansionism into sub-Saharan Africa in the 1890s. A useful point of departure for linking the well-known "scramble for Africa" to Egypt, however, might be the 1888 Anglo-French understanding over respective spheres of influence in the interior of Abyssinia. This agreement was kept secret for six years "to save the susceptibilities of the Egyptian and Turkish governments."[45] Essentially, it stemmed from British fears that Paris, having improved French port facilities at Djibouti, might take advantage of increased trade coming from Abyssinia to gain influence over parts of the Sudan lost to the Mahdi in the 1880s. Also, by 1890, Italy exhibited enough interest in similar inland expansion to alarm Britain's ambassador to Rome, none other than Lord Dufferin himself.

London's concern with keeping European rivals out of the hinterland of Africa's Horn seemed far removed from the Congo River basin. The arrival of Germany on the African colonial scene in the mid-1880s (in the Cameroons in 1884 and in German East Africa in 1886–87), however, created a new and ultimately vital element in British African policy. Tropical forest explorer Henry Stanley alerted British East Africa Company supporters that their plan to move into Uganda from South Africa was imminently threatened by conflicting claims, either from King Leopold's Congo State or from Germans in Tanganyika. Lord Salisbury soon found himself bombarded by colonial lobby pleas to secure Britain's claim over a north-south corridor linking South Africa to the Mediterranean. Although the foreign secretary initially referred to the Capetown to Cairo scheme as "a curious idea . . . lately become prevalent," he nonetheless sanctioned two colonial agreements (the May 1890 MacKinnon Treaty with Leopold and the July 1890 Heligoland Agreement with Germany) to assure minimum needs outlined by South Africa's Cecil Rhodes.[46] Within a fairly short period of time, the British government would find—particularly in the person of Joseph Chamberlain—other ways to stress the importance of maintaining as wide a field as possible open for free (or at least favorable) entry of British trade into and across future colonial zones.

One aspect of the importance of these developments for Egypt is well known. Great Britain decided to end talk of a phased withdrawal and began preparing politically for an imminent confrontation (which came at Fashoda in 1898) over France's bid to cut the Capetown-to-Cairo axis from west to east. Much too little attention is given to the internal Egyptian implications of these changes until the declaration of Britain's full protectorate in Egypt in 1914 and, in particular, negotiations over the later famous "Four Reserved Points." One of these points was the same question (legal responsibility for the protection of foreign private interests) that had been at the core of the Egyptian Question since the 1830s. Much more than its companion issues (the future status of the Sudan; security of British imperial communications; and defense of Egypt from foreign invasion), however, the third reserved point exercised a variety of effects on internal conditions of Egyptian society and economics. Precisely because of this fact—longevity of previous debates and obvious relevance to everyday concerns of many, if not all, Egyptians—the issues behind the future third reserved point before 1900 must be carefully studied to understand its eventual importance in the history of interwar Egypt.

The record of the 1890s shows that the British ended up appraising almost all capitulatory questions in Egypt in terms of external political needs. Certain estimates of Cairo's legal and legislative future were, as I have suggested, based on England's own international political maneuvers. Others aimed at preparing for what was perceived to be the inevitable and beneficial attraction—for local parties as well as foreigners—of facilitating links to the world market into which Egypt was destined to be submerged in the twentieth century. By following such guidelines for modern legal administration in the 1890s, the occupation in effect admitted that previous efforts to coordinate capitulatory and local legal reform were no longer relevant in Egypt. Equally importantly, this admission reduced Egypt's role in offering professional judicial models that were increasingly going to be needed throughout the Ottoman Empire.

11

The Interplay of Law and Economics in the 1890s

The entire decade of the 1890s was a period of prime importance for both the political and economic future of Egypt. In economic terms, trends set in locally and internationally that brought lasting consequences in the twentieth century. Politically, changes were less immediately perceptible. Open struggles between occupation authorities and Egyptian cabinet leaders subsided in the second half of the decade. Many key local politicians, symbolized by Mustafa Fahmi (prime minister during most of the decade), came to accept compromises, if only to guarantee their tenure in high office. Beneath the surface of political compromise, however, there were other sources for broader attitudinal changes by 1900. Some of these nourished the ideas of a generation that had not experienced the vicissitudes of internal reform issues that had been at the very core of the political careers of men like Nubar, Sharif, or Riadh.

This turn-of-the-century generation was forced by circumstances to leave behind not only personalities and issues, but certain outmoded values associated with the previous three decades. In some ways like the generation that came to maturity when Tanzimat rhetoric was still familiar to elite public figures, Egyptians by 1900 were anxious to adopt new ideas about politics and society. Many members of this generation became convinced that Egypt could once again adopt and adapt to new political and economic goals that testified to its continuing vital importance in the evolution of Ottoman affairs generally. One of the most important of these was a move away from mere institutional reformism as a primary means of promoting the much needed political and economic regeneration that had absorbed Tanzimat spokesmen a generation earlier.

Part of this conviction came from a realization that Egypt's future no longer depended on Ottoman reform models born in the Tanzimat and nurtured, for a certain time at least, by "concerned" European powers. Ultimately, however, attitudinal changes had their origin in ideas and issues that are less abstract or politically distant. Even cumulative economic forces in the 1890s, to which this chapter gives considerable attention, are difficult to portray as moving individuals to support views that distinguish them markedly from a preceding generation. A general lessening of the burden of the public debt, for example, did not cause Egyptians in general to proclaim a "new era." Nonetheless, certain sectors of Egyptian society by the mid-1890s could see ways in which economic and financial stabilization had positively affected their interests even under the politically abrasive conditions of a continuing British occupation. As certain elements of Egyptian society adapted to, and profited from, general economic trends in the 1890s, whole areas of earlier controversy ceased to be issues for debate by articulate local observers.

Similarly, reduced political attention to the previously major issue of judicial and legal reform gave way to different court-related questions. These would have as much meaning for certain sections of Egyptian society as the crisis of legal reform had ten years earlier. In fact, the changed social, economic, or even intellectual position of some groups or individuals had actually been brought about, in part, by new values and legal redefinitions implanted by the previous generation. It was not necessary, however, for those experiencing turn-of-the-century conditions consciously to realize either the original intentions that prompted earlier changes or the extent to which they were only partly successful.

From this point of view, much of Egypt's experience of two decades of effort and compromise in the area of legal reformism became abstract history by the middle of the 1890s. This does not mean, however, that various groups and individuals who depended on legal reform to move to another stage of social or economic development ceased to be concerned about effects wrought by the previous generation's efforts. Rather, they used them in a different way that was deemed more relevant to practical conditions around them. In this respect, shortcomings in earlier reformism produced some of the elements that went into later definitions of where Egypt's social, economic, and even political future should lead. As in the first stages of

Tanzimat more than half a century earlier, some of these definitions proved to be very relevant for other Middle Eastern and North African societies just entering upon experiences Egypt had a generation earlier.

Before approaching such obviously subjective factors in Egyptian social history by 1900, this chapter offers a review of concrete political and economic developments that confirmed the obsolescence of ideals and strategies pursued from the middle to late decades of the nineteenth century.

1892–93: WINTER OF DISCONTENT

The year 1892 ended on a mixture of new Anglo-Egyptian approaches to problems as old as the Egyptian Question itself. First Evelyn Baring (by then raised to the peerage as Lord Cromer) discovered that manipulation of cabinet leadership might not be as easy as he had thought when Mustafa Fahmi formed his first government. According to the French consul, a semiclandestine group of Egyptians who called themselves Young Egypt (Misr al-Fatat) had begun by mid-1892 to oppose a number of "rubber stamp" decisions imposed without Legislative Council agreement. Signs of discontent among "all sorts of functionaries . . . brutally spurned" by the Fahmi regime clearly pleased ᶜAbbas II.[1] The new khedive soon took advantage of Misr al-Fatat's anti-British tracts to encourage Husayn Fakhri (apparently one of Young Egypt's early spokesmen) to accept a new appointment, this time as cabinet head.[2] When this first preference did not work, ᶜAbbas called Riadh Pasha to resume the job he had resigned earlier.

Although this move embarrassed Lord Cromer temporarily, it clearly did not allay Misr al-Fatat's discontent. Riadh, after all, was a member of the old school of elites who had struck bargains with the British (only to be disappointed) on several previous occasions. His approach to two key ministries in 1893 indicated he was still motivated by similar considerations. Instead of bringing Husayn Fakhri back as justice minister, for example, Riadh chose one Ahmad Mazlum, grand master of ceremonies at the court of ᶜAbbas, to replace the technically trained but politically inexperienced Ibrahim Fuad. Butrus Ghali, who had served Dual Control and occupation interests in the Justice Department loyally for fifteen years, was also promoted to a full ministerial post. The fact that he was taken out of justice to become finance minister left little doubt that the British supported the move. The only new cabinet member who stated a desire to wrest back some of the authority that Fahmi's appointees had lost to British advisers was Mazlum Pasha. He seemed to be such a neophyte, however, that Lord Cromer counseled John Scott merely to ignore his politically expedient pronouncements.[3]

One result of ʿAbbas II's 1892 cabinet shuffle must have been to reduce support for Riadh as an opposition political leader. Probably already in January 1893 but certainly by the time the British succeeded in totally excluding Riadh from mixed justice renewal arrangements for another five years, anti-British spokesmen openly declared Husayn Fakhri to be their preferred opposition candidate.[4]

As usual, Egypt's foreign community talked about legal reform only when expiration of the "temporary" Mixed Court Charter approached in 1894. By then, not only main capitulatory rivals but newly visible local interest groups had begun to consider the impact of changing political and legal conditions set in the early 1890s. In fact, several new forms of activity connected with the law and its political importance were already well beyond the ken of the coterie of elites around Riadh and the main foreign consulates.

First, Egyptians who were interested could increasingly study their legal system through a number of written sources that had never before been available. The most technical was a French university doctoral thesis on the mixed courts by law student ʿAbdullah Simaika. Simaika's thesis was important mainly because it represented the first time a French law faculty had allowed an Egyptian to focus on the legal institutions of his own country in a high-level academic study.[5]

Simaika's thesis was primarily a documented history of technical provisions for mixed justice in Egypt before and since 1875. The author did, however, draw attention to issues that, as late as the 1890s, still "chilled" the Egyptian government's attitude toward the mixed courts and made it "anxious to replace them gradually by purely Egyptian courts."[6] It seems interesting, in light of what was to follow, that he did not complain that the courts had misused the principle of mixed interest to transfer almost all major Egyptian litigation to the mixed bench. Instead (perhaps to avoid any impression of wanting to reverse legitimate capitulatory guarantees), Simaika criticized technically unjustified mixed court decisions to accept cases from Ottoman subjects resident in Egypt (Tunisians and Tripolitanians in particular). He also discussed the status of subjects of noncapitulatory independent states that had business in Egypt (Iran and Morocco especially, but also some Latin American countries).

Egyptian-authored publications in Arabic were of course more likely to be read by locals who were not themselves students of law. Writings in Arabic were also less subject to critical review, especially by foreigners, and therefore freer to add political emphases to otherwise technical legal or administrative issues. Late in 1892, for example, *Al-Ustadh*, a Cairo journal with clear sympathies for Misr al-Fatat, announced that Amin al-Bustani, a member of the same generation of Syrian self-made lawyers as Shumayyil and Nicola Tuma, was preparing to publish a book on criminal law in Egypt. *Al-Ustadh* assured its general readers that, because of the importance of his subject for society as a whole, al-Bustani planned to write not for experts, but for educated people generally.[7] Al-Bustani's effort marked the beginning of a trend not only to cease limiting legal writings to specialized publications, but also to relate technical legal subjects to practical social and economic, as well as political, issues.

New types of emphases on legal questions by the mid-1890s were probably most visible in *Al-Ustadh*. It was no secret to the British that *Al-Ustadh* editor ᶜAbdullah an-Nadim already had a reputation for political activism from the pre-occupation period. Historians of Egyptian intellectual currents in this period consider An-Nadim something of a transitional figure linking early expression of nationalist consciousness between 1879 and 1882 (when he lent his journalistic skills to ᶜUrabi's cause) to new attempts to rouse antiforeign sentiments ten years into the British occupation.[8] This revived climate for political journalism in 1892 was part of ᶜAbbas II's early attempt to prove that some autonomy still remained in Egyptian hands. It appeared that some old-line nationalists were coming to believe in the power of popular social and economic causes to move Egyptians to defend themselves against both domestic and international sources of injustice ten years after Tell al-Kabir. Soon, however, An-Nadim's views were deemed too radical: Misr al-Fatat's first sympathetic journalistic organ was closed in less than a year. An-Nadim himself was banished to Istanbul, where he died in 1896. As we shall see, however, he helped establish a linkage between intellectual and social attitudes toward law in the first constitutional nationalist period that was picked up and developed by others at the end of the decade.

In its earliest issues *Al-Ustadh* treated Egyptian legal questions under fairly traditional rubrics. It praised Husayn Fakhri as retiring justice minister and insisted that John Scott had found Egyptian justice "firm . . . and carried out by judges who are not one degree beneath their European colleagues in the mixed courts." An-Nadim also congratulated ᶜAbbas II for personally inspecting the Khedivial Law School and encouraging its students to think of preparation for professional careers as a service to Egypt's future.[9] *Al-Ustadh*'s position on issues that gained more preeminence in the second half of the 1890s was clearer when it covered court cases that suggested possible manipulation in the Ministry of Justice. One of these confirmed Misr al-Fatat's view that cabinet politicians, as much as foreigners who depended on the *status quo* of the capitulatory regime, were responsible for the increasingly desperate economic plight of many average Egyptians.

The case in question, an *ahliyya* appeals plea involving what An-Nadim called "the Fatherland vs. its sons," was what would today be called a class action suit against the government for failing to protect the basic rights of its subjects. It began when a group of Cairene merchants and artisans tried and failed to obtain legislation to protect them from rising competition from cheap imported foreign goods. They then organized a shutdown that closed many shops. Since the strike also eliminated city taxes from normal sales operations, government prosecutors obtained a court order requiring shopkeepers to reopen. When the defendants took their case to appeals, their (unidentified) defense lawyer openly criticized the government for prosecuting protesters trying to improve their material lot. An obviously cynical brief was, the lawyer wrote,

> presented in the name of the sons of Egypt, whose main industry [is deemed by some to be] amusement, play and exhilaration . . . and whose poor now reside on the shores of the sea of depravity [or summer leisure, Ar., *khalaᶜa*]. These people tried to defend themselves by explaining they have closed their shops . . . and adopted . . . mockery and drink as their only business until they obtain rights due to anyone, whether poor or rich, weak or strong. . . . When a commission of experts was sent to investigate they alleged that there were plenty [of good business opportunities] and that the lawyers for the defense had been

> misled in their suppositions by their own inclination toward leisure as a primary activity.[10]

The *ahliyya* defense lawyer blamed the government for harming local business by losing the battle, year after year, to make changes in sorely outdated codes of law. Although this case focused on tariff privileges that created price advantages for foreigners, it ended on a broader note. A final unsuccessful plea moved from the specifics of the shopowners' strike to build a case for Egypt's general welfare:

> The [government] has drawn a picture of what it perceives to be just, as if it were blind to the thousands of sons of the fatherland seated in front of the wineshops and hashish shops . . . and hadn't seen the . . . soil and possessions that have passed over to European ownership as a result of [government] mismanagement. It also apparently has not seen the thousands of criminal cases and contraventions that grow out of quarrelsomeness and inability to cope with the country's declining state of affairs.[11]

Al-Ustadh supported the growing opposition view that the deplorable conditions symbolized by the shopowners' strike stemmed from the failure to challenge foreign domination of main provisions in the civil code. Again and again, its editorials came back to the mixed courts as a symbol of inequity protected by law. "Here are our eastern races" (i.e., Here we are), An-Nadim wrote months after the strike was over,

> . . . doing nothing to better general conditions of interaction [*mu'amalat*], but instead using many of the same methods that are used by Egypt's enemies. The merchant now resorts to lies and deceit, the moneylender relies on trickery . . . to extract the Egyptians' possessions and land even though this is the property of the nation. . . . Foreigners . . . act dishonestly and plunder the *fallah* in the mixed courts, the origin and powers of which the *fallah* does not understand. Foreign functionaries cling to their privileges under the capitulations to exclude Egyptians from government jobs. [These same privileged foreigners] horde houses and property, reducing Egyptian chances for legitimate access to many sources of wealth.[12]

RENEWAL, "PURE AND SIMPLE," OF MIXED JUSTICE FROM 1894 TO 1899

Egypt's foreign community remained unaware of such shifting emphases in the press away from reformism *per se* toward social and economic inequities supposedly supported by the capitulations and local court system alike. Until the spring of 1893, official circulars on mixed judicial questions dealt with *pro forma* issues that raised little or no public comment.[13] Finally, the British tried to return to specific issues left unresolved by the 1890 technical commission. The reform-weary press, however, this time simply dismissed Anglo-Egyptian threats to suspend the mixed courts unless something was done to curb their dominance in local property disputes, the biggest stumbling block in the last (1890) capitulatory commission.[14] In fact, the whole renewal issue was, from this date forward, decided behind the scenes. This served the cause of critics who suggested that guaranteeing stability more than equity in the judicial system was an accepted part of the changed political and economic environment of Egypt. As the decade unfolded, it also became clear that accommodation with imperfect legal reforms realized between 1875 and 1892 was attractive for certain sectors of local society, including many conservative lawyers. Debate over the meaning of such accommodations for the future, in terms of both individual and social material gains or losses, gradually displaced any remaining concern for the form or content of original reform goals.

Anyone who followed diplomatic rumors in 1893 could easily find sources for new cynicism surrounding old issues. One example came in conversations between the French and Danish consuls when Cairo tried to introduce much needed tariffs to make local products more competitive with foreign imports. The Danes, whose business with Egypt was minor in comparison with the French, promised to oppose new tariffs if the Quai d'Orsay supported appointment of a Danish judge to the mixed court of appeals.[15] Although Paris had obviously played the same game to obtain appointments in the past, de Reverseaux now claimed to be above such petty dealings.

In fact, the French had once again begun thinking of changes, if not in tariffs, then at least in other areas, to help overcome the helplessness of the Egyptian government in dealing with the capitulations. De Reverseaux must have sized up the political cost, for example, of renewing confrontations over Article 9 of the 1875 Charter and supposed mixed interest in all Egyptian property disputes. By 1893, the Quai d'Orsay seemed to realize that an extremist stand on this legal anomaly might only lessen chances to bargain over larger issues affecting Anglo-French interests, possibly even in other areas of the world. De Reverseaux therefore initially declared himself ready to grant a key compromise: assurance of continued mixed court jurisdiction *only* over the biggest land transfers that might touch upon foreign interests.[16] As we shall soon see, this would have satisfied the growing number of both Egyptians and foreigners who were investing by this date in larger agricultural holdings producing for an export demand market. Anything done to maintain a sense of security in this area, obviously necessary for the foreign-controlled credit market supplying mortgages to agricultural property owners, could contribute to Egypt's economic development in the future.

In short, even aggressive defenders of the Mixed Court Charter agreed that it was vital to avoid a repetition of the dilemma of the late 1870s, when large numbers of uninformed Egyptians had unnecessarily become involved in mixed court litigation. By the mid-1890s, it seemed more logical to let the mixed courts, as well as both Egyptian and foreign parties best prepared to use their codes, reach a natural level of legal activity occasioned by economic, not political, factors. It was too early in 1893 to predict the strong post-1895 world demand (and higher prices) for cotton produced on Egyptian farms. Nonetheless, depoliticization of the entire judicial reform question at least had a chance of support from both foreign and local entrepreneurs just beginning to readjust their sights on new business horizons in Egypt.

Events showed, however, that the same very local jealousies that had obstructed changes in the Mixed Court Charter since 1876 could still overpower logical economic considerations in the 1890s. In this case, it was again the "fickle mind" of judicial adviser Scott that guaranteed maintenance of the status quo, with all its recognized defects, for another five years. Probably without Agency consent, and certainly without consulting London, Scott made the mistake of repeating what he and many bureaucratic colleagues felt was still a main criterion in Anglo-Egyptian policy. He specifically discouraged the local foreign press from making distinctions between the long-term objectives of mixed and local court reform proposals in 1893. Any increase in the effective capacity of the latter, he felt, should help decrease Egyptian and foreign dependence on the former.[17]

This was enough to reawaken French suspicions that Scott was ready to use conciliatory gestures from supporters of mixed justice to strengthen British control over Egyptian justice. The result was that, although the Cairo Agency stayed out of the formal request for renewal of the mixed courts (by having the Egyptians circulate a new five-year charter that included revision of Article 9 directly to capitulatory capitals), only the German and British governments proved willing to sign without another plenary international conference. London apparently tried once again to pressure acceptance of minimal reforms by waiting right up to the technical expiration date. The British only succeeded, however, in obtaining French and Italian acceptance of "renewal, pure and simple," with the specific understanding that there would be no changes at all in mixed court operations at least until 1899.[18]

LINKAGE BETWEEN LAW AND EGYPTIAN ECONOMIC DEVELOPMENT IN THE 1890S

There is little point in asking what effect these capitulatory developments had on relations between European diplomatic representatives in Egypt. The 1894 Mixed Court Charter renewal process repeated in slightly altered form what had happened each time the Judicial Reform of 1875 came up for review. It is more important to ask how various Egyptian and foreign interests stood to be affected materially by the continued maintenance, throughout the 1890s, of a legal system originally designed to fit conditions at mid-century. What had changed to make this question as important as the politics that obstructed any reform in the 1875 Charter?

Studies of general economic patterns in the 1890s reveal developments that were bound to increase case loads in certain sectors of Egypt's court system, whether mixed or "native." The quite different nature of such pressures as compared to the 1880s was enough to convince British and Egyptian politicians that what had earlier seemed feasible or desirable for reform was simply no longer appropriate. The most obvious physical change by the 1890s was a sharp increase in Egypt's population, which went from about eight million in 1882 to over ten million by 1900.[19] This trend was not accompanied by a concurrent increase in cultivable land surfaces. Since population growth was most intense in rural zones, average available acreage per family began to decline, increasing problems of peasant subsistence.[20] As pressure on the land became more pronounced, there were more local disputes involving farm owners who entered into various short-term contracts with landless wage laborers who competed with traditional part-time sharecroppers. The same factor of crowding pushed rents up, making it materially attractive for some landowners to break existing long-term contracts and reassess future land-use patterns.[21] The growing number of such disputes may actually have encouraged some Egyptians to accept what was by then clear deflation in ambitious mixed and *ahliyya* legal reform expectations from the 1880s.

As long as minor civil cases remained within the reformed hierarchy of *ahliyya* courts, many agricultural contract disputes were being transferred from summary to district-level courts in several provincial Egyptian towns. Now that such an intermediate judicial apparatus finally existed, jurists whose more modest aspirations kept them from mixing into higher-level politics of legal reform stood to see their services (and remuneration) rise in importance in comparison with the first ten years of the occupation. Indeed, as we shall see in the concluding chapter, soon a literature focusing on small and intermediate rental and credit contracts began to replace worn-out political and reform issues formerly preached, but rarely practiced, among prominent advocates in Cairo.

If one combines this view of local justice with changes in landownership patterns by the mid-1890s, it is even easier to see why juridical and judicial problems left over from the Tanzimat lost much of their relevance. Precisely because Egypt progressed more quickly in certain economic and administrative areas, attitudes developed there in the 1890s foreshadowed changing approaches to basic legislative issues in other regions of the Ottoman Empire after 1900. Specifically, it was becoming increasingly apparent that a small but influential number of well-placed interests were posed to make gains in a large-scale commercial agricultural and diversified industrial market. This was often done with the aid of legal devices that previously seemed tailored to serve foreign capitulatory interests only.

Economic historians generally agree that patterns of concentrated large private holdings of land that became characteristic of many Middle East regions in the twentieth century assumed definite form in the 1890s. The process was especially clear in zones like the Nile Delta and regions of southern Iraq, which specialized in agricultural production for export markets. Roger Owen estimated, for example, that by the 1890s more than forty-two percent of Egypt's arable land belonged to large landowners who, in a twenty-year period, nearly doubled acreage cultivated for the international cotton market.[22] Increased investment in this sector alone contributed to both government and landowners' appreciation of an important fact: unlike other subregions of the Empire that still labored under only partially evolved legal systems, Egypt already had courts that could respond immediately to both European and Egyptian-initiated demands for all sorts of rising commercial import and export contracts. If investment trends continued to develop, Cairo's internationally guaranteed legal system had a real chance of gaining importance in the eyes of many who had vied against it for two decades.

On the strictly fiscal side, increasing export and import trade registered some positive notes in the mid-1890s. This occurred not because of increases in agricultural land tax obligations, but because levels of importation (and therefore indirect customs taxes) rose in tandem with agricultural export earnings.[23] Such added treasury receipts definitely helped lighten the overall weight of Egypt's public debt by the end of the decade.

Simple budgetary logic alone, therefore, would have discouraged occupation authorities from letting rumors of future mixed court instability menace revenue-producing import or export contracts, whether from England or other European countries. Foreign cotton buyers' investments, however, were likely to continue to be short-term commitments depending on supply factors unrelated to Egypt's capitulatory regime. Local landowners' involvement in the rising export market and extension of mortgage contracts, on the other hand, soon fostered legal interrelationships that tied Egyptian private-sector economic development to extraterritorial interests for generations to come.

One obvious effect of expanding export sales by large-scale agriculturalists, for example, was an increase in the importation of European goods into Egypt in the late 1890s. Such purchases were divided between consumer items, mainly luxury products, and capital goods either to boost agricultural production or to help fledgling Egyptian processing industries. Professor Tignor's observation that no less than twenty of twenty-three Egyptian manufacturing concerns in existence by 1901 were founded in the 1890s suggests a general rise in capital investment throughout the decade.[24]

One essential fact, however, would have governed attempts to use imported machinery for complementary processing plants for sugarcane or cotton by-products. Even relatively wealthy Egyptians needed to borrow funds to enter the cash crop sector at a high enough level to escape limited local marketing conditions in Egypt. In the absence of a locally controlled modern credit system, the only option was to borrow from foreign subscribed banks operating in Cairo or Alexandria. Once this was done, as it was, the principle of mixed interest tied all subcontracts of such Egyptian investors to the law and jurisdiction of the mixed bench. That a minority of well-to-do Egyptians accepted this prospect and went on to compound their level of private indebtedness to try to secure even more wealth is a matter of statistical fact. Foreign and Egyptian investment capital to found or expand existing mixed land development and mortgage companies continued to mount, at least until serious depression conditions struck midway through the first decade of the twentieth century.[25]

Most additional foreign funds that arrived in this period stimulated export-related transport and light industrial (agricultural-processing) ventures. Expansion in the nonagricultural sector, however, was largely accomplished by newly founded foreign businesses, whose financial needs absorbed most of the credit available in the limited banking sector. This brought to the local commercial field the same imbalance that characterized the institution of credit itself: increasingly numerous European businesses in the capital and main provincial towns (retail machinery and dry-goods stores, for example) became dominant, replacing traditional (mainly family-run) shops in all but the strictly artisan sector. The fact that foreign firms were primarily joint-stock ventures, however, meant that Egyptians who wished to diversify investment of profits that had orginated in agriculture could buy shares in European-controlled retail or industrial ventures without committing major sums or borrowing from foreign-controlled banks.

Both of these trends—concentration of capital in development and mortgage companies servicing investors in land and Egyptians' growing attraction to stocks in foreign companies—implied private-sector growth prospects that no other region of the Ottoman Empire had yet begun to see on a comparable scale. Indeed, positive signs in Egypt would appear even more attractive as political strains, culminating in an Ottoman-Greek war over Crete in 1897, caused general setbacks for entrepreneurs in other provinces.

The sudden impact of the 1897 war on the imperial treasury (and therefore on necessary tax reassessments) came at a time when European demand for Ottoman agricultural export commodities was peaking. Early signs of aftereffects probably left many potential large-scale growers in several provinces wondering if necessary local administrative support functions (import-export licenses, title registration, etc.) would long survive. There is no way of establishing a direct link between Abdulhamid's known tendency after 1896 to clamp down on already limited individual civil rights, including security of person and possessions under law, and a declining volume of trade contracts in various provinces. Figures covering exports from Turkish ports and Syria during the last five years of the century, however, show that, as far as grain shipments were concerned, both zones suffered depression (despite fairly constant levels of production) compared with the preceding decades.[26]

Obviously, one must consider many different causes for this decline in the export activity of Egypt's neighbors. Nonetheless, most surveys of trade patterns in Syria and Anatolia tend to suggest that many commercial agriculturalists were giving up hope that their interests would ever be adequately protected by an independent and disinterested civil judicial authority.[27] No doubt increased sultanic despotism by the mid-1890s exacerbated factors that, in combination, depressed investment in Levantine export markets. Although the same cannot be said of alternative North African sources for marketable agricultural commodities like wheat and olives, rising exports in the same period, especially in Tunis, tended to be dominated by a single foreign trade partner.[28] In those cases, the European partner, France, also enjoyed obvious legal benefits put in place by political forces well beyond either Ottoman or other European powers' control.

Seen by occupation authorities, therefore, Egyptian developments may have promised to be a long-awaited catalyst. Increased investment, under benevolent sponsorship, could bring better economic conditions for those sectors of Egypt's population most prepared to turn the unique legislative and judicial status of their province to local advantage. A good example of the direction many Anglo-Egyptians hoped would become general occurred in 1896, when an Egyptian-run company took over (from an original Belgian concessionaire) responsibilities for an entire provincial section of light (agricultural) railway construction and management.[29] Any additional support for such Egyptian investment meant, of course, that similar ventures would be encouraged to take whatever legal business they had to the mixed courts. Clearly, any hope that private English capital would join such moves would proceed from the assumption that mixed legal status would be as much expected by British as rival capitulatory investors.

Perusal of *The Times*' coverage of Egypt in the mid-1890s suggests that this must have been a very real consideration for veterans of Britain's fifteen-year-old anti-mixed court legal reform campaign. Within five years (corresponding to the rise of future colonial secretary Joseph Chamberlain's politics of increasing economic benefits for England in dealing with foreign producers of raw materials), a British cabinet that had previously concentrated on Egypt's political and administrative imbroglio definitely changed its tack. Many began considering the importance of opening investment prospects in subsectors of the Nile Valley economy that could possibly grow in tandem with larger-scale commercial agricultural pursuits on the part of Egyptian landholders. Beginning in 1895 with the first mention of dairy concerns and Egyptian trademark legislation, attention turned to infrastructural prerequisites for future light industrial development. Between 1897 and 1901, for example, *The Times* printed articles on Egypt's increased electrical generating capacities, sugar-processing mills, laws facilitating the establishment of limited (joint-stock) companies, local developments in the cotton spinning and weaving industry, and the availability of rolling stock for the movement of commercial goods—all observably new topics of interest for British readers.[30]

The best symbol of the developing interplay between private economic and legal matters before 1900, however, was Lord Cromer's support for the founding (in 1898) of the new, mainly British capitalized, National Bank of Egypt. Part of this internationally subscribed (and therefore juridically mixed) bank's aim was to encourage private interests to share in Egypt's investment and export market. One way of doing this was to offer familiar (British) terms to entrepreneurs who had previously been forced to deal with banks under rival capitulatory control. At the same time, this private credit institution began, with Agency support (and under a board headed by Elwin Palmer, Cromer's former financial adviser) to function somewhat as Egypt's first national bank. It received, for example, the main accounts of most government administrations (including the mixed courts) and followed lending policies that favored priority investment sectors, including commercial agricultural storage facilities.[31] It also held limited authority to issue bank notes. This apparent attempt to involve even wider sectors of the local population in freer-flowing commercial transactions still fell short (until 1914) of granting Egyptian bank notes full status as guaranteed legal tender. The move certainly indicated, however, that Cairo policymakers were trying to support more and easier interaction between Egyptian and British business (and therefore legal) interests than at any time in the previous two and a half decades.

Each of these trends encouraged politically articulate Egyptians to denounce the apparent failure of idealistic Anglo-Egyptian legal reforms during the first decade of the occupation. Some compared early failures with more pragmatic but apparently privilege-oriented substitute policies by the end of the 1890s. Eventually a formal nationalist opposition party would use specific and blatant irregularities such as the well-known "mock trial" following anti-British violence in the village of Denshawai in 1906, or collapse of the speculative Cairo investment market in 1907, to rally more widespread condemnation of dual standards in Egyptian justice. It should be obvious, however, that later events that gave definite shape to the use of court issues in anti-British Egyptian nationalism did not occur in a vacuum. Mounting cynicism was the product of gradual alienation and reaction to changes over the entire preceding decade. In fact, many of the same arguments used by the Watani (Nationalist) party after 1906 were already clearly visible in 1898. This one year witnessed several key developments that would contribute to the new politics of nationalism after 1900. One obvious event, Anglo-Egyptian reconquest of the Sudan, had a direct impact on the perception that Britain had become increasingly willing to accommodate necessities of capitulatory privilege in Egypt.

The concluding chapter of this book shows that together with reactions to this major event were a number of related stimuli for adjustment to earlier "moral" estimates of Egypt's legal future. If such different forms of expression had one thing in common by 1898, it was that they rejected the naive optimism and rhetoric that had helped, a generation earlier, to rationalize the presumably benevolent reformist tactics of Nubar, Sharif, or Dufferin and Northbrook. Egyptians who had witnessed typical inconclusive crisis situations in the Ministry of Justice saw no point in renewing such tactics when new dilemmas arose in 1898. In part this stemmed from a simple observation: what had appeared to be serious political commitments behind reformist measures a generation earlier no longer existed. Thus, anyone concerned about legal and legislative conditions after 1898 had to look elsewhere for issues more relevant than administrative reform rhetoric to the average (and some not so average) Egyptians' daily life experiences. In fact, as views of what was politically, economically, and socially relevant began to focus beyond 1900 rather than on the 1880s, Egyptian opinion was more and more willing to limit British judicial advisers to recognized important but essentially routine tasks.

FINAL FORM OF "NATIVE JUSTICE" UNDER THE BRITISH AFTER 1894

The British Agency was somewhat relieved by the resignation of Mustafa Riadh in April 1894, after sixteen months of unnotable culminating service as prime minister. A one-year interim government followed under Nubar Pasha, the last prominent veteran of ambitious legal reforms begun in the 1860s. During this 1894–95 cabinet, Nubar did not raise any of the issues that had made his reputation as founder of Egypt's Europeanized court system. Although Husayn Fakhri returned to loyal ministerial service at this date, Nubar decided to assign the second most active politician of legal reform in his generation to public instruction and public works. Whether the decision to reappoint the professionally qualified but politically disinterested Ibrahim Fuad as justice minister came from Nubar or from the British is not clear. What is clear is that neither Nubar nor Ibrahim Pasha (or any of their successors in official cabinet posts over the next few years) opposed Lord Cromer's now obvious desire to cancel priorities of court reform that had dominated the 1880s and early 1890s.

In fact the judicial advisers' reports during the mid-1890s showed that, following the 1890–91 shift of emphasis away from more ambitious plans, the needs of Egypt's majority rural population were being met. With the extension of summary jurisdictions (up to 37 by 1895), nearly twice as many provincial cases (31,000) were decided in 1894 as in 1892. What was most important, only 1,000 of these decisions were carried by plaintiffs to district courts for retrial. Lower numbers did not mean that district judges were underworked, but they did reduce claims (one of Husayn Fakhri's key points around 1890) that Egypt needed to train more professional jurists to staff courts in all district-level towns.[32]

Agency reports after 1895 recognized this trend and argued that, since more and more Egyptian court cases were beginning and ending at the summary level, the cabinet should cease trying to inflate the importance of Ministry of Justice activities. Cromer did not even mention that serious economic and social pressures were either under way or about to occur as a result of rising investment by landowners trying to expand cash crop agricultural production. By 1895–96, he must have accepted the fact that any increased demand for legal services growing out of such changing conditions would involve the firmly ensconced mixed courts. Thus, the Agency saw no point in nourishing assumptions that raising the numbers and professional competence of *ahliyya* jurists could seriously affect patterns of justice by the turn of the century. On the contrary, Cromer claimed that the "native judiciary have now passed the point of rapid promotion, and have got beyond the special interest which always attaches to new work. In fact, they have settled into harness and it remains to be seen if the present standard of excellence can be maintained."[33] The same report contained even more ominous prospects for a generation of Egyptians who increasingly regarded secular education, and especially legal studies, as a path to employment in occupations unknown before the 1880s. Cromer estimated that very few additional graduates in law would be needed in the Justice Department for a number of years. He even suggested that the Khedivial Law School would render a greater service if it concentrated on a purely administrative training program for future employees of the Ministry of the Interior.[34]

Only one brief issue arose before John Scott's retirement in 1898 to break the impression that many Ministry of Justice decisions were being made without serious concern for their effect on the ranks of Egyptian advocacy. Justice minister Ibrahim Fuad's appointment of one of his professional peers, Sabri Pasha, to replace departing Belgian attorney general Charles Legrelle brought a flush of enthusiasm in the Egyptian press. The tone of articles was reminiscent of Nubar's pride in the selection of Shafiq Mansur to fill the same post after Raymond West's resignation a decade earlier. Like Shafiq Bey, who had worked alongside West in 1885, Sabri had counted among John Scott's professional confidants in the early 1890s. After earning a French doctorate in law, he had moved from private practice to an important judgeship in Cairo. Sabri's appointment to replace Legrelle implied that he was presumed to be equal to previous European holders of the post. One problem was that there were now other qualified Egyptians behind Sabri who, without yet coveting the attorney general's job, saw that few new hirings were planned at the intermediate level. To make matters worse, Ibrahim Fuad's ministry was soon asked to make appointments above a certain rank from a list of British nominees only.

Lord Cromer apparently preferred to cover up the real reasons preventing recognition that Sabri was only one of a number of qualified local jurists expecting to fill high Egyptian judicial posts. Pending Scott's retirement, the Agency even tried to express indirect discontent with the new attorney general's appointment. Sometimes this was done by hinting that the high percentage of penal dismissals or acquittals in Egypt (by a somewhat forced comparison with European systems) proved that the Egyptian-directed *parquet* was not working up to expected levels.[35] Cromer may have hoped to convince British policymakers that, because clear distinctions between local and mixed justice finally existed, London had a responsibility to monitor the former much more directly. If this was intended, it soon became apparent that the Agency's conception of the proper location for such monitoring was not at the town or village level, where unprofessional handling of judicial cases was most likely to occur, but rather in the Cairo court of appeals.

Cromer's reasons for wanting to monitor Egyptian justice at the highest level may have been quite simple: increased British participation in the Cairo court would maximize Anglo-Egyptian ability to watch and react to mixed court deliberations. This was where key litigation involving large land transfers or investments was likely to be found. Having British judges study and compare all such cases, whether purely Egyptian or mixed, was, of course, a very different thing than asking them to assist in the review of lesser litigation originating at the village level.[36]

Tensions over Lord Cromer's suggested expansion of British participation in the high court remained under the surface until January 1897, when the Agency deliberately bypassed Scott and called for the appointment of three new British judges to the appeals bench.[37] There seems little doubt that John Scott was among the opponents of Cromer's interference in such personnel questions. His resignation early in 1898 came only one month after two more British judges were appointed to the Cairo bench. At the same time, a British judge took over Sabri Pasha's post as attorney general, reversing Scott's earlier attempts to Egyptianize the *parquet*.[38]

Although the circumstances surrounding Scott's resignation suggest (like the earlier cases of Benson Maxwell and Raymond West) a falling-out with Lord Cromer, there was no residual court reform controversy when he left. Even if Scott did not resign in protest, it is not difficult to imagine why no open rift appeared, either in *The Times* or in Lord Cromer's correspondence. By this date, no government in London, Conservative or Liberal, shared the previous generation's ambivalence about British commitments to stay in Egypt. Bigger questions, including an imperial axis from Capetown to Cairo, the first stages of a British protectorate arrangement in faraway Kuwait, and a much more aggressive search for trade and investment markets, certainly reduced any presumed controversy over local Egyptian justice to minor proportions.

The trend away from political tensions over judicial affairs became even clearer when John Scott was replaced by Malcolm McIlwraith. The man who would stay on as judicial adviser throughout the remainder of Lord Cromer's consulship had no prior experience of the internal complexities of the Egyptian Question. Unlike most of Lord Cromer's previous key aides, McIlwraith came from a traditional civil service position, deemed quite adequate for overseeing local justice. He definitely had not filled, like Scott (in the mixed courts in the late 1870s and then in India in the 1880s), a high judicial post where the interplay of professionalism and government influence trained one for politics in a protocolonial environment. This attribute, which qualified him for the routine judicial adviser's job after 1898, proved to be a rather negative one for Egyptians who had grown accustomed to a relatively high degree of political leverage between the Ministry of Justice and the British Agency.

McIlwraith's activities over the next few years, for example, proved he was mainly interested in completing the judicial decentralization process begun in 1890–91. By continuing the trend toward what eventually became known as *ᶜumda* justice, McIlwraith rediscovered the most effective way to keep the case load of the provincial courts down to a minimum. By 1900, all civil cases in which disputed sums did not exceed 100 piasters were deemed simple enough to be judged by local village heads. Further reductions in the right to appeal minor penal decisions cases had the same effect: local justice was moving back toward less formal judicial forms that had been characteristic of rural litigation before the entire legal reform process began in the 1860s. This trend would not be formally decreed until "cantonal courts . . . not . . . bound strictly . . . by established codes" were established in 1912.[39] By the key period between 1898 and 1904, however, even McIlwraith could see that what Lord Cromer now supposed to be purely administrative concerns affected Egyptian views of the workings of justice under the extended occupation. When the process of deemphasizing professionalism passed another major landmark—the establishment of trial by peer *assises* jurisdictions in the penal system in 1904—he warned Lord Cromer of widespread "abandonment of the judicial service as a profession in favor of . . . other administrations and a consequent . . . loss of the best of the young [Egyptian] legal talent."[40]

Anyone who read Agency reports summarizing McIlwraith's accomplishments would not have suspected that Britain's second official judicial adviser had any misgivings about the steady progress of "native justice." Simple statistics after 1900 proved that procedures for local justice adopted during the 1890s had solved earlier problems of judicial paralysis. Many segments of Egypt's increasingly articulate educated population, however, were disillusioned with London's apparent satisfaction. For those who were particularly aware of contradictions between ideal Ottoman Tanzimat schemes that had failed and observable realities in the 1890s, successes sometimes stressed the wrong factors. "Native justice," even if it had improved greatly, would never earn the type of recognition imagined when, in the Treaty of Paris of 1856, foreign sponsors of the Tanzimat had invited an earlier generation of Ottoman reformers to "participate in the advantages of the public law . . . of Europe." Of course the Judicial Reform of 1875, the original symbol of Egypt's desire to go beyond modest Tanzimat advances in the Empire as a whole, still functioned on a technical level unmatched in any other province. Egyptian frustrations over the obvious gap between mixed and local justice, however, were probably greater by the end of the 1890s than at any time over the previous two decades.

This gap had always existed in reality. Both before and after 1900, however, it tended to be camouflaged by opinions claiming to reflect modern ideas of reform. This had been most visible in the local ranks of legal professionalism since the mid-1880s. Moreover, there had been some, albeit limited, advances in Egypt's modern legal sector. As a consequence, benefits were being gained by locals who knew how to use the law to strengthen their material position in an increasingly commercialized society and economy. Again, this was an advantage not easily found, even by privileged classes, in other provinces of the Ottoman Empire. It was something not only to be maintained, but expanded, if Egypt (and elite groups by then emerging in Egypt) was to win the type of recognition many came to expect in the first decade of the twentieth century. The way in which concerns of these groups evolved often wedded them to quite different concepts of law. Such varying concepts, examined in the context of contemporary Arabic writings on law, offer a useful historical profile of these concerns, and those who held them, by 1900.

12

Conclusion: Social Perceptions of Law in Egypt by 1900

Several samples of turn-of-the-century writing help illustrate how and why local social politics, more than official policies, affected debates over the role of law and courts in Egypt after 1900. Certainly many different turn-of-the-century ideas linking law to essential social or economic functions reflected concerns not limited to Egypt alone. Because Egypt's experiences were particularly intensive, however, and because reactions at several levels of Egyptian society were quite well articulated, issues reviewed in this chapter stand out as early harbingers of currents that would spread to other regions of the Middle East and North Africa between 1900 and World War I.[1]

Some of these issues concern internal social and intellectual schisms visible long before the 1860–90 generation became preoccupied with the politics of court reform *per se*. To assign such views to tempting conservative or liberal categories, however, would be to underestimate the importance of many changes since the mid-nineteenth century. Broad economic or political studies, while documenting effects of change on local and foreign interest groups, too often overlook intellectual or social adjustments that do not lend themselves to simple classification as forward- or backward-looking.[2] Here a major theoretical premise from the introduction of this book should be recalled. In chapter 1 I suggested that observation of social and intellectual adjustment in modernizing Third World countries is most useful historically if one finds attitudes rationalizing changes that, although they ultimately affected society as a whole, had particular relevance for restricted subgroups. This tended to be the case in legal writing in Egypt around 1900. Sometimes adjustments were to changes initially opposed by conservative opponents of foreign borrowings or supported by progressive elements dissatisfied with a time-honored status quo. Once in place, however, new legal categories involving social and economic identity (property tenure, rental and credit contracts, etc.) often turn yesterday's opponents of the status quo into today's neoconservatives. When this happens, neoconservative defense of new status quo conditions may involve apologetics proving derivation from traditional values.

This chapter seeks to illustrate Egyptian neoconservative rationalizations, not of judicial reformism *per se*, but of the centrality of European law in several areas of social and economic change. Such concerns should be seen as early reflections of future patterns of Middle Eastern political history generally. There has been an overemphasis by historians on the study of early twentieth century nationalist politics primarily as a process of opposition. Neoconservative adaptation to "inevitable" processes of change, therefore, may not seem to be as political as the openly reactionary views of religious conservatives or positions expressed by purely secular nationalists. In the former case, defenders of the *sharicа* lamented the loss of presumed security in the past. True reactionism, unlike the mixture of past, present, and future characteristics in neoconservative opinions, faced an inevitable quandary: it lacked a conception of how a return to past values could, in practical terms, help deal with problems that were clearly in evidence in the present and likely to take on even more importance in the future.

Another source of opinion might be labeled "radical" because it openly espoused political nationalism. These ideas definitely stood a greater chance of gaining wide public recognition than did those of neoconservative interpreters of law and politics in Egypt after 1900. Direct opponents of the status quo, radical nationalists tried to force immediate change by denouncing observable injustices "caused" by foreign institutions borrowed since the 1870s. Those who viewed the social politics of law in these terms seemed to share dissatisfaction with their equally anti–status quo conservative religious counterparts. Also like religious conservatives (but unlike those who supported neoconservative views), they lacked, at least for another half-decade, a way to build within a system that was effectively operating. This concluding chapter does not seek to deny in any way the coming importance of more radical politics of dissent in Egypt after the turn of the century. Its main purpose is to show how neoconservative attitudes toward law and society tried, albeit unsuccessfully, to prevail over more actively dissident views as the new century began.

EARLY MODERATE AND RADICAL APPROACHES: QASIM AMIN AND MUSTAFA KAMIL, 1894–95

Among Egyptians involved in written campaigns on law around 1900, the best known, albeit for different reasons, were Qasim Bey Amin and Mustafa Kamil. Of these two, the former consciously shifted from identification with narrow professional apologetics—visible in *Les Egyptiens: Réponse à Monsieur le Duc d'Harcourt*—to underlining the social and economic attractions of sections of the *ahliyya* civil and commercial codes.[3] This transition was reflected in various articles by Qasim Amin appearing in *Al-Mu'ayyad* during the later 1890s. It apparently earned him a considerable following among neoconservative lawyers, including teachers at the Khedivial Law School in Cairo, several years before publication in 1899 of his landmark book, *Tahrir al-Mar'a*. Amin's neoconservative approach to legal questions was not as direct as his views on the social and economic cause of women in Egypt. Certain trends it reflected, however, were continued in the moderate nationalist Umma party shortly after the turn of the century.[4]

By contrast, Amin's younger contemporary Mustafa Kamil began, shortly after finishing his *licence en droit* in 1895, to use points of law to prepare politically for opposition to the occupation regime. Kamil's approach, which attracted a more militant following among Egyptian lawyers, received a strong stimulus during the 1898–99 Sudan campaign controversy. This sudden forward impetus helped guarantee that, despite more nuanced social and economic factors supporting neoconservative approaches to Egypt's legal system by 1900, the direct politics of law would attract adherents to Kamil's Watani Nationalist party after 1904.

The incomplete impression that remains is that rising numbers of lawyers in Egypt and other regions of the Middle East perceived their own and their respective polities' future in terms of declared militancy.[5] Part of the problem of interpreting the legacy of nineteenth-century politics of legal reform, then, stems from overemphasis on events that, like the Sudan controversy or, even more obviously, the Denshawai incident of 1906, marked turning points in Egypt's nationalist history.

Even while still a secondary school student, Mustafa Kamil was already divided between two rising concerns for young educated Egyptians in the 1890s: social advancement (for those who had the means to pay tuition) through specialized vocational training or becoming engaged in opposition politics. His privileged position as a scholarship student and *protégé* of education minister ʿAli Mubarak exposed Kamil to an earlier generation's attempts to revive popular nationalist sentiments left over from the pre-occupation era. Such exposure came from disgruntled politicians like Mubarak and Husayn Fakhri, both of whom had identified with *Misr al-Fatat* in 1892. Both senior figures were also associated with rising emphasis on the Khedivial Law School as a training ground for future Egyptian political leaders.

Another source for the views Kamil later made famous was his early law school contact with students who (like Fuad Salim) had taken inspiration from their own fathers' experiences in pre-1882 nationalist politics. Kamil soon found himself in an underground successor group to Misr al-Fatat that called itself the Society for the Renewal of the Fatherland.[6] By this time (1894, the year in which Qasim Amin published *Les Egyptiens*) some future Watanists already saw a need to set themselves apart from moderates who preferred moral or social and economic programs for Egypt's progress into a new decade and century.

Following transfer from the Khedivial School of Law to the recently founded Ecole des Frères Chrétiens in Cairo, Kamil arranged to continue his law studies in France.[7] This opportunity placed him in contact with a circle of influential Egyptians who were already trying to disseminate moderately progressive nationalist views without depending on sponsorship from the khedivial *diwan* (the case of the Watanists) or foreign assistance of any kind. Recent Khedivial Law School graduate Ahmad Lutfi as-Sayyid and Saʿad Zaghlul, who had temporarily left his post on the *ahliyya* bench to complete his *licence* in law in Paris, met in Geneva in 1895 with Shaykh Muhummad ʿAbduh and Qasim Amin (both *ahliyya* judges since the early 1890s). All four Egyptian jurists preferred to deemphasize the direct confrontation political strategy of the new Watani grouping then forming in Cairo. According to one account, it was at this time that Kamil decided to reject gradualist views expressed by Amin, ʿAbduh, and as-Sayyid.[8]

When he returned to Egypt, Kamil became engaged not in professional pursuits as a lawyer, but in pressing for closer Watanist association with ᶜAbbas II's "palace clique." He also sought various forms of foreign (including French and/or Ottoman) sponsorship for anti-British propaganda efforts. Apparently it was as a result of his being "discovered" by François Deloncle, a strongly antioccupation *député* visiting Egypt, that Kamil was able to revisit Europe to debate with his older gradualist-leaning lawyer colleagues. In speeches he gave in France, Kamil indicated that he believed direct French political pressure on the British, not various forms of social and economic development, was the quickest route to solving Egypt's problems.

A speech published by the *Nouvelle Revue* in December 1895 developed the kernel of what later became Watani party demands for formal court reforms as a minimal nationalist demand. First, French audiences heard what they, and perhaps Kamil, wished to believe: that, before 1882, "France had helped regenerate Egypt by introducing all sorts of progressive innovations . . . without harming either its autonomy or liberties, and without trying to dominate its local institutions."[9] Kamil then contrasted France's conveniently assumed "benevolence" in sponsoring for the mixed courts with historically observable attempts to manipulate Egyptian justice. He insisted that the only power able to monitor British exploitation of the position they had gained in Egypt was the internationally guaranteed mixed judiciary—again something with which the French were eager to agree. This type of language in 1895, then, set the stage for the later paradox of Egyptian nationalist tactics pursued by Mustafa Kamil, at least until the Entente Cordiale of 1904. His somewhat ironic call for France to increase its (equally imperialist-motivated) opposition to London's occupation regime alienated Egyptians who had no sympathy at all for a foreign "cooperative" component. Kamil, however, seemed obsessed with the idea that the mixed courts, through their international immunity from control by the occupying power, held the key to Egypt's political future. "The English," he proclaimed to his French audience,

> . . . have often manifested their hostility to the guarantees extended [under the capitulations] to Europeans. . . . They feel that these guarantees are obstacles preventing them from taking final possession [of Egypt]. For this reason alone they have sought jurisdictional unifica-

> tion, not to give the country a single set of laws, but to arrive at the suppression of the mixed courts . . . that they consider to be an intolerable barrier to their tyrannical caprices. Of course Egyptians will be happy the day when Europe will have confidence in their judges and will give to all, Europeans and local subjects alike, the same judge. But as long as the English continue to occupy Egypt, Egyptians will understand that it is in everyone's interest to maintain the mixed courts.[10]

Already in 1895 (a decade before the more famous Denshawai incident catapulted Watanist judicial grievances to the forefront of Egyptian politics), Kamil combined a surprisingly naive willingness to depend on the mixed courts with other, strictly local, concerns. Some of the latter held some chance of becoming popular nationalist issues. When he referred to continuing clashes between occupation soldiers and Egyptian villagers, for example, he attacked British unilateral decisions to create (as they had in 1882 and would again at Denshawai) special jurisdictions to try such cases outside normal court operations. Although the presumed victims of separate standards of justice in such cases were simple villagers, Kamil couched his condemnation in a way that invited his peers in the legal profession to speak out politically in their defense. "The English," he declared,

> . . . continue threats to create, as they did last winter [1894–95], special courts to hear cases that have any bearing, large or small, on their interests. . . . The setting up of such tribunals is a very serious violation of the law. . . . A great sadness overcomes one at the thought that such a court could have been put in place by people who know anything at all about the rights of people and who live in the nineteenth century.[11]

DIVISION OF VIEWS ON THE LEGALITY OF THE ANGLO-EGYPTIAN SUDAN CAMPAIGN

If informed opinion had been more favorable toward open attacks on revised legal reform policies in Egypt in the second half of the 1890s, several political issues should have aroused wider support for Mustafa Kamil's views. Ironically, the earliest such issue was actually debated in court over a three-year period during the planning and execution of Herbert Kitchener's famous reconquest of the Sudan Province.

Controversy over the possibility of mixed court intervention to frustrate Britain's clearly imperialist interests in the Sudan began when Lord Cromer committed £E 500,000 in Egyptian public debt reserves to extend railheads toward Khartoum. This move was presumably sparked by a call for international assistance following defeat of Italian forces at Adawa in March 1896. In fact, it was a first step toward reentering the Sudan to thwart planned French moves eastward to the Horn from territories already secured in West Africa.[12] Even if Cromer had tried to justify rail extension as an essential Egyptian development expense, however, debt law procedures had always required prior Caisse approval before using any reserve funds. When a majority of Caisse representatives approved a special request from the British Agency, the French and Russian commissioners claimed that unanimity was required in all such votes. Rather than bend to majority rule, the French and Russians broke rank and brought suit against the government in the mixed courts. The latter, still anxious to show the extent of their influence over Anglo-Egyptian policy decisions, supported the minority plaintiffs' view. Resurgence of the same controversies that had thwarted Lord Northbrook's use of sinking fund reserves in 1884 meant that all monies expended for rail expansion and then for actual troop movements into the Sudan were technically illegal. In fact, appeals proceedings were still pending when Kitchener's forces entered Khartoum in 1898!

What is essential here is not France's first major failure to use the international courts to obstruct British occupation policy priorities. Rather, one should look at Egyptian reactions to the last high-level judicial imbroglio of the century. Given inflammatory anti-British declarations already being made by Watanist sympathizers, mixed court intransigence on Sudan campaign funds should have had some attractive force. Especially when arrangements were imposed in 1899 to make the Sudan a separate Anglo-Egyptian "condominium," informed Egyptians were bound to condemn the move as a departure from the vague international legal status of the occupation itself. In fact, Watanist-leaning sheets like *Al-Mu'ayyad* continued to favor anti-British resentment over possible irredentist aspirations by arguing that the campaign itself had been illegal from the outset.

If anti-British propagandists hoped that different sections of opinion would line up behind the mixed courts on the Sudan issue, however, they were sorely disappointed. Egyptians were given a choice between trusting Britain's future good intentions and an obvious return to political manipulation of Egypt's mixed court system. Most moderate nationalist papers, including *Al-Huquq*, supported not England *per se*, but the administration's right to dispose of its own budget free from outside interference. Amin Shumayyil's editorials condemned the mixed courts and supported the efforts of the (now largely Egyptian-staffed) attorney general's office to squelch the appeals case of the French and Russian members of the Caisse. They thus became early examples of a preference to hold fast to moderate (but realistic) gains for general Egyptian interests that could be made through proper recognition of the limits of judicial authority.[13]

An essential question remains. Who, in fact, was politically interested in Ministry of Justice affairs in 1897–98, which also happened to be the year of British "rearrangement" of the Cairo appeals court, convenient removal of attorney general Sabri Pasha, and John Scott's resignation? In their separate approaches to the Sudan campaign and budgetary autonomy (questions that had been central to nascent Egyptian nationalism twenty years earlier), radicals and moderates alike seemed to be stressing legal technicalities that no longer held attraction for groups outside the narrow circles of Watanists or the professional lawyers' press. Ultimately, issues that would interest considerably less well-known individuals and groups by 1900 tended to be not necessarily apolitical, but certainly more socially relevant than the broad political causes that lawyers like Mustafa Kamil and even *Al-Huquq* editor Amin Shumayyil tried to address.

BEGINNINGS OF A MORAL-MATERIAL DILEMMA: SOCIOECONOMIC INTERRELATIONS OF *AHLIYYA* LAW IN 1898

The best source for documenting changing local identification with legal reform questions is again *Al-Huquq*, especially after the death of its original editor in 1897. Amin Shumayyil's successor, Ibrahim Jammal, initially dropped support for moderate reformist efforts that had been characteristic of *Al-Huquq*'s editorials for over a decade. Until sometime shortly after the turn of the century, one finds in its place a rising concern for direct private material advantages to be gained via provisions in the *ahliyya* and mixed codes. This seemed to reflect a professional bias that, unless handled in a very different way, neither Mustafa Kamil nor Qasim Amin (or their respective followers) could have supported as a basis for a broader political cause.

Signs of problems appeared when *Al-Huquq* began stating opposition to increasing restoration of village *ᶜumda* responsibilities for local justice. Jammal's bias also appeared when he questioned what some lawyers perceived to be Anglo-Egyptian willingness to expand, at their expense, the legal role of the Islamic *qadi*. Although the latter subject had also drawn comments from Amin Shumayyil earlier, it had not, until this date, seemed to represent a real challenge to the expertise and functions of the *ahliyya* judiciary. By 1898, however, several potential sources for friction between traditional *qadi* jurisdictions and *ahliyya* law appeared. The first definitely stemmed from Ministry of Justice moves (with tacit British support) to alter the *qadi*'s place in personal status justice. Only one aspect of efforts underway—which was picked up immediately by Jammal—stood to affect individual professional interests and the upcoming generation of trainees for *ahliyya* court service. Beneath the surface of this issue, however, there was a sign that lawyers were beginning to sense a very local need to discuss a number of *shari^{c}a*-related subjects that might be vitally attractive to their potential clients.

For one thing, Egypt had just experienced, in 1897, a significant administrative reform that caused reactions among *ahliyya* and traditional Islamic legalists alike. In November 1896, the Ministry of Justice decided, after thirteen years of multijurisdictional confusion in handling family successions, to abolish the traditional institution of the *bayt al-mal*.[14] Soon after suppression of this time-honored office for coordinating relations (and fees) between survivors of the deceased and the *qadi*'s *mahkama*, the ministry also expanded the responsibility of Egypt's first noncapitulatory mixed (shariatic and secular) judicial body, the *majlis al-hasbi*. Since 1889, a single *majlis* in Cairo had handled a large number of legal matters involving guardianship (of minors, orphans, or the mentally incompetent)—a major subsection of Islamic jurisprudence formerly monopolized by the *qadi*.[15] Two decrees in 1897 extended a "lay" guardianship court organization down to the district level. These stated that the Ministry of Justice and Ministry of the Interior would appoint, respectively, a local religious figure (not a *qadi*) and a lay notable to share expanded *majlis* responsibilities with the *ma'mur*, or district head.[16]

The *majlis al-hasbi* reforms and other primary source evidence from 1898 suggest that Egypt's lawyers were beginning to see a possibility of more and more overlapping between their own secular fields and lingering traditional element in *shari^{c}a* law. Soon not only activities of the guardianship courts but especially permutations in the supreme *mahkama* in Cairo itself promised other potential conflicts of interest between secular and shariatic legal professions.[17] When some lawyers sensed that such shifts in administrative policy might hamper their own professional edge in cases marginally affected by shariatic law, an actual anti-*mahkama* bias began to appear in the local press.

The maiden editorial of *Al-Huquq*'s new editor inaugurated a problem that would take on diverse forms in Egypt after 1900. Ibrahim Jammal launched what other lawyers considered excessive attacks on efforts to improve *qadi*-related justice. He specifically condemned plans to change the curriculum and open more places in the Khedivial Law School for trainees who sought appointments in the *mahkama*s. The way Jammal defended the exclusiveness of *ahliyya* training suggested he did not as yet appreciate the importance of overlapping grass-roots social and economic concerns. His editorial adamantly denied that any mutual ground existed that could possibly justify either a closer working relationship or an intellectual exchange between *shari^c^a* specialists and lawyers involved in secular civil justice. "We feel," Jammal wrote in 1898,

> that given the present areas of competence [of the *mahkama* courts] trainees for their jobs do not need education beyond what is available to them in Al-Azhar or the Dar al-^c^Ulum. The law school is not really a suitable place to teach the *shari^c^a*. Since today the *shari^c^a* courts exist only for questions touching religion and personal status of the believers, they should limit their benevolent labors to matters that concern them specifically.[18]

It did not take long for *Al-Huquq*'s new editor to realize that such extreme secularist views ran against opinions held among his colleagues at the bar. Although *Al-Huquq*'s challenge was directed specifically at Muslim jurists, responses to the narrowness of such views came from both Christian and Islamic sources. What all respondents had in common was avoidance of any suggestion that secular and sectarian laws were necessarily mutually exclusive or in opposition. Many even wanted to assure prospective students and clients that granting necessary recognition to principles of the *shari^c^a* would not harm but rather strengthen both social and individual material interests that were vital to Egypt's future.

An example of a Christian lawyer's approach to this problem appeared in an article signed by Najib Shuqra. Shuqra was a holder of a French *licence en droit* who soon founded *Al-Istiqlal* (Independence), a clear competitor for *Al-Huquq*'s readership. Until Shuqra realized how slow *Al-Huquq* would be to stress new forms of social and economic relevance in the law, he and others simply tried to reassert compatibility between their own obviously secular legal pursuits and basic Egyptian cultural values. In an article "On the Duties of Lawyers," published in *Al-Huquq* in September 1898, he raised standard questions of technical dealings between legal professionals (judges and lawyers) and their clients, along with a novel form of criticism of Egyptian lawyers for failing to respond to the standards of "moral conscience" expected by the majority of clients whose interests they held in trust.

Shuqra's attack on narrow professional training and tendencies to neglect traditional moral values may have reflected the added deference that a Christian lawyer could be expected to show toward clients from an Islamic majority community. It also prepared the way, however, for a form of legal and political rhetoric that would soon also be used by prominent Muslim members of the profession. Shuqra may thus have been the first moderate political spokesman of his profession to place such moral issues and their relationship to the law in the context of patriotism. Indeed, the term *wataniyya* became one that neoconservative interpreters of relationships between law and society in the key period between 1898 and 1904 used, albeit with different emphases, as frequently as their more radically engaged contemporaries.

In a very revealing paragraph, Shuqra summarized both a dilemma and a hope within the social politics of legal professionalism in his generation. "Many parents who are religious and firm in their conscience," he wrote,

> refuse to send their sons to learn law and . . . enter the profession. They imagine that their future success will depend on double-dealing and deception. . . . The actions of some lawyers who cannot find a way to achieve harmony between their consciences and their everyday practices have fixed this image in the minds of many. Some sacrifice their conscience out of greed, or because in their narrow-mindedness they lose good judgment. . . . Thus they bring shame to a profession that has been the hope of kings, ministers, and princes and pursued by proud people who care for freedom and humanity.[19]

NEOCONSERVATIVE SYNTHESES: LAW SCHOOL *MUDARRIS* MUHAMMAD RA'FAT

Najib Shuqra's approach to moral questions in law was symptomatic of positions expressed by several Egyptian lawyers during the next five or six years at least. Because Shuqra was a Syrian Christian, however, the issues he addressed—particularly concerning individual material gain and spiritual or religious conscience—required a degree of "Islamization" to open wider dialogue, either in the *ahliyya* bar or in Egyptian society as a whole. There is ample evidence to suggest that a number of Muslims, ranging from social thinkers like Judge Qasim Amin to surprisingly pragmatic teachers in the Khedivial Law School, recognized this need. Soon several tried to make it a priority over both technical legal reform debates and direct political confrontations favored by the Watanist faction. What emerged, largely on a model proposed in 1898 by Qasim Amin, was what I have referred to as a neoconservative approach to *ahliyya* law.

Neoconservatives would exhort awareness and use of the law in ways that nonspecialists could recognize as vital to general social and individual welfare, whether viewed from a religious or essentially secular perspective. Such awareness was meant to underscore the relevance of law to religious, political, and, in the end, a rather specific set of individual material concerns among identifiable Egyptian social sectors at the turn of the century. Indeed, more and more well-placed Egyptians, although they may have had no specific interest in technical questions that lawyers debated, had by this date various reasons to be concerned about the type of law that applied to their material interests. Most importantly, many were anxious to justify actions that could be taken to protect such interests in broader social or even nationalist terms. The surviving text that demonstrates this growing impetus best is Khedivial Law School professor Muhammad Ra'fat's book *On the Principles of Secular Law*, published by the Jaridat al-Islam press in 1898.[20]

Ra'fat's *Kitab usul al-qawanin* is a fitting focus for the conclusion of this book for several reasons. Most obvious is the fact that it was prepared (and presumably used for lectures) by a teacher in the law school that, by the mid-1890s, had already been identified as the "breeding ground" for Egyptian political leaders in the coming generation.[21] An equally important justification for focusing on this book is the support it received from Qasim Amin, himself by this date engaged in publishing (in the conservative Islamic newssheet *Al-Mu'ayyad*) articles reflecting similar theses.[22] Qasim Bey's role in writing an "Islamic" preface to Ra'fat's work was clearly to establish the otherwise unknown teacher's credentials. Ra'fat was identified as one among a number of professional *ahliyya* legalists dedicated to improving the moral and social welfare of Egypt as a whole. Beyond that ideal goal, his work had a practical orientation toward social and economic questions of reflected in post-Tanzimat laws applied in Egypt and other regions of the Ottoman Empire.

Qasim Amin's introduction indicated that he was frankly pleased that an Egyptian Muslim was anxious to continue the work of scholars who, like his *ahliyya* court colleague Muhammad ᶜAbduh nearly a generation earlier, had tried to define the place of secular law in the total cultural context of Islamic society. Ra'fat's book made it clear, he said, that lawyers could "bring to the Egyptian public the basic knowledge of the law that has become indispensable today not only for legalists, but for writers, journalists, business people, civil servants, and . . . for any man who needs, either because of his vocation or interests, to understand the juridical and philosophical principles that underline our contemporary social organization."[23] Amin saw in the *Kitab* a demonstration that Egypt's codified laws took essential inspiration from sources that could yield the same beneficial results as the Islamic *shariᶜa*. He complimented Ra'fat for "giving . . . to Egyptian youth a fine example . . . of devotion and attachment to our [Islamic] institutions." Amin felt that the *Kitab* provided insight into the sources of universal justice that are to be found in revealed law. Here the Ottoman Empire had more to learn from its own traditions than from the West. Without a tradition of revelation, he claimed, Christian Europe

> had lived in total ignorance [of broad principles of law]. About the time of the Crusades they brought together a specific body of written laws that soon proved to be insufficient. This led them to study the laws of other communities [Ar., *ummam*]. In this way they learned that the laws [they had themselves legislated] were feeble reflections of the laws of the Heavenly Legislator. They were astounded that they had proceeded in a piecemeal fashion without [a necessary firm grasp of the higher principles of revealed law]. . . . Many Westerners claim that the basic sources for [secular] legal science are two: practical need and the rational mind. . . . But I say, you who are rational men, consider that God gave reason to men so that they could bring about benefit and fend off evil [by using it]. Yet we know men to be victims of the two contradictory forces of lust and anger [that in the end taint the laws they legislate for themselves]. Some higher need exists, therefore, that is served by revealed law, brought by prophets to provide light and . . . support the weak.[24]

Such strong emphasis on the ultimate moral force of revealed law was only one suggestion that Ra'fat approached Egyptian legal issues in different ways than many of his predecessors. The *Kitab* was the first work that researched specific shariatic texts and considered how their analysis related to *qanun* laws being applied in Egyptian courts. Where contradiction could be identified, Ra'fat's introductory sections nearly obligated him to object to any foreign-inspired laws that departed from moral guidelines in the *sharīᶜa*. Of course, had the work been fully motivated by Islamic reactionism, the *Kitab* would have had to condemn many contradictions. This was far, however, from the essential aim of neoconservative *ahliyya* lawyers at the turn of the century.

Indeed, Ra'fat systematically avoided criticism of specific foreign-dominated (and *qanun*-supported) institutions that had been targets for Egyptian critics of abortive legal reform efforts in the 1870s. Treatment of circumstances leading to and resulting from the original Mixed Court Charter, for example, was brief, containing only one very oblique reference to efforts to reform the laws.[25] Still unresolved controversies over mixed interest and the long legal arm of the public debt commission (the most debated mixed court question in the year the *Kitab* was published) escaped any subjective evaluation. The epitome of apolitical treatment of foreign interventionism appeared in Ra'fat's cursory historical sketch of "legislative authority" in Egypt. It was here, of all places, that political obstructionism had prevented attempts to relate broad principles of shariatic tradition to civil laws. Not only was no serious distinction made, however, between Ismaᶜil's "responsible mixed ministry" in 1878–79 and the largely powerless legislative council put in place by Lord Dufferin in 1883: there was no mention at all of Egypt's abortive attempt to establish its own autonomous Majlis between 1879 and 1882.[26]

On the broadest level, the *Kitab usul al-qawanin* raised philosophical and moral questions that had been the main intellectual fare for the first generation of Tanzimat-educated lawyers. Long before publication of the *Kitab*, writers in *Al-Huquq*, for example, had tried to justify general abandonment of shariatic legal models by evolving a theory of compatibility of "legislative intent" between God, the supreme lawgiver, and legislators of secular civil law.[27] Although Ra'fat opened similar fields of inquiry, several marks distinguished his attempts to compare assumed sources and meaning behind revealed and legislated law. He devoted only brief attention to theories of the philosophical evolution of natural law from a rudimentary social contract to advanced levels. Ideally, in the latter, human legislators, through consideration of cumulative experience, gradually make an effort to institutionalize higher ethical values in systematic codes. Like *Al-Huquq*'s editorialists before him, Ra'fat was careful to cite arguments of Western philosophers like Bentham, Spencer, and Rousseau linking natural law, philosophy, and abstract political theory. Unlike previous writers, however, he simply refuted social contract theory, which he deemed "unprovable" as an original source for eventual higher evolutionary stages of civil law.[28] In its stead, the *Kitab* espoused the superiority of timeless principles of revealed shariatic law. Judging from the tenor of his introductory sections, then, Ra'fat purposely intended to show weaknesses in the Western origins of Egypt's codified law and call, in certain areas, for some form of return to the *shari^{c}a* as a guide for both moral and practical legal affairs.

The author's reasons for doing this selectively may have responded to needs that were essentially political in nature. No real purpose could be gained by applying to all foreign-styled laws the same type of Islamic critique that appeared, with measured regularity, at key points in the *Kitab*. Leveling more attacks on institutions that the British had tried but failed to reform since the mid-1880s would only lessen chances of official recognition of some worthy educational value in Ra'fat's teaching manual. In fact, *most* sections of the book indicate that, despite considerable rhetoric in support of the moral superiority of shariatic law, practical considerations of protecting modest status quo interests were becoming the most essential issues in Egyptian legal politics.

APPLIED NEOCONSERVATIVE INTERPRETATIONS

Sometimes the existence of well-known shariatic texts clearly necessitated comparisons between Islamic ideals and the reality of certain Egyptian legal practices. Here Ra'fat usually concluded that proper interpretation of *ahliyya* law could lead to adequate defense of essentially identical Islamic values. His method of reassurance, unique to this point, was to demonstrate such principles at work in the adopted codes. Before proceeding, Ra'fat borrowed a direct quote from his apparent mentor Qasim Amin, who was building similar arguments in the columns of *Al-Mu'ayyad*. The *Kitab*'s author declared himself prepared to defend codified secular law in addition to the *shari^c^a* for (in Qasim Amin's words)

> the power it has temporarily to entrust to the hands of others the preservation of what is actually ours [*ma ladayna*]. The term "civil law" means just that: an individual right is not assigned to someone else except when such transfer is necessary to guarantee respect for our right of action or our material right [of possession]. It has an added strength, which is that it enables us to call on outside authority to assist us in getting from others what is due to us. This channel is open even to those who have no wealth or power of their own . . . but closed to those without scruples, who do not understand its true meaning.[29]

Movement from this idealized world to the actual application of law involved several steps. Each was gauged to show Ra'fat to be a firm sponsor of any laws, whatever their origin, incorporating the broad moral objectives in Amin's definition of "civil law." Falling back on references to the higher authority of the *shari^c^a* sometimes proved necessary, especially when its limited but continuing jurisdictional precedence had to be considered (as in certain cases of family law). This was also true, however, when examination of certain effects of applied codes revealed moral shortcomings that begged debate beyond the literal provisions of the law.

Several articles in Egypt's penal law in the late 1890s inevitably fell into the latter category. It was a subject that was bound to incite high emotional identification with obvious problems of criminality in a society that had undergone so many internal strains during the previous generation. There had been many rumors of miscarriages in penal justice, often against anonymous violators (brigands of the 1880s and, as noted, village commoners condemned before special courts for violations against British troops). These certainly stood to arouse more general indignation over contradictions between ideal and reality than technicalities of civil law.

At the same time, the centrality of criminal law in Islamic tradition meant that certain shariatic provisions would be known to most educated Egyptians. Equally important, however, was one other key consideration: shariatic penal law was not being applied by an existing jurisdiction in Egypt. Thus, its defense as an ultimate criterion for deciding the justice of real court cases was purely moral, with no ground for direct practical application. This very fact, however, increased its possible political value: shariatic tradition stood above flaw-ridden Egyptian penal codes, whose foreign origins could always be blamed for causing intolerable injustices. Moreover, the emotionally sensitive realm of penal repression was likely to be very distant from the actual personal or material interests of Ra'fat's typical readers. This meant that claims of the sole validity of shariatic rulings could be accepted or rejected without any implication of practical consequences for readers' interests. As we shall see, this is a feature of legalistic neoconservatism at the turn of the century that did not carry over into the area of civil law.

Ra'fat's discussion of penal law focused on what constituted crime and proper punishment of criminal behavior. This was a subject for which extensive shariatic literature could be cited to measure standards in *ahliyya* law. The problem of premeditation, for example, invited controversy several stages removed from obvious day-to-day issues that—like the question of foreign penal immunities—could have been used (and had been a decade earlier) for more direct political purposes.[30] Premeditation involved internal or psychological factors that could not be measured according to immediate evidence. Ra'fat felt justified, therefore, in questioning certain practices of justice in Egypt according to criteria that were not in the specific texts of laws applied by the courts. The *Kitab* agreed, for example, with shariatic and Western commentators (in this case Bentham, as well as article 30 of Egypt's penal code) that, when a sign of intent to commit crime appeared, more good than harm was done by immediate penal detention, even if no specific violation had occurred. Such preventive measures were commonly practiced in Egypt without necessarily entailing prosecution or punishment. The status quo, therefore, technically guaranteed respect for both the letter of the law (punishment only of crimes actually committed) and intent behind the law (protection of innocents). Ra'fat felt, however, that this area of penal law required additional insight from practicing lawyers.

A case in point was the rising incidence of blackmail in Egypt. Some cases in this area were going unpunished if adroit lawyers could convince judges that the barely defined letter of the law on premeditation protected their clients from prosecution. This created loopholes that needed to be filled by completing the existing codes. By drawing attention to such selected combinations between the ideal (moral) and operative (codified) realms of law, neoconservative legalists could hope that a change for the better could be registered in the name of their profession. This was especially attractive if references to relevant shariatic provisions could be emphasized as guidelines for future legislators. In fact, *Mudarris* Ra'fat tailored at least three other subchapters of penal law (on intoxication, prosecution of accomplices to a crime, and nature and levels of punishment) to combine ideal shariatic issues and at least the promise of future practical objectives.[31]

It was not only comparisons of Egypt's penal law with the *shari^{c}a* that gave the *Kitab* its distinct neoconservative flavor. Penal sections did, however, introduce an abstract theme that eventually overshadowed all selected case studies of conflicts and gaps in the legal system. This theme, particularly dominant in the civil sections, invited distinctions between specific rights of individuals on the one hand and those of more abstract legal or social entities on the other. A number of topics of civil law that fell in this category focused on very current Egyptian concerns that were reflected in actual law cases. Some of these offered a broad basis for a form of neoconservative secular politics that appealed—much more than religious conservatism or open political nationalism— to many of Ra'fat's colleagues, to students, and, especially, to their existing or future clients.

Having established a mixed theoretical (moral) and nascent political approach to pitfalls in *ahliyya* law, Ra'fat lost little time shifting emphasis from defensive to positive associations with civil law. This occurred where a specific conjuncture of local socioeconomic circumstances in Egypt suggested that the status quo was already working to individual and general social advantage. Such benefits were clearly based less on higher moral than on purely material criteria. Controversial "moral" considerations (of acceptable limits of property and individual personal liability, for example) had always pervaded areas of civil law in which Egyptian and foreign interests definitely overlapped (usually to foreign advantage) by the 1890s. There were, however, a number of other, less publicized, areas in which practical problems experienced by Egyptian lawyers and their clients needed to be addressed without necessary reference to foreign interests or mixed law. The first such issue discussed was also the first that revealed the essentially secular nature of Ra'fat's neoconservative approach.

Practical advice was most plentiful in a subsection dealing with subleasing segments of real estate as well as other property rights.

Two key subjects, quarry leasing and well water use contracts, received particular attention. The way each was developed under a quasi-shariatic rubric of original property and attached property rights shows that some Egyptians were becoming very sensitive to possible liabilities that accompanied such contracts. What happened, for example, when subcontractees themselves entered into business arrangements that could affect the original property interests of lessors? Ra'fat's legal dissections in two cases—the process of bankruptcy of a quarry operating firm and of a company using leased land to carry out commercial agricultural exploitation with capital equipment purchased on credit—was clearly meant to encourage all parties strictly to define the limits of their liability in advance.[32] What is particularly interesting is the combination of practical legal advice on how to do this—a strictly technical question of provisions in the civil code—with a higher shariatic moral responsibility to see that secular laws served that end. In a number of cases, for instance, Ra'fat drew on shariatic discussions of the legal injunction to avoid *sharr* (individual or social harm) to evaluate the effectiveness of *ahliyya* civil procedures.[33]

From this point on, Ra'fat's exposé of *ahliyya* law could nearly be called a handbook for Egypt's rural landholding class. A subsection on two civil code articles referring to governmental rights of domain, for example, began as a discussion of the higher principle of eminent domain (a question of defining original rights and those of the government as trustee for the welfare of the abstract legal entity of society). It ended as a heated discussion of disregard for procedural laws governing private acquisition of domain land in Egypt at the turn of the century. The way in which the subject was framed (condemning arranged deals between administrative auctioneers of domain parcels and privileged private bidders) suggested Ra'fat was directing his remarks to parties who would see the relevance of a lawyer's expertise to their interests, especially when these were not fully protected by the existing codes.[34] If this was meant to associate Ra'fat's treatise with political liberalism present in pre-occupation (and pre-professional) opposition to arbitrary privilege, the intent scarcely showed through. Any opposition to *status quo* conditions was based mainly on a concern for defending existing private interests, which were then placed behind a symbol of higher public welfare. Referring specifically to the inadequacy of *ahliyya* law to monitor manipulation of domain sales contracts, for example, Ra'fat stated:

> [Legislative assumptions behind our codes] . . . do not have the same provisions that exist in foreign legal systems. . . . They require prior consultation with legislative bodies, whereas here a simple decree suffices. . . . Only a legislative body can properly guarantee full protection of public interest. Indeed if [bodies like the existing Legislative Council] do not work for the protection of the public good [through adequate laws], there is no real place for such anomalies in our institutional system.[35]

Aside from a few other similarly isolated vignettes, the *Kitab* reflected essentially conservative social and economic values, without espousing openly political views. If there was any general political tenor behind selected legal topics, it was a wariness of expanding government and administrative roles in a number of different areas deemed to be essentially within the sphere of private responsibility and thus subjects of civil law. Ra'fat's neoconservative devotion to the autonomous status of just codes, therefore, sought to avoid any legislative innovations that might affect chances of realizing benefits, however modest, from the local social and economic status quo that had evolved by 1900. No reader sympathetic to such goals should have been surprised to find that, in the remainder of its chapters, the *Kitab* underscored modes of clear legal protection in typical private contracts (transfer of usufruct rights and sharecropping are specific examples) that had become essential to Egypt's landowning elites. In all of these there was a striking absence of references to parallel shariatic literature or broader concern for the "public good."[36]

CONCLUSION

We may now turn, in conclusion, to a retrospective consideration of chances for survival of such views after 1900. There is, I believe, little doubt that the neoconservative current that Muhammad Ra'fat represented played a greater role in Egyptian society and politics than historians have generally recognized. For one thing, it emphasized the importance of legal analysis to shore up status quo operation of locally controlled economic activities. This would have been well received by a number of contemporary practitioners of *ahliyya* law. Some sought to profit from the new image of neoconservative thought reflected in their own profession and among other increasingly articulate social or economic semi-elites (the Khedivial Agricultural Society formed in 1898 and the soon-to-be-activated Committee for Reform of the Azhar are examples).

To do this, lawyers needed to make their concerns conform as much as possible to prospective clients' political as well as private social and economic identification with Egypt's future. Increasingly, lawyers published articles evaluating the importance of key social or economic institutions, both domestic and international, for determining Egypt's future development.[37] Generally these did not contain references to the narrow politics of judicial reformism or the negative political climate associated with the continued British occupation. This was true at least until London sealed its joint colonial understanding in the Entente Cordiale of 1904 with France, in essence proving that the domestic optimism of neoconservatives could never hope to exercise enough influence to affect high-level politics. Even after 1904, however, it was this form of indirect political expression (epitomized in the foundation of the Umma party and its official organ *Al-Jarida* in 1907) that accompanied the quiet transition of the politics of Egyptian law into the twentieth century.

Such a phenomenon, coming at the end of a long and complicated process of Egyptian legal reform in the nineteenth century, in many ways completes the theme introduced at the beginning of this book. The first chapter discussed the problem of analyzing responses to change that contact with Western reform models superimposed on Middle Eastern traditional local institutions, whether military, economic, or legal. A main element of the problem, I would argue, is to draw distinctions between levels and areas of perceptible change and levels and areas of response. In Egypt's legal reform experience, many of the responses documented in this book aimed at facilitating adaptation to new institutions governing interpersonal and intergroup material relationships that were deemed essential by certain segments of Egyptian society. As part of the process of adaptation, identifiable groups (so often referred to in less specific literature as "modernizers") consciously cease functioning according to traditional rules that still have meaning for others whose definitions of interpersonal or intergroup relationships appear poorly adapted to material changes that are obviously under way. Herein lies the internal dilemma of uneven levels of modernization, be it in the nineteenth-century legal system in Egypt or in other key social and economic institutions of formerly colonized countries generally.

This book has attempted to separate realistic from idealized or (intentionally) naive conceptions of changing circumstances of legal administration in Egypt over seventy-five years. Wherever possible, it has dealt with real people who influenced such conceptions and tried to make them reflect the interests of identifiable groups, whether relatively broad or narrow. Each chapter has focused mainly on two types of historically documentable social groups. Each, in one way or another, chose and pursued particular attitudes toward government-decreed legal reforms. The first group was comprised of consciously adapting interest groups that became Egypt's late nineteenth century political elite and landed property class. The second was formed by nascent specialists of new laws that were bound to affect the material (and therefore political) status of established elites. As legal reform became increasingly subject to externally controlled institutions and political forces, there was bound to be a perceived need to identify overlapping areas of interest between representatives of these two groups. By 1900, such perceptions of complementarism were best exemplified by positions taken in writing (and in courtrooms, of course) by neoconservative Egyptian lawyers.

One may also suggest that tacit conceptual alliances between conservative interpreters of the law and their clients encouraged the two groups to view many Egyptian political issues from similar perspectives. In the first few years after 1900, there was apparently little reason for either to articulate discontent or political opposition to the status quo. Neither bothered seriously to express positions on what had been before, and would become again, key nationalist issues, in either militant secular or Islamic terms. In an earlier, clearly abortive, period of attempted adaptation to changed material and political circumstances (specifically, between 1878 and 1882) this had not been true. In the heyday of politically volatile debate over changes in Egypt's legal system, however, the effects of institutional transition were not yet rooted enough for earlier comparable elite or semi-elite groups to espouse quiet conservatism based on essentially material interests. Tensions over legal reforms from the 1870s to the 1890s, therefore, fostered a politically ineffective joining of quite different interests, including modernizers, traditional secular and religious notables, and political elites in transition.

If this conclusion is correct, institutional changes that became well established in the late 1890s made it possible, not for the same combination, but for similar sorts of interests to elaborate more fully integrated conservative viewpoints just prior to the appearance of openly political nationalist pressures in Egypt. Beneath the rhetoric of such debates, one could see concerns for pragmatic issues and practical results brought by application of acceptable imported Western laws. For a decade at least, from 1897 to 1907, an aura of optimism prevailed, based on a sense of stability and expectations of continued evolutionary benefits to be gained.[38] Until such expectations received serious shocks, therefore, anyone looking for signs of politics surrounding Egyptian legal matters would be disappointed: pragmatism remained the predominant mode.

It was only when long-desired objectives were impossibly slow in coming (as when Britain's first move after conclusion of the 1904 Entente Cordiale was to give *carte blanche* to another renewal of the Mixed Court Charter, reopening at the same time the possibility of a capitulatory international legislative council to guide Egypt's basic lawmaking decisions), or when cumulative material gains were suddenly reversed and exposed to legal liability (when the 1907 depression and stock crash threatened to ruin many private investors in commerce and agricultural land), that political nationalist options would become more attractive to otherwise passive neoconservatives.[39] When such reactions finally came, socioeconomic adaptation to the "new justice" among Egyptian elites generally was much more fully developed than it had been in the last quarter of the nineteenth century. The resultant possibility was that security and expansion of status quo interests, not necessarily fully negative opposition, could become basic elements in Egyptian nationalism. This phenomenon, similar in some ways to the origins of nationalism in Western polities, is exemplified in the pattern of continuity in Egyptian lawyers' participation in the moderate politics of the prewar Umma and postwar Liberal Constitutionalist party. In both cases, one can find cohesive social and economic bonds linking Egyptian professionals and various influential nonprofessionals who depended on a legal perspective to defend their civil and political rights, both in and outside the courtroom.

Notes

Chapter One

1. Standard prototypes for modernization theory are too numerous to review here. Two general works from the 1960s by well-known political scientists are frequently cited: S. N. Eisenstadt, *Modernization: Protest and Change* (Englewood Cliffs, N.J., 1966) and Chandler Morse et al., *Modernization by Design* (Ithaca, N.Y., 1969). Studies dealing with the phenomenon of modernization in the Middle East proper are Robert Ward and Dankwart Rustow, *Political Modernization in Japan and Turkey* (Princeton, N.J., 1964); and William R. Polk and Richard L. Chambers, eds., *Beginnings of Modernization in the Middle East* (Chicago, 1968).

Of most concern here is the widely shared view among early theorizers that a primary and universal component of "modernization" is adoption of Western models to replace "traditional" modes of interaction. Such unilinear Westernization is superficially traceable, of course, in social and economic as well as political spheres. Less obvious, and the main target of theorists since the heyday of the modernization school, are the multiple levels of internal reaction and adjustment that make progress from traditional to modern something very different than unilinear Westernization.

2. See, for example, R. J. Moore, *Sir Charles Wood's Indian Policy, 1853–66* (Manchester, 1966), pp. 65–86; and Thomas R. Metcalf, *The Aftermath of the Revolt: India, 1857–1870* (Princeton, 1964), pp. 248–88.

3. There are several monographs devoted to the Eastern Question itself. A general and useful account is M. S. Anderson, *The Eastern Question, 1774–1923* (London and New York, 1966). One should also consult J. A. R. Marriott's classic study, first published in 1917 by Oxford University Press as *The Eastern Question: An Historical Study in European Diplomacy*.

4. The only general history of the Ottoman capitulations in English is Nasim Sousa, *The Capitulatory Regime of Turkey* (Baltimore, 1933). More detailed treatment appears in Gérard Pélissié du Rausas, *Le régime des capitulations dans l'Empire ottoman*.

5. See, as a typical textual example, article 24 of the "Final Treaty of Capitulations: Ottoman Empire and England" (September 1675), in J. C. Hurewitz, *The Middle East and North Africa in World Politics: A Documentary Record,* vol. 1, p. 35.

6. Omer Lutfi Barkan, *Osmanli imparatorlugunda zirai ekonominin hukuki ve mali esaslari* (Istanbul, 1943). See especially "Misir kanunnamesi," pp. 378ff.

7. François Charles-Roux, *Autour d'une route: L'Angleterre, l'Isthme de Suez et l'Egypte au 18me siècle* (Paris, 1922).

8. M. James Bruce, *Voyage aux sources du Nil en Nubie et en Abyssinie*, trans. J. H. Castera (10 vols.; Paris, 1790–91).

9. Charles-Roux, *Autour d'une route*, pp. 26–49. On ᶜAli Bey, see Daniel Crecelius, *The Roots of Modern Egypt: A Study of the Regimes of ᶜAli Bey al-Kabir and Muhammad Bey Abu Al-Dhahab*, pp. 54–103.

10. Charles-Roux, *Autour d'une route*, pp. 42–49 and 161–72.

11. Examples of such retrospective judgment of Muhammad ᶜAli's intentions are Henry Dodwell, *The Founder of Modern Egypt* (Cambridge, England, 1931), pp. 39ff.; Shafiq Ghorbal, *The Beginnings of the Eastern Question and the Rise of Mehemet Ali* (London, 1928), pp. 279–84; and, most recently, Afaf Lutfi al-Sayyid Marsot, *Egypt in the Reign of Muhammad Ali*, pp. 136ff.

12. See especially Helen Rivlin, *The Agricultural Policy of Muhammad Ali in Egypt* (Cambridge, Mass., 1961), pp. 137–200.

13. Lutfi al-Sayyid Marsot, *Muhammad Ali*, pp. 1–5.

14. Stanford J. Shaw, *Between Old and New* (Cambridge, Mass., 1971), pp. 71–72.

15. Gabriel Baer, *A History of Landownership in Egypt, 1800–1950* (London, 1962), pp. 4–6.

16. See Gabriel Baer, *Egyptian Guilds in Modern Times* (Jerusalem, 1964).

17. On this subject generally, see E. R. J. Owen, *Cotton and the Egyptian Economy, 1820–1914.*

18. On the origins and impact of the "Egyptian Crisis" between 1831 and 1839, see Sir Charles Webster, *The Foreign Policy of Palmerston, 1830–41* (2 vols.; New York, 1969) vol. 1, pp. 255–332; and vol. 2, pp. 619–76.

19. Egyptian occupation reforms in Syria, with their emphasis on standardization of previously fragmented and inefficient administrative practices, are treated in Yvonne Y. Haddad, "The Administrative and Economic Policies of Ibrahim Pasha in Palestine, 1831–1840," unpublished M. A. thesis, University of Wisconsin (Madison), 1971.

20. See L. Carl Brown, *The Tunisia of Ahmad Bey, 1837–1855* (Princeton, N.J., 1974), pp. 285–86; and Webster, *Foreign Policy*, vol. 2, chap. 8, especially pp. 639–40.

21. The text of the Balta Liman Trade Convention of 1838 is in Hurewitz, *Middle East*, pp. 265–66. See also Lutfi al-Sayyid Marsot, *Muhammad Ali*, pp. 238–48.

22. See Webster, *Foreign Policy*, vol. 2, pp. 665–737.

23. On evidence of foreign involvement in outbreaks of violence in areas of Syria and Lebanon in the last stages of the Egyptian occupation, see Iliya F. Harik, *Politics and Change in a Traditional Society: Lebanon, 1711-1845* (Princeton, 1968), pp. 245–53.

24. The text of the *Hatt-i Şerif* of 3 November 1839 is in Hurewitz, *Middle East*, vol. 1, pp. 269–71.

25. *Firman* of 1 June 1841, in ibid., pp. 276–78.

26. Ibid.

27. See Philippe Gélat, *Répertoire général annoté de la législation et de l'administration égyptiennes, 1840–1910*, vol. 2, pp. 853–56ff.

Chapter Two

1. Bernard Lewis, *Emergence of Modern Turkey* (London, 1961), pp. 107-13. Although begun in 1840, the Ottoman commercial code was not promulgated until the second formal Tanzimat ministry headed by Reşid Pasha, in 1849–50.

2. Compare Jasper Y. Brinton, *The Mixed Courts of Egypt*, p. 277; Pierre Awad, *Les pouvoirs des tribunaux mixtes d'Egypte* (Paris, 1930), p. 13; and Donald M. Reid, *Lawyers and Politics in the Arab World, 1880-1960*, p. 11.

3. Farhat Ziadeh, *Lawyers, the Rule of Law, and Liberalism in Modern Egypt*, p. 7.

4. Jean Deny, *Sommaire des archives turques du Caire* (Cairo, 1930), 27–31; Ahmad Fathi Zaghlul, *Tarikh al-muhamah*, appendices, pp. 63–66.

5. Lewis, *Emergence*, p. 106.

6. Gabriel Baer, "Tanzimat in Egypt: The Penal Code," *Bulletin of the School of Oriental and African Studies* (London), 26 (1963), 29–49; cf. Lutfi al-Sayyid Marsot, *Muhammad Ali*, pp. 108–9.

7. Zaghlul, *Al-Muhamah*, appendices, pp. 70–73.

8. Ibid., pp. 31–42. Dr. Abdel Karim Rafeq's research on Ottoman Syria indicates that an Egyptian tribunal of commerce had operated in Damascus up to the 1841 withdrawal. During the 1840s, this was replaced by a *diwan at-tujjar* composed, like its Egyptian counterpart, of Syrian merchants locally appointed by the Turkish governor and foreigners nominated by their consuls. Dr. Rafeq's sources on this subject are to be found in the archival records of the *Majlis al-wilaya* (Damascus) and in the Damascus consular records of the French *Ministère des Affaires Etrangères.*

9. Zaghlul, *Al-muhamah*, pp. 70–76.

10. Ibid., pp. 70–73.

11. On the planned spread of local provincial councils, see Roderic A. Davison, *Reform in the Ottoman Empire, 1856–76* (Princeton, 1963), pp. 56–67, 104.

12. Zaghlul, *Al-Muhamah*, pp. 196–97, and appendices, pp. 76–84.

13. Baer, *Landownership*, p. 8.

14. On the Ottoman imperial land law of 1858, see Davison, *Reform*, pp. 99–100.

15. Law of 5 August 1858, in Gélat, *Répertoire*, vol. 4, pp. 83–93.

16. See, in particular, Alan Richards, *Egypt's Agricultural Development, 1800–1980* (Boulder, Colo., 1982), pp. 36–37; and the same author's discussion of the literature on "peasant differentiation" in Alan Richards, ed., *Food, States, and Peasants* (Boulder, Colo., 1986), pp. 3–6.

17. F. Robert Hunter, *Egypt under the Khedives, 1805-1879,* pp. 51–54.

18. See especially decrees of Jumadi al-Ula/November 1865 and 22 Sha[c]ban 1282/January 1866, in Gélat, *Répertoire*, vol. 4, 97–99.

19. See Great Britain, Foreign Office, 78 (Turkey)/2186.

20. On contemporary Ottoman Ministry of Justice *nizamiyya* reform efforts, see Stanford J. Shaw and Ezel Kural Shaw, *History of the Ottoman Empire and Modern Turkey* (2 vols.; London and New York, 1977), vol. 2, pp. 118–19.

21. "Mudhakkirat Husayn basha Fakhri," in *Al-Kitab adh-Dhahabi* (2 vols.; Cairo, 1937–38), vol. 1, pp. 107–15.

Chapter Three

1. H. Mandelstam, *La justice ottomane dans ses rapports avec les puissances étrangères* (Paris, 1911), p. 96.

2. Shaw and Shaw, *Ottoman Empire*, vol. 2, pp. 118–19.

3. For the effects of the 1856 Treaty of Paris on the Ottoman regime and the "second-generation" Tanzimat Council, see Davison, *Reform*, chap. 2.

4. Ibid., pp. 83–84; and M. Sakir Ulkutasir, "Tanzimat Devrinin buyuk bilgini Cevdet Paşa (1822–1895)," in *Türk Kültürü*, 8, (1970), 406–90.

5. Shaw and Shaw, *Ottoman Empire*, vol. 2, pp. 6–13.

6. On the earliest stages of Suez Canal concession negotiations, see Ferdinand de Lesseps, *Percement de l'Isthme de Suez: Exposé et documents officiels* (Paris, 1855).

7. An excellent account of this phenomenon is in David Landes, *Bankers and Pashas*, pp. 69–101. See also Anouar Abdel Malek, *Idéologie et renaissance nationale: L'Egypte moderne*, pp. 72, 76.

8. Zaghlul, *Al-muhamah,* pp. 187–89, and appendix 4, pp. 43–45.

9. Mirrit Boutros Ghali, ed., *Mémoires de Nubar Pacha* (Beirut, 1983), p. 168.

10. Amin Sami, *Taqwim an-Nil*, vol. 2, p. 291.

11. See Reinhard Schulze, *Die Rebellion der ägyptischen Fallahin: 1919*, p. 48.

12. The most useful general account of the decline of capitulatory justice in Egypt after 1860 is Georges Douin, *Histoire du règne du khédive Ismaïl* (Rome, 1935), vol. 2.

13. Ibid., p. 177.

14. On the Ottoman *mecelle*, see S. S. Onar, "The Majalla," in Majid Khadduri and Herbert J. Liebesny, *Law and the Middle East* (Washington, D.C., 1955), pp. 292–308.

15. See Najib Makhluf, *Nubar basha wa ma tamma* *[c]ala yadihi*; and Ziadeh, p. 24; and Nubar's own *Mémoires*.

16. Douin, *Histoire*, vol. 2, pp. 168–73.

17. Ibid., p. 177. See a variation on this position that Nubar claimed to have communicated in a meeting with Isma[c]il in January 1867, in *Mémoires*, pp. 268–69.

18. Ministère des Affaires Etrangères (France), *Rapport présenté au Marquis de Moustier par la commission instituée à l'effet d'examiner les propositions faites par le gouvernement égyptien pour réformer l'administration de la justice en Egypte*.

19. Nubar, *Mémoires*, pp. 272–73, 317–18. Robert Hunter's discussion of growing rural elite desires to build "bureaucratic checks on traditional [central] absolutism" helps place the Judicial Reform issue in 1875 in a broader context (*Egypt under the Khedives*, pp. 179–80).

20. *Firman* of 8 June 1867, in Gélat, *Répertoire*, vol. 2, pp. 485–86.

21. *Rapport . . . au Marquis de Moustier*.

22. Nubar's autobiographical account of his meetings with de Moustier and other interested French parties (*Mémoires*, pp. 320–29) mentions at least one concession (the foreign judge majority). Nubar claims, however, that these ideas "were always in the back of my mind, but I had not dared announce them publicly at the outset" (p. 326). Cf. the de Moustier *Rapport*, and Charles de Lesseps, *Les capitulations et la réforme judiciaire en Egypte: Sa nécessité et son urgence*.

23. Ministère des Affaires Etrangères (Egypt), *Rapport de la commission internationale pour l'examen des réformes dans l'administration de la justice en Egypte* (Alexandria, 1870).

24. Nubar's memoirs reveal an interesting ambivalence concerning this very essential point. "It was difficult," he writes, "for me to understand the necessity of having *procureurs*. . . . I adopted the institution, however, because I had my own idea of the role of the *parquet*. Our governors were ignorant of anything having to do with [legal] procedure. The *procureurs* should have, in my mind, become counselors to the governors in any procedural question regarding execution of a sentence or of measures decreed by the government" (*Mémoires*, p. 373). By this time (April and May 1868) Tanzimat leaders [c]Ali Paşa and Fuad Paşa succeeded in establishing two new public bodies, a Council of State under Midhat Paşa, and a High Judicial Council under Cevdet Paşa. Although the latter had main responsibilities for handling cases governed by the Empire's new Westernized codes, it did not include a *ministère public*, or attorney general's office. See Davison, *Reform*, pp. 240–44.

25. Nubar, *Mémoires*, pp. 378–79.

26. Contrast Brinton's exposé of the one-man origins of the mixed codes (*Mixed Courts*, pp. 145–50) with the surprisingly brief treatment of

this major turning point in Ziadeh (*Lawyers*, pp. 27–28), and Reid, *Lawyers and Politics*, pp. 30–31. Nubar's own account of his dealings with Maunoury is found in his *Mémoires*, pp. 321–22, 374.

27. Evidence of the outmoded status of nineteenth-century French civil law by this period can be seen quite clearly in the context of contemporary European legislative reform. Especially when the unified states of Italy and Germany were formed (more than five years before the mixed codes went into effect in Egypt), many inherited principles of French law were replaced by statutes corresponding to conditions of credit, capital formation, and property ownership that had evolved primarily during the generation of Napoleon III, not Napoleon I.

28. On the *muqabala* law, see Baer, *Landownership*, pp. 7–12; and Gélat, *Répertoire*, vol. 3, pp. 498–508.

29. Ministère des Affaires Etrangères (Egypt), *Procès verbaux et rapport de la commission des délégués . . . instituée pour l'examen des propositions du gouvernement égyptien relatives à la réforme judiciaire* (Cairo and Istanbul, 1873).

30. Only a few minor areas of penal competence, including cases of fraudulent bankruptcy, were left to the proposed mixed jurisdictions following this 1873 conference. See title 2, articles 6–10, of the Mixed Court Charter. Nubar's account of efforts to avoid French procedures on *hypothèque judiciaire* is in his *Mémoires*, p. 426. Cf. chapter 4, note 25, below.

31. The first-instance courts were to be in Cairo, Alexandria, and Zagazig in Sharqiyya Province. Mansurah (the more active center of the cotton trade in the Delta) subsequently replaced Zagazig when the courts opened in January 1876. A mixed court of appeals was to sit in Alexandria, the "foreign capital" of Egypt.

32. On the terms of Egypt's 11 June 1873 loan, see Gélat, *Répertoire*, vol. 2, pp. 56–71. H. Oppenheim is discussed in Landes, *Bankers*, pp. 219 (note 2), 249–50, 306–9.

33. See Great Britain, Parliament, *Hansard's Parliamentary Debates* (Commons) (hereafter *Hansard*), third series, vol. 214, 13 February 1873, col. 369; vol. 220, 26 June 1874, col. 513; and vol. 225, 3 May 1875, col. 1953.

34. See E. R. J. [Roger] Owen, *The Middle East in the World Economy, 1800–1914*, pp. 104–8.

35. Gélat, *Répertoire*, vol. 4, pp. 470–74.

36. Nubar's *Mémoires* (p. 435) try to blame Sharif for accepting, on French insistence and at the last minute, unfavorable conditions for capitulatory nomination of foreign judges whose contracts, as Egyptian functionaries, would be signed by the minister of justice.

37. On Disraeli's unexpected purchase of the Egyptian government's shares in the Suez Canal, see Charles Louis de Saulces de Freycinet, *La question d'Egypte*, pp. 150–51.

38. The French draft convention of 27 September 1874 (ratified in December 1875) is in Gélat, *Répertoire*, vol. 4, pp. 466–67.

Chapter Four

1. See *Rawdat al-Akhbar* (Cairo), 16 January and 3 February 1876. A description of *Rawdat al-Akhbar*, a semiofficial organ of public opinion, appears in Abdel Malek, *Idéologie,* p. 178.

2. *Le Phare d'Alexandrie*), cited in *Rawdat al-Akhbar*, 13 April 1876.

3. Great Britain, Parliamentary Papers (hereafter, Accounts and Papers), Egypt No. 4 (1876) and Egypt No. 7 (1876).

4. Owen, *Middle East in the World Economy*, pp. 108–10.

5. Decree of 2 May 1876 in Gélat, *Répertoire*, vol. 2, pp. 74–76.

6. Decree of 7 May 1876, in ibid., pp. 81–83.

7. For details of the Carpi case, see *Recueil de la jurisprudence des tribunaux de la réforme en Egypte* (hereafter *RJTR*), vol. 1 (1875–76), pp. 43–49.

8. Article 11 of the original Mixed Court Charter, in Octave Borelli, *Choses politiques d'Egypte, 1883–1895*, pp. 522–35.

9. Paul Merruau, "L'Egypte sous le gouvernement d'Ismaïl Pacha: Les finances du khédive et les tribunaux mixtes," *Revue des Deux Mondes*, 228 (1876), 927.

10. Count Munster to Derby, London, 27 June 1876; and Lord Lyons to Derby, Paris, 25 July 1876, in FO 407/8.

11. Sir Charles Cookson to Derby, 3 July 1876 (confidential) in FO 407/8. On the early organization of European lawyers before the mixed courts, see Zaghlul, *Al-muhamah*, pp. 293–300.

12. Cookson to Derby, 29 July 1876, in FO 407/8. See Haakman's own account in *Le Caire et la justice internationale* (Paris, 1877).

13. For events surrounding the constitutionalist-backed coup in Istanbul in 1876, see Lewis, *Emergence*, pp. 156–63.

14. Lyons to Derby, Paris, 5 October 1876, in FO 407/8; and Mr. F. S. Reilly's memorandum of 3 December 1876, in Great Britain, Foreign Office Correspondence (Turkey), FO 78/3375.

15. Mr. Hussey Vivian to Derby, Cairo, 4 November 1876, in Accounts and Papers, Egypt No. 2 (1879).

16. Vivian to Derby, 4 November 1876, in FO 407/8.

17. Decree of 18 November 1876 in the *Moniteur Egyptien* of the same date.

18. Derby to Vivian, 21 December 1876, in Accounts and Papers, Egypt No. 2 (1879).

19. For Baring's full career, see *Dictionary of National Biography* (hereafter *DNB*), vol. for 1912–21, pp. 20–28.

20. Decree of November 1876, title 3, article 8.

21. Article 12 allowed for "additions and modifications" in the mixed codes only after an undefined mode of "approval by the magistracy."

22. Vivian to Derby, 13 January 1877, enclosing Sharif to Vivian, 23 December 1876, in FO 407/8.

23. See Vivian to Derby, 23 January and 7 April 1877, enclosing Baron des Michels to Sharif, 27 March 1877, in FO 407/8.

24. Emile Vercamer, *La juridiction mixte et ses attributions législatives* (Paris, 1911), pp. 97–98.

25. Vivian to Derby, 3 and 15 February 1878, plus the law officers' opinion on same, 27 March 1878, in FO 407/8. The effects of the *hypothèque judiciaire*, a procedure in French law transferred to Egypt via the mixed codes, were already visible in 1877. A *hypothèque judiciaire* enabled creditors to request sale by judicial auction of the landed property of individual peasant debtors. It should not be confused with a standard mortgage contract, which usually involved larger sums than the average *fallah* borrowed. See the (abortive) decree of 24 December 1877 modifying articles 507, 528, 622, and 639 of the mixed code of civil procedure on seizures and auctions, in *Moniteur Egyptien*, 5 April 1878.

26. Des Michels to Waddington, 12 July 1878 (confidential) in France, Ministère des Affaires Etrangères, *Documents diplomatiques Français* (hereafter MAE, *DDF*), first series, vol. 2.

27. Baring to Goschen, 21 and 28 December 1877, in Cromer Papers (hereafter CP) FO 633/5.

28. On Charles Rivers-Wilson, see Richard Atkins, "British Policy toward Egypt, 1876–1882" (Ph.D. dissertation, University of California, Berkeley, 1968), pp. 70–71; and Wilson's own book, *Chapters from My Official Life*.

29. Riadh's career is discussed by Charles Moberly-Bell, *Khedives and Pashas* (London, 1884), pp. 127, 130–41. See also Hunter, *Egypt under the Khedives*, pp. 158–65.

30. Baron des Michels, *Souvenirs de carrière*, p. 180.

31. Ibid., pp. 181–82.

32. Vivian to Salisbury, 24 May 1878, in FO 407/8.

33. The only published statistics on local judicial council activities during the first years of the international financial crisis appear in Sharif's report to the khedive dated 22 November 1877 (*Moniteur Egyptien*, 14 February 1878). This report indicates that the majority of *fallahin* and provincial town disputes were penal in nature and (although no clear distinction is made between prosecution for tax arrears and normal penal cases) were being settled without a judicial backlog.

34. Isma^cil to Riadh, 16 June 1878, cited in *Al-Watan* (Cairo), 20 July 1878.

35. The pros and cons of the Lapenna plan were summarized by Scott, Hills, and Law (all British consular or mixed court judges) in Vivian to Salisbury, 10 January 1879, enclosing the judges' report dated 29 December 1878, in FO 78/3375.

36. On *Al-Ahram*, see Abdel Malek, *Idéologie*, p. 179. *Al-Muqtataf* is discussed in Hourani, *Arabic Thought in the Liberal Age, 1798–1939* (London, 1962), pp. 246–47.

37. *Al-Watan*, 29 June 1878. *Al-Watan* is discussed by Anwar al-Jundi, *As-sihafat as-siyasiyya fi misr*, pp. 151–52.

38. See John Scott's biography in *DNB*, 2nd supplement, vol. 3, pp. 280–88.

39. Scott to Vivian, 29 June 1878, in FO 407/8.

40. Vivian to Derby, 19 August 1878, enclosing the Commission of Inquiry's Report, in Accounts and Papers, Egypt No. 2 (1879).

41. Some of the implications of the great power settlement of the 1877–78 Russo-Ottoman War for the Egyptian and Tunisian provinces are surveyed by Ronald Robinson and John Gallagher, *Africa and the Victorians* (New York, 1961), p. 82; and Jean Ganiage, *Les origines du protectorat français en Tunisie, 1861–1881* (2nd ed.; Tunis, 1968), pp. 401–21.

42. Des Michels, *Souvenirs de carrière*, p. 182; cf. Waddington to des Michels, 5 April 1878, in MAE, *DDF*, first series, vol. 2.

43. Salisbury to Vivian, 3 May 1878, cited in Atkins, "British Policy," p. 135.

44. *Phare*, 19 November 1878.

45. *Phare*, 22–23 December and 31 December 1878.

46. Vivian to Salisbury, 10 January 1879, in Accounts and Papers, Egypt No. 5 (1879).

47. *Phare*, 21 December 1878. See also *Rawdat al-Akhbar*, 7 July 1877, for an early example of public advertisements by European lawyers seeking Egyptian clients in need of contracts, translations, and other services connected with mixed court civil litigation.

48. See, for example, articles by Shaykh Muhammad [c]Askar of Mansurah in *Al-Watan*, 4 and 18 January 1879.

49. Vivian to Salisbury, 10 January 1879, enclosing Judge John Scott to Vivian, same date, in FO 78/3375.

Chapter Five

1. P. J. Vatikiotis, *The Modern History of Egypt* (New York, 1969), p. 135.

2. The social and intellectual milieu that nurtured this nascent stage of political liberalism in Egypt is described by Jacob Landau, "Prolegomena to a Study of Secret Societies in Modern Egypt," *Middle East Studies*, 1 (1965). A valuable impression of this same milieu is offered by Ahmad Effendi Samir, editor of *Sulafa' an-nadim fi muntakhabat as-sayyid [c]Abdullah an Nadim* (2 vols.; Cairo, 1914), vol. 1, pp. 6–11.

3. See *Al-Watan*, 21 December 1878.

4. *Al-Watan*, 11 January and 13 February 1879.

5. Memorandum from General Louis-Frederic Menabrea, Italian ambassador, to Salisbury, 2 April 1879, in FO 78/3375; and *Al-Watan*, 22 March 1879.

6. Vivian to Salisbury, 15 March 1879, in FO 407/15.

7. *Al-Watan*, 22 March 1879.

8. *Al-Watan*, 5 and 12 April 1879.

9. Isma^c^il to Sharif, 7 April 1879, in Accounts and Papers, Egypt No. 5 (1879).

10. Wilson to Salisbury, 5 April 1879, in Salisbury Papers (hereafter SP), A16.

11. Lascelles to Salisbury, 26 April 1879, enclosing a summary of the Commission's report and draft liquidation law compared with the Assembly's alternative plan.

12. Ibid., Commission of Inquiry report.

13. On the Three Emperors' League, see William L. Langer, *European Alliances and Alignments* (2nd ed.; New York, 1962), pp. 171–212.

14. Salisbury to Lascelles, 25 April 1879; in Egypt No. 5 (1879); and Waddington to Godeaux, 25 April 1879, in MAE, *DDF* (1871–1914), series 1, vol. 2.

15. Lascelles to Salisbury, 27 April 1879, in Accounts and Papers, Egypt No. 5 (1879); cf., Hunter, *Egypt under the Khedives*, p. 224.

16. *Masr* (Cairo), 23 April 1879; cf. *Al-Watan*, 3 May 1879.

17. See British and German political correspondence of May and June 1879 in Accounts and Papers, Egypt No. 3 (1879).

18. Atkins, "British Policy," p. 176.

19. Afaf Lutfi al-Sayyid [Marsot], *Egypt and Cromer* pp. 4–5.

20. *Firman* of 9 August 1879, in Gélat, *Répertoire*, vol. 2, pp. 492–93.

21. Reform initiatives associated with Mehmet Sa^c^id are discussed by Lewis, *Emergence*, pp. 178–84.

22. Ibid., p. 183.

23. *Phare*, 23 September 1879.

24. See Husayn Fakhri's biographical sketch in Fahmi, *Safwat al-^c^asr fi tarikh wa rusum mashahir rijal masr*, pp. 226–31.

25. *Phare*, 30 September 1879.

26. Baring to Salisbury, 25 October 1879, in SP, A/6; and same to same, Vienna, 1 November 1879, in CP, FO 633/2.

27. Cited in *Phare*, 31 October 1879.

28. De Ring to de Freycinet, 12 January 1880 (telegram), in MAE, Egypte/65.

29. Malet to Salisbury, 26 February 1880, in SP, A/6.

30. For two traditionalist views on the presumed grass-roots needs of Egyptian justice at this time, see *Al-Waqt* (Cairo), 22 December 1879; and Shaykh Husayn al-Marsafi, *Rasa'il al-kalim ath-thaman*.

31. F. S. Reilly memorandum dated 23 April 1880, in FO 78/3375.

32. De Ring to de Freycinet, 2 June 1880, in MAE, Egypte/66.

33. *Al-Waqt*, 2 June 1880.

34. *Arrêté* of 31 July 1880 in *Moniteur Egyptien*, 3 August 1880. Octave Borelli was head of the legal department of the Ministry of Finance. Alfred de Vacher was *procureur général* of the mixed courts.

35. Al-Waqt, 3 and 7 August 1880.

36. De Vacher to de Ring, Alexandria, 6 August 1880, in MAE, Egypte/67.

37. *Al-Waqt*, 6, 8, 9, and 10 December 1880.

38. *Al-Waqt*, 6 December 1879 and 11 May 1880. Surviving *dafatirs*, or registers of the *majalis* jurisdictions, demonstrate a revealing pattern in village-level disputes during this period. Random sampling from the 1880 *Deftar qaid* no. 2609 (*Fihrisat al-qadaya' bi majlis al-mansura*) shows that the most common rural cases of the 1870s—disputes over watering rights, petty theft, and crop sales—were gradually being replaced by peasant land disputes in which village heads (*ᶜumda*s) were often the second party.

39. Jacques Berque, *Egypte: Impérialisme et révolution* (Paris, 1967), pp. 130–31. Berque's analysis of conditions in 1880–81 helps explain the phenomenon of rural violence later characterized as brigandage. He suggests that Ismaᶜil's purposeful reduction in the "patriarchal authority" of the *mudir*s, who had traditionally maintained a forced equilibrium between rival villages and even groups within villages, allowed subsurface "clan" violence to emerge in the form of marauding and vendettas. One should add the obvious fact that peasants who had become destitute and had lost land to rising "notable" clans would have been naturally inclined to seek retribution, often through night robberies and attacks, inside or between villages.

40. *Al-Waqt*, 5, 10, and 11 January 1880.

41. *Al-Kawkab al-Masri*, 23 July 1880.

42. *Al-Waqa'iᶜ al-Misriyya*, 31 October 1880, in Al-Sayyid Muhammad Rashid Rida, *Tarikh al-ustadh al-imam ash-shaykh Muhammad ᶜAbduh*, vol. 2, pp. 71–73.

43. *Phare*, 23 September and 14 December 1880.

44. Ministère de la Justice (Egypt), *Procès-verbaux des séances de la sous-commission de la Réforme Judiciaire du* 11 *décembre* 1880 *au* 4 *février 1881* (Cairo, 1881), minutes of 11 December 1880.

45. Subcommission minutes of 15 and 22 December 1880; cf. *Phare*, 23 December 1880 and 14 January 1881.

46. On the French and Italian capitulatory pressure groups, see *Phare*, 10 and 30 November and 15 December 1880.

47. Subcommission minutes of 19 January 1881.

48. Ibid.

49. See the general description of Riadh's January 1881 clash with the *fallah* colonels led by Ahmad ᶜUrabi in Lutfi al-Sayyid [Marsot], *Egypt and Cromer*, pp. 8–9.

Chapter Six

1. See Shaw and Shaw, *Ottoman Empire*, vol. 2, pp. 217–18.

2. Monge to Saint Hiliare, 9 March 1881 (telegram), in MAE, Egypte/68; same to same, 8 April 1881; and Saint Hiliare to Monge, 17 April 1881 (telegram), in Egypte/69.

3. Lyons to Granville, Paris, 10 June 1881; Granville to Lyons, 23 June 1881, in FO 78/3376.

4. Early in 1881, Malet discovered that several members of the British Auxiliary Commission strongly disapproved of his and Cookson's handling of the capitulatory question. See Scott to Reilly, 18 and 29 January 1881, in FO 78/3376; and Malet to Granville, 26 January and 18 March 1881, in Granville Papers (hereafter GP), G & D 29/159.

5. On Sir Auckland Colvin, see *DNB*, supplement for 1901–11, pp. 395–97; and Colvin's own historical account, *The Making of Modern Egypt, 1881–1905*.

6. The local administrative implications of Britain's decision to follow up suppression of the Indian Mutiny in 1857 with direct colonial political controls at almost every level are discussed in Thomas Metcalf, *The Aftermath of the Revolt*: *India, 1857–70* (Princeton, 1964).

7. Malet to Granville, 20 July 1881, enclosing Sir Auckland Colvin's memorandum of 15 July 1881, in FO 78/3376.

8. Ibid.; cf. Malet to Sanderson, 24 July 1881, in GP, G & D 29/159.

9. The British Auxiliary Commission's reports dated 28 and 30 July 1881 are in FO 78/3376. As of this date, the specialized advisory body for Egyptian court reform questions included several highly placed personalities, such as Lord Tenterden, Sir Charles Dilke, Sir Julian Pauncefote, and Mr. F. S. Reilly.

10. Rivers-Wilson to Granville, 22 July 1881, enclosing Nubar to Wilson, Alexandria, 12 July 1881, in GP, G & D 29/170.

11. Nubar to Wilson, 12 July 1881.

12. On the traditional functions of *wukala'* in Egypt before the emergence of a distinct profession of advocacy in the mid-1880s, see ᶜAziz and Jamil Khanki, *Al-muhama qadiman wa hadithan* (Cairo, 1940), pp. 5–12.

13. *Al-Kawkab al-Masri*, 25 March 1881.

14. See, for example, Shaykh Muhammad ᶜAbduh's 19 June 1881 article in *Al-Waqa'iᶜ* entitled "Ikhtilaf al-qawanin bi ikhtilaf ahwal al-umami."

15. *Al-Watan*, 28 May 1881.

16. See Sharif's first official circular of 27 September 1881 to all provincial authorities and heads of local judicial councils, in *Majmuᶜat al-qararat* (vol. for 1880–82), pp. 83–85.

17. On Qadri, see Muhammad Husayn Haykal, *Tarajim misriyya wa gharbiyya*, pp. 109–18.

18. Malet to Granville, 29 September 1881, in FO 78/3376.

19. Ibid.

20. Decree of 17 November 1881, in *Moniteur Egyptien*, 21 November 1881.

21. Malet to Granville, 28 November 1881, FO 78/3376.

22. Ibid.

23. *Al-Watan*, 26 November 1881.

24. On Salim Bey's literary and political activities by 1881, see Abdel Malek, *Idéologie*, pp. 284, 286, and 320.

25. *Al-ᶜAsr al-Jadid*, 12 October 1881.

26. See, for example, "Hudud al-Huquq," *Al-ᶜAsr al-Jadid*, 26 October 1881.

27. *Al-Waqa'iᶜ*, 25 December 1881.

28. At this point, Qadri was already engaged in his own project of *shariᶜa* codification, possibly with the intention of presenting it to the Assembly for adoption (see Qadri's *Murshid al-hayaran ila maᶜrifat ahwal al-insan*).

29. *Phare*, 4–5 and 29 December 1881; and Gambetta to Sienkiewicz, 13 December 1881, in MAE, Egypte/71. One new Egyptian mixed court judge, Ismaᶜil Effendi Sami, was appointed from his post as translator for the Council of Ministers. A second, Saᶜid Bey Nasr, had been a teacher in the government's military college. The only reference to possible appointments to the *ahliyya* courts was Husayn Bey Wasif, then a functionary in the Ministry of the Interior (*Phare*, 29 December 1881). Although Husayn Bey had no formal legal training, he had served in the mixed attorney general's staff. See his biography in Fahmi, *Safwat al-ᶜAsr*, pp. 243–46.

30. Sienkiewicz to Gambetta, 4 January 1882, in MAE, Egypte/72.

31. See Sharif's speech to the newly convened Assembly in *Al-Ahram*, 7 January 1882.

32. Rivers-Wilson to Granville, 31 January 1882, in GP, G & D 29/171; and Wilson's memorandum of 13 February 1882, in FO 407/19.

33. Sienkiewicz to de Freycinet, 7 February 1882, in MAE, Egypte/72. For several months at least, the Sami cabinet did not include a minister of justice.

34. *Phare*, 25–26 February 1882. Some judicial appointments appear to have been made, and later canceled, by the Assembly (see *Phare*, 16 February and 18 March 1882).

35. Atkins, "British Policy," p. 311.

36. *Phare*, 19–20 February 1882.

37. *Phare*, 12–13 March and 2 May 1882.

38. Of eight appointments announced in the *Phare*, I have biographical references to five, or possibly six, personalities: Muhammad Pasha Qadri, president of the supreme court; Muhammad Faik (brother of Salim Pasha, a minister), Cairo court of appeals; Ibrahim Fuad (graduate of the University of Paris Law Faculty and a future minister of justice), president of the tribunal in Qalubiyya Province; Mustafa Effendi Fahmi (former bureau head, Ministry of Pious Foundations), and Shaykh ᶜAli Nayel (former member of the *majlis mahalli* in Cairo), judgeships in the Qalubiyya tribunal; and Yahya Effendi Qadri (related to Muhammad Qadri?), judgeship in the Cairo first-instance court.

39. See, for example, "Al Qanun," in *Az-Zaman* (Cairo), 6 March 1882.

40. *Phare*, 7 and 9 June 1882.

41. Raghib to Tawfiq, 20 June 1882, in *Recueil de tous les documents officiels du gouvernement égyptien* (hereafter *RDO*), 1882.

Chapter Seven

1. Robinson and Gallagher, *Africa and the Victorians*, pp. 122–28.

2. Tawfiq to Sharif, 20 August 1882, in *RDO*, 1882.

3. *Moniteur Egyptien*, 29 September 1882.

4. Consul de Vorges to Paris, 3 August 1882, in MAE, Egypte/75; and Malet to Granville, 13 September 1882, in FO 407/30.

5. Granville to Malet, 5 October 1882; and Malet to Granville, 11 October 1882, in FO 407/30.

6. Granville to Malet, 5 October 1882, in FO 407/30.

7. Cambon to d'Estournelles, Paris, 8 October 1882, in Paul Cambon, *Correspondance*: 1870–1924, vol. 1.

8. *Hansard*, third series, vol. 721 (1881), col. 1123.

9. Granville to Malet, 14 November 1882 (telegram), in FO 407/30.

10. Raindre to Duclerc, 4 November 1882, in MAE, Egypte/76.

11. Lyons to Granville, Paris, 6 December 1882, in FO 407/30.

12. The first person to fill the Anglo-Egyptian post of financial adviser was Sir Auckland Colvin, controller general in Cairo until 1882.

13. Granville to Malet, 17 and 30 December 1882 (italics added), in FO 407/30.

14. Cabinet minutes of 2 November 1882, in *Al-Kitab adh-Dhahabi* (2 vols.; Cairo, 1937–38), vol. 1, pp. 102–6.

15. Ibid.

16. *Mudhakkirat Husayn basha Fakhri*, 7 December 1882, in ibid., pp. 107–15.

17. Ibid., p. 112.

18. Cabinet minutes of 7 December 1882, in *Al-Kitab adh-Dhahabi*, vol. 1, p. 117 (italics added).

19. Dufferin to Granville, 20 December 1882, in GP, G & D 29/166.

20. Raindre to Duclerc, 25 December 1882, in MAE, Egypte/76.

21. *Phare*, 20 January 1883; cf. Dufferin to Granville, 29 January 1883 (telegram); and Granville to Dufferin, 29 January 1883, in FO 407/41.

22. Dufferin to Granville, 2 January 1883, in GP, G & D 29/166.

23. Dufferin to Granville, 22 January 1883, in GP, G & D 29/166.

24. *Egyptian Gazette*, 26 January 1883.

25. Raindre to Duclerc, 19 February 1883, in MAE, Egypte/77.

26. Dufferin's report of 6 February 1883, in Accounts and Papers, Egypt No. 6 (1883).

27. *Al-Burhan* (Cairo), 5 March 1883.

28. The *Egyptian Gazette* of 22 March 1883 claimed that London had tried to obtain the professional services of John Scott as the first *ahliyya* court prosecutor-adviser.

29. Dufferin to Granville, 25 April 1883; and same to same, 24 April 1883, in GP, G & D 29/166.

30. Raindre to M. Challemal Lacour, 9 May 1883, in MAE, Egypte/79.

31. *Gazette*, 25 August 1883.

32. *Phare*, 21–22 January 1883; *Gazette*, 30 January 1883; cf. *Al-Burhan* (Cairo), 5 March 1883.

33. See *Hansard*, vol. 279 (1883): col. 950 (28 May 1883), and col. 1331 (31 May 1883).

34. Malet to Granville, 1 September 1883, enclosing Maxwell's report to Sharif, 28 August 1883, in FO 407/41.

35. Ibid. Judge Sheldon Amos was the only British judge appointed to the *ahliyya* court bench in 1883. Amos's biography is in *DNB*, 1st supplement (London, 1921–22), vol. 22, pp. 44–45; and *Gazette*, 7 June 1883. Belgian judge T. Minnaert's account of his own appointment is the only published narrative by one of the original European judges in the Egyptian courts. See T. Minnaert, *Le Caire et la justice internationale en Egypte,* p. 308.

36. Baring to Granville, 19 September 1883 (telegram); and same to same, 26 September 1883, in FO 407/41.

37. See decrees of 28 October 1883 and 13 November 1883, in Gélat, *Répertoire*, vol. 4, p. 401; cf. *Gazette*, 7 November 1883; and *Al-Burhan*, 5 November 1883.

38. *Az-Zaman*, 6 September 1883.

39. Pauncefote memorandum of 20 November 1883; and Granville to Baring, 18 December 1883, in FO 407/41.

40. Baring to Granville, 27 December 1883 (telegram), in FO 407/41. The original appointees to the *ahliyya* courts are listed by Aziz Khanki, *Al mahakim al-mukhtalata wa'l mahakim al-ahliyya*, pp. 6–7.

41. Pauncefote memorandum of 7 November 1883.

42. Malet to Granville, 25 June and 2 July 1883, in FO 407/41.

43. Malet to Granville, 26 July 1883, enclosing Cookson's memorandum of 24 July 1883, in FO 407/41.

44. Raindre to Lacour, 18 July 1883; Lacour to Raindre, 24 July 1883; Lacour to Barrère, 13 October 1883, in MAE, Egypte/80.

45. Baring to Pauncefote, 5 October 1883, in CP, FO 633/5.

46. Baring to Granville, 23 October 1883, in FO 407/41.

47. Granville to Baring, 20 November 1883 (telegram), in FO 407/41.

48. Nubar's critical attitude toward Sharif's earlier handling of Ministry of Justice affairs is documented in his memoirs (see chapter 3, note 36, above). Unfortunately, the published memoirs do not go beyond 1879, creating an obvious historical gap that must be filled, as I have done here, by means of alternative primary sources.

Chapter Eight

1. *Phare*, 11 January 1884.

2. *Le Bosphore Egyptien* , 22 January 1884. After "promotion" from his key position as director of the Contentieux d'Etat to a nominal post as *avocat du gouvernement*, Borelli's name drops out of the official records. He seems to have devoted most of his time after 1883 to his Cairo daily newspaper, *Le Bosphore Egyptien*.

3. Baring to Granville, 26 January 1884, enclosing Maxwell's undated "Report on the Native Courts," in FO 407/42.

4. Baring to Pauncefote, 21 January 1884, in CP, FO 633/5; cf. Baring to Granville, 21 January and 5 February 1884, in GP, G & D 29/162.

5. Butrus Bey's biographical sketch is in Haykal, *Tarajim misriyya*, pp. 119–28.

6. Accounts of Lloyd's controversial tenure in Egypt from 1883 through 1884 may be seen in Milner, *England in Egypt*, pp. 112–14; and Robert Tignor, *Modernization and British Colonial Rule in Egypt, 1882–1914*, pp. 70–73.

7. Malet to Granville, 14, 18, and 29 August 1883, in GP, G & D 29/160.

8. *Az-Zaman*, 24 January 1884.

9. *Az-Zaman*, 11 and 18 March 1884.

10. Barrère to Ferry, 30 May 1884, in MAE, Egypte/86.

11. Baring to Granville, 11 March 1884.

12. Pauncefote to Granville, 9 April 1884, in GP, G & D 29/194. See also Portal Papers (Rhodes House, Oxford), Gerald Portal's diary entries for 5, 6, and 7 May 1884.

13. Pauncefote to Granville, 9 April 1884.

14. Decree of 28 April 1884, in *RDO*, 1885.

15. Gerald Portal diaries, entry for 26 May 1884.

16. Baring to Granville, London, 4 July 1884, in GP, G & D 29/162; cf. *Times* (London), 17 July 1884.

17. Barrère to Ferry, 4 February 1884, in MAE, Egypte/83; and Georges Martin-Sarzeaud, "Sur la Réforme Judiciaire en Egypte: Rapport à la commission internationale," *Journal de Droit International Privé* (Paris), 11 (1884), 300–15.

18. Baring to Granville, 7 February 1884, enclosing two undated circular memoranda by Judge Martin-Sarzeaud, in FO 407/42.

19. Baring to Granville, 10 February 1884, in GP, G & D 29/162; and same to same, 17 March 1884, in CP, FO 633/6.

20. The courts' changing stand is discussed in *Az-Zaman*, 25 and 27 March 1884; *Al-Burhan*, 28 April 1884; and *Gazette*, 1 May 1884.

21. In February 1884, for example, the Crédit Foncier, one of Egypt's principal (French-capitalized) land mortgage companies, barely escaped a *parquet* challenge (argued by an Egyptian lawyer) that its suits against *fal-*

lahin debtors should not continue to profit from special conditions offered by the mixed codes (see *Gazette*, 11 February 1884).

22. See de Ring's 1880–81 international capitulatory role, chapter 5 above.

23. Baring to Granville, 11 and 18 March 1884, in FO 407/42.

24. *Phare*, 16 May 1884, reprinting the subcommission's final report.

25. Enclosure in Comte d'Aunay to de Freycinet, 12 March 1887, in MAE, Egypte/105.

26. Egerton to Granville, 23 May 1884, in FO 407/42.

27. *Hansard*, vol. 291 (1884), 1 July 1884, col. 1792; 10 July 1884, col. 673–74; and 25 July 1884, col. 501.

28. *Hansard*, vol. 291 (1884), 31 July 1884, col. 1181; cf. 3 July 1884, col. 1871.

29. Berbera and the Somalian hinterland, taken by Khedive Isma^{c}il in 1875, had drifted toward anarchy and became possible prey for foreign rivals until Britain dispatched troops into the area from Aden in June and July 1884.

30. In 1885, the Paris Chambre voted to extend a French guarantee over the totality of the Tunisian beylicate's public debt. Italy, meanwhile, was building up forces for a (1885) campaign against the Red Sea enclave at Massawa.

31. On Northbrook's experience of internal reform and imperial politics in India, see *DNB*, 2nd supplement, vol. 1, pp. 93–96.

32. *Times* (London), 20 August 1884. An interesting sidelight on Samiullah Khan, "a willing servant of the British in India," appears in Nikkie Keddie's translation of Jamal ad-Din al-Afghani's writings, *An Islamic Response to Imperialism* (Berkeley and Los Angeles, 1968), pp. 179–80.

33. Cited in *Gazette*, 22 August 1884; cf. *Phare*, 25 August 1884.

34. *Times* (London), 6 October 1884.

35. *Gazette*, 10 December 1884; cf. Lord Northbrook's report of 20 November 1884, in FO 78/3690, and Barrère to Ferry, 8 December 1884 (telegram), in MAE, Egypte/90.

36. Barrère to Ferry, 18 November 1884, in MAE, Egypte/89.

37. *Az-Zaman*, 12 September 1884.

38. *Az-Zaman*, 11 September 1884; also *Al-Bayan*, 14 August 1884.

39. *Az-Zaman*, 4 October 1884

40. *Az-Zaman*, 24 October 1884.

41. *Gazette*, 21 October 1884; *Az-Zaman*, 23 October 1884.

42. *Az-Zaman*, 1 November 1884.

43. Lord Northbrook's report of 20 November 1884, in FO 78/3690.

44. Baring to Granville, 27 October 1884, in GP, G & D 29/163.

45. See the Declaration of 17 March and Convention of 18 March 1885, in Gélat, *Répertoire*, vol. 2, pp. 134–35. In March 1885, Lord Granville won a preliminary agreement on the revision of the 1880 liquidation law, which was not finalized until the Salisbury government returned to power in the summer of 1885. The judicial implications of the initial compromise

appeared in article 2, which stated that the mixed courts would continue to be the sole authorities competent to judge strict observation of Egypt's revised financial regime. This amounted to an additional guarantee that Britain could not seriously alter the Mixed Court Charter as long as the foreign debt remained outstanding.

46. *Bosphore*, 7 January 1885; *Phare*, 9 January 1885. On Raymond West himself, see *DNB*, supplement for 1901–11, vol. 1, p. 95.

47. Baring to Granville, 9 February 1885, enclosing West's memorandum of 6 February 1885, in FO 78/3800.

48. On the firing of judges already under way, see *Gazette*, 29 January 1885, and *Phare*, 14 February 1885.

49. Legislative Council Minutes of 9 August 1884, in *RDO*, 1885.

50. Legislative Council Minutes of 27 and 29 April, 9 May, and 9 June 1885.

51. Decree of 21 April 1885, in *Az-Zaman*, 29 April 1885; cf. *Gazette*, 4 and 5 May 1885.

52. On Qasim Bey Amin's work as an *ahliyya* court judge, see Haykal, *Tarajim misriyya*, pp. 109–18. Cf. chapter 12 for later developments in Amin's career.

53. Decision of 30 June 1885, in *RDO*, 1885; *Al-Ahram*, 24 August 1885; and decisions of 13 and 22 October 1885, in *RDO*, 1885.

54. Wolff to the Earl of Rosebery, 13 March 1886, enclosing West's memorandum of 19 August 1885, in FO 407/68.

55. West memorandum of 19 August 1885.

56. Salisbury to Egerton, 6 November 1885, in FO 407/42. See also Harold Perry, "Justice in Egypt," *Law Quarterly Review*, 1 (1885), 342–54.

57. *Phare*, 11 and 14 November 1885.

58. *Gazette*, 3 and 9 December 1885. Nubar's extension of the brigandage commissions in 1886 was accomplished by strengthening extrajudicial elements that had originally been meant to work side by side with *ahliyya* court representatives. He charged the *mudirs* of each province of lower Egypt with the ex-officio function of heading the draconian deliberations, with two *ᶜumdas* to serve as "assessors."

59. *Phare*, 30 January and 1, 14, and 15 February 1886.

60. Baring to Lord Rosebery, 15 February 1886, in CP, FO 633/6.

61. Ibid. (italics added).

62. *Times*, 15 March 1886.

63. *Al-ᶜAlam*, 17 January 1886; *Az-Zaman*, 16 and 24 February 1886.

64. *Al-Huquq* (Cairo), 6 March 1886. Of the original *ahliyya* lawyers who served on this self-appointed body, only three names—Amin Shumayyil, Saᶜad Zaghlul, and Husayn Effendi Saqr—provide biographical leads. Amin Shumayyil's biography appears in Jurji Zaydan, *Tarajim mashahir ash-sharq*, vol. 2, pp. 206–9; and in his obituary, *Al-Huquq*, 11 December 1897.

65. ᶜAbd al-Khaliq Muhammad Lashin, *Saᶜad Zaghlul: Dawruhu fi as-siyasat al-misriyya hatta 1914*, pp. 61–76.

66. *Al-Huquq*, 20 March 1886.

67. *Al-Huquq*, 3 April and 15 May 1886.

68. D'Aunay to de Freycinet, 30 April 1886 (telegram), in MAE, Egypte/99.

69. *Phare*, 5 May 1886; cf. *Bosphore*, 8 May 1886.

70. Baring to Rosebery, 13 May 1886, enclosing Nubar to Baring, 8 May 1886, in FO 407/67.

71. Baring to Pauncefote, 17 May 1886, in CP, FO 633/5.

72. *Al-Huquq*, 15 May 1886; cf. *Al-Qahira al-Hurra*, 21 June 1886.

73. Baring to Rosebery, 18 and 28 June 1886; and Drummond-Wolff to Rosebery, 19 June 1886, enclosing Consul Charles Cookson's note, "The Mixed Tribunals as a Political Instrument," 14 June 1886, in FO 407/43.

74. Baring to Pauncefote, 26 June 1886, in CP, FO 633/5.

75. Baring to Rosebery, 29 June 1886; and Rosebery to Baring, same date (telegram), in FO 407/68.

76. D'Aunay to de Freycinet, 3 July 1886, in MAE, Egypte/101.

Chapter Nine

1. See my original draft of the first section of this chapter, "Nubar Pasha, Sir Evelyn Baring, and a Suppressed Article in the Drummond-Wolff Convention," in the *International Journal of Middle East Studies*, 5 (1974), 468–83. Wolff was appointed British ambassador to the Ottoman Empire at the outset of Salisbury's 1886–92 government.

2. Iddesleigh to Baring, 13 October 1886, in CP, FO 633/7.

3. De Beaucaire to de Freycinet, 18 October 1886, in MAE, Egypte/101.

4. Baring to Iddesleigh, 24 October 1866; and same to same, 31 October 1886 in CP, FO 633/6.

5. See *Phare*, 26 October 1886, announcing ratification of draft modifications in the mixed laws (the first since 1876), including the notorious *hypothèque judiciaire*.

6. A letter from Nubar to Wolff in January 1887 is the only documentary evidence of the Egyptian's conversion to Salisbury's desire to maintain a clear distinction between mixed and *ahliyya* court priorities. After more than a decade of arguing to the contrary, Nubar urged the high commissioner not to pursue the course of simple jurisdictional unification, because, "unless fusion results in the . . . absorption of the mixed . . . into the native courts . . . it would cause disadvantages for Egypt" (Nubar to Wolff 30 January 1887, in Baring to Salisbury, 28 April 1887, in FO 407/43).

7. Legislative Council Minutes for 6 and 17 November 1886, 1 and 9 December 1886; and 5 January 1887, in *RDO*, 1886 and 1887.

8. Decree of 9 February 1887, in *RDO*, 1887.

9. *Al-Huquq*, 19 February 1887.

10. Wolff to Salisbury, 14 February 1887 (telegram); and Salisbury to Wolff, 14 February 1887 (telegram), in SP, A/51.

11. Salisbury to Wolff, 15 February 1887 (telegram), in SP, A/51.

12. Baring to Salisbury, 4 March 1887, in SP, A/52.

13. D'Aunay to de Freycinet, 20 March 1887, in MAE, Egypte/105.

14. Baring to Iddesleigh, 31 December 1886, in CP FO 633/6; and d'Aunay to de Freycinet, 24 March 1887 (telegram), in MAE, Egypte/105.

15. Wolff to Salisbury, 18 March 1887 in SP, A/51.

16. Wolff to Salisbury, 31 March and 5 April 1887, in Accounts and Papers, Egypt No. 7 (1887).

17. D'Aunay to de Freycinet, 2 April 1887, in MAE, Egypte/105; and Baring to Salisbury, 3 April 1887, in FO 407/43.

18. *Al-Huquq*, 9 April 1887.

19. *Bosphore*, 15 April 1887.

20. Baring to Salisbury, 28 April 1887, enclosing Nubar's note of 27 April 1887, in FO 407/70.

21. Ibid. The twelve original categories of bylaws included legislation governing the administration of land, dikes, and canals; sanitation and hygiene; waste disposal (*tanzim*); press and printing regulations; policing of public establishments (hotels, gaming places, etc.); sale and carrying of firearms and explosives; hunting regulations; carriages and other private means of transportation; policing of ports, navigation routes, and bridges; begging and street vendors; policing of dangerous sites and construction zones; and creation of new taxes, tariffs, and so forth.

22. Wolff to Salisbury, 4 April 1887, in SP, A/51.

23. D'Aunay to de Freycinet, 16 May 1887; and same to same, 22 and 23 May 1887 (telegram), in MAE, Egypte/106.

24. Text of the 22 May 1887 convention in Gélat, *Répertoire*, vol. 2, pp. 503–6.

25. Baring to Salisbury, 28 May 1887, in SP, A/52; cf. *Al-Fallah*, 3 June 1887.

26. Baring to Salisbury, 30 May 1887, in FO 407/43. On the high-level European diplomacy that blocked the Anglo-Ottoman Convention of 1887, mainly because of British insistence on a guaranteed unilateral reentry clause, see Langer, *European Alliances and Alignments*, pp. 428–49.

27. *As-Sadiq* (Cairo), 14 December 1886; see also *Al-Huquq*, 23 April 1887.

28. Portal to Salisbury, 3 October 1887; and Baring to Salisbury, 7 October 1887, enclosing a memorandum by Coles Pasha (deputy inspector of the Cairo Division, Egyptian Police) to Valentine Baker, 7 October 1887, in FO 407/71.

29. *Phare*, 20 and 21 October 1887. Shafiq's biography is in Zaydan, *Mashahir*, vol. 2, pp. 183–85. Trained in government secondary schools in the 1860s, Shafiq Bey studied mathematics and natural science in Switzerland between 1871 and 1877. During the first troubled years of Tawfiq's khedivate, he wrote articles for the scientific journal *Al-Muqtataf* and textbooks for use in the Egyptian public school system. This evidently helped him finance four more years in France, two of which were dedicated to formal studies of law. When the troubles of 1882 were over, therefore, Shafiq

Bey was one of the few formally trained Egyptians who served in the Ministry of Justice, first as an assistant in the foreign indemnities commission and then as one of Husayn Fakhri's first appointees to the new Cairo appeals bench. It was Raymond West who chose Shafiq when he was only twenty-nine years old to be his Egyptian deputy, a post that qualified him to become attorney general in 1886.

30. Baring to Salisbury, 10 November 1887, in FO 407/43.

31. Baring to Nubar, 21 October 1887, enclosing a letter from General Frederick Stephenson to Baring, in FO 407/43.

32. Baring to Salisbury, 18 December 1887, enclosing Baring to Nubar, 17 December 1887, in FO 407/43.

33. Baring to Cookson, Cairo, 31 December 1887, in CP, FO 633/5; and Baring to Salisbury, 31 December 1887, enclosing Scott to Baring, Bombay, 12 December 1887, in FO 407/44; cf. Salisbury to Baring, 23 December 1887, in FO 407/43.

34. Baring to Pauncefote, 22 October 1887, in CP, FO 633/5.

35. In January 1888, the government quietly suspended its investigation of conditions of rural justice under the *ahliyya* and brigandage jurisdictions. See *Phare*, 11 January 1888, and *Al-Qahira*, 5 January 1888.

36. Baring to Pauncefote, 30 January 1888, in CP, FO 633/5; cf. note 23, above.

37. D'Aubigny to Flourens, 16 and 25 February and 5 March 1888, in MAE, Egypte/109.

38. Salisbury to Baring, 17 April 1888, in FO 407/44; and Goblet to d'Aubigny, 11 April 1888, in MAE, Egypte/110.

39. *Al-Qahira*, 19 April 1888.

40. *Al-Qahira*, 23 and 28 August 1888.

41. *Al-Huquq*, 17 March and 7 April 1888.

42. Biographical notes on Tuma are in Zaydan, *Mashahir*, vol. 2, pp. 245–48; and Abdel Malek, *Idéologie*, p. 286.

43. *Phare*, 22 and 25 June 1888; and *Al-Qahira*, 3 July 1888.

44. *Phare*, 7 April 1888. Potentially affected were the khedive's *da'ira*s, the railroad and port of Alexandria administrations, and four provincial governorates.

45. *Al-Huquq*, 16 June 1888; cf., *Al-Qahira*, 3 June 1888.

46. *Al-Fallah*, 3 September 1888.

47. *Al-Ahkam*, 1 October 1888.

48. Baring to Salisbury, 2 and 5 July 1888, in FO 407/44.

49. Baring to Salisbury, 13 July 1888, in FO 407/44.

50. Salisbury to Portal, 17 September 1888, in FO 407/44.

51. Denant to Goblet, 12 October 1888 (telegram), in MAE, Egypte/112.

52. Baring to Salisbury, 13 and 15 November 1888, in FO 407/44; cf. *Hansard*, vol. 330 (1888), 22 November 1888, col. 1832; and vol. 332 (1888), 20 December 1888, col. 871–72. See listing of the bylaws originally proposed in note 21, above.

53. D'Aubigny to Goblet, 20 November 1888, in MAE, Egypte/112.

54. Vivian to Salisbury, Brussels, 1 December 1888, in FO 407/44; and Baring to Salisbury, 20 January 1889, in FO 407/91. According to *Al-Qahira* (14 January 1887), Portugal had already tried unsuccessfully to obtain a reserved spot on the appeals bench at the time of the Drummond-Wolff negotiations. For similar demands from the Belgians, see Salisbury to Vivian, 15 January 1887, in FO 407/70.

55. Circular of 19 December 1888, in *RDO*, 1888. The controversy over the status of Greek subjects in Egypt came soon after the shah in Tehran mounted pressures to obtain capitulatory status for Iranians who entered Egypt as foreign traders (see *Al-Qahira*, 24 July and 11 September 1888).

56. Baring to Salisbury, 4 and 22 January 1889, in FO 407/91.

57. See Monson to Salisbury, Athens, 29 January 1889 (telegram); and Salisbury to Baring, same date (telegram), in FO 407/91.

58. D'Aubigny to Goblet, 8 January 1889, in MAE, Egypte/113.

59. Baring to Salisbury, 7 January 1889 (telegram), in FO 407/91.

60. D'Aubigny to Goblet, 19 January 1889 (telegram), in MAE, Egypte/113.

61. Baring to Salisbury, 20 January 1889 (telegram), in FO 407/91.

Chapter Ten

1. Baring to Salisbury, 13 December 1888, in FO 407/44.

2. Legislative Council Minutes of 4 August 1888 and 6, 10, 13, and 27 October 1888, in *RDO*, 1888. Fakhri's 22 December 1888 report on the mixed courts noted a surplus of £E 47,000 in annual judicial fees over costs (*RDO*, 1889).

3. *Al-Huquq*, 9 February 1889.

4. *Al-Huquq*, 23 February 1889. By this date, the court of appeals in Cairo had accepted thirty-one lawyers, the Cairo tribunal thirty-five, Alexandria ten, Tanta eleven, Zagazig seven, and Banha five.

5. Legrelle's report is in the *Journal Officiel* of 2 March 1889. An example of an Egyptian who first served under the European attorney general of the mixed courts and then moved to the local *parquet* (from which he was promoted to a superior judicial post) is Husayn Bey Wasif.

6. See especially *Al-Adab* (Cairo), 30 March 1889; *Al-Qahira*, 16 March 1889; *Phare*, 30 April 1889. To upgrade the professional climate surrounding legal proceedings, Fakhri cut the number of auxiliaries assisting judges by one-quarter. He also fired many recorders and bailiffs who had been hired *en masse* without a real idea of how to divide tasks between clerks and professionally responsible members of the judiciary.

7. *Phare*, 30 March and 18 April 1889.

8. *Phare*, 27 April 1889; and *Al-Qahira*, 2 March and 14 May 1889.

9. *Gazette*, 23 May and 1 June 1889.

10. *Al-Muqattam*, 21 August 1889; and *Al-Huquq*, 24 August 1889.

11. Clarke to Salisbury, 27 July 1889 (telegram), in FO 407/92.

12. Clarke to Salisbury, 30 August 1889, in FO 407/92.

13. *Al-Huquq*, 21 December 1889; and *Al-Mu'ayyad*, 10 and 25 December 1889. On *Al-Mu'ayyad*, edited by Shaykh [c]Ali Yusuf, see al-Jundi, *Sihafa*, pp. 159–61.

14. *Al-Huquq*, 22 February 1890; Baring to Salisbury, 11 February 1890 (telegram); and Salisbury to Baring 25 February 1890 (telegram), in FO 407/04.

15. Charles Cookson's report, in Baring to Salisbury, 29 June 1890, in FO 407/104.

16. The amount invested in such land development and mortgage companies by the 1890s is summarized in Baer, *Landownership*, pp. 66–70.

17. The original text of article 9 appears in Borelli, *Choses politiques*, p. 524 (italics added).

18. One area of property law that was becoming a target for discussion by advocates of the status quo and exponents of a larger role for principles of Islamic law in the *ahliyya* courts was *shuf[c]a,* or preemptive buyers' rights.

19. Charles Cookson's report in Baring to Salisbury, 29 June 1890.

20. See *Al-Huquq*, 3 and 17 May 1890; and *Al-Mu'ayyad*, 9 and 16 June 1890.

21. Baring to Salibury, 27 June 1890, enclosing Scott to Fakhri, 14 June 1890, in FO 407/104.

22. Baring to Barrington, 27 June 1890, in SP, A/54.

23. Baring to Salisbury, 6 November 1890, enclosing Scott's memorandum of 5 November 1890, in SP, A/54.

24. Lytton to Salibury, Paris, 15 December 1890, in FO 407/104.

25. *Al-Watan*, 24 December 1890.

26. *Al-Huquq*, 27 December 1890.

27. *Al-Huquq*, 7 February 1891; cf. *Al Mu'ayyad*, 31 January 1891.

28. Baring to Salisbury, 19 January 1891, in SP, A/54.

29. Ribot to d'Aubigny, 13 February 1891 (telegram); and d'Aubigny to Ribot, 14 and 16 February 1891 (telegrams), in MAE, Egypte/120.

30. D'Aubigny to Ribot, 18 and 21 February 1891, in MAE, Egypte/120.

31. Baring to Salisbury, 19 February 1891 (telegram), in FO 407/105.

32. Fakhri's Egyptian nominees for the law school director's post were Husayn Bey Wasif and Ibrahim Pasha Fuad, both high-ranking judges in the *ahliyya* courts.

33. Denant to Ribot, 8 March 1891 (telegram), in MAE, Egypte/120.

34. Denant to Ribot, 8, 10, and 16 April 1891, in MAE, Egypte/121.

35. Denant to Ribot, 16 and 24 April 1891, in MAE, Egypte/121.

36. Eldon Gorst to Alfred Milner, 1 May 1891, and Palmer to Milner, 22 May 1891, in Alfred Milner Papers, Bodleian Library in Oxford (hereafter MP), boxes 186 and 187.

37. De Reverseaux to Ribot, 9 May 1891, in MAE, Egypte/121.

38. De Reverseaux to Ribot, 30 May 1890. In private correspondence with Alfred Milner, Baring mentioned his presumed disappointment with Scott's attitudes, claiming he was "full of good intentions, but [lacks com-

prehension in] dealing with the natives" (Baring to Milner, 27 June 1891, in MP, Box 186).

39. Legislative Council Minutes of 11 and 13 June 1891, in *RDO*, 1891, and Baring to Salisbury, 21 June 1891, in FO 407/105.

40. *Al-Mu'ayyad*, 13 June and 15 August 1891; and *Al-Huquq*, 20 June 1891.

41. *Journal Officiel* (Cairo), 8 July 1891; and *Al-Huquq*, 11 July 1891.

42. De Reverseaux to Ribot, 15 December 1891, in MAE, Egypte/124.

43. *Le Sphinx*, 17 January 1892; cf. de Reverseaux to Ribot, 19 January 1892, in MAE, Egypte/125.

44. Langer, *The Diplomacy of Imperialism*, pp. 3–4.

45. Ibid., p. 109.

46. Ibid., p. 119.

Chapter Eleven

1. De Reverseaux to Ribot, 10 June 1892, in MAE, Egypte/127.

2. Arthur Goldschmidt, Jr., "The Egyptian Nationalist Party: 1892–1919," in P. M. Holt, ed., *Political and Social Change in Modern Egypt* (London, 1968), p. 310.

3. De Reverseaux to Ribot, 28 January and 10 March 1893, in MAE, Egypte/129.

4. De Reverseaux to Ribot, 6 January 1893 (telegram), in MAE, Egypte/129.

5. Simaika, *De la compétence des tribunaux mixtes d'Egypte en matière civile, commerciale, et financière*. After earning his doctorate in Roman and French law, Simaika returned to Cairo to practice before the *ahliyya* courts. He participated in the lawyers' circle involved in the publication of *Al-Huquq*.

6. Ibid., pp. 16–20.

7. *Al-Ustadh*, 6 September 1892.

8. Hourani, *Arabic Thought*, pp. 196–97.

9. *Al-Ustadh*, 30 August and 22 November 1892.

10. *Al-Ustadh*, 18 October 1892.

11. Ibid.

12. *Al-Ustadh*, 20 December 1892.

13. Between 1890 and the spring of 1893, "low-key" procedural reform issues only appeared in official circulars.

14. De Reverseaux to Develle, 12 December 1892, in MAE, Egypte/128.

15. De Reverseaux to Develle, 25 April 1893, in MAE, Egypte/130.

16. De Reverseaux to Develle, 17 May 1893, in MAE, Egypte/130.

17. De Reverseaux to Develle, 24 June 1893, in MAE, Egypte/130; and 26 September and 1 October 1893, in MAE, Egypte/131.

18. Casimir-Perier to de Reverseaux, 8 December 1893, in MAE, Egypte/132.

19. Owen, *The Middle East*, pp. 217–18.

20. Richards, *Egypt's Agricultural Development*, pp. 58–59.
21. Owen, *The Middle East*, p. 218 (table 49).
22. Owen, *Cotton and the Egyptian Economy*, p. 306.
23. Owen, *The Middle East*, pp. 219–20, 234ff.
24. See Robert Tignor, "The Introduction of Modern Banking into Egypt, 1855–1920," *Journal of Asian and African Studies*, 15 (1981), 103–22.
25. Owen, *Cotton and the Egyptian Economy*, p. 288.
26. Ibid., p. 202 (table 40), 259–60, especially table 68.
27. Roger Owen surveys a variety of formal legal (and extralegal) and administrative problems afflicting Syrian modes of agricultural production by 1900, including persistence of *musha*ᶜ*a* (common) property rights in preference to individual holdings, as well as Sultan Abdulhamid's own intervention to create imperial estates on the best agricultural land (see ibid., pp. 253–64).
28. See Jean Poncet, *La colonisation et l'agriculture européennes en Tunisie depuis 1881: Etude de géographie historique et économique* (Paris, 1962), pp. 159–60, 167.
29. Owen, *Cotton and the Egyptian Economy*, p. 214.
30. See *Times*, 5 January, 16 August, and 9 September 1895; 7 April 1897; 2 May 1898; 1 and 17 April 1899; and 2 May 1901.
31. Tignor, "Introduction of Modern Banking," pp. 107–8.
32. *Report by Her Majesty's Agent and Consul General on the Finances, Administration, and Condition of Egypt and the Sudan Covering the Year 1894* (Egypt No. 1—1895).
33. *Report* for 1895 (Egypt No. 1—1896).
34. Ibid.
35. In 1896, Cromer cited statistics indicating that in France twenty-seven percent, of all penal cases submitted were dismissed for lack of sufficient evidence and another twenty-four percent were eventually acquitted. In Egypt, equivalent percentages in 1895 were forty-six percent and twenty-nine percent, respectively.
36. See *Al-Huquq*, 1 December 1894.
37. "La réforme des tribunaux indigènes [en Egypte]." *Bulletin du Comité de l'Afrique Française*, 7 January 1897, 110–13.
38. *Report* for 1897 (Egypt No. 1—1898).
39. Tignor, *Modernization and British Colonial Rule in Egypt*, p. 138.
40. *Report* for 1903 (Egypt No. 1—1904).

Chapter Twelve

1. Again, the fact that Tunisia underwent many experiences that can be compared with developments in Egypt (especially in the 1850s to the early 1880s) suggests that later trends visible in Egypt might have been transferred earliest to Tunisia. In fact, substantial reflections of many of the concerns discussed in this chapter, especially under the rubric of neoconservatism, are visible in works by ᶜAbdul ᶜAziz ath-Thaᶜalibi and a number of

representatives of the turn-of-the-century Young Tunisian movement who wrote for *Al-Hadhira*, *Az-Zuhra*, and their own (French- and Arabic-language) organ, *Le Tunisien*. See, for example, discussion of legalistically oriented neoconservatism in Arnold H. Green, *The Tunisian Ulama, 1873–1915* (Leiden, 1978), and my article "La constitution ottomane dans la stratégie politique jeune tunisienne, 1908–10," *Cahiers de Tunisie*, 29 (1981), 279–94.

2. A perfect example can be seen in the final chapter of Owen's 1969 study, *Cotton and the Egyptian Economy*. Instead of attempting analysis of the way major institutional changes affected local modes of expressing essential social and economic ideas (in Owen's case economic, here legal), discussion of changing views of economic phenomena is limited to European authors only.

3. See Kassem [Qasim] Amin, *Les Egyptiens: Réponse à Monsieur le Duc d'Harcourt* (Cairo, 1894), pp. 17–250; cf. note 23, below.

4. A concise and useful account of the origins of the Umma party is Goldschmidt, "Nationalist Party," pp. 308–33.

5. Examples of this generalization are too numerous to mention here. One should compare the views expressed in Ziadeh, *Lawyers*, chap. 4, with Goldschmidt, "Nationalist Party," and Reid's *Lawyers and Politics*.

6. Goldschmidt, "Nationalist Party," pp. 312–13.

7. On the Ecole des Frères, see Reid, *Lawyers and Politics*, pp. 22–23, and my "Social Tensions and the Teaching of European Law in Egypt before 1900," *History of Education Quarterly* (Fall, 1975), 299–315.

8. Lutfi al-Sayyid [Marsot], *Egypt and Cromer*, pp. 186–87.

9. *Conférence sur L'Egypte par Monsieur Moustapha Kamel* (Paris, 1895; Extracted from *La Nouvelle Revue*).

10. Ibid.

11. Ibid.

12. See Langer, *The Diplomacy of Imperialism*, pp. 281–91.

13. See *Al-Huquq*, 28 March and 21 November 1898.

14. Decree of 19 November 1896, in Gélat, *Répertoire*, vol. 3, pp. 410–18.

15. See decree of 16 Rabi[c] Awwal 1290 (1889), in ibid., pp. 403–9.

16. Decree of 19 November 1896, *Arrêté* of 26 January 1897, and Decree of 29 March 1897, in ibid., pp. 410–18.

17. An excellent example of what was to come was the appointment, in May 1899, of two *ahliyya* appeals judges, one Yussuf Chawki Bey and Ahmad Afifi (the latter a former lawyer on the mixed attorney general's staff) to sit on the (two-year-old) supreme *mahkama* court in Cairo. Within a year, the supreme court was itself suspended following a three-year testing of the (November 1897) general reorganization of *mahkama* justice (ibid., pp. 458–59).

18. *Al-Huquq*, 9 April 1898.

19. *Al-Huquq*, 15 September 1898.

20. Muhammad Ra'fat, *Kitab usul al-qawanin*.

21. De Reverseaux to Casimir-Perier, 10 March 1894, in MAE, Egypte/134.

22. A collection of Qasim Amin's (unsigned) articles for *Al-Mu'ayyad* between 1895 and 1899 appears in Muhammad ᶜAmarah, *Qasim Amin: Al-Aᶜmal al-Kamila* (Beirut, 1976). Of particular interest to the theme presented in this chapter are "Al-istiqlal fil maᶜisha qabla kulli al-istiqlal" (pp. 194–95); and "Limadha la yujadu fi Misr aghniya'?" (pp. 198–201).

23. Ra'fat, *Kitab*, preface, p. i.

24. Ibid., pp. 7–9.

25. Ibid., pp. 88–92.

26. Ibid., pp. 102–5.

27. Examples of various lawyers' treatment of the philosophical principles of civil law (Ar., *haqq madani*) can be seen in *Al-Huquq*, 17 November and 1, 8, 22 and 28 December 1888.

28. Ra'fat, *Kitab*, pp. 120–22.

29. Ibid., pp. 44–45.

30. Ibid., pp. 108–10

31. See ibid., pp. 132, 141, 169, 175.

32. See ibid., pp. 183–85, 194–98.

33. See Ra'fat's discussion of *sharr* as an ultimate moral concern for legalists in ibid., pp. 67–68, 203.

34. Ibid., pp. 199–202. Similar tensions between administrative agents of government domain property and individual agriculturalists seeking to obtain segments of government land through normal legal channels can be seen in turn-of-the-century Tunisia and Algeria. See, for example, my article "Le marché de location des *habous* publics en Tunisie, 1874–1902," in *Terroirs et sociétés au Moyen Orient et du Maghreb*, *Etudes du monde arabe*, Number 2, Maison de l'Orient, University of Lyon II, 1987.

35. Ra'fat, *Kitab*, p. 201.

36. Ibid., pp. 205–30.

37. A number of neoconservative interpretations of issues of obvious concern to Egypt's private rental or commercial agricultural export sector appeared in the Cairo lawyers' press between 1900 and 1904. In contrast to the anonymity that characterized standard judicial reform articles before the turn of the century, many of these were signed. This may indicate that *ahliyya* lawyers were (or sought to be) public figures associated with causes that had obvious political and economic importance for prospective clients. Several examples can be cited. First, there was a trend toward diversification of editorial interest in at least two of Cairo's specialized lawyers' journals after 1900. After a few very cautious feelers by *Al-Huquq* into the field of liberal political journalism (see "The Right of Election in Egypt," 18 June 1898), more and more articles edited by Ibrahim Jammal lent themselves to the neoconservative framework for socioeconomic commentary pioneered by Muhammad Ra'fat. An example would be a (8 June 1901) editorial suggesting that procedural reforms were needed to obtain quicker resolution of

local creditors' suits against recalcitrant debtors. As *Al-Huquq* continued to diversify its investigation of such subjects, Najib Shuqra's new journal *Al-Istiqlal* offered editorials that would attract attention from Egyptians whose interests had surpassed simple questions of courtroom proceedings and jurisdictions and encompassed general economic questions with more legislative than judicial relevance in post-1900 Egypt (e.g., "Freedom of Commerce and Its Protection," *Al-Istiqlal*, 15 June 1902).

Finally, the extent to which Egypt's new generation of *ahliyya* lawyers seemed prepared to offer "laymen's" legal analyses of an ever widening range of social and economic issues, some formerly reserved for strictly religious legalists, is exemplified in Aziz Effendi Khanki's article "On Egyptian Pious Foundations [*Awqaf*]" (*Al-Huquq*, 24 October 1903), and a series of anonymous articles on marriage laws, polygamy, and family relations (*Al-Huquq*, 7 and 14 May, 3 September, and 8 October 1904).

38. The most prominent example of this phenomenon in Egypt until his death in 1905 would be, of course, Shaykh Muhammad ʿAbduh. Much the same current of thought can be seen reflected after 1896 in writings and activities of the Khalduniyya Society in Tunis at the turn of the century (see Green, *Tunisian Ulama*, pp. 167–71ff). I have developed the main lines of this argument as it relates to Tunisia in "La constitution ottomane dans la stratégie politique," pp. 279–94.

39. Lord Cromer's last attempt to devise a plan for an "international legislative council" in Cairo is documented in Egypt No. 1 (1905), Cd. 2409. The impact of the 1907 depression on overextended Egyptian investors in commercial agricultural ventures (in the form of additional land as well as purchased shares in processing plants and other businesses that did not survive the 1907 crash) is outlined in Berque, *L'Egypte,* pp. 247–52.

Selected Bibliography

I. Documents and Unpublished Sources

A. Archives

1. Egypt

Dar al-Watha'iq: Registers of the *Diwan al-Haqqaniyya*.

Dar al-Mahfuzat: Registers of the *majalis mahalliyya* and the *mahakim ahliyya*.

2. France

Ministère des Affaires Etrangères: Correspondance Politique: Egypte.

3. Great Britain

Foreign Office: Consular Correspondence, Series 78 (Turkey).

Foreign Office: Confidential Print, Series 407 (Egypt).

B. Private Papers

Cromer Papers (Public Record Office, London).

Granville Papers (Public Record Office).

Milner Papers (Bodleian Library, Oxford).

Portal Papers (Rhodes House, Oxford).

Salisbury Papers (Christ Church College, Oxford).

C. Government Publications

1. Egypt

a. General

Bulletin des lois et décrets royaux. Cairo, 1876–.

Majmu^{c}a mahadir al-jalasat li majlis shura al-qawanin. Cairo, 1884–.

Majmu^{c}at al-qararat as-sadira min majlis an-nuzzar wa min an-nizarat wal manshurat. Cairo, 1880–82; 1885–. *Moniteur Egyptien*. Cairo (after 1887, *Journal Officiel Egyptien*).

Recueil de tous les documents officiels du gouvernement égyptien. Cairo, 1876–.

2. France

a. General

Parlement Français. Chambre des Députés. "Rapport à la Chambre des Députés sur la prorogation des tribunaux mixtes en Egypte." *Journal Officiel du Gouvernement Français*, 1408 (23 décembre 1882).

b. Ministerial Publications

Ministère des Affaires Etrangères. *Rapport présenté au Marquis de Moustier par la commission instituée à l'effet d'examiner les propositions faites par le gouvernement égyptien pour réformer l'administration de la justice en Egypte*. Paris, 1867 and 1870.

Ministère des Affaires Etrangères. *Documents diplomatiques français: Affaires d'Egypte: 1878-1880.*

Ministère des Affaires Etrangères. *Documents diplomatiques français: 1871-1914.* First series, second volume (1871–1900).

3. Great Britain

a. Parliamentary Papers (Accounts and Papers) and Debates

Great Britain. Parliament. *Hansard's Parliamentary Debates*. Third Series.

Correspondence Respecting Mr. Cave's Special Mission to Egypt.

Egypt No. 4 (1876) C 1396.

Report by Mr. Cave on the Financial Condition of Egypt. Egypt No. 7 (1876) C 1425.

Correspondence Respecting the Finances of Egypt: Egypt No. 8 (1876); Egypt No. 2 (1879); Egypt No. 36 (1884); Egypt No. 4 (1885); Egypt No. 17 (1885).

Correspondence Respecting the Affairs of Egypt: Egypt No. 3 (1879); Egypt No. 4 (1884); Egypt No. 26 (1884); Egypt No. 1 (1885); Egypt No. 20 (1885).

Reports by Her [or His] Majesty's Agent and Consul-General on the Finances, Administration, and Condition of Egypt and the Sudan:

Egypt No. 3 (1893) C 6957; Egypt No. 1 (1894) C 7308; Egypt No. 1 (1895) C 7644; Egypt No. 1 (1896) C 7978; Egypt No. 1 (1898) C 8815; Egypt No. 3 (1899) C 9231; Egypt No. 1 (1900) Cd. 95; Egypt No. 1 (1904) Cd. 1951; Egypt No. 1 (1905) Cd. 2409.

II. Reference Works

Aziz, Joseph. *Concordance des codes égyptiens mixte et indigène avec le Code Napoléon*. Paris, 1886–87.

The Dictionary of National Biography and Supplements. London, 1917–.

Fahmi, Zaki. *Safwat al-ᶜasr fi tarikh wa rusum mashahir rijal misr*. Cairo, 1926.

Gélat, Philippe. *Répertoire général annoté de la législation et de l'administration égyptiennes, 1840–1910*. Alexandria, 1906–11, 6 vols. and tables.

Haykal, Muhammad Husayn. *Tarajim misriyya wa gharbiyya*. Cairo, 1929.

Hurewitz, J.C. *The Middle East and North Africa in World Politics: A Documentary Record*. 2nd ed. New Haven and London, 1975. 2 vols.

Al-Naqqash, Salim. *Misr l'il misriyyin*. Alexandria, 1884. 9 vols.

Qadri, Muhammad Basha. *Murshid al-hayaran ila maᶜrifat ahwal al-insan*. Cairo, 1889.

Sami, Amin Basha. *Taqwim an-Nil*. Cairo, 1938. 5 vols.

Zaydan, Jurji. *Tarajim mashahir ash-sharq*. Cairo, 1920. 2 vols.

III. Contemporary Egyptian Press (including place and date of first publication)

Al-Adab, Cairo, 1888; *Al-Ahkam*, Cairo, 1887; *Al-Ahram*, Alexandria, 1876; *Al-ᶜAlam*, Cairo, 1885; *Al-ᶜAsr al-Jadid*, Cairo, 1880; *Al-Bayan*, Cairo, 1884; *Le Bosphore Egyptien*, Cairo, 1883; *Al-Burhan*, Alexandria, 1881; *Egyptian Gazette*, Alexandria, 1883; *Al-Fallah*, Cairo, 1886; *Al-Huquq* , Cairo, 1886; *Al-Istiqlal*, Cairo, 1902; *Al-Kawkab al-Misri*, Cairo, 1879; *Masr*, Cairo, 1877; *Mir'at ash-Sharq*, Cairo, 1879; *Al-Mu'ayyad*, Cairo, 1889; *Al-Muqattam*, Cairo, 1889; *Le Phare d'Alexandrie*, Alexandria, 1878; *Al-Qahira al-Hurra*, Cairo, 1885; *Rawdat al-Akhbar*, Cairo, 1874; *As-Sadiq*, Cairo, 1886; *Le Sphinx*, Cairo, 1890; *At-Tijara*, Alexandria, 1878; *Al-Ustadh*, Cairo, 1892; *Al-Waqa'iᶜ al-Misriyya*, Cairo, ca. 1822; *Al-Waqt*, Alexandria, 1879; *Al-Watan*, Cairo, 1877; *Az-Zaman*, Cairo, 1882.

IV. Published Memoirs, Biographies, and Correspondence

Blignières, Ernest-Gabriel de. *Le Contrôle anglo-français en Egypte*. Paris, 1882.

Cambon, Paul. *Correspondance: 1870–1924*. Paris, 1940–46, 2 vols.

Coles, Pasha, C. E. *Recollections and Reflections*. London, 1918.

Colvin, Sir Auckland. *The Making of Modern Egypt, 1881–1905*. London, 1906.

Cromer, Earl of. *Modern Egypt*. Second edition, London, 1911.

Freycinet, Charles-Louis de Saulces de. *La question d'Egypte*. Paris, 1905.

Leon, Edwin de. *The Khedive's Egypt*. New York, 1878.

Malet, Sir Edward. *Egypt: 1879–1883. London, 1908.*

Michels, Baron des. *Souvenirs de carrière*. Paris, 1901.

Milner, Alfred. *England in Egypt*. London, 1892.

Minnaert, T. *Le Caire et la justice internationale en Egypte*. Brussels, 1898.

Nubar Pacha. *Mémoires de Nubar Pacha*. Ed. Mirritt Boutros Ghali. Beirut, 1983.

The Political Correspondence of Mr. Gladstone and Lord Granville. Oxford, 1962. 2 vols.

Wilson, Sir Charles Rivers-. *Chapters from My Official Life*. New York, 1916.

V. Books and Articles

Abdel Malek, Anouar. *Idéologie et renaissance nationale: L'Egypte moderne*. Paris, 1969.

Amin, Kassem. *Les Egyptiens: Réponse à Monsieur le Duc d'Harcourt*. Cairo, 1894.

Amos, Sheldon. "Egypt in 1882." *Nation* (London), 34 (1882) 97–98; 440–41; 519.

——. "Spoiling the Egyptians, Revised Version." *Contemporary Review*, 42 (October 1882), 509–24.

Anderson, J. N. D. "Law Reform in the Middle East." *International Affairs* (London), 32 (1956), 43–51.

——. "Law Reform in Egypt: 1850–1950." In *Social and Political Change in Modern Egypt*, ed. P. M. Holt. London, 1968.

Asser, T. "Administration de la justice en Egypte." *Revue de Droit International et Législation Comparée*, first series 2 (1870), 564–72.

Baer, Gabriel. "Tanzimat in Egypt: The Penal Code." *Bulletin of the School of Oriental and African Studies* (London), 26 (1963), 29–49.

Batchelder, George. "The International Court of Egypt." *Albany Law Journal*, 19 (1879), 289–92.

Bemmelen, Pieter van. *L'Egypte et l'Europe par un ancien juge mixte*. Leiden, 1881–82. 2 vols.

Blunt, Wilfred S. *Atrocities of Justice under British Rule in Egypt*. London, 1906.

——. *A Secret History of the English Occupation of Egypt*. New York, 1922.

Bonzelly, Hippolyte. *Réflexions sur la réforme judiciaire en Egypte*. Alexandria, 1870.

Borelli, Octave. *Choses politiques d'Egypte, 1883–1895*. Paris, 1895.

Bousquet, G. "Les nouveaux tribunaux égyptiens." *Revue des Deux Mondes* (Paris), 238 (1878), 184–97.

Brinton, Jasper Y. *The Mixed Courts of Egypt*. First edition. New Haven, 1930.

Campbell, Sir George. "Our Dealings with Egypt and the Possible Results." *Fortnightly Review*, new series, 19 (1876), 137–73.

Crecelius, Daniel. *The Roots of Modern Egypt: A Study of the Regimes of ʿAli Bey al-Kabir and Muhammad Bey Abu Al-Dhahab*. Minneapolis, 1981.

Gatteschi, Domenico. "Le droit international public et privé en Egypte." *Revue Historique de Droit Français et Etranger*, 8 (1862), 573–95.
——. "Une nouvelle organisation judiciaire en Egypte." *Revue Historique de Droit Français et Etranger*, 14 (1867), 571–92.
——. "La Réforme judiciaire en Egypte." *Bulletin de l'Institut Egyptien*, first series, 12 (1873), 85–92.
——. *Della riforma giudiziaria in Egitto*. Alexandria, 1873.
Gavillot, J.-C. Aristide. *Les capitulations et la réforme judiciaire*. Paris, 1875.
Haakman, Jacques. *L'Egypte et les traités internationaux sur la réforme judiciaire*. Paris, 1877.
Hunter, F. Robert. *Egypt under the Khedives, 1805–1879*. Pittsburgh, 1984.
Issa, Hossam M. *Capitalisme et sociétés anonymes en Egypte*. Paris, 1970.
Jenks, Leland H. *The Migration of British Capital to 1875*. Second edition. London, 1963.
al-Jundi, Anwar. *As-Sihafa as-siyasiyya fi misr*. Cairo, 1962.
Khanki, Aziz. "At-Tashri[c] wal qada qabla insha al-mahakim al-ahliyya." Vol. l. Cairo, 1937.
——. *Al-Mahakim al-mukhtalata wal mahakim al-ahliyya*. Cairo, 1939.
Landes, David. *Bankers and Pashas*. Cambridge, Mass., 1958.
Lashin, [c]Abd al-Khaliq Muhammad. *Sa[c]d Zaghlul: Dawruhu fi as-siyasat al-misriyya hatta 1914*. Cairo, 1971.
Lesseps, Charles de. *Les capitulations et la réforme judiciaire en Egypte: Sa nécessité et son urgence*. Paris, 1867.
Lucovich, Antoine. *Comment on administre la justice en Egypte*. Paris, 1866.
Lutfi, [c]Umar. *Al-Imtiyazat al-ajnabiyya*. Cairo, 1904.
Lutfi al-Sayyid [Marsot], Afaf. *Egypt and Cromer*. London, 1968.
——. *Egypt in the Reign of Muhammad Ali*. Cambridge, England, 1984.
Makhluf, Najib. *Nubar basha wa ma tamma [c]ala yadihi*. Cairo, 1903.
al-Marsafi, Shaykh Husayn. *Rasa'il al-kalim ath-thaman*. Cairo, 1880–81.
Martin-Sarzeaud, Georges. "Sur la Réforme Judiciaire en Egypte: Rapport à la commission internationale." *Journal de Droit International Privé* (Paris), 11 (1884), 300–315.
——. "La Réforme Judiciaire en Egypte: De la fusion des tribunaux mixtes et tribunaux indigènes." *Journal de Droit International Privé*, 13 (1886), 270–72.
Maunoury, Jacques. *La réforme de l'organisation judiciaire en Egypte*. Paris, 1867.
——. "Rapport de M. Astrie-Rolland sur les communications de Monsieur Maunoury relatives aux tribunaux mixtes égyptiens." *Recueil de l'Académie de Législation de Toulouse*, 29 (1880–81), 443–55.

——. "Rapport sur le projet de loi relatif à la prorogation de la Réforme Judiciaire en Egypte." In *Recueil des Traités de la France*, 14 (1883–84), 90–105.

McIlwraith, Malcolm. "The Declaration of a Protectorate in Egypt and Its Legal Effects." *Journal of Comparative Legislation and International Law*, 39 (1917), 89–95.

Owen, E. R. J. [Roger]. *Cotton and the Egyptian Economy, 1820–1914.* Oxford, 1969.

——. *The Middle East in the World Economy, 1800–1914*. London, 1981.

Pélissié du Rausas, Gérard. *Le régime des capitulations dans l'empire ottoman*. Paris, 1910–11. 2 vols.

Perry, Harold. *The Future of Justice in Egypt*. London, 1881.

——. "France and Judicial Reform in Egypt." *National Review*, 1 (1883), 113–25.

——. "Justice in Egypt." *Law Quarterly Review*, 1 (1885), 342–54.

Ra'fat, Muhammad. *Kitab usul al-qawanin*. Cairo, 1898.

Reid, Donald M. *Lawyers and Politics in the Arab World, 1880–1960.* Minneapolis, 1981.

Rida, As-Sayyid Muhammad Rashid. *Tarikh al-ustadh al-imam ash-shaykh Muhammad ᶜAbduh*. Cairo, 1906–31. 3 vols.

Schölch, Alexander. *Egypt for the Egyptians*!. London, 1981.

Schulze, Reinhard. *Die Rebellion der ägyptischen Fallahin*: *1919*. Berlin, 1981.

Scott, J. H. "The Judicial System of Egypt." *Juridical Review*, 18 (1906), 386–98.

——. *The Law Affecting Foreigners in Egypt as a Result of the Capitulations*. Edinburgh, 1907.

Silvestre, Henri. *La réforme judiciaire devant l'Assemblée Nationale*. Marseilles, 1875.

Simaika, ᶜAbdullah. *De la compétence des tribunaux mixtes d'Egypte en matière civile, commerciale, et financière*. Paris, 1892.

Tagher, Jacques. "Nubar Pacha et la réforme judiciaire." *Cahiers d'Histoire Egyptienne*, 1 (1948), 373–412.

Tignor, Robert. "The Indianization of the Egyptian Administration under British Rule." *American Historical Review*, 68 (1963), 636–61.

——. *Modernization and British Colonial Rule in Egypt, 1882–1914.* Princeton, 1966.

——. "The Introduction of Modern Banking into Egypt, 1855–1920." *Journal of Asian and African Studies*, 15 (1981), 103–22.

West, Sir Raymond. "Egypt and the Judicial Adviser's Report." *Journal of the Society of Comparative Legislation*, new series, 6 (1905), 513–17.

Zaghlul, Ahmad Fathi. *Tarikh al-muhamah*. Cairo, 1900.

Ziadeh, Farhat. *Lawyers, the Rule of Law, and Liberalism in Modern Egypt*. Stanford, 1968.

Index